Families of Co. Dublin Ireland

From The Earliest Times To The 20th Century

Irish Family Surnames
With Locations & Origins

Including English, Scots, & Anglo Norman
Settlers And Settlements

O'LAUGHLIN

Published as a supplement and an addition to the original:
Book of Irish Families, great & small
Volume 7 of the set

i

The Complete Irish Family Library

Works below made possible by members of the IGF & OLochlainns Irish Family Journal. Membership starts at $54 per year for regular members, and $104 per year for gold members. Regular members receive the Journal 6 times yearly. Gold members 12 times yearly.
Your membership is invited. Thank You.

Hardbound Works By the Same Author:
Complete Book For Tracing Your Irish Ancestors. $26. (0-940134-02-0)
The Complete Book of Irish Family Names. 1987. $25. (0-940134-41-1)
The Irish Book of Arms. 1988. $75. (0-940134-07-1)
Irish Settlers on the American Frontier. $34.50. 1985. (0940134-43-8)
The Book of Irish Families Great and Small. 1992. $32.95. (0-940134-15-2)
Master Book of Irish Surnames. $26. 1993. (0-940134-32-2)
Master (Atlas) & Book of Irish Placenames. $24. 1994. (0-940134-33-0)
Families of Co. Kerry, Ireland. 1994. ($32) (0-940134-36-5)
Families of Co. Clare, Ireland. 1996. ($32)   (0-940134-37-3)
Families of Co. Cork, Ireland. 1996. ($32) (0-940134-35 -7)
Families of Co. Limerick, Ireland 1997. (0-940134-31-4)
Families of Co. Galway, Ireland . 1998. (0-940134-00-4)
Families of Co. Roscommon, Ireland. (in process)
Irish Genealogies..from Keatings History of Ireland. 1998. $29.95

Other published works by the author:
Beginners Guide to Irish Family Research. ($15) 1990.
Journal of Irish Families. 1986 - present. monthly. (ISSN 1056-0378)
Irish Families web bulletin. (monthly via the world wide web.)
Ortelius Map of Ireland 1572. ($20) (ancient map)

Rare Book Reprints Published by the I.G.F.:
Keatings' 'History of Ireland' 3 volume set. (0-940134-44-0)
The Poetry and Song of Ireland. O'Reilly. (1865). $45 (0-940-134-43-8)
Irish Names and Surnames. Rev. Patrick Woulfe $40 (0-940134-40-3)
Tribes/Customs of Hy-Many. O'Donovan. (orig.1873) $104. (0-940134-39-X)
Tribes/Customs of Hy-Fiachrach. O'Donovan. (1874) $129. (0-940134-38-1)
Gaelic Titles & Forms of Address. Duhallow. 2nd ed. $25.1997.(0-940134-27-6)
King James's Irish Army List. D'Alton. (0-940134-23-3)
A Social History of Ancient Ireland. Joyce. 2 v. set. (0-940134-24-1)

Volume VII of the *Book of Irish Families, great & small:*

The Families of County Dublin Ireland

Original First Edition

By

Michael C. O'Laughlin
president, I.G.F.
editor, *Irish Family Journal*
noted author & lecturer.

Over Four Thousand Entries
From the Archives of the
Irish Genealogical Foundation.

ISBN: 0 - 940134 - 30- 6
© 1999 Irish Genealogical Foundation.
Box 7575, Kansas City, MO. 64116 U.S.A.
All Rights Reserved. Write For Free Catalogue

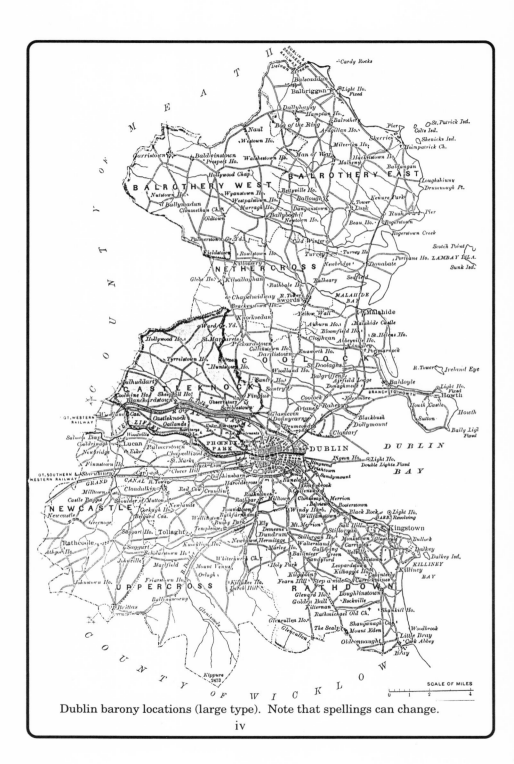

Dublin barony locations (large type). Note that spellings can change.

iv

Families of County Dublin, Ireland
Volume VII of the Book of Irish Families

Contents

Frontis (Map)
List of Books, ISBN data.................................. ii
Barony Map of County Dublin........................... iv
Ortelius Map of Dublin 1576............................. vi
Ancient Tribal Names Chart.............................. vii
Keatings History (illus)..................................... viii

Early Families... 9
Norman Invasion.. 10
Families by Parish... 17
Vikings.. 35
Famine and The New World............................... 41
Guide to Tracing Dublin Ancestors....................... 43

Families of County Dublin, Ireland....................... 53
   History and Locations Found.
   (Listed in Alphabetical order, disregarding the
   O', Mc, or Mac prefix before the name.)

Appendix... 211
Dublin Surname List   Dublin Placename List
Jewish Settlers List   County of Dublin (census)
City of Dublin (census)

Index of Family Names Found in Text.................... 231

Additional Maps and Illustrations

Ordnance Map: Stillorgan...... 12
Ordnance Map Merrion.......... 17
Orndance Map Tallaght.......... 21
Ordnance Map Palmerston...... 25
City of Dublin in 1611............42
Rocky Road to Dublin............ 50
Arms of Dublin Families......... 52
Arms of Dublin Families......... 230

Map of Co. Dublin in 1576.

What was known of Co. Dublin, represented in this extract from The Ortelius Map of Ireland, 1576 (reprinted ©1992 Irish Family Journal). Note the spelling of Dublyn. Family names appear on this map and in many records under older spellings as well. OTolo = O'Toole, Wykelo = Wicklow, Kyldare = Kildare, etc...

Ancient Tribes of Leinster
Old Irish Families Located In and Around County Dublin

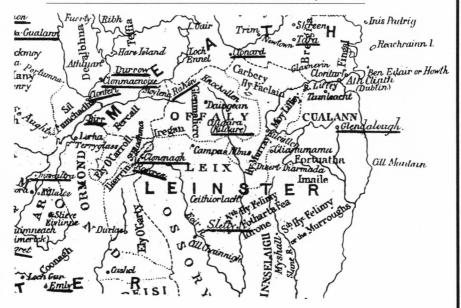

√ **Cineal Laoghaire -** The race of Laoghaire, son of Niall of the nine hostages, seated in the baronies of Upper and Lower Navan in Co. Meath. (There was also a Munster clan of the same name.)

√ **Clann Cholmain -** The race of Colman Mor, son of Diarmaid, son of Fearghus Cirrbel, son of Conall Cremhthainne, son of Niall of the Nine Hostages; the chief clan of the southern Ui Neill; and the clan name of the O'Melaghlens and their correlatives in Meath.

√ **Feara Cualann -** The men of Cuala, a clan whose territory included a great portion of the present counties of Dublin and Wicklow.

√ **Ui Faolain-** The descendants of Faolan of the race of Cathaoir Mor, King of Ireland; the clan-name of the O'Byrnes and the MacKeoghs who, prior to the Anglo-Norman invasion, were seated in the north of the present county of Kildare.

√ **Ui Muireadhaigh-** The descendants of Muireadhach, of the line of Cathaoir Mor, monarch of Ireland; and the clan name of the O'Tooles, whose territory prior to the Anglo-Norman invasion, comprised the southern half of the present county Kildare.

vii

8. O'HAIRT or O'Hart, O'Riagain or O'Regan, O'Ceallaigh or O'Kelly, and O'Conghalaigh, or O'Connoly—the Four Tribes of Tara are thus mentioned by O'Dugan:

" The princes of Tara I here record,
The royal O'Hart and likewise O'Regan,
The host who purchased the harbors,
Were the O'Kellies and the O'Connollies."

These tribes of Tara were also styled princes of Bregia, and appear to have possessed the territories about Tara in Meath, and also parts of the present county of Dublin.

15. The FAGANS, some of whom have been called O'Fagans and Mac Fagans, are considered by some to be of Irish origin, but according to others they were of English or Danish descent, and the name is still numerous in the counties of Meath, Westmeath, and Dublin.

16. The O'MULLENS are one of the Leinster clans, and were numerous in Meath, Dublin, and Kildare.

17. MAC GILLA-MOCHOLMOG and O'Dunchadha or O'Donoghoo, are mentioned in O'Dugan as lords or princes of Fine Gall, that is, of Fingall near Dublin; and it may be observed that there was another Mac Gilla-mocholmog, lord of a territory on the borders of Wicklow, and mentioned in the note on Cualan.

18. O'MURCHERTAIGH, or O'Murtogh, chief of the tribe or territory of O'Maine; and O'Modarn, chief of Kinel Eochain, are mentioned in O'Dugan as chiefs over the Britons or Welsh, and appear to have been located near Dublin.

19. MAC MUREGAIN, prince of East Liffey, is mentioned in our annals in some battles with the Danes in the tenth century.

In the County and City of Dublin the following have been the principal families of Anglo-Norman descent: The Talbots, Tyrrells, Plunketts, Prestons, Barnwalls, St. Lawrences, Cruises, Cusacks, Cogans, Whites, Walshes, Walls, Warrens, Wogans, Woodlocks, Darcys, Nettervilles, Marwards, Phepoes, Fitzwilliams, Fitzsimons, Flemmings, Archbolds, Archers, Allens, Aylmers, Balls, Bagots, De Bathes, Butlers, Barrys, Barrets, Berminghams, Bretts, Bellews, Blakes, Brabazons, Finglases, Sweetmans, Hollywoods, Howths, Husseys, Dowdalls, Dillons, Seagraves, Sarsfields, Stanihurts, Lawlesses, Cadells, Drakes, Graces, Palmers, Eustaces, Browns, Nangles, Tuites, Trants, Luttrells, Delahoydes, Ushers, Grattans.

From the book entitled *Irish Genealogies*, extracted from Keatings History, giving the ancient Families and their locations in Dublin .

The Invasions

In 'Irish Genealogies' (volume three of Keatings 'History of Ireland', I.G.F. edition) we read of the principal families settling in Dublin City and County subsequent to the 12th century invasions. They are given therein as listed below:

Talbot
Tyrrell
Plunkett
Preston
Barnwall
St. Lawrence
Cruise
Cusack
Cogan
White
Walshe
Wall
Warren
Wogan
Woodlock
Darcy
Netterville
Marward
Pheopoes
Fitzwilliam
Flemming
Archbold
Archer
Allen
Aylmer
Ball
Bagot
De Bathe
Butler
Barry
Barrets
Bermingham
Brett
Bellew
Blake

Brabazon
Finglas
Sweetman
Hollywood
Howth
Hussey
Dowdall
Dillon
Seagrave
Sarsfield
Stanihurt
Lawless
Cadell
Drake
Grace
Palmer
Eustace
Brown
Nangle
Tuite
Trant
Luttrell
Delahoyde
Usher
Grattan

One can see from this list that many settler families will be found in Dublin, including Viking, Welsh, Norman and English ones. It should be remembered however, that over time, Dublin drew its population mainly from the far flung parts of Ireland itself. Indeed, we have the most mixed population of the entire country right here in Dublin.

Due to the fact that it became the administrative center for the English government, there was continued settlement from England. Although the area now known as Dublin city was a stronghold for the Vikings and Normans anciently, the settlers became outnumbered by native Irish eventually.

Dublin Families

The mix of families and family names found in Dublin is extraordinary. Dublin was a center of government for the Vikings, and then for the Normans who invaded in the 12th century. It has also drawn families from every other part of Ireland in considerable numbers. It is important to be aware of families adjacent to Dublin, for they are very often found in Dublin itself.

Taking from the works of earlier days, O'Hart, in his "Irish Pedigrees", lists the chiefs and clans of Dublin, Kildare, King's, and parts of Meath together in the same section. O'Connor of Offaley; O'Toole of Co. Wicklow; O'Moore of Leix; and O'Dempsey of Clanmaliere were anciently given as chiefs of Co. Kildare, which is adjacent to Dublin. The O'Tooles and O'Byrnes were given in the mountainous areas in the south of Dublin.

MacFogarty of South Bregia is given as such by the four masters in the 10th century; O'Carey, is found as chief of Cairbre O'Ciardha in Kildare; O'Murcain or O'Murcan and O'Bracken are given possessing lands along the Liffey near Dublin; O'Gilbroin is given on the borders of Dublin and Kildare. O'Fiachra, O'Cullen, O'Colgan, MacDonnell, O'Dempsey, O'Dunn, O'Hea and O'Murtha are found in Kildare. O'Toole and O'Byrne are given as chiefs in Wicklow. O'Duffy is given originally in Kildare and Carlow but subsequently in Dublin, and they are found migrating to Louth, Monaghan, Cavan, Galway and Roscommon.

The O'Fagans or MacFagans (given to be the same family) are given as possibly of English descent by O'Hart, and D'Alton gives several of the name as high sheriffs in Meath and Dublin from the 13th to the 15th century. The Fagans of Feltrim, near Dublin are given with extensive holdings in early times. O'Murphy of Wexford is found numerous in Dublin and Meath. O'Mullen is given as numerous in Meath, Dublin and Kildare. Donohoe and Gilcolm are given as ancient chiefs of Dublin at Feltrim. O'Moriarty or O'Murtagh, was chief of the tribe of O'Maine; and together with O'Modarn they are given as chiefs of the Britons or Welsh apparently near Dublin.

New Settlers

DeLacy and his barons came to own the greater portion of the present county of Dublin subsequent to the 12th century Norman invasions. Hugh Tyrell got the land around Castleknock, held by his descendants as barons of Castleknock. The Phepoes got Santry and Clontarf, and according to MacGeogeoghegan, Vivian de Cursun got the area of Raheny near Dublin which formerly was held by the Irish family of Giollamocholmog.

The principal families of Dublin (both Irish and settlers) from the 12th to the 18th century are given by O'Hart as: Talbot; Tyrrell; Plunket; Preston; Barnwall; St. Lawrence; Taylor; Cruise; Cusack; Cogan; White; Walsh; Wall; Warren; Wogan; Woodlock; Darcy; Netterville; Marward; Phepoe; Fitzwilliam; Fleming; Fitzsimons; Archbold; Archer; Allen; Aylmer; Ball; Bagot; De Bathe; Butler; Barry; Barret; Birmingham; Brett; Bellew; Blake; Brabazon; Finglas; Sweetman; Hollywood; Howth; Hussey; Burnell; Dowdall; Dillon; Segrave; Sarsfield; Stanihurst; Lawless; Cadell; Evans, Drake; Grace; Palmer; Eustace; Fyan or Fynes; Foster; Gough; Berrill; Bennet;

Noted Families

Brown; Duff; Nangle; Woder; Tuite; Tew; Trant; Peppard; Luttrell; Rawson; Vernon; Delahoyde; Usher; Garnet; Hamilton; Domville; Coghill; Cobb; Grattan; Molesworth; Latouche; Putland; Beresford; Shaw; Smith; etc...

Many accounts of these families and others can be found in the Histories of Dublin by D'Alton and by Ball. The more recent nobility (19th century or prior) of Dublin is also given in the works of O'Hart.

More Recent Nobility

Among these nobility are given the Talbots, earls of Shrewsbury, centered at Malahide and Belgard in Dublin, they were created barons of Malahide and barons of Furnival. Of these lines were Richard Talbot, the duke of Tyrconnell, Lord Lieutenant of Ireland under King James II. The Plunkets were centered in Dublin, Meath, and Louth, and were created barons of Killeen and earls of Fingal. Preston is found as viscount Gormanstown, and as viscount Tara. The St. Lawrence family furnished some earls of Howth. Barnwall became viscount of Kingsland and barons of Turvey; De Coursey, baron of Kilbarrock; Fitzwilliam, viscount of Merrion; Rawson, viscount of Clontarf; Beaumont, viscount of Swords; Molesworth, viscount of Swords; Temple, viscount Palmerstown or Palmerston; Treacy, viscount of Rathcoole; Patrick Sarsfield, the commander under James II, was 'Earl of Lucan'; Bingham, earl of Lucan; Loftus, earl of Rathfarnham and viscount Ely; Luttrell, earl of Carhampton; Leeson, earl of Miltown; Harman, viscount Oxmantown or Ostmanstown in Dublin city; Parsons, earls of Rosse in King's

Monkstown

County were also barons of Oxmantown; Wenman, baron of Kilmainham; Barry, baron of Santry; Caulfield, earl of Charlemont who resided at Marino, Clontarf; Brabazon, earl of Meath with extensive possessions in Wicklow and Dublin; Thomas O'Hagan of Dublin was Lord Chancellor of Ireland under Gladstone and was in 1870 in the peerage of the United Kingdom, created 'Baron O'Hagan'.

The foregoing list is based upon several noted sources. Note that these names may be spelled differently today.

The following random notes on families in Dublin are arranged by civil parish. They are based largely upon the history of Dublin compiled by Ball. The comments are by no means complete, and are meant only to spark further interest and investigation by the reader.

MONKSTOWN PARISH

The Castle of Monkstown was granted to Sir John Travers, Master of the Ordnance in Ireland, by King Henry VIII, subsequent to 1539. It is given by Ball that Travers had a knowledge of the Celtic language and a generous nature which helped him amass a fortune here. He held a chief place among the military adventurers in 16th century Ireland. The Castle at Monkstown served as his residence and country seat in Ireland. His place at Monkstown was later taken by James Eustace, eldest son of the second viscount Baltinglass, who played a significant role in the Desmond Rebellions. The Castle would later pass to Sir Gerald Aylmer, of Donadea, Co. Kildare; then to Henry Cheevers; and then to General Edmund Ludlow.

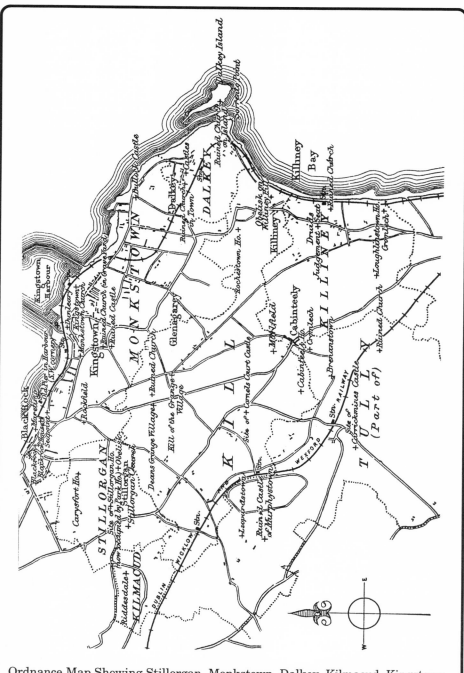

Ordnance Map Showing Stillorgan, Monkstown, Dalkey, Kilmacud, Kingstown...

12

Seapoint

In the middle of the 18th century we find at Monkstown one Dr. Robert Roberts (d.1758) and Mr. Robert Elrington, a West Indian merchant, probably a descendant of the well known Dublin actor, Thomas Elrington.

Seapoint and Templehill

On the dissolution of the Abbey, in 1539, the lands of Newtown, as they were then called, contained a small castle house and were held by John Moran. The lands were often owned in common with Monkstown. In the early part of the 18th century, 'Newtown Castle Byrne', as it was then called, served as a pleasure resort for the citizens of Dublin. Other distinguished residents included Edward Willes in 1757; James Stanyhurst: Speaker of the House of Commons Honourable Robert Marshall; Lt. General John Aldercron of the Huguenot family in 1762; and Edward Murphy (d.1777).

A boarding house with ballroom was built at Seapoint by Mr. William Jones towards the end of the 18th century.

Montpelier Area

In 1748 an auction was held for Mr. Thomas Byrne at Montpelier, near Newtown Castle Byrne....Rockfield was held by Lord Townshend circa 1772 and subsequently held by Thomas Manning; Sir Frederick Flood; and Edward Badham Thornhill. Also noted in the neighborhood are William Raphson; Christopher Myers, the architect; Joseph Atkinson; Sir Edward Newenham (d.1814); and Sir William Betham (d.1853) Ulster King of Arms.

Port of Kingstown

(formerly known as Dunleary) One of the principal residents of the small village of Dunleary was Mr. William Roseingrave, one of the secretaries in

Kill of the Grange

Dublin Castle in the 18th century, whose house stood on or near the site of Salthill hotel. His father had been organist of the Dublin Cathedrals, and his uncle was a composer...Sir James Taylor, Lord Mayor of Dublin in 1765 came to hold lands subsequently, as did George Glover. One 'humble' resident of note was of the name of 'Lawlor' who frequently swam from Dunleary to Howth in 1760.

Bullock

Two tenants are given as Patrick Bermingham and John Gaban who paid rent in fish. (Those lands were leased to Richard Edwards.) Peter Talbot later came to hold the lands and castle of Bullock. He may have been killed by a party of kerns while trying to protect his property in 1555. During the 16th century the land and castle was assigned to one of the great Dublin mercantile families of the day, the Fagans, whose principal residence was at Feltrim, near Swords. One of the principal residents in the Restoration period was Mr. Kenelm Livinglyhurst (d.1685).

KILL of the GRANGE Parish (formerly called Clonkeen) The lands and tithes of the manor, town, and fields of the Grange were leased in 1561 to Christopher Bassenet, John Brady and John Hore who was then the chaplain. The house known as Kill Abbey was built in 1595 by George Ussher, a merchant of Dublin, and it passed to the children of Walter Harold. In 1623 Christopher Wolverston was tenant for the farm, and William Gilbert was tenant for the mensal lands.

At Dean's Grange the chief house was occupied by Ralph and Nathanial Swinfield....The widow of Christopher

Rochestown

Merry, a Dublin baker, resided in the house built by George Ussher. The property later passed to the Fitzsimons family and was later assigned due to the penal laws to Mr. William Espinasse. Espinasse was of a French family who emigrated to Ireland after the revocation of the Edict of Nantes, and they had acquired much wealth. He died in 1740 leaving several children including his eldest, Isaac, who served as High Sheriff of Co. Dublin and was succeeded by his eldest son Richard.

Rochestown

About the middle of the 16th century lands of Rochestown on which a castle stood, were occupied by the son of the owner of Loughlinstown, James Goodman. The lands were held by the Talbots of Belgard, and may have been transferred to Matthew Birsell and Thomas Lawless in 1563 (per Ball). At the beginning of the 17th century the lands of Rochestown fell to other hands.

Lord Loftus is found disposing of Loftus Hill, and in 1778 it was occupied by Mr. Medlicott, and then by Mr. Minchin....'during the last century the neighborhood was much developed by Mr. Robert Warren' of Killiney Castle, whose name is recorded as restorer in 1840.

Cabinteely

Thomas Cusack was leased the lands at first, but in 1545 they were granted to Sir John Travers, later passing to the Eustace and then the Cheevers family. Subsequently the Byrnes or O'Byrnes became identified with Cornelscourt and Cabinteely upon Cheevers death. John Byrne married the only surviving daughter of Walter Cheevers.

Johnstown house was occupied in 1778 by Mr. Love Hiatt, and then by a Mr.

Dalkey

Williams.

Tipperstown

(town of the well). Among the tenants in the 13th and 14th centuries were the families of Whyte, Hacket, Wythir, Harold and Lagthenan....In 1561 these lands were leased to Bassenet, Brady and Hore....In 1623 they were held by William Wolverston, owner of Stillorgan and in 1645 they were in the occupation of Richard Swinfield of Murphystown....In 1724 Christopher Ussher (of Booterstown), leased the lands and at the time of the Union they belonged to Councillor O'Farrell, and were farmed by him with great skill.

Newtownpark

(originally known as Newtown Little)

The tithes of these lands were leased to Nicholas Cor and Gerald Long in 1564. In the 16th century the Wolverston family occupied a good slated house on these lands.

DALKEY PARISH

In 1326 John Kendal was tenant at the Priory at Dalkey. A holding at Dalkey was given in 1320 by Alice, wife of John de Dundrum, to Andrew Fitzrichard. Nicholas Pyn is found here in 1394. At the close of the 18th century the principal families were those of Sir John Hasler, William Macartney, Mr. John Patrickson, and Miss Charlotte Brooke.

KILLINEY PARISH

The lands of Killiney itself were occupied in the 14th century by John Milis. After the dissolution of the Priory the lands were held successively under the Cathedral by William Walsh alias McHowell; James Garvey; and the Goodman family. After the rebellion of

Loughlinstown

1641 the lands were held by Gilbert Wye of Belfast; the Mossoms; the Fawcetts; the Pocklingtons; and the Domviles. Towards the end of the 18th century a lodge was built by Mr. Peter Wilson who came there from Dalkey. Later a Mr. Fetherston was residing at Killiney and in 1800 the Rev. James Dunn was lodging in the area.

Loughlinstown

The lands of Loughlinstown belonged in the middle ages to the Talbots and were held under them by the Goodmans who were also early English settlers. It is noted at the passing of one of the name who was Catholic, that he was buried in 1575, as were all of his family, in the parish church of Killiney. Mr. John Lambert eventually came to occupy the Goodman's house there. With the Restoration came the Domville family to the area.

Hackettsland

These lands take their name from the Hackets who were in the 14th century one of the principal families in the south of Dublin. In the 17th century the lands were owned by the Wolverstons of Stillorgan, and in the following century, a family called Towson was resident on them.

Kilboggett

At the close of the 16th century we find one Alderman Gerald Young of Dublin leasing these lands. The lands were then owned by the Rochfort family, who were dispossessed for their part in the rebellion, and after the rebellion the lands were granted to William Domville.

TULLY PARISH

Carrickmines Castle was garrisoned by the Walsh family, who despite constant threats and encounters with the old Irish

Murphystown

families, by the 15th century came to be expert military defenders and farmers of the area. Several of the name are given by Ball in his history of Dublin. Among the deaths given in obituaries of the day were the wife of Anthony Robinson (1760) and a daughter of Thomas Morgan; in 1761, John Payne, an eminent livery lace weaver; in 1762 a daughter of Alderman Crampton; in 1772, George Carey, of Redcastle; in 1773 the Rev. Henry Wright; and in 1780 Samuel Murphy, Doctor of Music.

Laughanstown

Among the occupants from the 14th to the 17th century we find the family of Macnebury, (of Ashpoll, or Archbold). Thomas Smith, a fellow of Trinity College is also noted. At the time of the Restoration Edward Buller occupied a good thatched castle there. In 1795 Laughanstown was held by the tenants of Brenanstown, the Mercer family.

Brennanstown

The Walsh family probably held this area from the 14th century. At the beginning of the 17th century, William Rochfort married a Walsh and became tenant, as did subsequently Thomas Wolverston. After the Restoration we find one Dr. Lightburne, and in 1683 the castle was occupied by the Powell family.

Murphystown

The lands of the townland of Murphystown were probably leased in 1230 by Geoffrey Tyrel, and in 1326 held by Peter Howell. The lands comprised of the old townland of Ballyogan were held by Robert, son of Stephen and Gilbert Begg. Towards the end of that century these lands were leased, under the names of Ballymorthan and Farnecost, to Sir John Cruise, and in

Leopardstown

the 16th century were held by the Harolds.

Leopardstown

These lands were known up to the 18th century as 'Leperstown'. Ellena Mocton held the tithes to the land of the Church of St. Stephen there in the 14th century. In 1400 Simon Hacket occupied the lands; in 1571 Robert Walsh did so; a few years later James Wolverston did so. Not long before the Union, Leperstown came into the possession of Col. Charles Henry Coote, M.P. for Maryborough.

STILLORGAN PARISH

The first English owner of Stillorgan Park appears to have been Raymond Carew, who gave a portion of lands to St. Mary's Abbey. He was succeeded by members of the Hacket family. At the close of the 14th century the manor came into the possession of of Sir John Cruise and subsequently to the Derpatrick family, one of whom was killed in an expedition against the O'Tooles around the year 1410. In the 15th century we find John Loghenan as the principal tenant of the manor house. Richard Locumbe, an Englishman, is also given as a tenant at that time. The manor would eventually come into the possession of the Plunkets of Rathmore, and it was held by them for more than 150 years.

At the end of the 16th century we see the settlement at Stillorgan, a branch of the ancient family of Wolverston or Wolferston, and a granting of a lease to the Right Hon. Jacques Wingfield. Both of these families had ties to the nearby Travers family in the past. It is noted of William Wolverston, that he was Catholic, as were his neighbors the

Kilmacud

Cheevers, the Goodmans and the Walshes. His family had been Protestant, but through intermarriage with early English settlers, he had become Roman Catholic.

The first of the Allen family identified with Stillorgan was John Allen who came to Dublin from Holland and was a master builder in Dublin according to Ball, who gives a long account of the family. Also mentioned in this parish at Stillorgan House are Nicholas Le Fevre who was a lottery merchant in Dublin, who assumed the place after Lord Lifford's death in 1789.

KILMACUD PARISH

The lands of Kilmacud were granted after the 12th century invasions to Walter de Rideleford, Lord of Bray, along with other lands. They became part of the manor of Thorncastle, 'now represented by Booterstown' according to Ball. Sir John Cruise and the Fitzwilliams of Merrion, are later found in possession of some or all of these lands.

In the 16th and 17th centuries the Archbold family emerges here. They descended from some of the earliest English settlers in the area. John Archbold (d.1756), was the last of the family to reside at Kilmacud. At this time properties passed to Lt. Col. John Arabin, the father-in-law of General Aylercorn, of Seapoint.

The house known as Redesdale, at one time residence of Archbishop Whately, was originally the country seat of Sir Michael Smith. It was occupied for a short time by Lord Redesdale circa 1799, having passed from Smiths ownership.

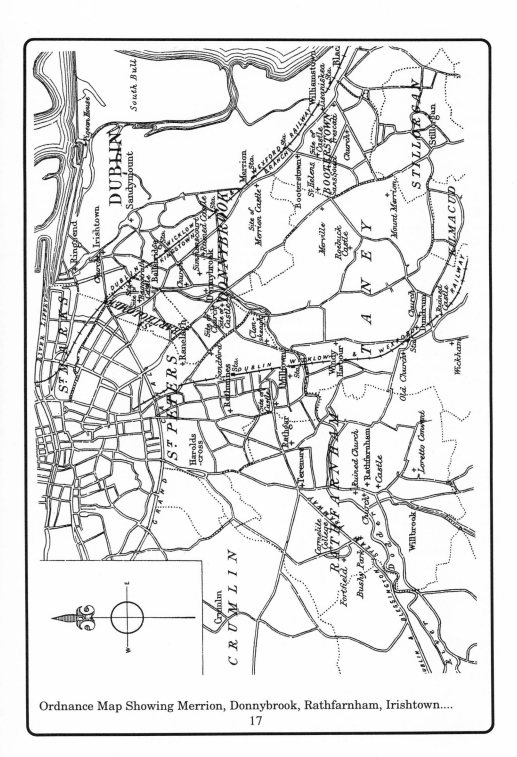

Ordnance Map Showing Merrion, Donnybrook, Rathfarnham, Irishtown....

17

Merrion

Merrion Castle & Lands

Merrion is now a suburb of Dublin. It was the home of a family 'foremost' among the the landed proprietors in the metropolitan county. One of the principal mediaeval castles of Dublin county also stood here, now long since removed. The Fitzwilliams of Merrion were one of the few early settler families in Ireland to 'retain all their property' through all the revolutions and troubles.

The first of the name was said to have arrived here with King John. They claim descent from the English family to which Earl Fitzwilliam, the inheritor of the Earl of Strafford's estates in Yorkshire and in Co. Wicklow belonged. At any rate they stopped using a separate coat of arms in the 17th century and adopted the arms of Earl Fitzwilliam.

The Fitzwilliams were firmly established in the south of Co. Dublin in the 14th century. By the 15th century they held no less than four manor houses and the lands of Merrion came under Fitzwilliam possession. By the end of the 15th century these lands were controlled by the branch of the family seated at Dundrum. The castle was in ruins and disassembled in 1780, and the seat of the family had earlier been established at Mount Merrion.

Nearby we find Walter de Rideleford at Thorncastle, who by the 13th century founded powerful allegiances with the Fitzgerald, Fitzmaurice and Carew families.

Booterstown
(also known as 'The Town of the Road')

To the southeast of Merrion, this was part of the ancient manor of Thorncastle. The Rideleford family is here early, and we find the Fitzwilliams would come to own these lands as well as Merrion.

Simmonscourt

The principal resident in Booterstown at the time of the rebellion of 1641 was Thomas Fox, a gentleman farmer. By the 18th century we find Mr. Richard Colley, who later assumed the name of Wesley and was made Lord Mornington, and Christopher Ussher at Booterstown. Part of the lands were being cultivated by an extremely successful farmer called Isaiah Yeates. By mid century the neighborhood was transformed from agricultural to residential. Among 18th century noted residents were Cooley; Doherty; Gough; O'Reilly; LaTouche; Doyne; Wight; Bradstreet; and Fitzgerald.

Note the mention of 'Castle Dawson' among the villas erected between Blackrock and Booterstown.

Simmonscourt

(Located northwest of Merrion, on the opposite side as Booterstown) The name of Simmonscourt is given to have come from the Smothe family, who succeeded the Morville family there. In the 14th century we find John Mynagh, Robert Serjeant, and Roger Kilmore in the area. At the time of the 1641 rebellion George Hill occupied these lands. Towards the end of the 18th century Counsellor Whittingham and Mr. Trulock are mentioned as chief residents at Simmonscourt.

Sandymount

A village called Brickfield town sprung up here, and not far from the sea was a pretty thatched inn kept by one Johnny Macklean.

Ringsend

In the 17th century this was a landing place for passengers bound for Dublin.

Baggotrath

Where Upper Baggot Street stands was the mediaeval castle of Baggotrath. The

Donneybrook

early tenants included: Ralph de Mora; William de Flamstead; and in 1255 Maurice Fitzgerald; and subsequently the lands passed to Philip de Hyndeberge. The first of the house of Bagod to reside there was likely Sir Robert Bagod (d.1336), chief justice of the bench in Ireland.

We also find one Robert Jans, a merchant of Dublin in 1547 described as 'of Baggotrath'. Thomas Fitzwilliam is also found making the castle his principal residence. We also find note of the widow of John Cashell, a Drogheda merchant. She died at the castle in 1574.

Donneybrook

Prominent early names connected with this area include Walter de Rideleford, and Walter de Lacy, the brother of the Earl of Ulster. The latter granted lands to Walter Missett here. Also found in the 13th century are de Verneuil; Butler or de Verdon; and de London. In 1524 the lands passed to the Ussher family. The owners of two farms at Donneybrook, (Richard Winstanley and Robert Woodward), were depositioned regarding the 1641 rebellion.

The Ussher family held the mansion house of Donnybrook into the 18th century. Subsequently in that century we find the names of Twigg, Stoyte, Jocelyn, and Sterne at the manor.

Among residents in the 18th century we find Sir Robert Barry of Barry House on the main road to Dublin. In 1777 it became the residence of Robert Hellen. Lt. Gen. Lewis Dejean is found on the Donnybrook road, as are the Downes family who were seated there as well. Sir Wm. Fortick died at Coldblow in 1789 and that was also the home of Denis George, Recorder of Dublin.

Taney

TANEY PARISH

(commonly called Dundrum) Among early tenants here are found Edmund Hackett, Richard Chamberlain and John Locumbe, subsequent to the lawless period in the early 14th century. The Fitzwilliams are found here at the same time and they erected a castle at Dundrum.

During the Rebellion of the 17th century we read of Richard Leech who was murdered at Churchtown and of Robert Turner, a traveling clothier, who was robbed on the road by Donagh Cahere of Dundrum. Lt.-Col. Isaac Dobson of the Parliament Army repaired and occupied Dundrum Castle by 1653. In the middle of the 18th century we find these among the few 'names of importance' in the parish of Taney: Fitzwilliam at Mt. Merrion; Foster; Carmichael; Rogers; Crowe; Hunt; Thwaites; Moulds; Messit; and Rinkle.

Some of the deaths announced at Dundrum were: in 1756 the wife of Anthony Perry; in 1757 Lt. John Kellie; in 1760 Mr. William Litton, a silk weaver; and in 1771 the wife of Mr. Shea, a linen draper.

At the end of the 18th century we find Dundrum was the home of Mr. John Giffard. At Churchtown Mr. Edward Mayne resided and in the vicinity were Stephen Stock, Daniel Kinahan, and Nathaniel Hone.

Balally

Given by some as originally a Danish settlement, later ruled by the Harolds. Names associated subsequently with the area were de Walhope; Othyr; Howell; Taunton; and the Walshes of Carrickmines, who built a Castle in a grant from the crown in 1407. Mr. John Borr held the lands in the 17th century.

Roebuck

Roebuck

Early names in the area around the 13th century were 'Basset', of the great Norman family, and 'le Brun'. Mr. William Nally is also noted in this area as occupying a house rated as containing two hearths, which was probably part of the castle. Those mentioned in connection with villas built at the close of the 18th century were John Exshaw; James Potts; Alexander Jaffray; Dr. Robert Emmett; and Henry Jackson. The Croftons are found residing in the castle at that time.

Mount Merrion

The Fitzwilliams are traditionally associated with these lands and much information is given in Balls History of the County Dublin.

ST. PETER PARISH (part)

(formerly part of St. Kevins Parish) Of various names found in the work of Ball, we find Capt. Wm. Shore who was connected to Co. Fermanagh; Sir Henry Brooke; and Thomas Radcliffe who was involved in legal proceedings in 1668 regarding Rathmines. At the beginning of the 18th century the Temple family, holding the title of Palmerston, came to possess Rathmines.

Ranelagh and Sandford

(formerly called Cullenswood) Many incursions on the settlers of Dublin were made from these woods in more ancient times. In the 17th century the land was held by Sir Wm. Ussher of Donnybrook and in 1641 the lands were occupied by Yeoman Thomas Ward who was taken captive along with one Mr. Parnell.

Milltown

Held by the Brigg family in the 14th century, and by the Loftus family in 1641 when John Bacon was principal

Rathfarnham

resident at Milltown. In the 18th century the town was the property of the Leeson family. Other noted names in the 18th century include: Mr. Heavisid; Classon; Burr; Hugh Johnston; Randall; Dogherty; Tomlinson; King and Walcot.

RATHFARNHAM PARISH

Names connected are: In the 14th century 'le Bret'; 14th & 15th centuries - Harold; Galvey; Hall; Cornwalsh; Loftus; In the 18th century - Palliser, O'Callaghan, Cramer, Coghill, Stannard, Fountain, Ward, Geering, How, Boyle; and Blackburne into the 20th century. In the 17th century we find Burgoyne, Bishop, Wilks and Graham in the village. Dixon and a large farmer 'Henry Walsh' are given in Butterfield.

Rathgar

In the 16th century we find these lands held by James Richards and later by Nicholas Segrave. The Cusacks occupied the castle in 1608 for several generations.

Terenure and Kimmage

In the 17th century Peter Barnewall held the castle and 6 dwellings, and Thomas Mason was a tenant who was robbed by John Woodfin. Wm. Dickinson was also a tenant. Terenure House was seat for the Deane family after its purchase in 1671 from Richard Talbot. In the latter 18th century Terenure House was taken by Mr. Robert Shaw, which formed a connection to the area for generations.

Fortfield House on the lands of Kimmage was built in 1785. In 1811 the lands passed to Sir Wm. McMahon. In 1858 they passed to John Hatchell, the grandfather of Mr. Louis Perrin-Hatchell, who was resident in the early 20th century.

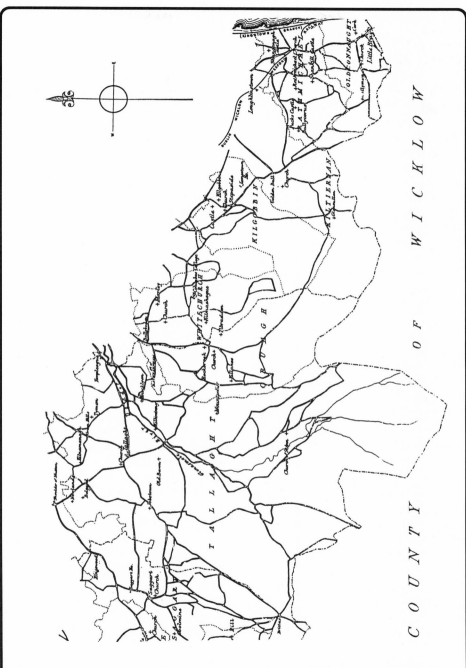

Ordnance Map Showing Tallaght, Whitechurch, Kilgobbin, Old Connaught....

21

Tallaght

TALLAGHT PARISH

The Castle at Tallaght was occupied by the Archbishops, dating back to the 14th century when it was erected. The principal resident in the village of Tallaght in 1650 was John Jones.

Jobstown

Also known as Rathmintin, these lands were acquired by Richard Fitzwilliam in 1326, from Ralph Aubry. and it remained in the family till the 17th century when the Archbold, and later the Whitshed families are found there.

Belgard

In the 15th century Talbot of Feltrim is at the Castle. In the 18th century it was in possession of the Dillon family, then passing to Dominick Trant and later to a Dr. Kennedy.

Newlands

Here find the Cole, Arthur, Wolfe, Ponsonby and O'Brien families of note.

Kilnamanagh

Here find the Talbot, Belgard, Parsons, Fitzwilliam, and Hawkins families.

Tymon

Anciently the lands of O'Mothan, we find Loftus, and one Barnaby Relly (a devout Roman Catholic) in the 17th c.

Templeogue

Alexander and King are given here in Balls History (1905). The Harold clan is found here early, and the Talbot families who were Roman Catholic, and later the Domvilles in the 17th century.

Knocklyon

Among owners we find Rideleford, Burnell, Bathe, Nugent, Talbot, Deering, Loftus and Handcock. Archbold, Relly, and Fieragh are noted.

Killininny

Rideleford, de Marisco, Cosyn, Immaulouz, Ashbourne, Newcomen, Briscoe, Cottle and Allen are noted.

Whitechurch

Old Bawn

Bulkeley, and others in his service, also of Welsh birth, are noted in 1641. Judge Worth (d.1721), and several of the Tynte family are found in later times.

Tallaght Hills

Long under control of the Irish, in the 16th century it was granted to the Luttrells, and to the Talbots of Belgard. After 1641 we find Loftus, Parsons, Bulkeley, and Allen of Wolstans. One Henry Hackett inhabited a house at Oldcourt then. O'Byrne and Fitzgerald caused some trouble there in 1717. The 'Hell Fire Club' (18th c.) was erected by the Conollys of Castletown.

CRUAGH PARISH

(formerly Creevagh) Noted families at Killakee are those of Henry Joy, Guinness, St. Michael, and Mr. Lundy Foot. In the 13th century we find Butler, Wallis, Finglas, and Fitzgerald. In the 16th century we find Luttrell and Talbot of Belgard. The Loftus family made many improvements here and after 1641 we find 'British Protestants' Thomas Price, John Whyte, and William Thomas suffering damages. Richard Greene of Cruagh, Samuel Brown of Newtown and Luke White of Woodlands are noted.

WHITECHURCH PARISH

Marlay House, the seat of the La Touche family, was later owned by R. Tedcastle. Glensouthwell was built by the Southwells; Hollypark by Jeffrey Foot; Hermitage was home to Hudson and Moore families. In 1335 Robert De Moenes leased lands. The Harold family is closely identified with the area. Loftus, King, Burgoyne, Taylor, LaTouche and John Philpot Curran are subsequently found.

Kilgobbin

KILGOBBIN

The Harolds are the first owners of Kilgobbin after the 12th century invasions, which later passed to the Hackets, and was occupied by the Howell family as well. The Derpatricks of Stillorgan are at Balyofryn and the Dawe family are at Jamestown in this era.

A branch of the Walsh family of Carrickmines, the Harolds' comrades in protecting the Pale, settled at Kilgobbin, and were succeeded by Adam Loftus in 1641. Subsequent names are Talbot; General Monk; Dr. Harding; Radcliffe; Wandesforde; Eustace of Harristown; McDonnell of Antrim; and Nutley.

KILTIERNAN PARISH

Before the Norman conquest Kiltiernan and Glencullen were the lands of MacGilamocholmog. Passing from Carew and later the religious Abbots, we find Walter Goulding; Walter Peppard; Edward Bassenet; and subsequently in 1577, Fitzwilliam of Merrion, with these lands. In the 17th century we find Wm. Nally of Roebuck as a principal farmer, and 'Murtagh' was 'ye ploughman' at Glencullen. Glencullen went to the FitzSimons and Kiltiernan to the Johnsons. In the 18th century Adair and Anderson are found.

RATHMICHAEL PARISH

We find the Lawless family being supplanted by the Walsh family in the 15th century. In 1537 we find Talbot and Walsh in need of assistance against the incursions of the O'Tooles. Barnewall is found at this time here. Shanganagh was occupied by Baxters and later by Walsh again after Restoration.

Saggart

OLD CONNAUGHT PARISH

Old Conna Hill, residence of Capt. Riall, and Connaught House of Lord Plunket, were noted in Balls time. Bray served as the seat of Manorial government for de Rideleford after the invasions.

In the 13th century we find R. Chapman and P. Makagan. In the 14th century Geoffrey Crump, and R. deBray are noted. Bray was burned by the O'Tooles and O'Byrnes in 1313 and was considered wild territory. Among the largest tenants at Bray in 1284 were Wm. le Deveneis, John Clements, Robert the Baker, and W. de Belinges.

The Archbolds who were protectors of the Pale with Harold and Walsh, are in Bray in the 14th century and it is given that they and the Lawless family were prominent at that time. In old Connaught Garret Warren was schoolteacher for the Catholic residents.

After the Commonwealth, Walsh lands in Old Connaught passed to Major Henry Jones, and then to John Baxter. Edward Billingsly was prominent there, as was Henry Bennett at Ballyman.

The Roberts family appears in the mid 18th century in Old Connaught, and they were of ancient Welsh descent.

SAGGART PARISH

As was the case in Bray, a leading mercantile family in Dublin borrowed the parish name as their own, becoming in 1282 'John and Richard de Tasagart' (per Ball). Coolmine in the 13th century belonged to the Berminghams and Hackets. The O'Tooles and O'Byrnes made many incursions in the 14th century. In the 15th c. we note the Dens, the Founts, the Prestons and the Handcocks. Savage and Ffolliott were

Newcastle

granted property there, and some land was forfeited by Ed. Byrne. In the 17th c. Sir William Parsons had many lands here and residents named Jackson, Allen and Graham are noted by Ball. The Den family were of note through the 18th c..

RATHCOOLE PARISH
The Scurlock family had residence here from the 15th century, and Johnstown House was the seat of Sir John C. Kennedy. Names noted here are Meldiric (Mulderick), Aubry, Marshall, and those that took their cognomen from Rath by the 13th century. In the 16th c. and later we note John Mey; James Bathe; the FitzGeralds; and the Darlases of Maynooth. In 1641 it was a stronghold of the Irish, supported by the Scurlocks and the Hetheringtons as testified to by Digory Cory and widow Honor Pooley. We then find Wharton; Chambers; Willion; Barry; Robinson; Moses Reyly; Lovelace; Eaton; Murphy; Lawlor; Leedom; and Walsh of note.

NEWCASTLE PARISH
In the 13th century 'MacGillamoch-olmog' still ruled as chief. Early names were; St. John; de Revell; le White; Yerward the Welshman; Elias of Winchester; Godiman; Carrick; Russell; and le Marshall. In 1562 cows were stolen from William Clinch. The Locke family of Athgoe and Colmanstown was of note here beginning in the 16th c., as were the Reynolds and Russells. In 1612 the first city officials were Reynolds; Parsons; Rolles; Kenny; Frend; Davies; White; Burton; Grible; Bridges; Rutledge; and Lushe. We find Scurlock and McDaniel giving place to R. Scarborough and Morgan Jones. Nowlan and Lawless are found later.

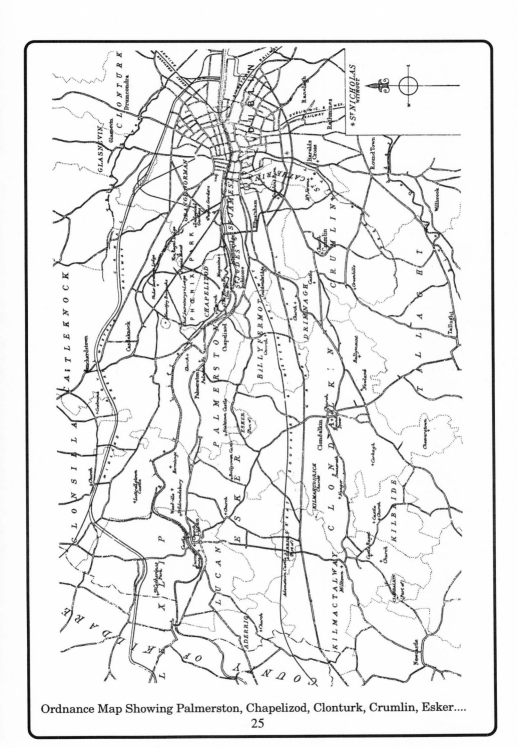

Ordnance Map Showing Palmerston, Chapelizod, Clonturk, Crumlin, Esker....

25

Clonsilla

CLONSILLA PARISH

Luttrellstown was from the middle ages until the 19th century, the home of the Luttrell family Their lands served as the county boundary on its Meath and Kildare borders. The first of the name to come to Ireland was Sir Geoffrey Luttrell who arrived around 1204. From him descends the noble family of Luttrell of Dunster Castle, in Somersetshire in England.

Col. John Hewson, once Governor of Dublin and past shoemaker in Westminster, is found here in the 17th century. The east end of the Clonsilla church was found as an 18th century burial place for one branch of the Slingsby family, of whom one is given as 'alias Finglas'. One 'Mr. Luke White, ancestor of Lord Annaly' changed the name of the place for a while to 'Woodlands'.

LEIXLIP PARISH

Sir Nicholas White came to control St. Catherine's Park here in the 16th century. He appears to be the son of James White, the steward of the household of James, ninth Earl of Ormonde. Sir Nicholas White, from whom the Whytes of Loughbrickland descend, was married first to a lady called Sherlock and later, in 1587, to Mary Brereton. The latter would subsequently marry Sir T. Hartpole, of Carlow .

The Davys are found here in the early 18th century, as are the Cooke family.

LUCAN PARISH

On the south side of the walls of the old parish church, which was connected to the castle by a door, was a burial place of the Vesey family. In 1204 Lucan was granted to Wirris Peche, who

Kilmactalway

appears to have been a native of Hampshire. Others of the name are noted in Ireland at that time as well, including Richard Peche in the reign of Richard II. Subsequent names here are: Hanstede; Pippard; de Nottingham; Gernan; Rokeby; and the Fitzgeralds held the castle till the 16th century. Sir William Sarsfield made Lucan Castle one of the principal houses in Co. Dublin. Sir Theophilus Jones rules here subsequently, and we find Nicholas Hide in a house here. The old castle was home to the Vesey family until 1772, when the new house was erected.

ADERRIG PARISH

In this parish lay the isolated townland of Adamstown. Adamstown Castle is named for the Adam family which was established in the 16th century in the parish of Esker.

We find le Marshall; Douces; Pedelow; and Philip in the area with holdings in the 14th century. At the beginning of the 15th century the Fitzgeralds have holdings at Aderrig.

Subsequently we find Thomas Sedgrave, of the Dublin mercantile family in a house here. After the Restoration we find the Whites and Allens once more owning lands in Aderrig, along with Arthur, 2nd Viscount Ranelagh. Robert Scarborough is given as a principal resident in the townland of Aderrig.

Backweston House is given as the residence of Sir Bryan O'Neill, a descendant of the 'Chiefs of Claneboy.'

KILMACTALWAY PARISH

Castle Bagot is found here. The beginning of the 17th century saw many lands in the hands of the Russell family.

Kilbride

Other noted family names here are Walse; Mey; Bassenet; Eustace at Milltown; Harte at Jordanstown; and Thunder at Grange. The Bagots arrive in the later part of the 18th century.

KILBRIDE PARISH

The castle of which little remains was built before the 16th century. It was leased to John Gibbons in 1537; and to Thomas Bathe in 1570. At the time of the Restoration the family of Carberry assumes the land, from whom one of the townlands takes its name, and the Luttrells appear as owners of Baldonan.

KILMAHUDDRICK PARISH

The names of Patrick Holder (1539); Sedgrave of Cabra (17th c.); Nicholas Wolverston (1650); and Patrick Thunder of Kilmahuddrick (1666); are given.

ESKER PARISH

MacGillamocholmog, the Irish chieftain was granted lands here after helping to route the Danes for the Anglo-Norman forces. Gregory Tweddell, yeoman and soldier, is here at Ballydowd in the mid 16th century. The Browne family is still resident in the parish in the 17th century as are Christopher Taylor and 'Lamerick Nottingham'.

Sir Robert Kennedy was a much noted person here, with a small house on the lands of Kishoge and other lands. Gerrard Archbold is on Kishoge in 1641. Before the Restoration we find Capt. Peasley with lands that would go back to the Nottinghams, and at this time the Forsters are found along with Mr. Drape, Mr. Burton and Mr. Harbourne. Ballyowen would pass to Col. Bellew and then to Rochfort.

Ballyfermot

Hermitage was the residence of Maj.-Gen. Robert Naper which passed to Hon. Robert Butler in 1739. Ballydowd Castle, the home of the Forster family appears to have been occupied by the Ulster King of Arms, John Hawkins, in the 18th century.

PALMERSTON PARISH

The Castle of Irishtown, (built by Patrick Browne), was the only surviving relic in Balls History of Dublin. Palmerston is a place name found more than once in Dublin and Kildare.

The Allen family held Palmerston lands into the 17th century. Prior to 1642 the lands of Irishtown were farmed by the Ussher family and a yeoman called John Lawless. Among principal residents of 17th century Palmerston were William Smith; Walter Archbold; a wealthy Englishman Thomas Vincent; Eustace; and Keatinge. The latter were buried in Palmerston churchyard.

Subsequently we find the Temple family; the Wilcocks; the Hutchinson family; and the Rev. Philip Smythe.

BALLYFERMOT PARISH

Among the early owners of these lands were the de Clahull and Burnell families in the 14th century. The Barnewalls are mentioned in connection with the area as well. In 1578 we find a Richard Wespey here. Robert Newcomen arrived in Ireland in 1585 and resided at the castle, founding a family noted in Ireland for more that 200 years. Other houses in the parish housed the families of Verveer; Styles; Carden; Ryves; Exham; and Talbot of Templeogue. The Domviles were noted in the 17th century. At the close of the 18th c., Mr. Prossor kept a school in the castle.

Clondalkin

CLONDALKIN PARISH

The Comyns of Balgriffin and Laurence Blundell held these lands early. In 1393 we find John Shillingford; and in 1345 John FitzSimons 'late guardian of trade' in Ireland. The Neills, the family from whom the townland in the parish takes its name, were prominent in the area. We also find one Roger Bekeford, grandson of Simon Neill.

Subsequently we find here the country house of the Molyneux family seated here in the 17th century. We also find Mr. Caldbeck and Barry Yelverton here. In the 18th century the Finlay family settled at Corkagh, and we find Arthur Wolfe at Newlands noted as well.

DRIMNAGH PARISH

Drimnagh Castle was for centuries the seat of the great Anglo-Norman family of Barnewall. We read that the founders of the family in Ireland settled in Munster at Bearhaven, but they were slaughtered, with only one member escaping, and he was the first of the name to possess Drimnagh. Hugh de Barnewall is found there in 1216. They held lands here into the 18th century at least.

In the 17th century at the Castle we find Lt.- Col. Ferneley. Subsequently we find the Archer family (1735). The lands of Robin Hood appear to have been the site of a well known house of entertainment at the time. In 1780 Mr. Reilly occupied the castle and said that Mr. Ennis was the grandfather of the owner before him.

CRUMLIN PARISH

Crumlin was known as Crum or Trum in earlier times. At the close of the 16th century the Purcell family was seated

St. James & St. Jude

near the village and remained so for several hundred years. The Brereton family is found here, as is Sir Patrick Fox. A branch of the Ussher family settled here in the reign of James I. Most of the lands came into the possession of the Deane family in the latter 17th century. We also find a Mathew family. Andrew Trench (d.1750), and John Rider (d.1762) both lived to be 100 years old. In 1766 Thwaites and Purcell are noted. In 1798 Arthur Orde and Thomas Jones kept a boarding school at Crumlin.

Portions of the Parishes of
ST. Catherine & St. Nicholas Without
Harold's Cross originated from a cross which marked the boundary of the lands of the Archbishop of Dublin and warned the Harolds, the wild guardians of the Pale near Whitechurch, that they must not encroach on these lands.

Two of the earliest tenants were Wm. Moenes of Rathmines and Nicholas Sueterby. Mount Jerome, in the early 18th century was occupied by Mr. Daniel Falkiner, the father of John Falkiner of Nangor Castle in Clondalkin. The Falkiners of Abbotstown descend from these as well. In the mid 18th century Mt. Jerome was occupied by the Wilkinson family. The Weld family was at Harolds Cross for many years. In 1784 Mt. Jerome was purchased by John Keogh (d.1817), an early leader for Catholic emancipation.

ST. JAMES & ST. JUDE PARISH

(formerly included in an extinct parish called St. John of Kilmainham.) The district known as Dolphins Barn probably was named for the Dolphin or Dolphyn family. In the 17th century we

Chapelizod

find Chillam's Farm, the name taken from a Drogheda family of the name that owned it before the rebellion. William Budd and Sampson Holmes are given. John Stephens, eminent tanner and weaver, died there in 1761.

Names given in connection with Kilmainham in the 18th century were: Fownes; Cope of Loughgall; the Annesley family at Inchicore; and Bradstreet. A brewery was established at Island Bridge by John Davies who died in 1704, and another was afterwards owned there by Richard Pockrich. Andrew Haubois is also noted as owner of a celebrated nursery. At Island Bridge we find the names of Crowe (1720); Curtis (1724); Cox (1736); Ford (1738); Noy (1746); Jones (1749); (1764) Green; (1768) Pennefather; Keightley (1786); and Trail in 1799.

CHAPELIZOD PARISH

In Lord Valentia's time a great artificer, Edmond Tingham, resided here. In the 18th century John Dawson is noted as a host; in 1760 John Ryan was an entertainer; in 1787 Thomas Morris advertised stabling for 60 horses; William Conolly of Castletown planted golden Oziers along the Liffey; John Rutty discovered wells of petrifying waters; a spa was founded by Dr. Bellon; Richard White, mayor of Dublin died here in 1747; in 1754 we find Rev. Walter Chamberlain; in 1761 Capt. R. Aylmer, a centenarian; and in 1776 Dr. Richard Reddy.

O'Connell Monument, Glasnevin.

Howth

Howth

The St. Lawrence family held the lands of Howth from the time of the Anglo-Norman invasions down unto the 20th century. According to legend the founder of the family was a brother-in-law of the Anglo-Norman conqueror of Ulster, John De Courcy. His original name was said to have been 'Tristam', and legend gives that Howth was granted to him on the feast of St. Lawrence, hence the change of name.

Ball, in his History of Dublin, gives the pedigree of the family and of its cadet lines, 'correcting' some errors of the past. The seat of the family for over 700 years was Howth Castle, not far from the isthmus on the northern shore of the peninsula.

It is given that the names of several families connected with the peninsula tell of a Norse (Viking) heritage. The family of Harford, 'still there in considerable numbers', were distinguished as a race by their tallness, fair complexion, and bright blue eyes. Ball also gives the family names of Thunder, Waldron and Rickard as being of suggested Norse descent.

During mediaeval times little is known of the inhabitants other than the St. Lawrence and Cornwalsh families. It was given that a family named Sutton likely resided on the southern lands of the area.

William Howth slew John Gernon, the strongest man in Ulster as given in ancient legend.

In the 16th century Corr Castle was held by the White family and another Castle stood on the lands of Sutton and was held by the Hackett family. The Shergoll name also appears several times in the 17th century. Around 1660 in the House of Howth we find Peter Wynne and William Fitzwilliam. In the town of Howth the tituladoes were Thomas Lea and Richard St. Lawrence. 'In the Walls' was Thomas Dongan. In 1664 John Burniston was rated for five hearths and in 1667 Thomas Lightfoot was rated for two; Abraham Ellis for four; and Col. Newcomen for six hearths.

John Burniston and Col. Newcomen came to hold the lands of Sutton successively. Before the commonwealth they were held by William Gough. The names of Swift and Grattan, of note, are connected here in latter times as well.

In the 19th century many changes and much rebuilding came about. Sutton House was rebuilt and was the residence of Mr. Justice Jackson and then Rev. W. Lawrenson and later it passed to Mr. Andrew Jameson 'who built a modern house near its site'. Carrig Breac was long the home of physician Wm. Stokes. Drumleck was formerly the residence of Wm. McDougall, by whom it was built. Kilrock, formerly the residence of Lord Justice FitzGibbon; and St. Fintan's was the property of the Hawkins family.

The fourth Earl of Howth (d.1909) was buried at Howth in the tomb of his ancestors. On his death the barony and earldom of Howth lapsed. The estates passed by will to his nephew Julian Gaisford of Offington, who assumed by royal license the arms and names of St. Lawrence.

Southern Fine Gall

Here we glance quickly at ten parishes north of the River Liffey in Dublin County. The lands of the north of Co. Dublin have been called Fingal for over 900 years. Its exact extent has changed over time, but it is earliest referred to in the Annals when the Northmen, Danes, or Vikings were in control of it. Before the 12th century invasions, according to O'Dugan, Fingal was ruled by MacGillamocholmog, the Irish chieftain who also held lands of south Dublin.

CASTLEKNOCK PARISH

The principal seat of the parish is Abbotstown, the home of the family of Hamilton, who held the title of HolmPatirck. At the time of the invasions the fort of Castleknock was selected by Rory O'Conor, King of Connaught, as his headquarters while fighting the invaders in Dublin in the summer of 1171.

Among those cited by Ball in the 14th century are: the Deuswell family; the de la Feldes at Corduff; the Woodlocks at Cappoge; Walter Kerdiff (note Cardiffsbridge); the Porter and Renville families who held Porterstown and Renvelstown; John Owen who held Diswellstown; and the Luttrells at Luttrellstown.

The Burnells were seated at Ballygriffin but some of the family appear at Castleknock in the 15th and 16th centuries. Porterstown was occupied centuries later by William Muschamp; at Diswellstown, Nathanial Leake occupied a house, as did James Enos.

In the early 16th century William Rowles was of Blanchardstown and Robert Ball is a principal man of the area as well. At the time of the 17th century rebellion Martin Dillon is given

Mulhuddart

at Huntstown. At Pelletstown John Connel was resident, and he also held the lands of Ashtown; at the time of the rebellion, Robert Bysse, high sheriff of Dublin is resident there.

The Falkiner family became seated at Abbotstown, and the first of the name there was Frederick Falkiner, a leading Dublin banker. His grandfather was the first to settle in Ireland and the family was early on identified with Leeds.

The Arthurs are found continuing their residence at 'Much Cabragh' in the first half of the 18th century. At that time the Warrens resided at Corduff; and the Kennan family had long held Diswellstown. Hillbrook, near Abbotstown, was the home of Lt. Col. Robert Sampson (d.1764) who seems to descend from a Scots family identified with Co. Donegal. Other residents of note included Capt. Nixon; Stearne Tighe; Mrs. Blanchfort; and Mrs. Harpur. By the end of the century we find Elm Green as the residence of Richard Malone who was interested in pictures and prints. Scribblestown was the home of the Rathborne family. The ancestors of Lord Holmpatrick settled in the parish at this time with the coming of the Hamilton family.

MULHUDDART PARISH

From the 14th to the 16th century we find the names of Cruise of Cruiserath; Blanchfield; Plunkett; Tyrell of Powerstown; Scurlagh; Dowdall; Hunt; Fleming; and Bellings among those prominent in the area. In the bloody 17th century Powerstown is noted as belonging to William Freeme; John Jordan occupied Tyrrellstown; Nicholas Carte occupied Damastown; and Gilbert Ferris occupied Paslickstown.

Cloghran

In that century we also find the name of Povey who came into possession of Powerstown. At Damastown we find Hudson and Proby in the 1660's.

CLOGHRAN PARISH

(Note that there is another parish of this same name in Dublin County.) During the rebellion of 1641 all the buildings were demolished. Robert Hackett, a tanner, is noted as a prior owner of Ballycoolen. Mathew Barry assumed the lease of these lands subsequent to the mayor of Dublin in 1682.

WARD PARISH

After the 12th century invasions these lands were in the possession of the family of le Bank. During the first half of the 16th century the castle was occupied by Richard Delahide and subsequently held by the barons of Howth. Walter Segrave is also found at the castle. White and Ware are also mentioned in the area. At the middle of the 18th century New Park was the residence of George Garnett, and Spricklestown of Mr. James Hamilton.

St. MARGARET PARISH

Before the Anglo-Norman invasions Dunsoghly and Dunbro had a notable history, now lost. For five-hundred years after the 12th century invasions it served as residence for notables, before becoming so forgotten. The Plunkets are noted here in the 16th - 17th centuries. Dunsoghly castle then came under the possession of Tichborne and then to John Avery in 1672. At Dunbro we find Col. F. Willouby, a poor cavalier, of a well known family. A branch of the Warren family is given as

Finglas

as holding lands at Harristown around this time. At the beginning of the 18th century Dunbro was occupied by John Linegar, a citizen of Dublin.

FINGLAS PARISH

In the 16th century the principal resident here was named as Walter Kerdiff, and George Carey is given as the chief person in Finglas. Amongst prominent residents at the end of Elizabeths reign we find: the head of the Chamberlain family at Kilreesk; and at Ballygall we find Walter Ball, sometime mayor of Dublin. The most notable resident of that time was Sir Ambrose Forth.

In the 17th century we find: John England, village inn owner at Finglas; the Netervilles; Edward Capper; Wm. Baily who was driven from his mill at Finglas Bridge; and Robert Benison who lost cows, horses and carts. After the Restoration there were many new residents, the most notable of whom were cavaliers. Of the school at Finglas, Williams, Teebay, and Smith were licensed as masters, around the end of the century or shortly thereafter.

In the 18th century Thomas Wyndham was a noted resident, whose body was laid to rest in Salisbury Cathedral under a monument sculptured by Michael Rysbrack. Other residents included Boyle More; a son of Squire Robert Ball and it was given that the seat of the Ball family was moved to Drogheda from Ballygall; John Jephson; Ignatius Nugent; Sir N. Whitwell; Paul Barry; Lewis Layfield the Dublin actor; William Empson and Phineas Ferneley.

In that century we also find Ballygall in the occupation of Rev. Darley; and Johnstown in that of Robert French, the

Glasnevin

ancestor of Lord de Freyne. At Finglaswood House we find Thomas Savage who established there a tannery; at Jamestown we find Wm. Odlum; at Finglasbridge, Charles Vipont; at Cardiffsbridge, Wm. Rathborne; at Kilreesk, William Swan; and in the village Edward Lely, The Hon. Clotworthy Rowley, Thomas Towers, and John Ball.

GLASNEVIN PARISH

In the 20th century Glasnevin was well known for the cemetery there which held Daniel O'Connell, the liberator, and for the Botanic Gardens.

In the 16th century leases are found here held by Thomas Stephens, Alson FitzSimon, and Oliver Stephens; James and John Bathe; Braghall's farm went to John Quartermas and later to John Forster; the Seven farms to Thomas Lockwood and Richard Fagan; and Draycott's farm to Arland Ussher.

In the 18th century Dorothy Berkeley is found in the principal residence here, but was shortly replaced by Sir John Rogerson. Henry Mitchell succeeded John Putland in Glasnevin House, he was a banker and had great horticultural talents. Noted in the area we also find Thomas Egerton, a member of the Tatton family who died in 1756; Samuel Fairbrother a publisher who died in 1758; William Purdon; Col. Peter Renourd (d.1763); and Charles Davys (d.1769).

At the close of the 18th century Thomas Tickell's house and lands were sold by his grandson to the Dublin Society, and made the nucleus of the Botanic Gardens; and thirty years later the great cemetery was designed.

Grangegorman

GRANGEGORMAN Parish

(The parts that join on the north the parishes of Finglas and Glasnevin). In the 16th century we find Francis Agard residing here, and he was replaced by his son-in-law Sir Henry Harrington.

In the early 18th century Grangegorman became the residence of Charles Monck, who also possessed Charleville, in Co. Wicklow, through the family of his wife. At the time of his death in 1751, few houses are found in the northern part of the parish, and one of the earliest to be erected was given to be the Female Orphan House, built in the opening years of the 19th century.

ST. GEORGE PARISH

Stephen Lawless ruled the Abbey here in the 15th century, lands of which were granted in 1539 to Walter Peppard. At the time of the Commonwealth survey we find Mr. Munn in possession of a stone house and subsequently it was held by Mr. Leeson. Tristam Fortick, the founder of Fortick's alms house held Clonlife also known as 'the Grange' in the first half of the 18th century. Latter under the name of Fortick's Grove, the land was occupied by Taylor, Irwin, and Jones.

Eccles Mount was the country residence of Sir John Eccles, sometime Lord Mayor of Dublin. It was afterwards the residence of Joseph Damer, knight of the shire for Co. Tipperary; and later of the widow of Sir Sheffield Austen; and in 1757 of Nicholas Archdall. At the same time near it was a house called Mountjoy, which in 1761 was occupied by Henry Gavan.

Clonturk

CLONTURK PARISH

John Bathe (d.1586) had the castle at Drumcondra which was subsequently the residence of the noted Sir William Warren. He married the widow of John Bathe. He was the son of an English 'possessioner' known as valiant Capt. Humphrey Warren, who appeared in Ireland under Edward the Sixth as an official in Munster, and afterwards was an official in Ulster.

A few other names at random of note in the area include 'Marmaduke Coghill' in Georgian times; Harry Singleton; and Charles Moore, second Lord Tullamore.

In 1718 a Jewish burying ground had been made at Fairview. Around 1748, Joseph Dioderici came to live there. Sir Edward Newenham came to live on a house on the site of Drumcondra Castle around 1780. He succeeded there his aunt, Mrs. O'Callaghan, a wealthy lady who died in 1779. About 1773 Drumcondra House was leased to Alexander Kirkpatrick, a leading Dublin citizen.

Conclusion

This concludes the family notes based upon the history of Dublin by Elrington Ball. The reader should note the changes in places names and in surnames. Examples: the place name of Leperstown being changed to Leopardstown; families taking the surname of 'Rath' from the place name of Rathcoole in Ireland; and the use of an alias, as in "Walsh alias McHowell".

Could you guess: that Mr. Richard Cooley, would change his name to 'Wesley' and later still to Lord Mornington; or that the Wolverstons, Cheevers, and Goodmans settled in Dublin early and later became Catholic?

Family Locations

Dublin is in the eastern province of Ireland known as Leinster. On the east is the Irish Sea, on the north and west is the County of Meath, to the west and southwest is Co. Kildare, and to the south is Co. Wicklow.

The historian Ptolemy gives us the first account of peoples of the area. He gave them the name of Eblani or Blanii, and placed them in the counties of Dublin and Meath.

The first well known settlers from abroad were the Danes or Vikings. They established holdings well into the county of Dublin, and continued to live on in peace there after the noted Battle of Clontarf, which broke the military power of the Dublin Vikings.

According to Lewis, in his Topographical Dictionary, a considerable portion of the county north of the River Liffey was in the possession of the Danes and was called 'Fingal' denoting the lands of these foreigners. Traditionally it was given that the lands to the south of the Liffey were noted as 'Dubhgall', denoting another group of Danes. Henry II granted all of Fingall to Hugh de Lacy, Lord of Meath.

Two of the early Irish chieftains in the area were the O'Birnes (O'Byrnes, etc..) and O'Tooles. They were continuosly pushed from Dublin, and the county of Wicklow to the south was formed by the English in part to contain the old Irish.

The baronies within Dublin county were those of: Balrothery, Castleknock, Coolock, Nethercross, Newcastle, Half Rathdown, and Upper Cross, exclusive of those of St. Sepulchre and Donore which are parts of the liberties of the city of Dublin, a county unto itself. (see barony map in this introduction).

Notable 19th century towns and places

The Parish

included the: corporate towns of Swords and Newcastle; the seaport and fishing and post towns of Howth, Kingstown, Balbriggan and Malahide; The fishing towns of Rush, Skerries, and Baldoyle; the inland post-towns of Cabinteely, Lucan, Rathcool and Tallaght; the market town of Ballymore-Eustace, and the town of Rathfarnham, (both of which had a penny post to Dublin). There were many large villages near the town of Dublin, and many villages scattered throughout the county.

The Parish

The researcher will note that there are several territorial divisions to be aware of. There are Roman Catholic parishes. They are separate from the Church of Ireland parishes which closely follow the civil parish outlines in most cases.

The Church of Ireland was the established church, holding the responsibility for many record keeping duties now performed by the government. Hence those records are of interest, particularly for prominent families which settled in Dublin. (Several denominations have been buried in Church of Ireland graveyards,)

Landmarks

The county measures only about 30 miles long, from north to south, and at its narrowest from east to west it was less than 7 miles wide.

There were round towers at Lusk, Swords and Clondalkin. Cromlechs (standing stone monuments) were given at Glen Druid near Cabinteely; Killiney; Howth; Mount Venus; Glen Southwell; and Larch Hill. All these were enumerated by Lewis in the 19th century. Even though Dublin was the

Vikings

center of English power in Ireland, the entire county was dotted with castles, necessary to control and survive the rebellions of the older families.

Dublin City is given as the metropolis of Ireland, and it was designated as a county in and of itself, found within the County of Dublin. As mentioned in the 'Families of Co. Galway, Ireland', a line was often drawn in legend, as well as in reality, between Dublin and Galway, dividing Ireland into two halves.

The Vikings

Although present as traders earlier, the Vikings or Danes in the year 836 are given as arriving at the River Liffey' with a fleet of 60 ships furthering the efforts of savage raids made inland. They controlled Dublin now, which was their stronghold for the entire province of Leinster. 'Fin-Gal', to the north of the river took its name denoting the territory of the 'White Stranger' or Norwegian. Lands to the south were called Dubh-Gal, after the territory of the 'Black Strangers' or 'Danes'. (Both groups have been referred to as Vikings in modern day works.).

The 'control' of the area was fleeting, and many battles are recorded over the next two centuries. Often the Irish took the town from the Danes for a short period, until the 'foreigners' returned in force to regain control.

It is noted that, at the Battle of Clontarf (1014), the power of the Dublin Danes was broken, but they remained on in the everyday life of the Dublin area. The battle was not just one of Irish vs. Dane, for there were Danes and Irish supporting both sides of the battle.

When the Norman forces arrived to gain control of Dublin and Wicklow

The Norman Invasion

after the invasions of 1169, it was the 'Danes' who are most often mentioned as being defeated in battle, although Roderic, King of Ireland is found gathering forces too. (per Lewis)

Shifting Alliance

To illustrate the confusion and bloodshed, it was given by Lewis that as the Danes retreated from the victorious 'English' forces, they were further 'cut to pieces' by the Irish peasantry throughout the country, in retribution for their former cruelties to the Irish. Some 'English' writers seem to mark this as the true 'defeat of the Danes in Ireland'. (The battle of Clontarf is one of epic proportion in Irish legend - but it did not 'drive the Vikings out of Ireland.')

After the Normans subdued the Danes, the Danes served the Norman military. They accompanied Strongbow in an early incursion into the province of Munster. They were defeated however, by Donald, the Irish Prince of Ossory. Subsequently Roderic O'Conor, heading Irish forces, ravaged the countryside even to the doors of Dublin. The fighting would continue back and forth for centuries.

In 1312 the O'Byrnes and O'Tooles attacked Dublin City from the hills to the south. The forces of the city had been sent to Louth or Orgial, to quell an insurrection of the Verdons. The Irish retreated as those forces returned.

The back and forth battle would continue. In 1402 John Drake led a party against the O'Byrnes whom he defeated and they were forced to surrender the Castle of Newcastle-MacKynegan. In 1410 the lord-deputy made incursions into O'Byrne territory but retreated when

Wild Geese

his 'kernes' (Irish mercenaries) deserted en masse. In 1413 the O'Byrnes defeated the citizens of Dublin and carried off many prisoners. In 1516 the citizens of Dublin routed the O'Tooles of the mountains, slew the chief and sent his head as a present to the mayor. The victory was short lived, for they were defeated on a second incursion into the Irish chieftains territory.

Not until the final defeat of the Irish in the 17th century would power be fully vested in the English authorities. There would be a wholesale transfer of land and power at that time. The Cromwellian settlement of Ireland at that time brought an end to Gaelic power and society.

Wild Geese

The 'wild geese' are generally conceived of as the Irish who fled to the continent and joined the armies of Europe, principally in France, beginning in the 17th century. Thousands were forced to do so, being deprived of lands and liberty at home. It was always believed that one day, like the wild geese, they would return home to Ireland. Thousands of these Irishmen and their family histories in Ireland are recorded in <u>King James Irish Army List</u> by D'Arcy.

Surname Distribution

The 17th century was a tumultuous one for all of Ireland, and indeed for Dublin. It is fitting here to look at the more numerous names found in Dublin. First, we will look at the Irish "census of 1659" and we will compare that with the 1890 birth index of Ireland. (The latter recorded surnames having 5 or more births in the year of the survey.)

Remember that the 'Mac' and 'O' before Irish names can disappear at will.

1659 Census

Following this page is a chart of the families in County Dublin, according to the barony in which they were located in 1659. (Note that the 1659 'census' is by no means a 'complete' census.)

The 'principal' families in the census of 1659 are listed along with the total of each name (by barony) on the following pages. Among the most numerous names in Dublin were:

Birne (208) {Byrne, Burnes, O'Byrne}
Kelly (158) (Kelley)
Doyle (118)
Walsh, Welsh (87)
Murphy & Morphy (72)
White (55)   (Whyte)
Farrall (53)   {Farrell}
Connor (53)   {Conner}
Browne (53)   (Brown}
Nowland (53)   {Nolan, Noland}
Smyth(e) (50) {Smith}
Cavenagh, Cavenah, Keavenagh (48)
Realy, Reyly (40) {Reilly, Riley}
Bryan (39) {Brien, Brian, etc..}
Neal (39)   {Neill}
Quinn(e) (36)   (Quin)
Moore (35)   {More}
Martine, Martyn (34)
Davis (32)   (Davies)
Callen, Cullan, Cullin (27)

(Names such as McTeige, McShane, McDaniel, McDonogh and McEdmond are sometimes used only for one generation.) I have added names in brackets {}, to show other ways of spelling the names given above.

Compare Dublin names with the names in other counties and you will find differences. The Mac and O prefix before so many Irish names - has been dropped. Only McAllen, Mccann McDaniell, McAdam, McDonell and McGlorye are found, and in small numbers. No 'O' names are given at all.

Modern Surnames

By contrast, the most popular names in Dublin at the time of the 1890 birth index of Ireland were:

Byrne (301)
Kelly (194)
Doyle (162)
Murphy (132)
Smith (106)
O'Brien (105)
Kavanagh (97)
Dunne (93)
O'Neill (93)
Reilly (93)
Nolan (89)
Connor (82)
Walsh (77)
Farrell (73)
Carroll (71)
Ryan (65)
Moore (63)
Cullen (62)
Keogh (60)
Murray (60)
Whelan (59)
Brady (52)
Kennedy (51)

The number of births recorded in 1890 is given in parenthesis after the name. There was more than one way of spelling any of these names. They are grouped under the most common spelling found.

Mc Adam, etc.. 6 *Dublin City*

Allen & McAllen 14 *Dublin City*

Archbould 12 *Cowlock*

Barnewall 6 *Castleknocke*

Barry 8 *Dublin City*

Birne 86 *Newcastle & Upp.*

Birne 28 *Rathdowne*

Birne 13 *Nethercross*

Birne 11 *Balrothery*

Birne 26 *Cowlock*

Birne 5 *Castleknocke*

Birne 39 *Dublin City*

Boorke 9 *Newcastle & Upp.*

Bourke 5 *Dublin City*

Boylan 7 *Balrothery*

Boyle 6 *Dublin City*

Brayne 11 *Balrothery*

Brimingham 12 *Nethercross*

Brin 5 *Dublin City*

Browne 10 *Balrothery*

Browne 19 *Dublin City*

Browne (Eng. & Irish) 24 *Newcastle & Upp.*

Bryan 17 *Newcastle & Upp.*

Bryan 9 *Cowlock*

Bryan 13 *Dublin City*

Burne 8 *Newcastle & Upp.*

Butler 10 *Dublin City*

Butterly 8 *Nethercross*

Callen 11 *Balrothery*

Callen & Cullan 10 *Rathdowne*

Callin & Cullin 6 *Dublin City*

Carroll 6 *Newcastle & Upp.*

Carroll 5 *Dublin City*

Casey 10 *Nethercross*

Cassy 8 *Cowlock*

Casy 6 *Dublin City*

Cavenagh 12 *Dublin City*

Cavenah 12 *Rathdowne*

Clarke 11 *Dublin City*

Coleman 9 *Nethercross*

Coleman 7 *Balrothery*

Connor 14 *Newcastle & Upp.*

Connor 10 *Nethercross*

Connor 11 *Balrothery*

Connor 10 *Cowlock*

Connor 8 *Dublin City*

Corbally 9 *Balrothery*

Cruise 10 *Balrothery*

Daly 10 *Nethercross*

Mc Daniell 7 *Dublin City*

Daniell and McDaniell 13 *Newcastle & Upp.*

Daniell & Donell 12 *Nethercross*

Davis 13 *Dublin City*

Davis Eng. & Irish 19 *Newcastle & Upp.*

Dermott 10 *Balrothery*

Doly, etc.. 8 *Dublin City*

Donell and McDonell 8 *Newcastle & Upp.*

Donn 7 *Balrothery*

Dowdall 9 *Nethercross*

Dowdall 12 *Balrothery*

Doweing 7 *Newcastle & Upp.*

Doyle 48 *Newcastle & Upp.*

Doyle 29 *Rathdowne*

Doyle 8 *Nethercross*

Doyle 13 *Cowlock*

Doyle 20 *Dublin City*

Duff 9 *Balrothery*

Duff 8 *Dublin City*

Dunn 18 *Newcastle & Upp.*

Dunne 6 *Castleknocke*

English 15 *Balrothery*

Ennis and Ennos 16 *Newcastle & Upp.*

Farrall 8 *Rathdowne*

Farrall 12 *Balrothery*

Farrall 9 *Cowlock*	Malone 12 *Newcastle & Upp.*
Farrell 19 *Newcastle & Upp.*	Martin 8 *Dublin City*
Farrell 5 *Dublin City*	Martine 7 *Newcastle & Upp.*
Fitzgerald 6 *Newcastle & Upp.*	Martyn 13 *Balrothery*
Fitzgerald 4 *Dublin City*	Martyn 6 *Castleknocke*
Flemming 8 *Dublin City*	Moore 13 *Newcastle & Upp.*
Fulham 8 *Balrothery*	Moore 7 *Rathdowne*
Fullam 8 *Dublin City*	Moore 6 *Castleknocke*
Garrett 5 *Dublin City*	Moore 9 *Dublin City*
Mc Glorye 6 *Dublin City*	Morphy 12 *Rathdowne*
Gormly 8 *Newcastle & Upp.*	Morran 7 *Newcastle & Upp.*
Harford 17 *Balrothery*	Murphy 30 *Newcastle & Upp.*
Hughs 9 *Dublin City*	Murphy 7 *Balrothery*
Kearovan - Kearogan 13 *Newcastle & Upp.*	Murphy 10 *Cowlock*
Keavenagh - Cavanagh 24 *Newcastle & Upp.*	Murphy 11 *Castleknocke*
Kelly 34 *Newcastle & Upp.*	Murphy 10 *Dublin City*
Kelly 12 *Rathdowne*	Murrey 9 *Nethercross*
Kelly 36 *Nethercross*	Murrey 14 *Balrothery*
Kelly 26 *Balrothery*	Neale 6 *Rathdowne*
Kelly 23 *Cowlock*	Neale 13 *Dublin City*
Kelly 11 *Castleknocke*	Neale - O'Neale 20 *Newcastle & Upp.*
Kelly 16 *Dublin City*	Nowland 6 *Rathdowne*
Kenedy 8 *Newcastle & Upp.*	Nowland 17 *Dublin City*
Kenedy 9 *Dublin City*	Nowland - Nowlane 30 *Newcastle & Upp.*
Kernan 6 *Dublin City*	Plunkett 8 *Newcastle & Upp.*
Laundy 8 *Balrothery*	Quinn 8 *Newcastle & Upp.*
Lawces 10 *Newcastle & Upp.*	Quinn 10 *Balrothery*
Lawler, etc... 16 *Newcastle & Upp.*	Quinn 7 *Castleknocke*
Lawlis 9 *Cowlock*	Quinne 11 *Nethercross*
Lennan 7 *Nethercross*	Realy 10 *Newcastle & Upp.*
Loghlin 9 *Balrothery*	Realy 11 *Balrothery*
Lynch 9 *Balrothery*	Reyly 9 *Nethercross*
Lynch & Lynchy 10 *Nethercross*	Reyly 10 *Dublin City*
Maccan 10 *Nethercross*	Roe 10 *Newcastle & Upp.*
Maccan 10 *Balrothery*	Roe 7 *Dublin City*
Mahowne & Mahon 9 *Balrothery*	Russell 15 *Balrothery*
Mallone 7 *Dublin City*	Ryan 11 *Nethercross*

Ryan 6 *Castleknocke*

Smyth 16 *Newcastle & Upp.*

Smyth 23 *Dublin City*

Smythe 11 *Cowlock*

Toole 12 *Newcastle & Upp.*

Toole 11 *Rathdowne*

Toole 6 *Dublin City*

Wade 10 *Balrothery*

Walsh 16 *Newcastle & Upp.*

Walsh 11 *Rathdowne*

Walsh 19 *Nethercross*

Walsh 14 *Balrothery*

Walsh 8 *Cowlock*

Welsh 19 *Dublin City*

White 12 *Nethercross*

White 17 *Balrothery*

White 11 *Cowlock*

White 15 *Dublin City*

Williams Eng.-Irish 12 *Newcastle & Upp.*

The New World

Several place names attest to Dublin connections in the new world. Dublin, New Hampshire (U.S.A.) was so named by Matthew Thornton (b.1714) an Irish born immigrant. There is yet today a fine Irish festival at the town of Dublin, Ohio, also named after early settlers.

There were a great number of famous Dubliners abroad in North America and Australia. Victor Herbert, was born in 1859 of a Dublin family and came to reside in the U.S.. He was hailed as a great creative artist of this century. (JAIHS. vol. 24., 1925.). Many would not recognize 'Herbert' as an Irish name.

John Burns (b. 1730), a native of the city of Dublin,was the first governor of Pennsylvania. Charles Phipps was a schoolmaster from Dublin found in Philadelphia in 1729. (JAIHS. 1906).

Ships

We read of the Ship 'Erin' from Dublin under the command of Mr. Murphy in early issues of the "Shamrock" newspaper (circa 1810 -17). This was one of a growing number of ships that would come from Dublin, particularly from the famine era (post 1845). New York, Philadelphia and Boston were favored ports.

We note earlier records between Providence, Rhode Island and Dublin. In 1786 the Ship 'Tristam' under Captain Russell departed for Dublin. It was a trip she would make many times. Its' arrival in Dublin, Ireland, was noted at the same time as the Ship 'Mary' and the Brig 'Little John' of Newport, Rhode Island. (JAIHS VI. 1906.) In October, 1809 the Brig 'Orient' arrived at New York, in 53 days from Dublin.

These are a few of thousands of references to Dublin in the new world.

Famine

The Famine

The major upheaval of land ownership subsequent to the 17th century confiscation's, came with the great famine of 1845-1852. The famine continued to drive the growth of the city.

The height of the famine came in 1847, and quickly sent thousands from rural Ireland into Dublin city. This would result in a net increase in population for Dublin, as most of the country dwindled. Many lived and died in Dublin. Some left for North America, Australia, Scotland and England.

Note that ships departed from Dublin carrying our ancestors who were not from Dublin at all. The same is true for all the Irish ports, but particularly so for Dublin during the famine years.

Sometimes the names, ages and occupations of fellow travelers prove to be more important than the port of departure itself.

Miscellaneous Records

Among the numerous scattered records in Dublin, are those for the Rotunda Maternity Hospital, founded in 1745. These records include the name and age of the wife; the name and occupation of the husband; and in many cases the date of Baptism and name of the child.

Current I.G.F. member Harry Dunn estimates some 300,000 listings for the hospital exist, and he gives that they can become a truly detailed (although tedious) part of reconstructing the members of a given family.

The registers for the period of 1797 to 1882 (omitting 1809-1819) have been filmed and are available through the LDS Family History Center program.

This is but one example of a source to augment local parish records in Dublin.

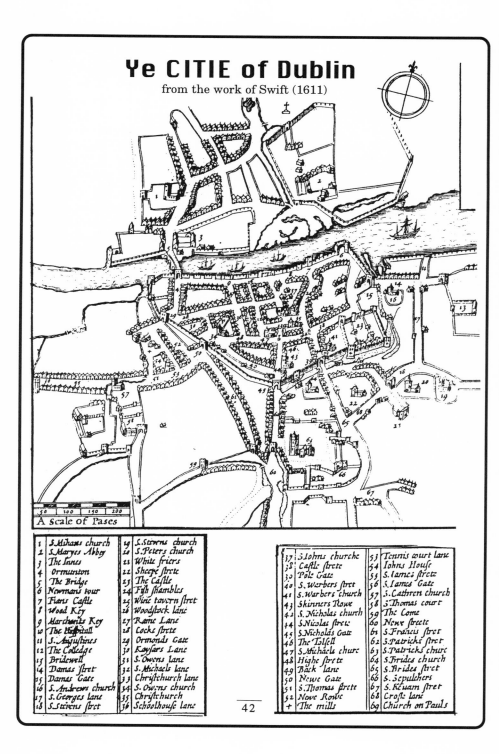

Ye CITIE of Dublin

from the work of Swift (1611)

A scale of Pases

1	S.Mihans church	19	S.Stevens church
2	S.Maryes Abbey	20	S.Peters church
3	The Innes	21	White friers
4	Ormunton	22	Sheepe strete
5	The Bridge	23	The Castle
6	Newmans tour	24	Fish shambles
7	Fiers Castle	25	Wine tavern stret
8	Wood Key	26	Woodstock lane
9	Marchants Key	27	Rame Lane
10	The Hospitall	28	Cocke strete
11	S.Augustines	29	Ormonds Gate
12	The Colledge	30	Kaysars Lane
13	Bridewell	31	S.Owens Lane
14	Damas stret	32	S.Michaels lane
15	Damas Gate	33	Christchurch lane
16	S.Andrews church	34	S.Owens church
17	S.Georges Lane	35	Christchurch
18	S.Stevens stret	36	Schoolhouse lane

37	S.Iohns churche	53	Tennis court lane
38	Castle strete	54	Iohns House
39	Pole Gate	55	S.Iames strete
40	S.Werbers stret	56	S.Iames Gate
41	S.Warbers church	57	S.Cathren church
43	Skinners Rowe	58	S.Thomas court
42	S.Nicholas church	59	The Come
44	S.Nicolas stret	60	Newe strete
45	S.Nicholas Gate	61	S.Francis stret
46	The Tolsell	62	S.Patricks stret
47	S.Michaels churc	63	S.Patricks churc
48	Highe strete	64	S.Brides church
49	Back lane	65	S.Brides stret
50	Newe Gate	66	S.Sepulchers
51	S.Thomas strete	67	S.Keuam stret
52	Newe Rowe	68	Crofs lane
+	The mills	69	Church on Pauls

Tracing Dublin Roots
Spellings

One common problem found with the arrival of emigrants in past centuries has been the 'spelling' of the family name. This should be remembered when researching any record, including passenger lists. The name could have been misspelled in the ships record, or could have been changed completely by the emigrant himself. (The latter is not common, but definitely a possibility in 'problem' research cases).

Other changes found in the spelling of our surnames bears repeating. Moloney was earlier found as Mullowny. So, remember to search for your family or place name phonetically - that is, by the sound of the name. The precise spelling was often changed, either by design or at the whim of the record makers!

Names like McShane, McTeige, McDonnogh and McDaniel are found often in 17th century Ireland - but they are not always considered true surnames. They were sometimes used more as nicknames- as in 'the son of' Rory O'Connor being recorded as a McRory instead of an O'Connor.

It is said that these names could be used for a generation - and then be dropped or changed altogether. When true, this poses a great challenge for the researcher.

If you are interested in the many spellings and variant spelling groups of Irish family names, you should consult the book, "The Master Book of Irish Surnames", (by O'Laughlin), which holds the largest compilation of Irish family names in print.

The arms of Irish families pictured in this volume have been largely taken from the IGF edition of the 'Irish Book of Arms', and the IGF member library.

Church Records

Church records are a primary source for tracing your Irish ancestor. While the majority of the population in Dublin is Catholic, there are also notable records for the Church of Ireland (CoI). We also have records to a lesser extent for Presbyterian, Methodist, Jewish, Baptist and Quakers in Dublin.

Civil registration for births, deaths and marriages did not begin until 1864, hence church records of these events are vital. (Non-Catholic marriages were recorded beginning in 1845).

The Dublin records that survive vary from parish to parish, but in general Church of Ireland registers begin earlier than Catholic ones. Most existing Church of Ireland records begin after the mid 18th century, and all fall within the 'Diocese of Dublin' for that denomination. Existing Church of Ireland (CoI) registers can be found at the local church, at the National Archives of Ireland, or at the Library of the Representative Church Body. Some registers are in the process of being recorded by the local heritage centres in the area. (see address list this section).

Presbyterian registers are used most often to record marriages. Deaths and births were not usually documented.

Huguenot registers were mostly destroyed in the Public Record Office fire early in the 20th century, but some exist in published form. The French Huguenots arrived in Ireland in the mid 17th century, a time when Protestants were being encouraged to settle here, and again in some numbers in the early 18th century. Many were tradesmen and successful merchants.

Methodist registers have also been indexed in part by the heritage centres in Dublin, and tend to begin in the latter

Church Records

half of the 19th century, although some begin earlier.

Quaker

While the population was never large for the Quakers (the 'Society of Friends'), they did keep excellent records. Those for Dublin can be found at the Friends Historical Library, Swanbrook House, Morehampton Rd., Dublin 4, Ireland. Many of these records begin around the start of the 19th century.

Baptist

The Baptist population in Ireland was always very small, but records can be found in the National Library in Dublin. You may also wish to contact the Irish Baptist Historical Society, 117 Lisburn Rd., Belfast BT9 7AF, Northern Ireland.

Jewish

For Jewish records in Dublin we suggest you consult the book entitled "A History of the Jews in Ireland" by Louis Hyman, 1972; and A Short History of the Jews in Ireland,by Schillmans, 1945. Some existing records may be found at the Irish Jewish Museum, 3/4 Walworth Road, South Circular Drive, Dublin 8, Ireland.

Lutheran

Some records are found in the General Registrars Office at Lombard Street in Dublin. The church is found in Dublin from the end of the 17th century.

Catholic

The majority of church records in Dublin are Catholic, as they are in the rest of Ireland. Most can be researched at the local parish with the permission of the parish priest. The local heritage centers have also indexed these registers, and they can also be viewed on microfilm at the National Library in Dublin, or through the LDS library available in many countries.

Other Records

Directories

Although the mix of peoples is greater here than in the rest of Ireland, the number of surviving records is greater as well. There are a great number of directories, business lists and governmental reports. Notably you will find a series of directories by Thom's, which lists householders in Dublin in certain years. Early directories tend to list merchants, nobility and traders in the area.

Some of these directories are found in the National Archives and in the National Library of Ireland in Dublin. The Gilbert Library has a collection of specific Dublin directories as well.

Wills

Many wills were destroyed in the fire at the Public Record Office in 1921. Remnants can be found at the National Library and National Archives in Dublin, at the Valuation Office and at the Registry of Deeds in Dublin. The Testamentary Card Index at the National Archives is a valuable source of information here. (see also book list at end of this section for printed sources.)

Gravestone Inscriptions

Since few church registers actually record death records, gravestone inscriptions are a valuable resource. Many gravestone inscriptions are being recorded today, and many have been published in the past. There are over 200 known graveyards in Dublin. Note that other denominations were also buried in Church of Ireland graveyards, so these should be checked regardless of religious affiliation. The following are available in printed form: Memorials of the Dead, Dublin City and County by

Land Records

Egan and Flatman, a multi volume set published by the Irish Genealogical Research Society; Journals of the Association for the Preservation of Memorials of the Dead in Ireland (1888-1921); and the Directory of Graveyards in the Dublin Area which was published in 1988.

Land Records

Various surveys exist to record land ownership and holdings. The appendix to this book lists the 1659 census, showing the old and new owners of land in Dublin. The Registry of Deeds holds some records from 1708 onwards; The Tithe Applotment Books record a survey begun in 1821; Griffiths Valuation recorded the occupiers of land and began in 1848; Estate records in the National Library in Dublin cover a wide span of time. The "Index to surnames of Householders in Griffith's Primary Valuation and Tithe Applotment Books" is a very valuable surname locator for the 19th century. It was compiled by the National Library of Ireland and is available for consultation by researchers.

Newspapers As Sources

Although formal notices in newspapers are often limited to the wealthiest of families, other items of interest may appear for working class families. The National Library in Ireland has a good collection of surviving newspapers for Dublin, along with several indexes to the same. The Gilbert Library in Dublin holds an excellent collection as well.

Among newspapers most often noted in the 18th century are the *Freeman's Journal, Faulkner's Dublin Journal,* and the *Dublin Evening Post.*

Periodicals

Dublin Periodicals

There are several periodicals in Ireland of interest. The local journals from county historical and archaeological societies contain a wide variety of topics, some of which bear directly on genealogical research. The *Irish Genealogist,* The *Irish Ancestor,* and the *Journal of the Preservation of Memorials of the Dead* are of obvious interest.

The *Reportorium Novum* concerns Dublin Diocesan History and the *Dublin Historical Record* is published by the Old Dublin Society (see address list). In the latter you will find articles on topics like the following :

Topic of Interest	Vol.: issue
...William Bligh in Dublin	(XLIV:1)
Corballis-Corbally families	(XLV:2)
..Funeral of Wm. Dargan	(XLVI:1)
Corbally family of Dublin	(XLVI:1)
Oliver Sheppard, sculptor	(XLVIII:1)
Emily Lawless	(XLVIII:2)
John Boyd Dunlop	(XLIX:1)
the Fannins of Dublin	(XLIX:1)
Charles Wye Williams	(XLIX:1)
Survey of Tipper Graveyard	(XLIX:2)
Delamain family in Ireland	(XLIX:2)

In the *Reportorium Novum* you will find items such as: The Wolverstons of Sillorgan (1960); The Seagraves of Cabra (1956); The Nottinghams of Ballyowen (1956); and The Bathes of Drumcondra (1956).

The value of such articles varies greatly, but they do prove useful to the family historian. As more indexing projects are completed, these records will become even more accessible.

Sources

The following works, found in the I.G.F. library, are good examples of published sources available to those researching their Dublin roots.

A History of the County Dublin. Elrington Ball. 6 v. set. 1902...

The History of County Dublin. 1838. D'Alton.

Dublin City and County from prehistory to present. Aalen & Whelan. 1992.

The Landowners of Ireland. 1878. de Burgh.

Topographical Dictionary of Ireland. Lewis. 1837.

Census of Ireland. 1659. ed. by Pender. pub. 1939. Dublin. (see appendix)

The Master Book of Irish Surnames. I.G.F. With specific sources linking names to Co. Dublin and elsewhere.

The Master Book of Irish Placenames. I.G.F. With place names indexed and keyed to detailed maps. 17th & 19th c.

The Book of Irish Families, great & small. I.G.F., 1998. O'Laughlin. (Master volume to the Irish Families series) ISBN 0940134152.

Irish Genealogies. From Keatings History with additional materials. IGF. ISBN 0940134497.

The Journal of the American Irish Historical Society. JAIHS. 1898 -... Published in book form annually.

Sources for Genealogical Research in the Dublin Corporation Archives. Mary Clark. *The Irish Genealogist*. 1987.

King James Irish Army List d'Arcy. ISBN 0940134233. reprinted 1997.

Irish Pedigrees. John O'Hart.

Irish Names and Surnames. Rev. Patrick Woulfe. IGF. 1992. ISBN 0940134403

Directory of Graveyards in the Dublin Area....1988. ISBN 0946841063.

Genealogical History of the Tyrells of Castleknock in Dublin.....J. H. Tyrell. 1904. London.

The Dublin Tweedys..... Owen Tweedy. 1956 . London.

...Cooke, Ashe and Swift Families, of Dublin. *Journal of the Association for the Preservation of Memorials of the Dead...* (1912-1916):503.

Dix Family of Dublin (as above) (1921-25):490.

The Magees of Belfast and Dublin. F. Bigger. 1916. Belfast.

Dublin Almanac & General Register of Ireland. Pettigrew and Oulton. A directory published annually 1834-49.

New City Pictorial Directory of Dublin.. Henry Shaw. 1850. Includes list of some residents.

The Dublin Historical Record.. Periodical published by the Old Dublin Society. 58 S. William St., Dublin.

Address List

Additionally one may wish to consult with the following repositories:.

The National Library of Ireland
Kildare Street
Dublin 2, Ireland
(holdings include Griffiths Survey, microfilm of parish registers, newspapers, estate papers, directories...)

National Archives of Ireland
Bishop Street
Dublin 8, Ireland
(holdings include Griffiths Valuation and Tithe Applotment Books)

Dublin City Archives
South William Street
Dublin
(Corporation Records)

Public Records Office of Ireland
Four Courts
Dublin 7, Ireland
(holdings include Tithe Applotment Books, estate records, court records.....)

Genealogical Office
2 Kildare Street
Dublin 2, Ireland
(includes a variety of materials on Irish families, a part of the National Library.)

Registrars General's Office
8 - 11 Lombard St
Dublin 2, Ireland
(the official birth, death and marriage records of Ireland from 1864 onwards)

Registry of Deeds
Henrietta Street
Dublin 1, Ireland
(Property transactions since 1608)

Irish Genealogical Foundation (I.G.F.)
Box 7575
Kansas City. Missouri 64116

Gilbert Library
138-142 Pearse Street, Dublin 2, Ireland
(major repository for Dublin research)

LDS Family History Centre
The Willows, Finglas Road, Dublin 11.

Irish Baptist Historical Society
117 Lisburn Road
Belfast, BT9 7AF Northern Ireland

Genealogical Office
2 Kildare Street, Dublin, Ireland
(now part of the National Library)

Represent. Church Body Library
Braemor Park, Churchtown, Dublin 14.
(records of the Church of Ireland)

Royal Irish Academy
19 Dawson Street
Dublin 2, Ireland
(manuscripts and other holdings)

Fingal Heritage Group
Carnegie Library, North Street
Swords, Co. Dublin
(The official centre for North Dublin.)
The main towns covered by this centre are Balbriggan, Malahide, Howth, Clontarf, Blanchardstown, Portmarnock, Donabate, Baldoyle, Skerries, Rush, and Lusk.
Current phone: (353) 1 8403629

Dublin Heritage Group
2nd Floor, Cumberland House,
Fenian St., Dublin
(The official center For Dublin City)

Dun Laoghaire Rathdown Heritage Society. Moran Park House,
Dun Laoghaire, Co. Dublin
(The official centre for South Dublin)
The main towns covered by this centre are Ballybock, Booterstown, Cabinteely, Dundrum, Kingstown (Dun Laoghaire), Blackrock, Dalkey, Glasthule, Monkstown and Donnevbrook. Fax: (353) 1 2806969

Spellings

One common problem found with the arrival of emigrants in past centuries has been the 'spelling' of the family name. This should be remembered when researching any record, including passenger lists. The name could have been spelled wrong in the ships record, or could have been changed completely by the emigrant himself. (The latter is not common, but definitely a possibility in 'problem' research cases).

Other changes found in the spelling of our surnames bears repeating. Moloney was then often found as Mullowny. So, remember to search for your family or place name phonetically - that is, by the sound of the name. The precise spelling was often changed, either by design or at the whim of the record makers!

Names like McShane, McTeige, McDonnogh and McDaniel are found often in the census of 1659 in Ireland - but they are not always considered true surnames. They were sometimes used more as nicknames- as in 'the son of' Rory O'Connor being recorded as a McRory instead of an O'Connor.

It is said that these names could be used for a generation - and then be dropped or changed altogether. When true, this poses a great challenge for the researcher.

If you are interested in the many spellings and variant spelling groups of Irish family names, you should consult the book, "The Master Book of Irish Surnames", which holds the largest compilation of Irish family names in print.

The arms of Irish families depicted in this volume have been taken from the IGF edition of the 'Irish Book of Arms'.

Format

The spelling of names and places will appear here in more than one form. Hence, at times, O'Connor and O'Conor refer to the same family name. Likewise you may see Dublin spelled as it was in one older record, as 'Dublyn'.

We have left some old English spellings alone, leaving the reader to make educated judgments as to places and persons. Chronicled here are compiled works of earlier historians and researchers. Hence, within these pages, conflicting statements and claims may appear, sometimes side by side.

A few families will have the notation "according to an undocumented source" appearing in their listing. This means that we have not confirmed the information. Many of these names are found in "A Genealogical History of the Milesian Families of Ireland" by DeCourcy - a dubious source at times, but included here as a possibility.

We will publish additional research and opinions in our monthly *Journal of Irish Families*, should you have new material or corrections to this text. In this way old errors can be corrected for all to see. This will be true for all 32 volumes of this set of Irish family histories.

Those interested in further research should consult the works listed at the end of this section, particularly the History by Ball, from which I have freely taken.

Let the reader understand and uncover errors and misstatements made within these pages, it is the best I could do.

-Michael C. O'Laughlin
11/7/98

Foundation Aids

For those wishing to further research their Dublin family roots, the Irish Genealogical Foundation offers help with a variety of publications.

Americans need to research in America first, a point sometimes forgotten. Birth certificates and obituary columns, etc... sometimes yield the key to success.

The small, but very directly written *Beginners Guide to Irish Family Research* is for those just beginning the search. OLochlainns *Journal of Irish Families* is the Foundations monthly membership publication, which receives timely information from all points.

It is through the Foundation and the Irish Family Journal that this work has been published. A sincere thank you goes out to all Foundation members once again, for your continued support.

Dedicated To

Brandon Sieve and Brittany Sanders

the next generation

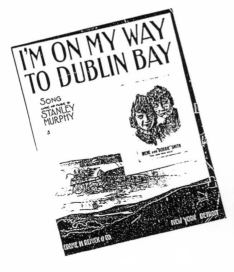

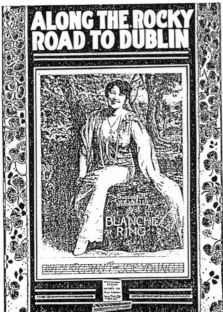

"Pat McGee, now listen to me
I've heard you fellows brag
about your beauties over here,
and the girls you love so dear.

They may be swell,
that's all very well
at wearing fancy clothes.
But I'd a queen, a fair colleen
as sweet as any rose........"

Dublin was immortalized in America through plays and sheet music
as shown above in <u>Along the Rocky Road to Dublin</u>. (1915)....;
Note also the songe entitled: I'm On My Way to Dublin Bay;
Dublin Daisys; and I'll Be With You When Its Daisy Time in Dublin, etc...

Families of County Dublin, Ireland

Listed in alphabetical order.
Mc, Mac and O' names are alphabetized
by the first letter after the Mc, Mac or O'.
(i.e. O'Connell is sorted as Connell etc...)

KEY:

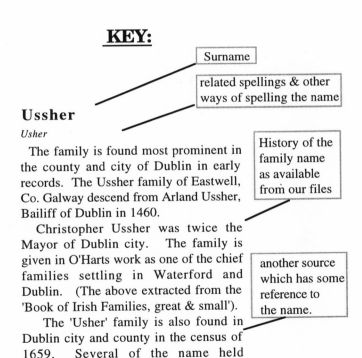

Surname

related spellings & other
ways of spelling the name

Ussher

Usher

The family is found most prominent in the county and city of Dublin in early records. The Ussher family of Eastwell, Co. Galway descend from Arland Ussher, Bailiff of Dublin in 1460.

History of the family name as available from our files

Christopher Ussher was twice the Mayor of Dublin city. The family is given in O'Harts work as one of the chief families settling in Waterford and Dublin. (The above extracted from the 'Book of Irish Families, great & small').

another source which has some reference to the name.

The 'Usher' family is also found in Dublin city and county in the census of 1659. Several of the name held considerable lands in the 17th century....

51

Arms of Some Dublin Families

Taken from the Irish Book of Arms (IGF edition)

Fitzwilliam

Gaisford-St. Lawrence

MacNeale of Portrane

Fitzwilliam

Guiness

Domvile of Loughlinstown

Fagan of Feltrim

O'Carroll of Athgoe

O'Connor of Rockfield

Westby

Vernon of Clontarf

Rowley

52

Abbecaces Of Morocco
A settler name given in Dublin city, of Jewish origins. (per OLochlainns Journal of Irish Families).

Abbott
Abbot, Abott, Abot
Abbot is a common English name which is often found in Dublin. (see the 'Book of Irish Families, great & small').

Ackley
Milesian Families gives the Ackley name as settled in Dublin and Wexford, of English extraction.

Acton
See "Acton Papers" from Analecta Hibernia. 25. (periodical)

Adair
In the 18th century the Adair family is found in Kiltiernan parish.

Adam
Mac Adams Adams
Adamstown Castle in Aderrig parish was named for the Adam family which was established in the 16th century in the parish of Esker.

McAdams
Mac Adams Adams
In Dublin and Belfast the name and its variants are often of Scots heritage.

Adams is of course, a common name in England and some of the name have settled in Ireland over the centuries. It is as well of Irish origins.

Arms for various families of the name, are found in the 'Irish Book of Arms', published by the I.G.F.)

McAdam is also found as a principle name of Dublin city in the 17th century.

Adrian
Adryan, Adrien, Adrain, Drain, Drean,
Some of the name of Adrian etc...may actually be of the old Irish family of O'Drean. Subsequently the name may be found as Drean and Drain.

Additionally, the name spelled as "Adryan" in the 17th century is found in Co. Dublin, although it is more traditionally linked to the province of Ulster. (see the 'Book of Irish Families, great & small').

Agard
In the 16th century we find Francis Agard residing in Grangegorman parish.

Aghwell
A family found in the city of Dublin in the 17th century. (see the 'Book of Irish Families, great & small').

Ahlborn
A family name of settler origins given in Dublin city, of Jewish extraction. (per OLochlainns Journal of Irish Families).

Aiken
Ekin, Aikens, Aikins, Aicken, Aitken,
Families of the name are found centered in Co. Antrim in the 19th century and are of Scottish and English descent, originating in many cases from the English name of Aitken. Several of the name are found in Dublin. (see the 'Book of Irish Families, great & small').

Alexander Aikens is found in St. Werburgh's parish in the Dublin City Pipe Water Accounts of 1680.

Alan
Allen Allan
Milesian Families gives this spelling in Dublin in 1640, of Scots origin.

Albert
Milesian Families gives the family in Dublin, of Norman origins.

Albun
The 'Albun' family name is given to be of Jewish heritage in at least one instance and is found in Dublin city.

Aldercron
Aldercorn
Lt. Gen. John Aldercron, of a Huguenot family is found in the area of Seapoint and Templehill in 1762.

Alding
The name of a family found in the city of Dublin in the 17th century. (see the 'Book of Irish Families, great & small'). See also appendix page 223.

Aldworth
We find one reference to the name being in Dublin and Cork, of English extraction.

Alexander
Alexandar Alex,elshinder

The family of Alexander is assumed to have arrived here from Scotland and is assumed to be of the province of Ulster when found in Ireland. In the 17th century it is documented as well in Dublin City under the spelling of Allexander.

Alexander is also an English name, with many variants found in older records, such as Elshinder, Mac Calshender and Kalshander.

The name is further given as one of the principal families of Ireland in the 1600's.

The surnames of Alexander and King are given in relatively modern times in Templeogue according to the works of Ball.

(see the 'Book of Irish Families.').

Strongbow's Monument—Christ Church.

Mac Allen
Allen Alen Alan

Families of the name may be of Scottish or English origins. Much confusion may result from the spellings of Allen, Allan, McAllen, etc.... All have been found in Dublin city, which should be no surprise.

Allen is found in the 1890 birth index in Dublin. McAllen is found as a principal name in Dublin City in 1659.

Numerous listings are found in the works of O'Hart and Burke.

One John Allen (1476 - 1534) was Archbishop of Dublin and Lord Chancellor of Ireland. He was assassinated by the followers of Lord Thomas Fitzgerald.

In the Irish Book of Arms we find one Joshua of the name who was a viscount, seated at Palmerstown, Co. Dublin. We also find one John Allen (living in 1618), of Rathlumney in O'Harts work. (see the 'Book of Irish Families, great & small').

We find the Whites and the Allens once more owning land at Aderrig parish after the 17th century Restoration.

James and Mathew Allen are also found holding a total of over 1400 acres in 17th century Co. Dublin. This was the family that inherited the lands at Palmerstown and St. Wolstans. The two individuals above were said to have been Irish Catholic.

The 'Allen' family is also given as a principal one of Anglo-Norman descent, settling in Dublin City and County, according to Keatings 'History of Ireland'. See also 'Allen'.

Allen
Mac Allen Allan
(See also MacAllen)

The first of the Allen family at Stillorgan was John Allen who came to Dublin from Holland, and was a master builder. Allen is found in the 1890 birth index in Dublin. They are given as a family of note in Dublin by Keating as well.

Allen is also noted at Killininny and the Allens of Wolstans are given at Tallaght Hills, both locations are in the parish of Tallaght.

At Saggart parish residents named Allen are noted in the History of County Dublin by Ball.

The Allen family held Palmerston lands into the 17th century.

Allison
Alison, Ellison, Alleson, Allisson

Scottish immigrants of the name account for many 'Allison' families in the north of Ireland today. The Scottish name of Ellison has often been used interchangeably with Allison.

We find mention of the name in Dublin and Limerick in the 16th century. (see the 'Book of Irish Families, great & small').

William Allison is found in St. Werburgh's parish in the Dublin City Pipe Water Accounts of 1680.

Alloway
Halloway Holloway

A surname found in Quaker records in Dublin city in the 18th century. Perhaps confused with the surname of Halloway or Holloway.

Allsworth

Milesian Families lists this family name settling in Dublin in the 17th century, of English extraction.

Alpine

Milesian Families gives the family in Dublin, of Scottish origins.

Altman

A family name found in Dublin city, given to be of Jewish heritage in at least one instance. (per 'OLochlainns journal of Irish Families').

Alwoodhouse

A family name found in the city of Dublin in the census of 1659.

Amansham

A family name found in the city of Dublin in the census of 1659. See Appendix.

Ambrose

Miss Ambrose, a Catholic Belle of Dublin Castle is given in, 'Families of Co. Kerry, Ireland.).

Amery
Amory

A family that settled in Ireland with the coming of the Norman invasions, found in Dublin according to Milesian Families.

McAnally
Mc Nally

A family name found in Dublin at the time of the Birth Index of 1890.

Anderson
Andersen

Anderson is a family name found commonly in Scotland, and in the north of Ireland. The most common locations for the name in the 19th century were in Antrim, Down, Dublin and Derry. Some 175 births of the name were recorded in 1890. (see the 'Book of Irish Families, great & small').

In the 18th century an Anderson family is found in Kiltiernan parish.

Anger
Angier, Aungier

The spelling of the name as "Anger" is found in Dublin city in the census of 1659. See listing for Aungier. (see the 'Book of Irish Families, great & small').

Anketel

Milesian Families gives the name in Dublin in the 17th century, of Anglo-Saxon origins.

Anncham

Capt. Nicholas Anncham is found in St. John's parish in the Dublin City Pipe Water Accounts of 1680.

Annesley

The Annesley family at Inchicore is given in connection with Kilmainham in the 18th century.

Anthony

Milesian Families finds the name in Dublin, of English origins. (no documentation given).

Arabin

Lt. Col. John Arabin assumed properties at Kilmacud. He was the father-in-law of General Aylercorn, of Seapoint.

Archbold

Archbald Archibold Archibald

In the 17th century the Archbold family held the lands of Jobstown and subsequently the Whitshed families are found there.

The Archbolds are in Bray in the 14th century, and along with the Lawless family, they were quite prominent. See introduction.

Gerrard Archbold is found on Kishoge in Esker parish in 1641. (see also Archibald)

Archdall

Eccles Mount was the residence of Nicholas Archdall in 1757. See St. George Parish.

Archer

Le Archer, Larcher

The name arrived in Ireland with the coming of the Norman invasions of the 12th century, and they were originally an Anglo-Norman family.

In the 12th century we have found one 'Ralph Larcher' from le Archer, as a burgess in Dublin city.

Keatings History gives the Archer family as a principal one of Anglo-Norman descent.

In the 17th century the name is found in Armagh and Kilkenny. By the time of the 1890 index the name is given in Counties Armagh, Dublin and Antrim as most numerous. (see the 'Book of Irish Families, great & small').

The family is also given as a principal one of Anglo-Norman descent, settling in Dublin City and County, according to Keatings 'History of Ireland'.

Archibald

Archbould Archbold

The family is also given as a principal one of Anglo-Norman descent, settling in Dublin City and County, according to Keatings 'History of Ireland'.

Garrett Archbold of Stillorgan, is given as a substantial landowner in 17th century Co. Dublin. The family is found in Kilmacud Parish in the 16th and 17th century, and they descended from some of the earliest settlers in Ireland. See introduction.

A principal name of County Dublin in the 17th century spelled as Archbould in that document. Also found in Dublin in the 1890 birth index. See also Archbold.

Ardagh

Ardough, Ardogh

A rare name in Ireland,. The spelling of the name of Ardough is found in Dublin city in the 17th century and may represent the Ardagh family. (see the 'Book of Irish Families, great & small'). See 1659 census in appendix as Ardogh.

Arnold

A family name found in Dublin at the time of the Birth Index of 1890. Also consult the "Journal of the Association for the Preservation of Memorials to the Dead" for article entitled "Arnold of Dublin" 1910.

Arnop

A family name found in the city of Dublin in the census of 1659.

Arthur
Mac Aurthur, Arthurs, Arthure, Aurthur,

Those of the Arthur family name in Ireland may spring from the Scottish name of MacArthur.

John Arthur of Hackettstown is listed among those transplanted from Dublin in the works of O'Hart.

The census of 1659 gives Arthur as a principal name of Co. Clare, as well as being found in Limerick city, Dublin, Kings, and Wexford.

In 'King James's Irish Army List' we find listed as a Dublin assessor, one Capt. Robert Arthur.

Some of the name from Ireland are also found in France in the 18th century.

Arms for the families of the name of Arthur are given in the Irish Book of Arms. (see the 'Book of Irish Families, great & small').

Arthur was a name of note at Newlands in Tallaght parish.

The Arthur family is found continuing their residence at Much Cabragh in the first half of the 18th century, see Castleknock in the introduction to this book.

Arundall
Spelled as Arundall we find the family in Dublin city in the 1659 census. One family of the name is said to have arrived here in the 16th century. Also spelled as Arundell.

Asbury
Milesian Families finds the name in Dublin, of English origins. (no documentation given).

Ashbourne
The name of Ashbourne is noted at Killininny.

Ashbrook
Milesian Families finds the name in Dublin, of English origins.

Ashe
Ash

Thomas Ashe (b.1885) was of Co. Kerry, but came to teach at Kilduff, Co. Dublin and founded the Black Ravens Pipers' Club. (see also 'Families of Co. Kerry, Ireland.).

See also "Notes on the Cooke, Ashe and Swift Families" (Dublin), in the "Journal of the Association for the Preservation of Memorials for the Dead." 9, 1912+.

Ashly
Ashley

Found in Dublin City in the census of 1659. See appendix.

Ashton
Milesian Families finds the name in Dublin, of English origins. (no documentation given). Aston is found in the 1659 census in Dublin.

Askins
Haskins

Several families of the name are found in Sandymount, Irishtown, Co. Dublin.

Assin
A family name found in the city of Dublin in the census of 1659.

Aston
Found in Dublin in the 1659 census. See appendix.

Attwood
Atwood

John Attwood is found in St. Nicholas Parish 'Within the Walls', in the Dublin City Pipe Water Accounts of 1680.

Aubry
Richard Aubry held the lands of Jobstown or Rathmintin until 1326 when they were acquired by Richard Fitzwilliam.

The family name is found several times in the 1659 census of Ireland.

Meldiric, Aubry, Marshall, and Rath families are given early in Rathcoole parish in the History of the County Dublin by Ball.

Audley
Ouldley Adley

Milesian Families finds the name in Dublin, of English origins. (no documentation given).

Aungier

Angier, D' Aungiers

In at least one instance given to be a Huguenot family settled in Ireland of long standing in Dublin. (see the 'Book of Irish Families, great & small').

Austin

Austen, Austine, Auston, Austan Aston

The Austin family name is found scattered throughout Ireland. It is considered to be, for the most part, of English origins here. The name has been in Ireland since the 12th century, the time of the Norman invasions.

The birth index of the last century gives Antrim and Dublin as principal locations for the family.. (see the 'Book of Irish Families, great & small').

Aston is a family name given in Dublin in the census of 1659, and it is found in Quaker records in Dublin city in the early 18th century.

Henry Aston is found in St. Michael's parish in the Dublin City Pipe Water Accounts of 1680.

Eccles Mount is found as residence of the widow of Sir Sheffield Austen prior to 1757.

Avery

Avory

Avery is given in Dublin city in the census of 1659, and Avory is found in Dublin County at that time as well. Both spellings have been interchanged.

Dunsoghly Castle came under the possession of Tichborne before being transferred to John Avery in 1672.

Aylercorn

Lt. Col. John Arabin assumed properties at Kilmacud. He was the father-in-law of General Aylercorn, of Seapoint.

Aylmer

Ailmer, Aylemer, D'aylmer

Keatings History gives the family as a principal one of the city and county of Dublin of Anglo-Norman descent. they are also given as an English family found settled in Dublin by at least the 17th century, where they held noted lands at that time.

Sir Gerald Aylmer of Donadea, Co. Kildare, came to hold the Monkstown Castle, replacing James Eustace.

Capt. R. Aylmer was a centenarian noted at Chapelizod parish.

"The Aylmers of Ireland" by F. J. Aylmer, was published in London in 1931. Mention of the family is also made in the Kildare Archaeological Society.(see the 'Book of Irish Families, great & small').

O' B

An abbreviated family name found in the city of Dublin in the census of 1659.

Babbitt

Milesian Families gives this name in Dublin, settling there in the 17th century from England.

Bacon

Milesian Families finds the name in Dublin, of English origins.

Milltown, Co. Dublin was held by the Brigg family in the 14th century, and by the Loftus family in 1641, and at that time John Bacon was principal resident.

Badham

Found in Dublin as given on page 13.

Bagot

Baggott Bagod

The family is given as a principal one of Anglo-Norman descent, settling in Dublin City and County, according to Keatings 'History of Ireland'.

It is given in King James' Irish Army List that in 1280 Robert 'Bagod' obtained a grant of the manor of Rath near Dublin, on which a castle was erected and became known as Baggot-rath. The name is then given to have spread over the counties of the Pale, and into Kildare.

Ball gives Sir Robert Bagod (d.1336) as the first to reside there.

Castle Bagot is given in Kilmactalway parish. Ball also gives the Bagots as arriving in the 18th century. See introduction.

Bagworth

A family name found in Dublin in the census of 1659.

Bailey

Bayley Bayly Baily

Milesian Families finds the name in Dublin, of English origins. In the 17th century we find one Wm. Bailey at Finglas who was driven from his mill at Finglas Bridge. See other spellings.

Bain

Milesian Families finds the name in Dublin, of Scottish origins. (no documentation given).

Baird

Milesian Families finds the name in Dublin, of Scottish origins. (no documentation given).

Baker

Le Bakere, Le Baker

The Birth index shows Dublin and Antrim as locations for the name in the 1800's. Interestingly enough, Rooney finds the name coming from Scotland in 1642 and settling in Dublin, Cork and Tipperary.

Among the major tenants at Bray, Co. Dublin, in 1284 were: Wm. le Deveneis; John Clements; Robert the Baker; and W. de Belinges.

It is also a surname found in Quaker records in Dublin city in the late 17th century, where Samuel Baker is given as a Tallowchandler.

One 'Richard Baker' in 'Copper Alley' is found in St. Werburgh's parish in the Dublin City Pipe Water Accounts of 1680.

(see also the 'Book of Irish Families.').

Baldwin

Milesian Families finds the name in Dublin, of settler origins. (no documentation given).   It is also a surname found in Quaker records in Dublin city in the late 18th century.

Bale

A family name found in the city of Dublin in the census of 1659.

Malahide Castle.

Ball

One noted family of the name originates in Dublin from Major Robert Ball (d.1637). The 1659 census finds the family in Dublin as well. The main locations for the family in the 19th century were Antrim, Meath and Dublin.(see the 'Book of Irish Families, great & small').

Robert Ball is found at Blanchardstown in the early 16th century.

The family is also given as a principal one of Anglo-Norman descent, settling in Dublin City and County, according to Keatings 'History of Ireland'.

The Ball Family of Dublin is also briefly noted in O'Harts "Irish...Landed Gentry".

Among the chief residents in Finglas at the end of the Elizabethan period, we find Walter Ball at Ballygall, sometime mayor of Dublin.

Boyle More, was the son of Squire Robert Ball. It was given that the seat of the Ball family was moved to Drogheda from Ballygall.

Bamford

'Bamford's House' is found in St. John's parish in the Dublin City Pipe Water Accounts of 1680.

Banks
Le Bank

Some of the name of Banks found in Ireland are of English extraction. Others descend from old Irish families by means of "translating" their name into English as Banks. The census of 1659 finds the family centered in Dublin City.(see the 'Book of Irish Families, great & small').

After the 12th century invasions of Ireland the lands of Ward Parish were held by the family of le Bank.

Banning

Milesian Families finds the name in Dublin, of English origins. (no documentation given).

Barber, Barbour
Barbador, Le Barbour, Barbier

Note the place name of Barberstown in Co. Dublin, where the name has been on record for some time in Dublin City.

Most of the name can be found centered today near the cities of Dublin and Belfast. Some of the name are of Scottish heritage having settled centuries ago in Ulster.

Older records find some families of the name spelled as le Barbour . (see the 'Book of Irish Families, great & small').

Barclay
Barcly Barkley

A surname found in Quaker records in Dublin city in the early 18th century belonging apparently to a family of merchants there in that century.

Barcroft

A surname found in Quaker records in Dublin city in the 18th century. A merchant and a weaver of the name are given circa 1730 there.

Bargerett

Nicholas Bargerett is found in St. John's parish in the Dublin City Pipe Water Accounts of 1680.

Barlowe

A family name found in the city of Dublin in the census of 1659.

Barnard
Bernard

A surname of a merchant found in Quaker records in Dublin city in the early 18th century. The spelling of a surname as 'Bernard' is also given in those records. (See major entry in 'The Families of Co. Kerry').

Barnes

A family name found in the city of Dublin in the census of 1659.

It is also the surname of a chandler found in Quaker records in Dublin city in the early 18th century.

Barneville

Barnewall

At the beginning of the 13th century, we read in *King James Irish Army List* of one Ulfran de Barneville, who obtained estates in 'the Vale of Dublin', which were held by the family until the reign of James I, when they were granted to James Loftus.

De Barnwall

Barnewall, Barnwell

According to "Keatings History" the name is of Anglo-Norman origins and they were styled Lords of Bearhaven with large possessions in that area. They were subsequently expelled by the O'Sullivans and settled in Dublin and Meath, and founded the families of Barnwall who became Barons of Trimblestown and Turvey, and viscounts Kingsland.

Drimnagh Castle was for centuries the seat of the Barnewall family, holding that place at least until the 18th century.. Hugh de Barnewall is found there in 1216.

According to Keating the name spelled simply as Barnwall, was that of a principal family of Dublin city or county. Today, of course, the name is found largely only as "Barnwall", with the "de" prefix removed.

Nicholas Barnewall, Lord Kingsland, served as an officer in Lord Limerick's Dragoons. This family is found settled at Turvey in Co. Dublin for some time. (see the 'Book of Irish Families, great & small').

In the 16th century the Barnewall family is noted at Rathmichael Parish.

In the 17th century Peter Barnewall held the castle at Terenure and Kimmage along with 6 dwellings.

The Barnewalls are often mentioned in connection with Ballyfermot.

Barnewall is given as a principal name of Dublin City in the census of 1659. See also "Barnewall" in the "Irish Genealogist" (5) 2. 1975.

"The Barnewalls of Turvey" are also given in the "Reportorium Novum" 1 (2). 1956.

Barrett Barrytt

Barett, Barret, Barnett, Barrat, Bartnett,

Barrett families spring from more than one source. Some of the name arrived in Ireland from England.

Several of the name arrived in Ireland with the 12th century Anglo-Norman invasions. They have been said to be Welsh by some, Normans by others, and Anglo-Saxon by others. The main areas of early settlement were in Co. Cork, and the Galway-Mayo areas of Ireland. In 1659 we find the family centered in Dublin City and Cork City.

Subsequent to the 17th century rebellions we find the names of Wharton; Chambers; Willion; Barry; Robinson; Moses; Reyly; Lovelace; Eaton; Murphy; Lawlor; Leedom; and Walsh in Rathcoole parish, Co. Dublin.

Sir Robert Barry was resident at Barry House at Donneybrook in the 18th century.

A century ago the name was fairly widespread, with Dublin and Cork heading the list of counties most populated with Barrett families.

The Irish Book of Arms gives one family of the name as Barrett-Hamilton of Kilmanock House, Co. Wexford. (see the 'Book of Irish Families, great & small').

The family is also given as a principal one of Anglo-Norman descent, settling in Dublin City and County, according to Keatings 'History of Ireland'. The family is listed as part of the 'more recent nobility' by O'Hart where they are given as barons of Santry, Co. Dublin.

Barrington

Milesian Families finds the name in Dublin, of Norman origins. (no documentation given).

A surname of a chandler found in Quaker records in Dublin city, in both the 18th and 19th century.

Barrow

A family name found in the city of Dublin in the census of 1659.

Barry
Bary

The Barry family of Dublin is briefly noted in O'Harts "Irish...Landed Gentry", and they are there given as 'Lords of Santry'. Of this line was Sir James Barry, Lord of Santry and Lord Chief Justice of the Kings Bench, (died 1673.)

Mathew Barry assumed a lease of the lands of Ballycoolen subsequent to the mayor of Dublin in 1682. (See major entry in 'The Families of Co. Cork').

Barton

A family name found in Dublin in the Birth Index of 1890.

Bary
Barry

A family name found in Dublin in the census of 1659. (see Barry)

Basill

A family name found in Dublin in the census of 1659.

Basnett
Bassenet

A name found in Dublin in older records. (see the 'Book of Irish Families, great & small').

Christopher Bassenet, John Brady, and John Hore, in 1561, are found leasing the lands of Kill of the Grange parish. See introduction.

Bassenet
Basnet

In 1561 we find lands of Tipperstown leased to Bassenet, Brady and Hore.

Edward Bassenet is given with the lands of Kiltiernan parish. The name is also noted in Kilmactalway parish. See introduction.

Basset
Bassett

Basset, of the great Norman family, and le Brun, were two of the families noted in the 13th century at Roebuck, Co. Dublin.

Bateman
Batemen

The 19th century birth index gives the name centered in Cork and Dublin. The name is most often found associated with Co. Cork in our records.

Several of the name have arrived from foreign shores here, beginning with the 12th century Norman invasions of Ireland. (see the 'Book of Irish Families, great & small'). (See major entry in 'The Families of Co. Kerry'). In 1876 John Bateman of Dublin is found as a landowner in Kerry.

Bates

A family name found in Dublin at the time of the Birth Index of 1890. George Bates is found in St. Nicholas Parish 'Without the Walls', in the Dublin City Pipe Water Accounts of 1680.

Bath
Bathe   De Bath

The 'de Bathe' family is also given as a principal one of Anglo-Norman descent, settling in Dublin City and County, according to Keatings 'History of Ireland'.

James Bathe held a considerable estate in Drumcondra in Co. Dublin.

Bathe

Among the owners of Knocklyon in the parish of Tallaght we find Bathe.

Among the names noted at Rathcoole parish from the 16th century onwards are: John Mey; James Bathe; the Fitzgeralds; and the Darlasses of Maynooth.

The castle at Kilbride parish was leased to Thomas Bathe in 1570.

In 16th century in Glasnevin Parish leases are found held by Thomas and Oliver Stephens, Alson FitzSimon, and James and John Bathe.

John Bathe (d.1586) had the castle at Drumcondra in Clonturk Parish.

Bather

A family name found in Dublin in the census of 1659.

Bathripp

A family name found in the city of Dublin in the census of 1659.

Bathurst
A family name found in the city of Dublin in the census of 1659.

Battersby
The 1890 birth index finds the family most numerous in Co. Dublin, with 5 recorded births of the name at that time. (see the 'Book of Irish Families, great & small').

Baulman
A family name found in Dublin at the time of the Birth Index of 1890.

Baxter
Macbaxter, Bacstar, Bagster
The census of 1659 finds the family of Baxter centered in Donegal and Dublin. Fairly common in Irish records, the name is traditionally linked to the province of Ulster. (see the 'Book of Irish Families, great & small').

We find that Shanganagh, in the parish of Rathmichael was occupied by the Baxters in the 17th century, before the Restoration.

After the Commonwealth, the lands of the Walsh family in Old Connaught parish passed to Henry Jones and then to John Baxter.

Bayly, Bayley
Bailey Baily
One branch of the Bayly family arrived from Yorkshire and settled in Ireland under Cromwell's regime. They are found early in the parish of St. Bride, Dublin in the 17th century; and one of the family is found in Fisherstown, Queens Co. subsequently. Another family of the name settled in Canada, coming from Dublin around 1836, settling in the township of Oro originally. See also Baily.

The family of Bayly of Ballyarthur, Co. Wicklow, was founded in the early 19th century, and they are found in the Irish Book of Arms. (see the 'Book of Irish Families, great & small').

Beaghan
Began Behan
John Beaghan is found in St. Werburgh's parish in the Dublin City Pipe Water Accounts of 1680. (see Behan)

Bealing
A family name found in the city of Dublin in the census of 1659. One family of the name held over 11,000 acres in Dublin, and held lands near Swords.

Beame
A family name found in Dublin in the census of 1659.

Beatty
Beattie, Beaty, Betagh, Batey
Beatty families are traditionally found in the province of Ulster.

Spelled as Beattie, the name is centered in Antrim and Down. Spelled as Beatty the name is found in Dublin, Armagh and Tyrone in the 1890 birth index. (see the 'Book of Irish Families').

Beaumont
The family is listed as part of the 'more recent nobility' by O'Hart where they are given as viscounts of Swords, Co. Dublin.

Becket
A family name found in the city of Dublin in the census of 1659.

Beebe
A surname of a chandler found in Quaker records in Dublin city in the 18th century.

Begg Beggs
Beg, Beggs, Bigg, Bigge, Begge, Big,
In Ulster some of the name descend from English families of the name (often spelled as Bigge in England). Others are thought to be of old Irish extraction, where the name may have sprung from the old Gaelic word of "beg" meaning small.

They are also given as an English family found settled in Dublin by at least the 17th century, where they held noted lands at that time.

The Begg family is found early at Murphystown. See introduction.

In the 19th century the spelling of Beggan was found mainly in Monaghan, and the name of Begg was numerous in Antrim and Dublin. (see the 'Book of Irish Families').

Behan

Beghan Beahan

The name is traditionally linked to counties Dublin, Kildare and Kerry. The 1890 birth index gives the family name in Dublin as well. (see the 'Book of Irish Families, great & small').

Bekeford

Beckford

We find one Roger Bekeford, grandson of Simon Neill, at Clondalkin.

Belgard

At Kilnamanagh the Talbot; Belgard; Parsons; Fitzwilliam; and Hawkins family are given of note.

Belinges

Among the major tenants at Bray, Co. Dublin, in 1284 were: Wm. le Deveneis; John Clements; Robert the Baker; and W. de Belinges.

Bell

Bell is a family most often found in the province of Ulster, and of likely Scottish origins there, "Bell" was given as a principal name of Co. Antrim in 1659, and subsequently found in Antrim, Down, Tyrone, Armagh and Dublin. (see the 'Book of Irish Families, great & small').

A surname of a merchant and several other individuals found in Quaker records in Dublin city in early to mid 18th century records.

Bellew

Bellow

According to "Keatings History" the name is among the "great families, either of English or Norman descent, settled in Meath in early times. The family is also given in that source as a principal one of Anglo-Norman descent in Dublin City and County.

In 1445 Philip Bellew is found as Bailiff of Dublin, and later generations produced a mayor of that city and other notables. A branch of the family is found in Castlebar and in Ballinrobe, Co. Mayo circa 1829.

Ballyowen in Esker parish, is found in the possession of Col. Bellew, presumably in the 17th century.

The main location for the Bellew family in the 19th century was in Co. Louth. (see the 'Book of Irish Families'). See also "The Bellews of Mount Bellew" a book by Karen Harvey, 1998.

Bellingham

A family name found in the city of Dublin in the census of 1659.

Bellings

The Bellings are given by Ball to be one of the families located in Mulhuddart parish from the 14th -16th centuries.

Bellon

A spa was founded at Chapelizod parish by Dr. Bellon.

Bender

A family name found in Dublin city, given to be of Jewish heritage in at least one instance. (per 'OLochlainns journal of Irish Families').

Benison

In the 17th century at Finglas parish we find Robert Benison who lost cows, horses, and carts.

Benmohel

A family name found in Dublin city, given to be of Jewish heritage in at least one instance. (per 'OLochlainns journal of Irish Families').

Bennell

A family name found in the city of Dublin in the census of 1659.

Benner

As given in 'Families of Co. Kerry, Ireland', Samuel Benner was a solicitor in Dublin, descended from a Palatine family there.

Bennett

One noted family of the name was from Banffshire, Scotland, one member of which went on to found the "New York Herald" Newspaper in America.

In 1890 the family is found in Cork, Dublin, Antrim, Armagh and Down. (see the 'Book of Irish Families.').

One 'William Bennett' is found in St. Werburgh's parish in the Dublin City Pipe Water Accounts of 1680.

Although not given in other sources, O'Hart finds the family as a principal one settling in Dublin subsequent to the 12th century invasions of Ireland.

Henry Bennett is given as prominent at Ballyman in Old Connaught parish.

Benson

A family name found in the city of Dublin in the census of 1659.

Beresford
Bearsford

As the name suggests, members of the Beresford family arrived in Ireland with the plantation of Ulster. One of the name is found in charge of the London Company there.

Several of the name are found in official records of the past, including Rt. Hon. J. Beresford, John Claud Beresford and Marcus Beresford, who all served in the "Irish" House of Commons in 1797.

The name is also given as a principal family name in the County and City of Dublin , at some time from the 12th to the 18th centuries.

Families found in the Irish Book of Arms include those of Pack-Beresford of Fenagh, Co. Carlow, and those of Beresford-Ash of Ashbrook, Co. Londonderry. (see the 'Book of Irish Families, great & small').

Berford
Bereford Beresford Birford

A family name found in the city of Dublin in the census of 1659.

Berg

A family name found in Dublin city, given to be of Jewish heritage in at least one instance. (per 'OLochlainns journal of Irish Families').

Bergin

A family name of Dublin as given in the birth index of 1890.

Berkeley

In the 18th century Dorothy Berkeley is found as the principal resident at Glasnevin Parish, but was shortly replaced by Sir John Rogerson.

Bermingham
Birmingham

A family name given in Dublin in the birth index of 1890. The family is also given as a principal one of Anglo-Norman descent, settling in Dublin City and County, according to Keatings 'History of Ireland'.

The Bermingham family of Lusk, Co. Dublin are given as noted gentry in the 17th century. Patrick Bermingham is given at Bullock, and was noted as paying rent in fish. See introduction. See also Birmingham.

Bernard

William Bernard (d.1828) was buried at Tallaght, Co. Dublin, and was of a Kerry family. (see 'Families of Kerry')

Berrill
Beryl

Although not given in other sources, O'Hart finds the Berrill family as a principal one settling in Dublin subsequent to the 12th century invasions of Ireland.

Berry
Barry

A family name given in Dublin in the census of 1659. See also Barry.

Berstow

A family name found in the city of Dublin in the census of 1659.

Bertram

Milesian Families finds the name in Dublin, of Scottish origins. (no documentation given).

Best

Bestwill

Families of the name of Best are found to have arrived in Ireland, coming from England, no later than the 17th century. Families of the name are found at that time in Dublin, Kilkenny and Cork in Ireland. Curiously the family name is not often found in or near the province of Ulster, where, by the end of the 19th century, the name is found most numerous in counties Antrim and Tyrone. (see the 'Book of Irish Families, great & small').

Alderman Elias Best is found in St. Nicholas Parish 'Within the Walls', in the Dublin City Pipe Water Accounts of 1680.

Betham

Sir Wm. Betham (d.1853), the Ulster King of Arms, is found in the Mountpelier area. See introduction.

Bettin

A family name found in the city of Dublin in the census of 1659.

Bettsworth

Richard Bettsworth of Dublin is found at Middleton, Co. Cork in 1727 (see also 'Families of Co. Cork, Ireland).

Betzold

A family name found in Dublin city, given to be of Jewish heritage in at least one instance. (per 'OLochlainns journal of Irish Families').

Beuchamp

A family name found in the city of Dublin in the census of 1659.

Bevan

A surname found in Quaker records in Dublin city in the early 18th century.

Bewley

A surname found in Quaker records in Dublin city in the early 18th century.

Bickford

Milesian Families finds the name in Dublin, of Saxon origins. (no documentation given).

Bicknell

Milesian Families finds the name in Dublin, of Saxon origins.

Bilder

Milesian Families finds the name in Dublin, of German origins. (no documentation given).

Billings

Milesian Families finds the name in Dublin, of English origins.

Billingsly

Edward Billingsly was given as prominent at Old Connaught parish in Dublin.

Billington

Mr. William Billingham is found in St. Catherine's parish in the Dublin City Pipe Water Accounts of 1680.

Billinsley

A family name found in Dublin in the census of 1659.

Bingham

The family is listed as part of the 'more recent nobility' by O'Hart where they are given as 'earls of Lucan', Co. Dublin.

Bird

A family name found in the 1890 birth index in Dublin.

Birford

A family name found in Dublin in the census of 1659.

Birmingham

Bermingham, Berminghan, Bremigan,

Of Anglo-Norman descent, the first of record to arrive here was Robert de Bermingham, of Castle Bermingham in Warwickshire. He arrived with Strongbow at the time of the invasions.

The family name is found most often in Leinster and Munster in Ireland.

A century ago 23 births were recorded under the spelling of Bermingham, and 17 bore the name of Birmingham. At that time the principal locations for the name were Dublin, Kings (Offaly), and Cork counties.

Arms for members of this family are found in the Irish Book of Arms. (see the 'Book of Irish Families, great & small'). See also Bermingham. A major entry on the name is found in 'The Families of Co. Galway'.

Birsell

The lands of Rochestown may have been transferred to Matthew Birsell and Thomas Lawless in 1563. See introduction.

Bishop   Bishopp

We find the family name in Dublin city and in Dublin County in the 17th century. In the 17th century village at Rathfarnham we find: Burgoyne; Bishop; Wilks; and Graham.

Bisse

A family name found in the city of Dublin in the census of 1659.

Black

Blake, Blacker...

Black is a family name most often found in the province of Ulster. It may be of either Scottish or English origins, outside of a few of the name who translated their names into Black from an original Gaelic name.

Several other names have likely been shortened into Black on occasion. Names like Blackand of Dublin, Blackbourne, Blacken, Blackender, Blackham, Blacker, Blacknell etc.., can all be of foreign origins when found in Ireland.

In the Irish Book of Arms several families of the name of Blake, and Blacker are given. (see also Blake). (see the 'Book of Irish Families.').

Blackand

A family name found in the city of Dublin in the census of 1659.

Blackburn

Milesian Families finds the name in Dublin, of Scottish origins. Names connected to Rathfarnham parish in the 18th century were Palliser; O'Callaghan; Cramer; Coghill; Stannard; Fountain; Ward; Geering; How; Boyle; and Blackburn was given into the 20th century in Dublin.

Blackhall

Blackall

The name of a settler family, who likely arrived here from England, found in Limerick in the 17th century and in Dublin and Clare subsequently. (see the 'Book of Irish Families, great & small').

Blackney

One George Blackney, described as an Irish Catholic, is found as a substantial landowner in 17th century Co. Dublin. He is given as holding Rickenhore with 718 acres of land at that time.

Blackwell

Families of the name of Blackwell are found in counties Clare, Dublin, Cork, and in Dublin city in 1659. (see the 'Book of Irish Families, great & small').

Bladen

A family name found in the city of Dublin in the census of 1659. One 'Dr. Thomas Bladen' is found in St. Werburgh's parish in the Dublin City Pipe Water Accounts of 1680.

Blake

Black De Blaca

The Blake family is given as a principal one of Anglo-Norman descent, settling in Dublin City and County, according to Keatings 'History of Ireland'. (see also Black)

One 'Widow Blake' is found in St. Nicholas Parish 'Without the Walls', in the Dublin City Pipe Water Accounts of 1680. (See major entry in 'The Families of Co. Galway').

Blanchfield

Milesian Families finds the name in Dublin, of Saxon origins. The Blanchfields are given by Ball to be one of the families located in Mulhuddart parish from the 14th -16th centuries.

Blanchfort

A Mrs. Blanchfort is given resident at Castleknock parish. See introduction.

Bligh

Bleigh

A family name found in the city of Dublin in the census of 1659.

Blum

Blume

A family name found in Dublin city, given to be of Jewish heritage in at least one instance. (per 'OLochlainns journal of Irish Families').

Blundell

Blondell

A family name found in the city of Dublin in the census of 1659.

Boas

A family name found in Dublin city, given to be of Jewish heritage in at least one instance. (per 'OLochlainns journal of Irish Families').

Bodley

Milesian Families finds the name in Dublin, of Saxon origins. (no documentation given).

Bold

Roger Bold is found in St. Werburgh's parish in the Dublin City Pipe Water Accounts of 1680.

Boles
Boales

A surname found in Quaker records in Dublin city in the late 17th century and onwards.

Bollard
Bullard

The name of a family, often found in Dublin, of whom several were noted as merchants. The census of 1659 finds the family in Dublin City, and the name remained centered in Dublin in the 1890 index. (see the 'Book of Irish Families, great & small').

Bolton
Bolten

The name of Bolton was fairly widespread in Ireland by the time of the census of 1659. It is found then in counties Down, Dublin, Queens, Louth and Waterford.

Bolton itself is a name of English origins, and it is generally given to be a name of English extraction when found in Ireland. The Bolton family of Castle Ring, Co. Louth is given in the Irish Book of Arms. (see the 'Book of Irish Families, great & small').

Bond

A family name found in Dublin in the birth index of 1890.

Bonole

A family name found in the city of Dublin in the census of 1659.

Bonorly

A family name found in the city of Dublin in the census of 1659.

Boorke
Bourke Burke

A family name found in Dublin in the census of 1659. (see also other spellings such as Burke, Bourke, etc..)

Booth

A family name found in Dublin in the birth index of 1890.

Borden

A family name found in the city of Dublin in the census of 1659.

Borr

A family name found in Dublin in the census of 1659. Names associated with the settlement of Balally in Taney parish were: de Walhope; Othyr; Howell; Taunton; Walsh in 1407 and Borr in the 17th century. It was given originally as a Danish settlement.

Boudler

A family name found in the city of Dublin in the census of 1659.

Bould
Bold

A family name found in the city of Dublin in the census of 1659.

Boulton
Bolton

A family name found in the city of Dublin in the census of 1659.

Bourne
Burne Beirne

A name we sometimes find in Dublin and Kildare.

Bowe
Bowe, Boe, Buo, O'bowe, O'bough, Bowes

The sometimes unrelated name of Bowes is found located mainly in Co. Dublin in the 19th century. (see the 'Book of Irish Families, great & small').

Bowker

Richard Bowker is found in St. John's parish in the Dublin City Pipe Water Accounts of 1680.

Bowman

Milesian Families finds the name in Dublin, of English origins. (no documentation given).

Bowye

John Bowye is found in St. John's parish in the Dublin City Pipe Water Accounts of 1680.

Bowyer
Bowyr

The name of an English family most often found in the city of Dublin, and also in Co. Longford for several centuries. (see the 'Book of Irish Families, great & small').

Boyd
Boid

A name most often found in the province of Ulster in Ireland, and assumed to be of Scottish origins when found there. In the census of 1659 Boyd was found as well in Monaghan and Dublin City .

The spelling of "Boyde" (it is common in earlier days to find an "e" on the end of many names),

The Irish Book of Arms gives the family of Boyd-Rochfort of Middleton Park, Co. Westmeath. (see the 'Book of Irish Families, great & small').

Boylan
Boyland, Boreland, Bullion

The ancient territory of Oriel marks the Boylan territory in Ireland. The families center of power is to be found in the barony of Dartry, in Co. Monaghan.

In the 17th century the Boylan name is found in Dublin, Kildare, Louth and Drogheda and Meath in the census of 1659. (see the 'Book of Irish Families, great & small').

Boyle

A name found in the city of Dublin in the census of 1659. Names connected to Rathfarnham parish in the 18th century included Boyle; and Blackburn.

Boyne
Boyn

In the 19th century birth index we find the Boyne family centered in Co. Dublin in Ireland. The family name can be found in several locations in Ireland. (see the 'Book of Irish Families, great & small').

Brabazon
Brabzon

According to "Keatings History" the name is that of a principal family of Dublin city or county, and of Anglo-Norman descent.

One noted family of the name is found in Ballinasloe, Co. Roscommon in the early 17th century. (see the 'Book of Irish Families, great & small').

The family is listed as part of the 'more recent nobility' by O'Hart where they are given as earls of Meath with large possessions in Wicklow and Dublin.

O' Bracken
Braken

Both the names of Brackane and Bracken were found as principal names of Kings Co. (Offaly) in the census of 1659. The name is given in that county and in Dublin in subsequent records. The name stems from O'Breacain when of possible old Irish origins. (see the 'Book of Irish Families, great & small').

The Brackens (O'Bracain) were chiefs of Moy Liffey along with the O'Murcains. This area is apparently near Dublin, and given as meaning lands along the Liffey, near Dublin. (per Keatings 'History of Ireland', I.G. F. edition.)

Bradbury

Milesian Families finds the name in Dublin, of English origins. (no documentation given).

Braddock

A surname found in Quaker records in Dublin city in the 18th century. Those of the name given above were merchants or weavers.

Alderman John Braddock is found in St. Nicholas Parish 'Without the Walls', in the Dublin City Pipe Water Accounts of 1680.

Bradley
Bradly, O'bradly, O'brolchain, O'bolchan

Bradley, a well known name found both of English and of native Irish extraction in Ireland.

Many of the name are to be found in Dublin in the 19th century records. (see the 'Book of Irish Families.').

Bradshaw

Bradshaw is assumed to be a name of English origins when found in Ireland, and is found settled here from the 17th century. The name is found in Dublin city and Fermanagh in the census of 1659, and in Antrim, Tipperary and Dublin in the 1890 birth index. (see the 'Book of Irish Families, great & small').

'Widow Bradshae' is found in St. Werburgh's parish in the Dublin City Pipe Water Accounts of 1680.

Bradstreet

Among the noted residents of Booterstown in the 18th century were included the names of Cooley; Doherty; Gough; O'Reilly; LaTouche; Doyne; Wight; Bradstreet; and Fitzgerald.

The Bradstreet family is given in connection with Kilmainham in the 18th century.

Mac Brady
Briody, Bradey, Mac Bradey

The powerful and respected Brady family is traditionally linked with the old territory of Breffni in Ireland. Here they were centered near the town of Cavan, in Co. Cavan.

Brady ranks among the top 100 most numerous surnames in all of Ireland. With over 200 births shown in the 1890 index, Co. Cavan leads the list for the name, with Dublin, Antrim, Meath and Longford also given as locations with many of the name. In fact it ranks among the 25 most numerous names of Dublin in the 1890 birth index.

Arms for members of the Brady family can be found on plates 67, 146, and 226 of the Irish Book of Arms. (see the 'Book of Irish Families.).

Christopher Bassenet, John Brady, and John Hore, in 1561, are found leasing the lands of Kill of the Grange parish.

In 1561 we find lands of Tipperstown leased to Bassenet, Brady and Hore. See introduction.

Bragg

A family name found in the city of Dublin in the census of 1659. Joseph Bragg is found in St. Werburgh's parish in the Dublin City Pipe Water Accounts of 1680.

Braghall

Braghall's farm, in Glasnevin Parish, went to John Quartermas and later to John Forster.

Braham

A family name found in Dublin city, given to be of Jewish heritage in at least one instance. (per 'OLochlainns journal of Irish Families').

Note also the name of Branham found in Dublin in 1659.

Brampton

A family name found in the city of Dublin in the census of 1659.

O' Branagan
Branigan, Brannigin

The Brannigan name is said to have been taken from O'Brannagain most anciently, and the family is found in Armagh and Monaghan in the 1890 birth index. Spelled as Branagan the name is given in Dublin at that time. (see the 'Book of Irish Families.').

Brandon

Milesian Families finds the name in Dublin, of English origins. (no documentation given).

Branham
Branam

A family name found in the city of Dublin in the census of 1659. Note also the name of Braham given in Dublin city.

Braun

A family name found in Dublin city, given to be of Jewish heritage in at least one instance. (per 'OLochlainns journal of Irish Families').

Bray
O'bree, De Bri, Di Bre, Bree

The Bray family is found in the wake of the Norman invasions, in Clonmel, with several prominent persons of the name there. This family name may have several origins in Ireland. One century ago the name is given in Counties Cavan and Dublin.

Keatings History cites the name as O'Bree, as the chief of the free Moy Sedna, of Irish origins. (see the 'Book of Irish Families, great & small').

Brayne

A family name found as a principal name in Dublin in the census of 1659.

O Brazzil

Brazil, Brassil, Brazel, Brassell, O'bressyl

In more modern times 'Brazil' is found as being of Dublin and Wexford at the turn of the century. It has many apparent variant spellings of which are included MacBrassill, which hailed from Galway in more ancient times. (see the 'Book of Irish Families.').

Breen

Brien, Briene, Obraein, Brawne, Bruen

The 'Breen' family of Ireland is an old and respected one.

O'Hart gave Mac Breen as a chief in Kilkenny, and as present in Tyrone.

A century ago the name was found most popular in Wexford, Dublin and Kerry (see the 'Book of Irish Families, great & small').

O Brennan

Brennan, Brannan, Briane, Brenon,

Brennon families represent one of the 30 most numerous families in all of Ireland in modern times. The name may stem from either MacBrennon or O'Brennon.

One century ago the name was fairly widespread as one might expect, with Kilkenny, Dublin, Sligo and Mayo heading the list of counties with most of the name. (see the 'Book of Irish Families, great & small').

Brereton

Brerton, Breerton

In 19th century records we find the name centered in Dublin and in Kings Co. (Offaly).

Many of the name settled here coming from England. (see the 'Book of Irish Families, great & small').

One noted family of the name is found in the barony of Uppercross, Co. Dublin, in the 17th century.

One Brereton family is found at Crumlin parish. See introduction.

Brett

Bret Le Bret

According to "Keatings History" the name is that of a principal family of Dublin city or county, and of Anglo-Norman descent.

The main location for the name in the 19th century was in Co. Sligo, and in Co. Dublin. (see the 'Book of Irish Families, great & small').

In the 14th century le Bret is noted at Rathfarnham parish. A Thomas Brett is found in Dublin City on High Street in the 17th century.

Breviter

One of the name is found at Irishtown, Co. Dublin in the latter 18th century.

Brewster

Sir Frances Brewster was Lord Mayor of Dublin in 1764 and is noted in 'Families of Co. Kerry, Ireland'.).

Brice

A family name given in Dublin in the Birth Index of 1890. John Brice is found in St. Audeon's parish in the Dublin City Pipe Water Accounts of 1680.

Bridges

A family name found in Dublin city in the census of 1659. Capt. Robert Bridges is found in St. Werburgh's parish in the Dublin City Pipe Water Accounts of 1680.

At Newcastle in 1614 among the first city officials were: Parsons; Rolles; Kenny; Frend; Davies; White; Burton; Grible; Bridges; Rutledge; and Lushe.

O Brien
O'bryan, O'brian, O'brein,

One of the most outstanding of all the great families of Ireland, most O'Briens can trace their descent back to the 10th century when the great high king, Brian Boru, came to prominence. It is he from whom the name is taken.

One of the most popular names in all of Ireland, it is to be found widespread throughout the entire country today. In 1890 O'Brien ranked among the top ten most numerous names in Dublin county.

O'Brien was a name of note at Newlands in Tallaght parish.

(see the 'Book of Irish Families, great & small' and 'The Families of Co. Clare, Ireland'.). (See major entry in 'The Families of Co. Clare').

Brigg
Brig Briggs

Milltown, Co. Dublin was held by the Brigg family in the 14th century, and by the Loftus family in 1641, and at that time John Bacon was principal resident there.

Brighness
A family name found in the city of Dublin in the census of 1659.

Bright
A family name given in Dublin in the Birth Index of 1890.

Brimingham
Birmingham Bermingham

A family name found in Dublin in the census of 1659.

Brin
Breen

A family name found in Dublin in the census of 1659.

O' Briody
Brady, Brody, Macbrody

One Maolin MacBrody is given as helping to translate the New Testament into Irish, as published by Ussher, in Dublin in 1602.

(see the 'Book of Irish Families, great & small').

Briscoe
Briscoe is a name of settler origins when found in Ireland and it is most often linked with Dublin in our records. It is here where we find the name in the 17th century as well. (see the 'Book of Irish Families, great & small').

Briscoe is also noted at Killininny.

Brocas
Brokas, Brocas

One of the rarer names found in Ireland, the family is traditionally linked to Dublin, where several of the name are found as noted artists. Families of the name here are of English descent, but the name is as well found among the Huguenots who settled in Great Britain. (see the 'Book of Irish Families, great & small').

Consult also " The Brocas Family, Notable Dublin Artists" as found in the "University Review" 2 (6), 1959.

Broderick
A family name given in Dublin in the Birth Index of 1890.

Broe
Brew, Broo, Broghe, De Berewa, De Bruth

Families of the name of Broe are found in Kildare and Dublin in the 1890 index for Ireland. (see the 'Book of Irish Families, great & small').

Bromagen
Milesian Families finds the name in Dublin in the 12th century of Norman descent. (no documentation given.)

Brooke
See also Brooks.

At the close of the 18th century the principal families of Dalkey Parish were those of Sir John Hasler; Wm. Macartney; John Patrickson; and Charlotte Brooke.

Sir Henry Brooke is found at St. Peters Parish. See introduction.

Brookfield
A surname found in Quaker records in Dublin city in the late 17th century, where one of the name is found employed as a 'tanner'.

Brooking

A family name found in the city of Dublin in the census of 1659. William Brooking is found in St. Audeon's parish in the Dublin City Pipe Water Accounts of 1680.

Brooks

Brook, Brooke, Brookes, Brooks

The name of Brooks is found under several spellings. Brooks, is the favored spelling today. The spelling of Brookes is found in Tipperary, Cork, Dublin City, Londonderry, Kildare and Kilkenny.

'Brooks' is also found in Cork and Dublin in the 1890 birth index. Note that these spellings have changed over time. 'Brooks' today could stem originally from Brookes, etc..

One source gives Brooke as settling in Dublin in 1690 and of English origins.

Two Brooke pedigrees are found, those of Leicestershire, England, and those of Navan, Co. Meath, who were originally from Chesire, England. Arms for the English family are given by O'Hart. (see the 'Book of Irish Families, great & small').

It is also a surname found in Quaker records in Dublin city in the 18th century, where one of the name is listed as a 'baker'.

Edward Brookes is found in St. Werburgh's parish in the Dublin City Pipe Water Accounts of 1680.

At the close of the 18th century the principal families of Dalkey Parish were those of Sir John Hasler; Wm. Macartney; John Patrickson; and Charlotte Brooke.

Brophy

The Brophy name is said to have come from O'Broithe, originally of Co. Leix (Queens County). The name is found most often in Dublin, Kilkenny, Queens and Tipperary in the 1890 birth index. (see the 'Book of Irish Families, great & small').

Broughall

Brothel, Brohel, Broughill, Brohale,

The census of 1659 finds the family in Dublin. (see the 'Book of Irish Families, great & small').

Broun

Broune Browne

Both Broun and Broune are found in Dublin City in the 1659 census. (see also Browne).

Browne

Broune, Brown

Brown(e) families comprise one of the 10 most numerous names in Scotland and England, and one of the 50 most numerous names in Ireland. Often a name of English or Scottish origins when found in Ireland, the final 'e' in the name appears common in Ireland.

'Brown' was found in 1659 mostly in Cork, Mayo, Wexford and Dublin and 'Browne' mostly in Ulster and Dublin.

Estate papers in the National Library in Dublin, relate to Browne families.

Several families of the name are found in the Irish Book of Arms. (see also the 'Book of Irish Families, great & small').

The 'Brown' family is also given as a principal one of Anglo-Norman descent, settling in Dublin City and County, according to Keatings 'History of Ireland'.

Thomas Browne is found in St. Werburgh's parish in the Dublin City Pipe Water Accounts of 1680. One of the same name is also found as a Councilor at Law in St. Nicholas Parish 'Within the Walls', in the Dublin City Pipe Water Accounts of 1680.

Samuel Brown of Newtown is given in the introduction of this book. In Esker parish the Brownes are noted as still resident in the 17th century.

Patrick Browne is given as the builder of the castle at Irishtown.

In 'King James's Irish Army List, 1689' we find listed as a Dublin assessor, one Thomas Browne, Esq.. (See major entry in 'The Families of Co. Galway'). (See major entry in 'The Families of Co. Kerry').

Bruister

Brewster

A family name found in the city of Dublin in the census of 1659.

Bruton

A family name found in Dublin at the time of the Birth Index of 1890. The name is traditionally found in the Union of Edenderry and the Union of Parsonstown in Ireland.

Bryan

O Bryan O Brien Brian

The Bryan family is most often associated with Co. Kilkenny in Ireland. Much confusion exists as to the spelling, for it is easily confused with Brien, O'Brian etc...

By the time of the 1890 birth index of Ireland the name was dispersed in several counties, with Dublin and Kilkenny heading the list.

The Bryan family of Upton and Borrmount Manor, Co. Wexford are given in the Irish Book of Arms. (see the 'Book of Irish Families.').

Bryscoe

Briscoe

A family name found in Dublin in the census of 1659.

Buck

Milesian Families finds the name in Dublin, of English origins. (no documentation given).

Buckarton

A family name found in the city of Dublin in the census of 1659.

Buckingham

Milesian Families finds the name in Dublin, of English origins.

Buckley

O'buhilly, Boughla, Bohelly, Buckeley,

Buckley is one of the top 100 most numerous names in all of Ireland. It is as well a common English name, from which some of the name in Ireland have sprung. O'Hart gives the name as arriving with the 12th century Norman invasions.

In the 17th century we find the family name in Queens Co. (Leix) as Buckly, in Dublin as Buckley, and in Louth and Drogheda as Bulkely. One century ago the name was most often found in Cork and Kerry, being followed by Dublin and Tipperary as well.

Arms for the family of Bulkeley are found in the Irish Book of Arms plate 9. One noted Bulkeley family in France is said to be of English origins. (see Bulkeley). (see the 'Book of Irish Families, great & small').

Budd

William Bud is found at St. James and St. Jude parish. See introduction.

Buggle

Bugle

The name of an English family found in Dublin and Kildare in our records. (see the 'Book of Irish Families, great & small').

Bulkeley

Buckley Bulkley

One family of the Bulkeley name can be traced back to William Bulkeley, Archdeacon of Dublin. (see the 'Book of Irish Families, great & small').

(see also Buckley)

Bulkeley and others in his service, also of Welsh birth are noted in 1641 at Old Bawn in the parish of Tallaght.

Buller

At the time of the 17th century restoration Edward Buller is given in a 'good thatched castle' at Laughanstown. See introduction.

Burbridge

Thomas Burbridge is found in St. John's parish in the Dublin City Pipe Water Accounts of 1680.

Burgess
Burges

The Burges family of Parkanaur, Co. Tyrone is found in Co. Dublin in the late 17th century. The 1890 birth index finds the family most numerous in Co. Dublin, under the spelling of Burgess. (see the 'Book of Irish Families, great & small').

Burgoyne

Milesian Families finds the name in Dublin, of English origins. Also found in Dublin in the census of 1659.

In the 17th century village at Rathfarnham we find: Burgoyne; Bishop; Wilks; and Graham. They are also noted in Whitechurch parish. See introduction.

Burke
Burgh, De Burgh, Bourke, Burk

One of the 20 most numerous names in Ireland, Burke was one of the most common names arriving in Ireland as a result of the 12th century invasions.

The original spelling of de Burgo was replaced by Burgh, Burke, Bourke etc.. but the older form of de Burgo remained for several centuries in Irish records. In the 17th century 'Burk' was a principal name of Kings Co., 'Burke' was found in Galway, Cork and Dublin, the spelling of 'Bourk' was a principal name in Limerick, and Bourke was such in Clare at the time of the 1659 census.

Galway, Cork and Dublin were centers for the name for centuries. A century ago the spelling of 'Bourke' was centered in Tipperary, Limerick and Mayo. (see the 'Book of Irish Families').

For more on the Galway family of the name see 'Families of Co. Galway, Ireland'. De Burgo (Burke) is often credited with establishing the town of Galway subsequent to the Norman invasion.

Burne
Bierne Byrne

A family name found in Dublin in the census of 1659. (see also variant spellings)

Burnell

Burnell is given by O'Hart as a principal family of Co. Dublin between the 12th and the 18th century. Among the owners of Knocklyon in the parish of Tallaght we find Burnell.

The De Clahull and Burnell families were early owners of Ballyfermot in the 14th century.

Although the Burnells were seated at Ballygriffin, but some of the family are found at Castle Knock in the 15th and 16th centuries.

Burnett

A family name given in Dublin in the census of 1659..

Burniston

In 1664 John Burniston was rated for 5 hearths near Howth.

Burns Beirne
Byrnes, O'byrne, Burns, O'beirnes,

The names of Burn(s), Byrne(s), Beirne, etc.. represent several different families. Many of the same family will spell their names differently. Due to similarity in sound and spelling these names are used interchangeably.

The spellings of "Byrne" and O'Byrne account for one of the top 10 names in Ireland. Originally of Co. Kildare, they were forced into Wicklow, being centered in Ballinacor. Today the name is numerous there, and in Dublin. The original "O" before the name was generally dropped. This family held lands within the pale in Ireland, and fought constantly against the "invaders".

The name of "Beirne" or Biernes, represents a separate family. (see the 'Book of Irish Families, great & small').

Burr

Noted names in 18th century Milltown, Co. Dublin, included: Mr. Heavisid; Classon; Burr; Hugh Johnson; Randall; Dogherty; Tomlinson; King; and Walcot.

Burrilow

Nicholas Burrilow is found in St. Nicholas Parish 'Within the Walls', in the Dublin City Pipe Water Accounts of 1680.

Burrowes
Burrows

A family name found in the city of Dublin in the census of 1659.

Burt

A family name found in the city of Dublin in the census of 1659.

Burton

The census of 1659 finds the family in Dublin. The 1890 birth index finds the family most numerous in Dublin and Antrim. (see the 'Book of Irish Families, great & small').

It is also a surname found in Quaker records in Dublin city in the 18th century, where one of the name is given as a 'weaver'.

At Newcastle in 1614 among the first city officials were: Parsons; Rolles; Kenny; Frend; Davies; White; Burton.

One 'Mr. Burton' is found at Esker parish in the 17th century.

Busby

Milesian Families finds the name in Dublin, of Saxon origins.

Bush

A family name found in Dublin City in the census of 1659. John Bush is found in St. Nicholas Parish 'Within the Walls', in the Dublin City Pipe Water Accounts of 1680.

Bushell

A family name found in the city of Dublin in the census of 1659.

Buston

A family name found in the city of Dublin in the census of 1659.

Butler
Buttler

One Butler family descends from 'Theobald Fitzwalter' who arrived in Ireland in 1177 with Henry the II. He was appointed Chief Butler of Ireland in 1177. His younger brother, Thomas, came with Prince John of England to Waterford in 1185. This family is referred to as the 'Ormond Butler' family.

In the 13th century we find Butler, Wallis, Finglas, and Fitzgerald at Killakee.

An entry in King James Irish Army list shows one John Butler, an obscure miller of Westpalstown, Co. Dublin, who was attainted circa 1642.

A century ago the name was most common in Dublin, Kilkenny, Tipperary and Waterford in Ireland. (above extracted from the 'Book of Irish Families, great & small').

In 13th century Donneybrook we find: de Verneuil; Butler or de Verdon; and de London.

The family is also given as a principal one of Anglo-Norman descent, settling in Dublin City and County, according to Keatings 'History of Ireland'.

In Esker parish Hermitage was the residence of Maj. Gen. Robert Naper which passed to the Hon. Robert Butler in 1739.

Butterfield

A name found in Dublin in the Birth Index of 1890. Milesian Families finds the name in Dublin of English extraction.

Butterly

A name found in Dublin as a principle name there in the census of 1659.

Butterton

Jonathan Butterton is found in St. Michael's parish in the Dublin City Pipe Water Accounts of 1680.

Bygins
Biggens Biggins

Found in Dublin in the 1659 census. See appendix.

Byland

Widow Byland is found in St. Audeon's parish in the Dublin City Pipe Water Accounts of 1680.

O'Byrne, Byrnes
O'byrne, Burn, Bierne, Byron,

A name prominent throughout Irish history, the family is traditionally associated with the province of Leinster in Ireland. As the 7th most common name in all of Ireland, it (Byrne) was also THE most numerous name of Dublin County in the 1890 birth index.

Several pages are devoted to the O'Byrne family of Cabinteely, Co. Dublin, in the works of John O'Hart. Thomas Cusack was leased the lands of Cabinteely, which were subsequently held by Sir John Travers in 1545, and then by the Eustace, Cheevers and O'Bynre families. See introduction.

The O'Tooles and the O'Byrnes were two of the leading Irish chieftains to wage war in Dublin for centuries after the 12th century Norman invasion. They were feared by their opponents, and at times ravaged the entire countryside.

In 1313 they burned Bray, which was considered 'wild territory' by the settlers. Such acts were not isolated.

In the early part of the 18th century Newtown Castle Byrne was a noted resort for Dubliners. In 1748 an auction was held for Mr. Robert Byrne at Mountpelier, near Newtown Castle Byrne.

Published materials:
"The O'Byrnes and their Descendants" published in Dublin in 1879.

"History of the Clan O'Byrne and other...septs", by Rev. P. L. O'Toole. published in Dublin in 1890.

(extracted in part from the 'Book of Irish Families, great & small').

Byron
O'byrne, Burn, Beirne, Byron,

Spelled as 'Byron' the name is given a century ago as centered in Dublin and Antrim. In the census of 1659 we find the spelling of Byrine in County Carlow. (above extracted from the 'Book of Irish Families, great & small').

Bysse
At the time of the 17th century rebellion Robert Bysse was high sheriff of Dublin and was resident in Castleknock parish.

Mac Cabe
Macabe, Mac Cabe, Mac Caba

The great fall of the family came in 1691 when their lands were confiscated as a result of the Battle of Augrim. Indeed, the whole order of the country had been reversed in that century.

Mac Cabe also ranks among the top 900 most common names in America.

A century ago the name was most common in Cavan, Monaghan and Dublin. Two centuries prior, it is found in Fermanagh, Monaghan and Louth. (above extracted from the 'Book of Irish Families, great & small').

Caddell
Cadell Gadell Caddle

The Cadell family is given as a principal one of Anglo-Norman descent, settling in Dublin City and County, according to Keatings 'History of Ireland'.

Richard Caddell, ale brewer, is found in St. Audeon's parish in the Dublin City Pipe Water Accounts of 1680. The Caddle family of Naul, Co. Dublin is given among the minor gentry in the 17th century.

See also *'Families of Co. Galway'* where the name is also prominent, and many took on the name of Blake in place of Caddell.

Cadmore
A family name found in the city of Dublin in the census of 1659.

Cadwell
A family name found in the city of Dublin in the census of 1659.

Cady
Milesian Families finds the name in Dublin, of English origins. (no documentation given).

Mac Caffrey

Mac Cafferky, Mac Goffrey, Caffreys,

The name is found as Caffrey however, in Dublin, Meath and Cavan in the 1890 index.

Several are found among the fighting men of Corcorans Irish Legion and Meaghers Irish Brigade of civil war fame in the U. S. A..

The name is said to come from MacGafraidh originally, from which some took the name of MacGoffrey instead of MacCaffrey.

This family name is often confused with Mac Cafferty and Mac Cafferky of Co. Mayo. (above extracted from the 'Book of Irish Families.').

O Cahan

Keane, O'kane, Kane, Kean, Cahane

Modern day members of the O'Cahan family most often spring from the old Irish family of O'Cathain. The name is found both as O'Cahan and Mac Cahan in Irish records and variant spellings are most numerous.

Moving into more modern times, when Kane and Keane have been substituted for the above spelling we find 'Kane' in Antrim, Londonderry and Dublin. Keane was in Galway, Clare, Kerry and Mayo at that time.

Origins may be difficult to trace due to the interchanging of these names. (above extracted from the 'Book of Irish Families, great & small').

O Cahill

Mccahil, Mccall, Cahil, Cahill

Families of the O'Cahill name in Ireland spring from several origins, and have almost always dropped the 'O' prefix from the name.

At the turn of the century the name was most popular in Cork, Kerry, Dublin and Kilkenny.

(above extracted from the 'Book of Irish Families, great & small'). (See major entry in 'The Families of Co. Galway').

Calbs

A family name found in Dublin city, given to be of Jewish heritage in at least one instance. (per 'OLochlainns journal of Irish Families').

Caldbeck

We find Mr. Caldbeck and Barry Yelverton at Clondalkin in the 17th century or later.

Caldwell

Coldwell, Calwell, Colavin, Cawldwell,

A well known name of foreign origins in Ireland, some native Irish families have adopted the name as well. Of foreign origins the name may have come from Scotland or England.

The Irish Book of Arms gives Caldwell of New Grange, Co. Meath, and this family was of original Scottish heritage, and earlier settled in Dublin. (above extracted from the 'Book of Irish Families, great & small').

O Callaghan

Callahan, Callihan, Calahan, Calaghan,

One of the 50 most numerous names in all of Ireland, the 'O' prefix before the name had largely been dropped by the time of the great immigrations to America. Today in Ireland the 'O' prefix is being assumed once again. In 1890 the name was most numerous in Cork, Kerry and Dublin. (See major entry in 'The Families of Co. Cork').

Several families of the name became armigerous. Arms for one family of the name are found in the Irish Book of Arms. The chief of the name into modern times was also given as being a citizen of Spain.

(above extracted from the 'Book of Irish Families, great & small').

Names connected to Rathfarnham parish in the 18th century were Palliser; O'Callaghan; Cramer; Coghill; Stannard; Fountain; Ward; Geering; How; Boyle; and Blackburn.

Mrs. O'Callaghan (d.1779), is noted at a house on the site of Drumcondra Castle.

Callan
Callen, Calan, Callin
   The name of O'Callan was a principal one of Monaghan, Callan a principal name of Dublin, and McCallan a principal name of Fermanagh in the census of 1659. (above extracted from the 'Book of Irish Families, great & small').
   The spelling of 'Callin' is given as a principal name of Dublin City in the census of 1659.

Mac Callery
   The MacCallery family name is traditionally linked to Co. Sligo in Ireland. It is as well found in Dublin city records. (above extracted from the 'Book of Irish Families, great & small').

Callisher
   A family name found in Dublin city, given to be of Jewish heritage in at least one instance. (per 'OLochlainns journal of Irish Families').

Candit
   A family name found in the city of Dublin in the census of 1659.

Mac Cann
Macanna, Canny, Maccanna
   McCann was centered in the north of Ireland and in Dublin in the 1890 birth index. In the 17th century 'McCan' was a principal name in Dublin and Londonderry, McCanna was found in Fermanagh and McCann in Armagh at that time.
   Arms for one family of the name are found in the Irish Book of Arms on plates 147 and 246.
   For more information the book entitled 'Origins of the McCanns' by A. Mathews, (1978) Ireland, will be of service.
   (The above extracted from the 'Book of Irish Families, great & small').

O Cannon
Cannan, Gannon, Kennon, Maccannon
   Traditionally the name is often identified with the county of Donegal.
   Mac Cannan and Mac Cannon families are still found in the ancient territory of Oriel, and the name is found in Dublin city and Meath in our records. (The above extracted from the 'Book of Irish Families, great & small').

Cantrel
   Milesian Families finds the name in Dublin, of Norman origins. (no documentation given).

Cantwell
   Tipperary and Dublin have become the main locations for the name. Some of the name are of Anglo-Norman origins, coming originally from the name of de Kentwell. (The above extracted from the 'Book of Irish Families, great & small').

Capper
   In the 17th century we find Edward Capper of Finglas Parish.

Carberry
Carbry
   In the census of 1659 Carbery was a principal name of Waterford, O'Carbry a principal name of Armagh, and the name was also in Kildare, Dublin and Meath at that time. (The above extracted from the 'Book of Irish Families, great & small').
   At least one family of the name held lands in Co. Dublin in 1640. At the time of the 17th century Restoration the Carberry family is given as holding the lands of Kilbride.

Carden
   Among houses noted at Ballyfermot were those of: Verveer; Styles; Carden; Ryves; Exham; and Talbot of Templeogue.

Cardyff
Cardiff
   A family name found in the city of Dublin in the census of 1659.

Carew
   Raymond Carew is given to be the first English owner of Stillorgan Park. (See entry in 'The Families of Co. Kerry').

O Carey

Cary, Carie, Keary, Kary, Mccarey,

Ruling as 'Lords of Carbury' in Co. Kildare until the Norman invasions, the name is more properly spelled as O'Keary.

The arms of Cary-Cadell of Harbourstown, Co. Cork, are found in the Irish Book of Arms, with some information.

Many can be found in fighting brigades in Europe and the name is one of the top 500 in America.

The 1800's birth index finds Carey centered in Cork, Dublin, Tipperary, Mayo and Kerry.

(The above extracted from the 'Book of Irish Families, great & small').

In 1772 in Tully parish obituaries we find George Carey of Redcastle.

George Carey is given as the chief person in Finglas in the 16th century.

Carley

Milesian Families finds the name in Dublin, of English origins. (no documentation given).

Carlis

Milesian Families finds the name in Dublin, of Scottish origins. (no documentation given).

Carlton

A surname found in Quaker records in Dublin city in the 18th century, where two of the name are given as 'weavers'.

Carmichael

Carmichael is given as among the few names of importance in Taney parish in the mid 18th century.

Carnett

Garnett

Milesian Families finds the name in Dublin, of English origins. (no documentation given).

It is a surname found in Quaker records in Dublin city in the early 18th century as Garnett.

O Carolan

Carrolan, Carrollan, Kerlin, Carleton

The O'Carolan family in Ireland has at least two distinct origins.

The 'O' prefix before the name has generally been dropped. Moving into modern times the name is found in Mayo and Cavan in the 1890 index, with representatives as would be expected in Dublin.

Arms for the name are found in the Irish Book of Arms plate 249. (The above extracted from the 'Book of Irish Families, great & small').

Carpenter

Found in the Birth Index of 1890 in Dublin. Milesian Families finds the name in Dublin, of English origins.

Carr

O'carr, Macelhar, Kerrane, Kerr,

The origins of the Carr family in Ireland can be difficult to trace.

'Carre' is a likely spelling given in the 1659 census in Dublin city. The 1890 birth index shows the name to be of Donegal, Galway and Dublin.

Today Carr ranks as the 203rd most popular name in America with an estimated count of 110,700 individuals. (The above extracted from the 'Book of Irish Families, great & small').

One Edward Carr is given in the Quaker records in Dublin as a 'harness maker'.

Carre

Carr

A family name found in the city of Dublin in the census of 1659. (Be aware of the possible spelling of 'Carr' as well).

Mc Carrig Carricke

Carrick

The similar names of McCarrick or Carricke, are found in Co. Kerry and Dublin City in the census of 1659. (The above extracted from the 'Book of Irish Families, great & small').

Early names at Newcastle parish after the 12th century invasions included Carrick; Russell; and le Marshall.

O Carroll
Carrol, Caroll, Carol, Mac Carroll,

One of the top 25 surnames of Ireland, several families use the name. It is among the 20 most numerous names of Dublin in the 1890 birth index. The Carroll family of Ashford, Co. Wicklow, are earliest found in Co. Dublin in the 18th century. (The above extracted from the 'Book of Irish Families.').

The O'Carrolls of Athgoe Park, Co. Dublin are found in the Irish Book of Arms, and they are given as of Ely O'Carroll lineage.

Carruthers
Carrothers, Caruth

The name of Caruthers is given to be a settler name in Ireland, coming from a place name in Scotland. As may be expected, the family is found centered in the province of Ulster, although it has also been found in Dublin City and in Waterford at a fairly early date. (The above extracted from the 'Book of Irish Families, great & small').

Carson
Curson

The traditional location for the name was in Antrim, Down and Tyrone in the 1890 birth index. Other sources find the name in Limerick and Dublin in the 16th century. (The above extracted from the 'Book of Irish Families, great & small').

Cart
Carte

A family name found in Dublin in the census of 1659. Nicholas Carte occupied Damastown in the 17th century.

Carter
Macarthur

In the more modern 1890 birth index, Dublin and Galway are listed as principal counties of residence.

The Irish Book of Arms give the family of Carter of Shaen Manor, Co. Mayo. (The above extracted from the 'Book of Irish Families, great & small').

Mac Cartney
See Macartney.

Carton
A family name given in Dublin in the Birth Index of 1890.

Caruthers
Milesian Families finds the name in Dublin, of Scottish origins.

Casement
Maccasmonde, Casmond, Casmey

Some of the name are found in counties Dublin and Limerick early.

The Casement family of Magherintemple, Co. Antrim is given in the Irish book of Arms. (The above extracted from the 'Book of Irish Families, great & small').

O Casey   Cassy
Casey, Maccasey, O'cahassy, Kasey Casy

Several completely separate families bear the name of Casey in Ireland today. In Co. Dublin they are found as 'Lords of Suaithni' and they were centered there in the barony of Balrothy west.

The 1800's birth index shows some 254 Casey births, with Cork, Kerry and Dublin heading the list as the most numerous counties of the name.

(The above extracted from the 'Book of Irish Families, great & small').

O'Hart also gives the Casey family of Dublin, Westmeath and Longford as of the same descent as the above mentioned branch from Suaithni. They were also known as Lords of Magh Breagh or Bregia, a territory which contained 'Suithni', according to O'Hart and others. These Dublin Casys were dispossessed by De Lacy at the time of the Norman invasions.

Casy is given as a name of Dublin City in the 1659 census, and the likely variant spelling of Cassy is found in Dublin at that time as well.

Cashell
We find the widow of John Cashell, a Drogheda merchant who died at the castle of Baggottrath. She died in 1574.

Caskin
Gaskin, Askin, (gascoigne)

In the census of 1659 Gaskin is found in County Louth, and in the 1890 birth index in Dublin. The original form of the name is said to be Gascoigne i.e. originating in Gascony. Caskin may be a form of Gaskin. (The above extracted from the 'Book of Irish Families, great & small').

O Cassidy
Casaday, Casidy, Casley, Cassedy,
The 1890 index finds the family in Donegal, Dublin, Antrim and Fermanagh.
Arms for some families of the name appear on plates 148 and 255 in the Irish Book of Arms. (The above extracted from the 'Book of Irish Families, great & small').

Cassilly
Milesian Families finds the name in Dublin, of Norman origins. (no documentation given).

Castleton
Alderman John Castleton is found in St. Audeon's parish in the Dublin City Pipe Water Accounts of 1680.

Casy
Casey
Casy is given as a name of Dublin City in the 1659 census, and the likely variant spelling of Cassy is found in Dublin at that time as well.

Catelyn
Catelline, Catlin
Sir Nathaniel Catelyn, served as speaker for the Irish House of Commons in 1634 and died in 1637, being buried at St. Nicholas's in Dublin. (The above extracted from the 'Book of Irish Families, great & small').

Caufield
Cawfield, Caulfield, M'caulfield,
It is certain that Caufield is a variant of Caulfield, which in turn, often comes from the Irish name of MacCawell in Ireland.
Passenger Lists for Caufield:
Cathne. Caufield. age 17, female, seamstress. aboard 'Perseverance', May 18, 1846. Dublin to New York.

Caulfield
Mccall, Caffrey, Gaffney, Calfhill,
The census of 1659 finds the Caulfield name in Dublin city, and in the Poll Money Ordinance Survey. (The above extracted from the 'Book of Irish Families, great & small').
The family is listed as part of the 'more recent nobility' by O'Hart where they are given as earls of Charlemont who resided at Marino, Clontarf.
It is certain that Caufield is a variant of Caulfield, which in turn, often comes from the Irish name of MacCawell in Ireland.
Passenger Lists for Caufield:
Cathne. Caufield. age 17, female, seamstress. aboard 'Perseverance', May 18, 1846. Dublin to New York.

Cavan
A family name given in Dublin in the census of 1659..

Cavanagh
Cavenagh Cavenah
A family name given in Dublin as a principal name in the census of 1659..

Cecil
Milesian Families finds the name in Dublin, of English origins. (no documentation given).

Chabner
A family name found in Dublin in the census of 1659.

Chaffee
A name linked in one document to Kilrisk, Dublin.

Chalkwright
Christopher Chalkwright is found in St. Catherine's parish in the Dublin City Pipe Water Accounts of 1680.

Chamberlain
Chamberlayne

According to "Keatings History" the name is given among the chief Anglo-Norman and English settlers in Ulidia, under DeCourcey and his successors. Among noted families of the name in our files are Chamberlayne of Kilrisk and Kilmacree Co. Dublin, and Chamberlayne of Athboy, Co. Meath. Under the spelling of Chamberlyn we find the family in Dublin in the 1659 census.

One of the name has been traced back to Richard Chamberlain or Chamberlen etc.. who lived in the 14th century. This family is found settled in Kilrisk and Kilmacree in Co. Dublin. (The above extracted from the 'Book of Irish Families, great & small').

Among the early tenants of Taney parish were Edmund Hacket, Richard Chamberlain and John Locumbe in the 14th century.

Elijah Chamberlin is given in the first half of the 18th century as a merchant who is found in the Quaker records in Dublin.

In 1754 we find Rev. Walter Chamberlain at Chapelizod parish.

Among the chief residents in Finglas at the end of the Elizabethan period are: the head of the Chamberlain family at Kilreesk.

Chambers
Chambres

In the 17th century we find the name in Dublin City, Armagh, Cork and Kerry.

The Irish Book of Arms gives Chambers of Fosterstown, Trim, Co. Meath, as descended from Joseph, of Taylorstown, Co. Wexford.

One pedigree for the name is found in O'Hart. The Chambre family of Dungannon House, Co. Tyrone is given in the Irish Book of Arms. (The above extracted from the 'Book of Irish Families, great & small').

Subsequent to the 17th century rebellions we find the names of Wharton; Chambers; Willion; Barry; Robinson; Moses; ·Reyly; Lovelace; Eaton; Murphy; Lawlor; Leedom; and Walsh in Rathcoole parish, Co. Dublin.

Champines
A family name found in the city of Dublin in the census of 1659.

Chandlee
Chandley

Assuming the spelling is correct (i.e. not mistaken for Chandler, etc..) some of the name are given as Quakers in Dublin records in the 18th century.

Chandler
A family name found in the city of Dublin in the census of 1659.

Chapman
A family name given in Dublin in the Birth Index of 1890. In the 13th century we find R. Chapman at Old Connaught parish. See introduction.

Charlton
A family name found in the city of Dublin in the census of 1659.

McChayer
One Willelmus McChayer is found at Glenasmole in prior centuries.

Chaytor
A surname found in Quaker records in Dublin city in the late 18th and 19th centuries.

Cheevers
One family of the name is found in Mountaine, Co. Dublin in the 17th century. (The above extracted from the 'Book of Irish Families, great & small').

Walter Cheevers of Muncktown is listed among those transplanted from Dublin in the works of O'Hart. Elsewhere we also find a Walter Cheevers of Monkstown, an Irish Catholic, holding over 800 acres of land in Dublin in the 17th century. Henry Cheevers is given as holding the Castle at Monkstown subsequent to Sir Gerald Aylmer.

Thomas Cusack was leased the lands of Cabinteely, which were subsequently held by Sir John Travers in 1545, and then by the Eustace, Cheevers and O'Bynre families. See introduction.

Chesterman
A surname found in Quaker records in Dublin city in the late 17th century.

Chetten

Milesian Families finds the name in Dublin, of Norman origins. (no documentation given).

Chichester

A family name found in Dublin City in the census of 1659.

Chillam

In the 17th century we find the Chillam Farm, the name taken from a Drogheda family who owned it before the rebellion, at St. James and St. Jude parish. See introduction.

Christian

A name found in the city of Dublin in the census of 1659. Michael Christian is found in St. Michael's parish in the Dublin City Pipe Water Accounts of 1680.

De Clahull

Clahull Clayhull
See introduction for the name in Dublin.

Clapham

A family name found in the city of Dublin in the census of 1659.

De Clare

Clare
The main location for the name of 'Clare' in the 19th century was in Co. Dublin. (The above extracted from the 'Book of Irish Families, great & small').

Claridge

A surname found in Quaker records in Dublin city in the late 17th century.

Clarke

Clarke, Clairke, Clarkins, Cleary,
The counties with the largest numbers of the name in 1890 were Antrim, Dublin, Mayo, Cavan and Louth.

Clarke was a numerous name by the 17th century and it was found as a principal name in Dublin city and elsewhere by that time.

The arms for Clark of Largantogher, Co. Londonderry, who settled there in 1690, are given in the Book of Arms.

(The above extracted from the 'Book of Irish Families, great & small').

Classon

Clausson
Noted names in 18th century Milltown, Co. Dublin, included: Mr. Heavisid; Classon; Burr; Hugh Johnson; Randall; Dogherty; Tomlinson; King; and Walcot.

Clay

A family name found in Dublin in the census of 1659.

Claypoole

A family name found in the city of Dublin in the census of 1659.

Clayton

Robert Clayton was Bishop of Clogher and was born in Dublin in 1695. Only 12 births of the name were recorded in the 1890 index. (extracted from the 'Book of Irish Families, great & small').

Cleabear

A family name found in the city of Dublin in the census of 1659.

Cleary

A family name given in Dublin in the Birth Index of 1890.

Clemens

A family name found in the city of Dublin in the census of 1659.

Clements

Among the major tenants at Bray, Co. Dublin, in 1284 were: Wm. le Deveneis; John Clements; Robert the Baker; and W. de Belinges.

Wm. Clements of Dublin is found as M.P. for Cork in 1761. (see 'Families of Co. Cork, Ireland'.)

Clere

A family name found in the city of Dublin in the census of 1659.

Clibborn

Claiborne, Clairborne, Cliborne, Clibborn

Spellings for the name are numerous, Clibborn is found at Moate Castle, Co. Westmeath, and "Clibborn" is found of Bath, England and of Dublin, Ireland. (The above extracted from the 'Book of Irish Families, great & small').

The Clibborn family of Bath, England and of Dublin Ireland is given in the works of John O'Hart. The Dublin line descends from the family settled earlier at Moate Castle, Co. Westmeath. Arms and pedigree are given in the works of O'Hart. It is also a surname found in Quaker records in Dublin city in the early 18th century.

Cliff

A family name found in the city of Dublin in the census of 1659.

John Cliffe, a stabler, is found in St. Catherine's parish in the Dublin City Pipe Water Accounts of 1680.

Clinch

Clench, Clenche, Clinchey, Clinchy

Families of the name of Clinch are found in Dublin in the census of 1659. Often spelled as Clench in earlier records, the name is thought to be of English origins, and is most often found in Dublin and the surrounding area of the pale. (extracted from the 'Book of Irish Families, great & small').

In 1691 Peter and Simon Clinch of the College, Dublin, were outlawed, according to an entry for Capt. James Clinch, in King James' Irish Army List.

In 1562 at Newcastle parish we find one William Clinch from whom cattle was stolen.

Clinton

According to "Keatings History" the name is given among the chief Anglo-Norman or British families settling in Louth quite early. The main location for the name in the 19th century was in Co. Dublin and in Co. Louth. (The above extracted from the 'Book of Irish Families, great & small').

Thomas Clinton's house is found in St. Werburgh's parish in the Dublin City Pipe Water Accounts of 1680.

Clotworthy

A family name found in the city of Dublin in the census of 1659.

Mc Cloud

One John McCloud, who was a fisherman at Rush in Co. Dublin is found in the mid 19th century. He moved to America, landing in New York and settling in Norwich, Connecticut. (extracted from the 'Book of Irish Families, great & small').

Mc Cluskey

Mccluskey, Mcclosky, Mcloskey

In the 1890 index McCloskey is found mainly in Londonderry (Derry) and McCluskey in Antrim and Dublin.

Arms for the name are found on plate 262 in the Irish Book of Arms. (The above extracted from the 'Book of Irish Families, great & small').

Coan

Coen Cohen

A name found in Dublin for some time, often spelled as Cohen or Coen. (Some of the name may be of Jewish heritage).

Coates

Cotes, Coats

In modern times the name is found in Dublin and Ulster.

Burke gives the seat of the name as being in Rathmore, Co. Antrim. (The above extracted from the 'Book of Irish Families, great & small').

Cobbe

Cobb

The Cobbe family of Newbridge House, Co. Dublin settled there, coming from Southampton originally. (The above extracted from the 'Book of Irish Families, great & small').

O'Hart gives the 'Cobb' family as a principal one settling in Dublin from the 12th to the 18th century.

Cochrane

Cochran, Corcoran, Cuggeran, Cockrane,

The name of Cochrane is said to have its origins in Scotland.

Two particular locations for the name were given as : Balrothery Union, in Dublin County and in Newry Union of Counties Armagh and Down. (The above extracted from the 'Book of Irish Families, great & small').

Coddington

A family name found in Dublin in the census of 1659.

O Coffey
Coffee, Cowhey, Cowhig, Cofee

There are several families that go by the name of Coffey etc.. in Ireland.

Keatings gives the family in an ancient genealogy which traces the family to the son of Ith. The O'Cowhys, (O'Coffeys), are cited as anciently powerful, with 7 castles on the coast in the barony of Ibane and Barryroe. They were found as 'Lords of the country of Triocha Meona, of the white-stoned shore, valiant foes in sea fights'.

In more modern times the 1800's birth index finds the name Coffey in Kerry, Tipperary, Dublin, Cork and Roscommon. (The above extracted from the 'Book of Irish Families, great & small').

Coghill

O'Hart gives the family as a principal one settling in Dublin from the 12th to the 18th century.

Names connected to Rathfarnham parish in the 18th century were Palliser; O'Callaghan; Cramer; Coghill; Stannard; Fountain; Ward; Geering; How; Boyle; and Blackburn.

Marmaduke Coghill is found in Clonturk parish in Georgian times.

Mac Coghlan
Coughlan, Coughlan, Coghlane, Cohalan,

Those of the Coughlan name today may properly be of either Mac Coughlan or O'Coughlan origins.

In the 1890 index the most common spelling of the name was as Coughlan, with Coghlan running a fairly close second. Both were most common in Cork at that time, but the later is found in Dublin in some numbers.

(The above extracted from the 'Book of Irish Families, great & small').

Cohen
Coan Coen

The names of 'Cohen' and 'Cohen of Poland' are given found in Dublin City of Jewish heritage. (per the 'Journal of Irish Families')

Colby

Milesian Families finds the name in Dublin, of Norman origins. (no documentation given).

Colcott

John Colcott is found in St. Audeon's parish in the Dublin City Pipe Water Accounts of 1680.

Isaack Colcott is found in St. Werburgh's parish in the Dublin City Pipe Water Accounts of 1680.

Cole
Coal

One noted Cole family is found at Newlands, Co. Dublin. The main locations for the name in the 19th century were in counties Dublin, Londonderry, Armagh, Down and Kings. (The above extracted from the 'Book of Irish Families, great & small').

Michael Cole is found in St. Werburgh's parish in the Dublin City Pipe Water Accounts of 1680.

O Coleman
Colman, Coalman, Clovan, Cloven,

Families by the name of Coleman in Ireland may stem from one of at least three separate origins. Some of the name are of English heritage.

Mac Colman, one independent family of the name, is found as a chief clan of Co. Louth more anciently.

In 1659 the name is listed as a principal one of Waterford, Dublin and Meath. Also given is Ralph Coleman of Dublin City.

In the 1890 birth index some 128 births are recorded primarily in Cork, Roscommon, Dublin and Waterford, mainly in the province of Munster.

Arms for the name are found in the Irish Book of Arms plate 248. (The above extracted from the 'Book of Irish Families, great & small').

Mac Colgan

Colgen, Colgun, Coligan, Colligan,

Originally there were at least two families, Mac Colgan and O'Colgan. O'Colgan appears to have been discarded as a surname and the more numerous Mac Colgan was adopted by members of both families.

In the 1800's birth index 'McColgan' is found as the preferred spelling of the name in Donegal and Londonderry. 'Colgan' (without the 'mac') was found more often in Dublin, Kings (Offaly) and Antrim. (The above extracted from the 'Book of Irish Families, great & small').

Collett

Milesian Families finds the name in Dublin, of Norman origins. (no documentation given).

Colley, Cooley

Cooly, Maccolly, Collie, Coley, Cowley,

Most of the Colley name in Ireland are of Anglo-Norman extraction, although some of the name may actually be of the Irish family of "Mac Cuille".

"Robert Cowley or Colley" was bailiff of Dublin in the year 1515, and was likely of English descent. There is a discussion of this by O'Hart. (The above extracted from the 'Book of Irish Families, great & small').

Gerrard Cooley is found in St. Michael's parish in the Dublin City Pipe Water Accounts of 1680.

In the 18th century Richard Colley, who later assumed the name of Wesley, was made Lord Mornington. He is found at Booterstown. See introduction.

Among the noted residents of Booterstown in the 18th century were included the names of Cooley; Doherty; Gough; O'Reilly; LaTouche; Doyne; Wight; Bradstreet; and Fitzgerald.

Collier

Le Collier, Colyer

The Collier name is usually of English origin when found in Ireland, and it has been on record here since the 14th century. The census of 1659 finds the name as a principal one of County Meath, and also in Dublin city.

'le Collier' was an older spelling of the name. (The above extracted from the 'Book of Irish Families, great & small').

Collins

Collen, Culhane, Cullane, Cullen,

One of the most numerous names in all of Ireland, Collins ranks among the top 30 names in the country. Although this is a recognized English name, it is also of Irish origins.

Counties Cork and Limerick are the most highly populated with the name in modern times, with Dublin, Galway, Antrim, Kerry and Clare also being given in the 1890 birth index.

Arms for some families of the name are found on plates 59 and 229 in the Irish Book of Arms. (The above extracted from the 'Book of Irish Families, great & small').

Collis

The family can also be found among the merchants of Dublin through two centuries at least. Several are found receiving lands in Cromwellian times. (The above extracted from the 'Book of Irish Families, great & small'). (See entry in 'The Families of Co. Kerry').

Charles Collis is found in St. Werburgh's parish in the Dublin City Pipe Water Accounts of 1680.

Colvin

Colvan, Colvil, Colville, Colven. (colavin)

In the 1890 birth index there are 6 recorded births of the name, listed in scattered locations. Some of the name may actually be of the "Colavin" family, who used "Colvin" as a variant spelling of the name. When the Colvin family name is found in Ulster, or in the city of Dublin, the likelihood of being of foreign origins increases.

Individuals of the name:
From The Duffy Family Pedigree, Of County Monaghan. 'mary Duffy Who Married A Mr. Colvin, Of Dublin'.
(The above extracted from the 'Book of Irish Families, great & small').

Combes

A family name found in the city of Dublin in the census of 1659.

Comerford

Commerford

An old English family of the name is given in Wexford, but we find the family most numerous in Kilkenny and Dublin in the 19th century. (The above extracted from the 'Book of Irish Families, great & small').

Compton

Milesian Families finds the name in Dublin, of English origins.

Comyns

Commins Cummins

The Comyns of Ballygriffin and Laurence Blundell held the lands of Clondalkin early. (see other spellings).

Condron

Condran, Conran

The main location for the name in 1890 was in Carlow, and in Cos. Dublin, Kildare and Kings. (extracted from the 'Book of Irish Families, great & small').

Conley

Conly, Connolly, Connell, Kinnealy,

This name is a variant spelling of several more common names.

We do find the name of ' Conly ' in the census of 1659 listed as coming from the city of Dublin. (see spellings given) (The above extracted from the 'Book of Irish Families, great & small').

O'Connell

O Connoll Connell Conel Conol

Given in the birth index of 1890 in Dublin. John Connell was resident at Pelletstown at the time of the 17th century rebellion, and he also held the lands of Ashtowne.

The cemetery at Gleasnevin was noted for holding the remains of the famous Daniel O'Connell, the liberator. (See major entry in 'The Families of Co. Kerry').

O Connolly

Conneely, Connolly, Conoly, Connoly,

The O'Connolly name is one of the top 30 names in all of Ireland. This family name is often confused and interchanged with similar sounding names such as Coneely and Conly.

The 1800's birth index finds Conneely in Galway and Connolly in Cork, Monaghan, Galway, Antrim and Dublin.

The arms of Conolly of Castletown, Co. Kildare are given in the Irish Book of Arms. They descend from the same line as William Conolly, 18th century speaker of the House of Commons in Ireland. (The above extracted from the 'Book of Irish Families, great & small').

The O'Connolly family is one of the noted "Four Tribes of Tara", along with O'Hart, O'Kelly and O'Regan. These tribes of Tara are also described as princes of Bregia, and appear to have possessed territories near Tara in Meath, along with areas in Co. Dublin. They were known as "Lords of Teffia". (per Keatings 'History of Ireland' IGF edition).

O'Connor

O Conner Connor Conor

'O'Connor was a family name given in Dublin in the Birth Index of 1890, and combined with Connor, etc..it was among the top 15 most numerous names of Dublin County at that time.

'Connor' was family name given in Dublin in the census of 1659 and in the 1890 birth index. Thomas Connor of Dublin is given obtaining lands in Co. Kerry according to "Families of Co. Kerry, Ireland", which is volume two in our Irish Families series. (See major entry in 'The Families of Co. Kerry'). (See also major entry in 'The Families of Co. Clare').

O'Connor of Rockfield, Co. Dublin is given in the 'Irish Book of Arms' (IGF edition)

Conolly

The Conollys of Castletown erected the noted 'Hell Fire Club' in the 18th century at Tallaght Hills.

Conrane

Conran

Walter Conrane of Curragh and Phillipp Conrane of Wyanstown are listed among those transplanted from Dublin, in the works of O'Hart. The Conran family of Wyanstown were of some note in 17th century Dublin.

Conroy

Given in the 1890 birth index of Ireland as centered in Dublin, Galway and Queens counties. (See major entry in 'The Families of Co. Galway').

Constantine

Robert Constantine is found in St. Catherine's parish in the Dublin City Pipe Water Accounts of 1680.

Conway

Conaway, Mcconway, O'conway,

One family of the name in Co. Kerry was actually of Welsh heritage, being settled there in the 16th century. They held lands at Killorglin in Kerry and in Co. Dublin. This family also donated sons to King James' Irish army.

The 1800's birth index gives the name primarily in Mayo, Tyrone and Dublin.

One of the Conway arms illustrated in the Irish Book of Arms gives the motto "Fide-et-amore" . (From the 'Book of Irish Families'). (See major entry in 'The Families of Co. Kerry').

Coogan   Cogan

A family name found in Dublin at the time of the Birth Index of 1890.

The 'Cogan' family is also given as a principal one of Anglo-Norman descent, settling in Dublin City and County, according to Keatings 'History '.

Cooke

Cook

The 1659 census finds at least one family of the name represented in Dublin City. The Birth Index of 1890 also finds the family in Dublin.

See also "Notes on the Cooke, Ashe and Swift Families" (Dublin), in the "Journal of the Association for the Preservation of Memorials for the Dead." 9, 1912+.

O Cooney

Coony, Coonahan, Coonan, Cooihan,

In the census of 1659 Cooney is found as a principal name of Clare, and by 1890 it is found centered in Mayo and Dublin.

Arms for the name can be found in the Irish Book of Arms plate 253. (The above extracted from the 'Book of Irish Families, great & small').

Cooper

The birth index of 1890 finds the family centered in Antrim and Dublin counties. (The above extracted from the 'Book of Irish Families, great & small').

Coote

Coot

The Coote family of Mt. Coote, Co. Limerick is given in the Irish Book of Arms. The birth index of 1890 finds the family name centered in Co. Dublin. (The above extracted from the 'Book of Irish Families, great & small').

Not long before the Union Col. Charles Coote held the lands of Leperstown, Co. Dublin.f

Cope

John Cope is found in St. Werburgh's parish in the Dublin City Pipe Water Accounts of 1680. Cope of Loughgall is given in connection with Kilmainham in the 18th century.

Copeland

Milesian Families finds the name in Dublin, of English origins. (no documentation given).

Corballis

One family of the name is found in the County of Dublin and the barony of Balrothery. The family lost their lands during Cromwellian times and came to settle in Dublin, where one became a Timber Merchant. (per the 'Book of Irish Families, great & small').

Corbally

A family name given as a principal name of Dublin in the census of 1659.

Corbett

Corban, Corbane

Families of the name of Corbett in Ireland may be either of old Irish or English extraction.

Several Irish families have changed their names to the more common name of Corbett, making early family history sometimes difficult to trace.

In the 17th century we find the name given in Carlow, Dublin, Westmeath and Cork. (extracted from the 'Book of Irish Families, great & small').

Corcoran

Maccorcoran, O'corcaran, Corckron,

In 1659 Corckron is given as a principal name of Kilkenny; Corkerin was found in Waterford; and O'Corkerane was found in Cork. In modern times the name hailed from Mayo, Cork, Tipperary, Dublin and Kerry, according to the 1890 index. (The above extracted from the 'Book of Irish Families, great & small').

Mac Cormack

Mccormick, Mccormac

MacCormack is a numerous name in Ireland. The name may come originally from O'Cormac, Mac Cormack, or may have Scottish origins when found in Ulster as well.

McCormack is the spelling favored in Dublin, Mayo, Roscommon and Limerick.

Arms for the name are found on plates 238 and 264 in the Irish Book of Arms. (The above extracted from the 'Book of Irish Families, great & small').

Cornwalsh

Names connected to Rathfarnham parish in the 14th and 15th centuries were Galvey; Hall; Cornwalsh; and Loftus.

During mediaeval times they are one of the few noted families in the area of Howth along with the St. Lawrence family.

Corr Corry

Curr, Corra, Corry, Curry, Corrie Corey

The 19th century records show the name centered in Dublin and Tyrone.

Much confusion can come about for some of the name, for Corr can serve as a shortened form of O'Corry, Curry, and MacCorry. (extracted from the 'Book of Irish Families, great & small').

Corey is found in Dublin City in the Census of 1659.

Nicholas Corr and Gerald Long in 1564 leased the lands of Newtownpark and in that century the Wolverston family occupied a good slated house.

O Corrigan
Carrigan, Corigan, Corrican, Corregan,

Most Corrigan families today may trace their origins to Fermanagh.

The 1890 birth index shows 74 births for the name in Dublin, Mayo, Fermanagh, Monaghan and Louth.

Arms for the name are found in the Irish Book of Arms plates 149 and 218. (The above extracted from the 'Book of Irish Families, great & small').

Corscadden
A family name extremely rare in our records, in which we find a few of the name in Co. Dublin, in relatively recent times. (The above extracted from the 'Book of Irish Families, great & small').

Cory
Corry

Digory Cory gave testimony in the 17th century concerning the 1641 rebellion, as found in the History of the County Dublin by Ball. See 'Corr'.

O' Cosgrave
Cosgrove

According to "Keatings History" the name is given as coming from O'Cosgraidh, being translated into both Cosgry and Cosgrave. Spelled as Cosgrave, the name is found most often in Dublin and Wexford in the 19th century. (The above extracted from the 'Book of Irish Families.').

We also read of one Edward Cosgrave of Dublin who obtained lands in Co. Kerry. (per 'Families of Co. Kerry, Ireland').

Cossart
David Cossart is found in St. John's parish in the Dublin City Pipe Water Accounts of 1680.

Mac Costello
Costolloe, Costelo, Costellow, Costillo,

Costello families are most often of early Norman descent when found in Ireland. Most will trace themselves back to Gilbert de Nangle in the 12th century.

According to "Keatings History" the name is given as an Irish name which was also adopted by Anglo-Norman or English families in lieu of their original surnames.

We find 'Costleloe' in Dublin City in the census of 1659. In more recent times Costello was most popular in Mayo, Dublin and Galway. (The above extracted from the 'Book of Irish Families, great & small').

Mac Costigan
Costigin

The name of Costigan is centered in Dublin, Kilkenny and Queens in the 19th century. (The above extracted from the 'Book of Irish Families').

Cosyn
Cosyn is noted at Killininny in the parish of Tallaght.

Mac Cotter
O'cotter, Cotter, Cottor, Kotter, Maccottyr,

We have one early reference to Mac Oitir in the 12th century, of the Hebrides, who ruled in Dublin.

Sir James Laur. Cotter served in the Irish House of Commons in 1797. (The above extracted from the 'Book of Irish Families, great & small'). (See major entry in 'The Families of Co. Cork').

Cottingham
Mr. James Cottingham is found in St. Werburgh's parish in the Dublin City Pipe Water Accounts of 1680.

Cottle
A family name found in Dublin in the census of 1659. Cottle is also noted at Killininny.

Cotton
A family name given in Dublin City and county in the census of 1659.. Samuel Cotton is found in St. Werburgh's parish in the Dublin City Pipe Water Accounts of 1680.

 © 1999. IGF. Families of Co. Dublin, Ireland- Box 7575, K.C., MO. 64116

Coulter

One source finds the name in Dublin and Cork of German origins, with no documentation.

Coultry

Milesian Families finds the name in Dublin, of Norman origins.

Courtney

The Irish of the name are traced into Co. Kerry. In the 19th century the family is mainly found in Kerry, Antrim and Dublin. (The above extracted from the 'Book of Irish Families, great & small'). It is also a surname found in Quaker records in Dublin city in the early 18th century.

Cowell

One noted family of the name is found as being of Logadowden, in Co. Dublin, in the 18th century.   (per the 'Book of Irish Families, great & small').

This family is also given in the works of O'Hart. The arms for this family were entered in the year 1771 in Dublin Castle, Office of Arms. Some 18th century wills of this family were proved in the Prerogative Court in Dublin,.

Cowman

In Dublin, a Quaker family of the name is found.. (The above extracted from the 'Book of Irish Families, great & small').

Cowse

A family name found in Dublin in the census of 1659.

Cox
Cocks, Quill, Koch, Mac Quilly

Traditionally linked with Co. Roscommon, it is here and in Dublin where the name is most often found in modern times. The old spelling of MacQuilly has fallen by the wayside in modern times. In older days the family served as Co-arbs of St. Barry of Kilbarry in Co. Roscommon.

In the 17th century "census" of 1659 Cox was given in Dublin city, Louth and Limerick. (The above extracted from the 'Book of Irish Families').

At Island Bridge we find the names of: Crowe in 1720; Curtis in 1724; Cox in 1736; Ford in 1738; and Trail in 1799.

McCoy
Coy, Mac Cooey, Makay, Coonahan,

Numerous in Ireland, it is considered a name of the north, concentrated in the counties of Armagh and Monaghan. The name usually comes from Scotland.

Sir Frederick MacCoy (1823 -1899) was born in Dublin. (The above extracted from the 'Book of Irish Families, great & small').

Coyle
Cool, Mccool

The family is found in some numbers in Donegal, Cavan, Londonderry, Dublin, Tyrone and Cavan. (per the 'Book of Irish Families, great & small').

Crabb

A family name found in Dublin city, given to be of Jewish heritage in at least one instance. (per 'OLochlainns journal of Irish Families').

Crafton

Milesian Families finds the name in Dublin, of English origins.

Cramby

A family name found in the city of Dublin in the census of 1659.

Cramer

Names connected to Rathfarnham parish in the 18th century were Palliser; O'Callaghan; Cramer; Coghill; Stannard; Fountain; Ward; Geering; How; Boyle; and Blackburn.

Crampton

At Tully parish in 1762 we find in the obituary notices the daughter of Alderman Crampton.

Cranwell

A family name found in the city of Dublin in the census of 1659.

Crary
Creary

Milesian Families finds the name in Dublin, of Saxon origins.

Creamer

Creemer, Cramer, Creamor, Kramer

Several families of the name are found with lands in Co. Kilkenny. The family name is also found in the city of Dublin in the 17th century spelled as "Creamer". Some confusion may arise as to the origins of the name, for, when spelled as "Cramer" it represents some families which are unrelated. The name of Creamer is also the name of an English family, that might have settled in Ireland over time. (per the 'Book of Irish Families, great & small').

Creighton

A family name found in Dublin at the time of the Birth Index of 1890.

Critchet

One John Critchet is found in the Quaker records in Dublin City in the 18th century, and is listed as a 'weaver'.

Crofton

The family is given to be of English extraction originally. In the 17th century we find the name in Roscommon, Leitrim, and the city of Dublin as well. (extracted from the 'Book of Irish Families, great & small').

Philip Croft is found in St. Werburgh's parish in the Dublin City Pipe Water Accounts of 1680.

The Crofton family is found residing in the Castle at Roebuck at the close of the 18th century.

Crosby

Crosbie

The birth index of 1890 finds the family centered in Dublin, although it is noted in Kerry as well. (The above extracted from the 'Book of Irish Families'). (See entry in 'The Families of Co. Kerry').

Cross

A family name found in Dublin in the Birth Index of 1890.

Crostenton

A family name found in the city of Dublin in the census of 1659.

Crowe

Crowe is given as among the few names of importance in Taney parish in the mid 18th century.

At Island Bridge we find the names of: Crowe in 1720; Curtis in 1724; and Trail in 1799.

O Crowley

Krowley, Crowly, Croly, Crole, Crolly

The Crowley families today may trace their line back to 'Cruadhloach'.

Rev. George Croly, was a poet, author and novelist born in Dublin in 1780, and he was a 'staunch Tory'.

Arms for the name are found in the Irish Book of Arms, plates 150 and 212. (The above extracted from the 'Book of Irish Families, great & small'). (See major entry in 'The Families of Co. Cork').

Cruise

Cruys Cruse

According to "Keatings History" the name is one of a noted family in Meath. Of this line we find the Cruises of Cruisetown and of Cruise-Rath.

The family is also given as a principal one of Anglo-Norman descent, settling in Dublin City and County, according to Keatings 'History of Ireland'.

One Christopher Cruise of Naul, is found with 600+ acres of land in the north of Dublin county in the 17th century.

The Cruise family of Cruiserath is given at Mulhuddart parish around the 14th - 16th century.

Sir John Cruise is given as holding lands at Murphystown. See introduction.

Many families of the name of Cruise are found in Co. Dublin in the 19th century. (extracted in part from the 'Book of Irish Families, great & small').

Crump

In the 14th century we find Geoffrey Crump and R. de Bray at Old Connaught parish in Dublin County.

Cudahy
Cuddihy, Cudihy, Cudahey, Cuddahy,
  Cudahy (Cuddihy) is a name traditionally associated with Co. Kilkenny in Ireland. The name remains distinct in that area today, as well as in the capital city of Dublin. (The above extracted from the 'Book of Irish Families, great & small').

Cuff
Cuffe
  A family name found in Dublin city in the census of 1659.

O Cullen
O'cullen, Cullin, Mccullin, Culloon,
  Among the 90 most numerous names in Ireland, it is among the 20 most numerous surnames of Dublin in the 1890 birth index. Several families have assumed 'Cullen, or Cullin' as the spelling of their names.
  The most populous family is that of O'Cuilinn of Glencullen by the Dublin and Wicklow border.
  The counties of Dublin and Wexford have held most of the name in 1890.
  The Irish Book of Arms lists several Cullen arms. (The above extracted from the 'Book of Irish Families, great & small').

Cumming
Cummings Cummins Comyn
  Milesian Families finds the name in Dublin, of Scottish origins. See other spellings.

Cummins
Comyn, Commons, Cummings,
  The English spelling of the name more often includes the 'g' at the end of the name, as Cummings, or Cumming. That spelling was most popular in Antrim, Dublin, Cork and Tipperary in 1890.
  Comyn is the spelling of an Norman family of the name found in Ireland. Note that one John Comyn was Archbishop of Dublin in the 12th century.
  Arms for the name can be found in the Irish Book of Arms plate 203. (The above extracted from the 'Book of Irish Families, great & small').

Cunningham
Counihan,connaghan,cunningham,
  Cunningham is one of the top 75 most numerous names in all of Ireland. The name may be of Irish, English or Scottish origins.
  O'Hart also gives one Rodger O'Cunnivane (b. 1680), whose descendant was living in Dublin in 1887 as John Cunningham. This family was also connected to Co. Clare.
  Arms for the name are found on plate 107 of the Irish Book of Arms. (The above extracted from the 'Book of Irish Families, great & small').

Mac Curley
Turley, Kerley, Curling, Turly, Terry
  In the 1890's index Curley is found in Roscommon, Galway and Dublin (The above extracted from the 'Book of Irish Families, great & small').

Curragh
Curraugh
  Individuals of the name of Curragh are found in the city of Dublin in the 16th century in our records.   (per the 'Book of Irish Families, great & small').

Curran
  A family name given in Dublin in the Birth Index of 1890.

Currid
  Early records give the family in Co. Sligo, and subsequently the name is found in Dublin. (extracted from the 'Book of Irish Families, great & small').

Curson
De Curson
  According to MacGeogeoghegan, Vivian de Cursun received the lands of Raheny near Dublin, formerly held by the Irish family of Giollamocholmog.

Curtis
  At Island Bridge we find the names of: Crowe in 1720; Curtis in 1724; Cox in 1736; Ford in 1738; and Trail in 1799.

Cusack
Cusacke, Cusake, Cussack, Cussacke

One Thomas Cusack is found as mayor of Dublin in 1409. Thomas Cusack was leased the lands of Cabinteely, which were subsequently held by Sir John Travers in 1545, and then by the Eustace, Cheevers and O'Bynre families. See introduction.

The Cusacks held the castle at Rathgar in 1608 for several centuries.

The 'Irish Book of Arms' gives the arms of Cusack of Gerardstown, (of Abbeyville House, Co. Dublin) (The above extracted from the 'Book of Irish Families, great & small').

The family is also given as a principal one of Anglo-Norman descent, settling in Dublin City and County, according to Keatings 'History of Ireland'. They are also given as an English family found in Dublin in the 17th century, where they held noted lands at that time.

The Cusack family is given in several articles in the "Irish Genealogist" as published in the 1970's -1980's.

Cuthbert
John Cuthbert is found in St. Werburgh's parish in the Dublin City Pipe Water Accounts of 1680.

Cutter
Milesian Families finds the name in Dublin, of English origins.

Cyrch
A family name found in the city of Dublin in the census of 1659.

Dagg
Dag

Families of the name are found in both counties Wicklow and Wexford, as well as a good amount of the name in Dublin. (The above extracted from the 'Book of Irish Families, great & small').

Dalton
Alton, Daltin

In the 1890's index Dalton is found in Dublin, Waterford, Limerick and Kilkenny. D'Altons 'History of Dublin' may be of special interest to those of the name. (The above extracted from the 'Book of Irish Families, great & small').

O'Daly
Daily, Dawley, Dawly, Dayley, Dealy,

The 1890's birth index finds Daly in Cork, Dublin, Kerry, Galway and Kings Counties. O'Daly was rare by then.

The Daly families of Castle Daly, Co. Galway are found in the Book of Arms. (See major entry in 'The Families of Co. Galway'). (See major entry in 'The Families of Co. Cork').

'The O'Dalys of Muintuavara: a story of a bardic family", by Dominic Daly was published in Dublin in 1821. (extracted from the 'Book of Irish Families').

Damer
Eccles Mount was the residence of Joseph Damer, knight of the shire for Co. Tipperary.

Danaher
Danagher Dannaher

Danaher is a family name found in Dublin at the time of the Birth Index of 1890. See also Dannaher.

Dancer
A family name found in Dublin in the census of 1659.

Dandridge
Milesian Families finds the name in Dublin in the 12th century, of Norman origins. (no documentation).

Daniel
Daniell

A Huguenot family name according to one source, the Daniell family of New Forest, Co. Westmeath, descend from Bridges Daniell of Dublin in the 18th century.

Most of the name are found in Dublin, Limerick and Waterford in the 19th century. (The above extracted from the 'Book of Irish Families, great & small').

McDaniell is found in the census of 1659 in Dublin and is fairly widely scattered throughout the country at that time.

We also find Scurlock and McDaniel at Newcastle parish giving place to Scarborough and Jones. See introduction.

Dannaher
Danaher

'Danaher' is also a family name found in Dublin at the time of the Birth Index of 1890. (The above extracted from the 'Book of Irish Families, great & small').

Darcy
De Arcy, De Arci, O'darcey, Mac Darcy

In more modern times, the 1890's birth index finds Darcy in Dublin and Tipperary most often. Some of the name may be of the Dorcey family, which is of Irish origins. For more detail see 'The Families of Co. Galway' where the family is covered in some depth.

The Irish Book of Arms shows the arms for D'Arcy.

The book entitled 'Complete Pedigree of the English and Irish Branches of the D'Arcy Family' was published in London in 1901.

(The above extracted from the 'Book of Irish Families, great & small').

The family is also given as a principal one of Anglo-Norman descent, settling in Dublin City and County, according to Keatings 'History of Ireland'.

Dardis
Dardes

Milesian Families finds the name in Dublin, of English origins. (no documentation given).

Dargan
Dorgan, Dargen

The birth index at the end of the last century shows the name of Dargan in Dublin. (The above extracted from the 'Book of Irish Families, great & small').

Darin

Milesian Families finds the name in Dublin, of French origins.

Darlas

Among the names noted at Rathcoole parish from the 16th century onwards are: John Mey; James Bathe; the Fitzgeralds; and the Darlases of Maynooth.

Darling

A family name found in the city of Dublin in the census of 1659.

Darly
Darley

The name is often traditionally linked with the city of Dublin, and most of these families are considered to be of English extraction having taken their name from a place in England. (per the 'Book of Irish Families, great & small').

We find Ballygall in the occupation of Rev. Darley. See introduction.

Henry Darley of Dublin is given as a landowner in Kerry in 1876.

Dason
Dawson

A family name found in the city of Dublin in the census of 1659.

Daton

Milesian Families finds the name in Dublin, of Norman origins.

Dauson
Dawson

A family name found in the city of Dublin in the census of 1659. Perhaps 'Dawson' would be a modern day spelling.

Davidson Of Poland

A family name found in Dublin city, given to be of Jewish heritage in at least one instance. (per 'OLochlainns journal of Irish Families').

Davies
Davys

At Newcastle in 1614 among the first city officials were: Parsons; Rolles; Kenny; Frend; Davies; White; Burton; Grible; Bridges; Rutledge; and Lushe.

A brewery was established at Island Bridge by John Davies who died in 1704. See also Davys.

Davieson
Davison

A family name found in Dublin city, given to be of Jewish heritage in at least one instance. (per 'OLochlainns journal of Irish Families').

Davis
Davies

Davis was a principal name of Dublin in the 17th century and remained there at the time of the 1890 index. The name is also given to belong to at least one family of Jewish heritage in Dublin City.

Nathanell Davis is found in St. Audeon's parish in the Dublin City Pipe Water Accounts of 1680. Rees Davis is found in St. Werburgh's parish in the Dublin City Pipe Water Accounts of 1680.

Davys
Davies

The Davys family and the Cooke family are found in Leixlip parish in the early 18th century.

Charles Davys who died in 1769 was from Glasnevin parish. See Davies.

Dawe

The Dawe family is given at Jamestown. (See introduction under Kilgobbin parish).

Dawkins

A family name found in Dublin in the census of 1659.

Dawson

A surname found in Quaker records in Dublin city as a merchant in the early 18th century.

Note the reference to Castle Dawson among the villas erected between Blackrock and Booterstown. See introduction.

John Dawson is noted as a host at Chapelizod in the 18th century.

De Bray
Bray

In the 14th century we find Geoffrey Crump and R. de Bray at Old Connaught parish in Dublin County.

De Clahull

The De Clahull and Burnell families were early owners of Ballyfermot in the 14th century.

De Clare
Clare

The main location for the name of 'Clare' in the 19th century was in Co. Dublin. (The above extracted from the 'Book of Irish Families, great & small').

De Coursey
De Courcey

The family is listed as part of the 'more recent nobility' by O'Hart where they are given as barons of Kilbarrock in Dublin. (See major entry in 'The Families of Co. Cork' as de Courcy).

De Flamstead

Among the early tenants at Baggotrath was William de Flamstead. See introduction.

De Groot

A family name found in Dublin city, given to be of Jewish heritage in at least one instance. (per 'OLochlainns journal of Irish Families').

De Hyndeberge

The lands of Baggotrath passed to Philip de Hyndeberge from Maurice Fitzgerald who held the lands in 1255.

De London

In 13th century Donneybrook we find: de Verneuil; Butler or de Verdon; and de London.

De Long
Long

The census of 1659 shows the family in Roscommon, Dublin, Clare and Kilkenny. The 1890 birth index shows Cork and Dublin to be the counties of residence at that time. (The above extracted from the 'Book of Irish Families, great & small').

De Marisco

De Marisco is noted early at Killininny in the parish of Tallaght.

De Moenes

Robert De Moenes, in 1335, leased lands in Whitechurch parish. Two of the earliest tenants noted at 'St. Catherines and St. Nicholas Without' are Wm. Moenes of Rathmines and Nicholas Sueterby.

De Mora
Mora

Among the early tenants at Baggotrath was Ralph de Mora. See introduction

De Tasagart

Sagart

According to Ball, A leading mercantile family in Dublin borrowed the parish name of Saggart as their own, becoming in 1282 'John and Richard de Tasagart'.

De Verdon

In 13th century Donneybrook we find: de Verneuil; Butler or de Verdon; and de London.

De Verneuil

In 13th century Donneybrook we find: de Verneuil; Butler or de Verdon; and de London.

De Walhope

Names associated with the settlement of Balally in Taney parish were: de Walhope; Othyr; Howell; Taunton; Walsh in 1407 and Borr in the 17th century. It was given originally as a Danish settlement.

Dean

Deane

The census of 1659 finds the spellings of Dean and Deane in Dublin. It is also a surname found in Quaker records as a weaver in Dublin city in the late 17th century. (See major entry in 'The Families of Co. Galway').

Terenure House in Rathfarnum parish was the seat for the Deane family after its purchase in 1671 from the Talbots.

Most of the lands of Crumlin parish came into the possession of the Deane family in the latter 17th century.

Deave Deaves

It is a surname found in Quaker records in Dublin city in the 18th century.

Debart

A family name found in the city of Dublin in the census of 1659.

Dee

A family name found in the city of Dublin in the census of 1659.

Deegan

Deagan, Dugan, Degane

The name is found most numerous in Dublin, Kings and Queens counties in the 19th century. (extracted from the 'Book of Irish Families, great & small').

Deering

Deering, Dearing

The 19th century birth index finds the name centered in Co. Monaghan, but we find several of the name in earlier days in Dublin, Kings (Offaly), Carlow and Kildare. (extracted from the 'Book of Irish Families, great & small').

Among the owners of Knocklyon in the parish of Tallaght we find Deering.

Dejean

Lt. Gen. Lewis Dejean is found resident on the Donneybrook road in the 18th century. See introduction.

Delacy

See Lacy

Delahoyde

Delahoid, Delahyde Delahide

"Keatings History" gives the name as that of a principal family of Dublin, and of Anglo-Norman descent. This work also gives the family of Delahoid, as one of note in Co. Meath. Delahoyd is also found in Dublin in the census of 1659. The 'Delahide' family is noted among the minor gentry of Dublin in the 17th century. (The above extracted in part from the 'Book of Irish Families, great & small').

During the first half of the 16th century the castle in Ward Parish was occupied by Richard Delahide.

O'Delaney

Dulany, Delane, Dillane, Dellany,

The primary locations for the name in 1890 were in Dublin, Queens, Tipperary and Kilkenny.

The Irish Book of Arms gives Delany arms. (The above extracted from the 'Book of Irish Families, great & small').

Delap

In 1735 Mrs. Agnes Delap of Dublin is given in 'Families of Co. Kerry, Ireland.'.

Delasale
Delasalle
A family name found in the city of Dublin in the census of 1659.

Dempsey
A family name given in Dublin in the Birth Index of 1890.

Den
Dean Denn
Milesian Families finds the name in Dublin, of English origins. In the 15th century we note the Den family at Saggart parish, where they were of note through the 18th century.

One J. Denn is found in the 1659 census. See appendix.

Dent
A family name found in the city of Dublin in the census of 1659.

Derbon
A family name found in the city of Dublin in the census of 1659.

Mac Dermot   Dermott
Dermott, Dermitt, Dermody, Mc Dermitt,
One of the 100 most numerous names in Ireland,

The 1890 index finds Mc Dermott had 189 births in Roscommon, Dublin, Donegal, Galway and Tyrone.

In 1659 the name is found in Dublin, under various spellings.

(The above extracted from the 'Book of Irish Families, great & small').

Derpatrick
The Derpatrick family held the manor at Stillorgan Parish subsequent to the 14th century. See introduction.

Derry
A name found in the city of Dublin in 1659. Nathaniel Derry is found in St. Werburgh's parish in the Dublin City Pipe Water Accounts of 1680.

Desmineer
Desminiers
The spellings of Desmineer and Desmineers is given in Dublin in the 1659 census.

John Desminieres is found in St. Audeon's parish in the Dublin City Pipe Water Accounts of 1680.

Deuswell
The Deuswell family is found at Castleknock parish in the 14th century.

Deveneis
Among the major tenants at Bray, Co. Dublin, in 1284 were: Wm. le Deveneis; John Clements; Robert the Baker; and W. de Belinges.

Devery
Devry
Found in the Birth Index of 1890 in Dublin.

O'Devine
Devin, Davine, Devane, Divine
Devine ranks as the most popular spelling of the name in 1890 and was found in Tyrone, Dublin and Roscommon. (The above extracted from the 'Book of Irish Families, great & small').

Widow Devine is found in St. Werburgh's parish in the Dublin City Pipe Water Accounts of 1680.

Mc Devitt
Mac Davitt, Davison, Mac Daid, Devitt,
To this day McDevitt remains a name of Donegal, as it was in the 1890 birth index.

Without the 'Mc' prefix, spelled as Devitt, the name was found in Clare and Dublin in the 1890 index. These locations are distinct from those found with the Mc prefix. (extracted from the 'Book of Irish Families.').

Devitt or Devett, is also a surname found in Quaker records in Dublin city in the early 18th century.

O'Devlin
Develin, Divelin
The name has always been considered one of the province of Ulster. Families are found in Antrim, Tyrone, Armagh, Dublin, and Londonderry in the 1890 birth index. (The above extracted from the 'Book of Irish Families, great & small').

Dexter
See "The Dexters of Dublin and Annfield, Co. Kildare" as found in the periodical "Irish Ancestor" 2 (1), 1970.

Diamond
Diamont Dimond

A family name found in Dublin city, given to be of Jewish heritage in at least one instance. (per 'OLochlainns journal of Irish Families').

Dickinson

Wm. Dickinson was a tenant in the 17th century at Terenure and Kimmage. See introduction.

Diggs

A family name found in the city of Dublin in the census of 1659.

Dillon, Dillion
Dillon, Dillion, Dillane, Dologhan,

Keatings History cites the name as a principal one of Galway and Dublin cities. This work also speaks of a Dillon who traveled to France in the 17th century and became Duke of Aquitane. His descendants returned to Ireland as 'de Leon'. (extracted from the 'Book of Irish Families, great & small').

The family is also given as a principal one of Anglo-Norman descent, settling in Dublin City and County, according to Keatings 'History of Ireland'. They are given as substantial landowners in 17th century Dublin.

In 'King James's Irish Army List, 1689' we find listed as a Dublin assessor, one Garret Dillon, Esq. Recorder.

In the 18th century Belgard castle was held by the Dillion family, and subsequently to Dominick Trant and then Dr. Kennedy.

At the time of the 17th century rebellion Martin Dillon is given at Huntstown in Castleknock parish.

Dioderici

Around 1748 Joseph Dioderici came to live in Clonturk Parish. See introduction.

Dix

See the "Dix Family of Dublin....", in the 'Journal of the Association for the Preservation of Memorials to the Dead' 11, (1921-25).

Dixon
Dickson, Dick

The Dickson family of Co. Limerick is found in the Irish Book of Arms.

The 'Dixon' spelling is found centered in Dublin and Mayo in the 1890 birth index. (The above extracted from the 'Book of Irish Families, great & small').

The spelling of Dixson is given in Dublin City in the 1659 census.

In the 17th century at Butterfield we find reference to the family name of Dixon as well.

Doane

Milesian Families finds the name in Dublin, of Saxon origins.

Dobson

A family name found in the city of Dublin in the census of 1659. Lt. Col. Isaac Dobson of the Parliament Army repaired and occupied Dundrum Castle by 1653.

Dockrell
Dockerell

A family name found in Dublin at the time of the Birth Index of 1890.

Dodson

A family name found in the city of Dublin in the census of 1659.

Doe

In 'King James's Irish Army List, 1689' we find listed as a Dublin assessor, one Lewis Doe.

Dogherty
Doherty

Noted names in 18th century Milltown, Co. Dublin, included: Mr. Heavisid; Classon; Burr; Hugh Johnson; Randall and Dogherty. See also the spelling of Doherty, etc..

Doherty
Dogherty Dougherty

Among the noted residents of Booterstown in the 18th century were included the names of Cooley; Doherty; Gough; O'Reilly; LaTouche; Doyne; Wight; Bradstreet; and Fitzgerald. See also Dogherty, Dougherty, etc..

Dolan
Dolane Doolan

A family name given in Dublin in the Birth Index of 1890.

Dolphin
Dolphyn

The district know as Dolphins Barn was probably named for the Dolphin or Dolphyn family at St. James and St. Jude parish, formerly called St. John of Kilmainham).

Doly

A family name found in the city of Dublin in the census of 1659.

Domville
Domvile

We find the Domvile family of Loughlinstown, Co. Dublin, given in the Irish Book of Arms. (The above extracted from the 'Book of Irish Families, great & small').

After the rebellion of 1641 the lands of Killiney parish were held by Gilbert Wye of Belfast; the Mossoms; the Fawcetts; the Pocklingtons; and the Domviles. With the coming of the restoration the family is also found in Loughlinstown.

The Domvilles are also found at Templeogue and Ballyfermot in the 17th century.

We find the family at Kilboggett being dispossessed for their part in the rebellion, their lands being subsequently granted to Wm. Domville. See introduction.

O'Hart gives the family as a principal one settling in Dublin from the 12th to the 18th century.

McDonald
Mack, Mac, Mcdaniel, Mcdonnell, Mcdonold

In the 1890 index the family name is found in Dublin, Antrim, Cavan, Wexford and Carlow.

The McDonald name can be considered a name of the province of Ulster as a rule.

Documented Passenger from Ireland include:

William M'donald- Aboard The 'belisarius'-dublin To New York. Before July 5, 1811.

(The above extracted from the 'Book of Irish Families, great & small').

Donell
Mc Donell Daniel

The 'Donell' surname is found in Dublin in the census of 1659.

Dongan

We find the family given as an English one, in Dublin by at least the 17th century, where they held noted lands at that time.

'In the Wall' at Howth we find Thomas Dongan. See introduction.

Donn

A family name found in Dublin in the census of 1659.

MacDonnell
Mcdaniell, Mcdonald, Donnell, Donel

One of the 100 most numerous names in Ireland, McDonnell may be traced to one of several origins.

Some of the name descend from the McDonnells of Argyllshire, Scotland.

Some of the name of MacDonald, may have changed their name to MacDonnell, simply due to the similarity in sound.

In the 17th century McDonell was a principal name of Antrim, as well as being found in Armagh, Fermanagh, Cork, Limerick, Dublin and Kings Counties etc...The name was numerous in the 1890 index, in Dublin, Mayo, Antrim, Galway and Cork at that time.

McDonnell of Antrim is given at Kilgobbin parish in County Dublin.

The Irish Book of Arms includes the McDonnell. (The above extracted in part from the 'Book of Irish Families, great & small').

O'Donnell
O'donell, Donnal, Donal, Donel, Donnell

One of the 50 most numerous names in Ireland, the O'Donnells are a most notable family of Ulster. As would be expected with such a numerous name, it can regularly be found in Dublin City.

(The above extracted from the 'Book of Irish Families, great & small').

O'Donnellan
Donlan, Donlon, Donelan, Donnellen

In the census of 1659 Donellan is found in Dublin. (The above extracted from the 'Book of Irish Families, great & small'). (See major entry in 'The Families of Co. Galway').

 © 1999. IGF. Families of Co. Dublin, Ireland- Box 7575, K.C., MO. 64116

O Donnelly
Dannelly, Donaldson, Donelly, Donely,

The O'Donnelly family is primarily from the province of Ulster in the north of Ireland. .

The name is found often in Dublin as well. (The above extracted from the 'Book of Irish Families, great & small').

Donnogh
Thomas Donnogh is found in St. Nicholas Parish 'Without the Walls', in the Dublin City Pipe Water Accounts of 1680.

Donohoe
Donohue Donahoe

Donohoe is family name found in Dublin at the time of the Birth Index of 1890. Keatings 'History of Ireland' (IGF edition) gives a branch of the O'Donoghue name as ancient chiefs of Fingall, near Dublin (per the works of O'Dugan). This family of the name would presumably be separate from the well known O'Donoghues of Co. Kerry. (See major entry in 'The Families of Co. Kerry').

O'Hart gives the Donohoe and Gilcolm families as ancient chiefs of Dublin at Feltrim.

Doogan
It is a surname found in Quaker records in Dublin city in the late 17th century, where one of the name is given as a 'skinner'.

O'Dooley
Dooly, Dowly

The 1890's birth index shows the name in Dublin and Offaly. (The above extracted from the 'Book of Irish Families, great & small').

Doolin
Doolan Dolan

Doolin is a family name given in Dublin in the Birth Index of 1890.

O'Doran
Dorian, Doran, Doren, Dorane

By the time of the 1890 birth index Doran is found in Dublin, Wexford, Down and Armagh.

(The above extracted from the 'Book of Irish Families, great & small').

Dore
Dores

Milesian Families finds the name in Dublin, of French origins. (no documentation given).

We find Dores in the 1659 census in Dublin. See appendix.

Dorland
Milesian Families finds the name in Dublin, of Saxon origins. (no documentation given).

Douces
The Douces family is given at Aderrig parish in the 14th century.

McDougall
Drumleck, near Howth, was given as the residence of Wm. McDougall, by whom it was built.

Dover
William Dover is found in St. Catherine's parish in the Dublin City Pipe Water Accounts of 1680.

O'Dowd
Doody, Duddy, Dodd, Doud, Dowds,

Spelled simply as 'Dowd', without the 'O' prefix, the birth index lists the family as found in Roscommon, Dublin, Kerry and Galway. In modern times the 'O' has been added back onto this name in many instances.

For interesting and more detailed accounts see : 'The Tribes and Customs of the Hy Fiachrach". (The above extracted from the 'Book of Irish Families, great & small').

'Hy Fiachrach' gives the 'famous family of the Dowds of Dublin'.

Dowdall
According to "Keatings History" the name is that of a principal family of Dublin city or county, and of Anglo-Norman descent. From the same source we find that the name was of a noted family in Meath, where they were centered in Athlumney.

The birth index of 1890 finds the family centered in Dublin and Louth. (The above extracted from the 'Book of Irish Families, great & small').

The Dowdalls are given by Ball to be one of the families located in Mulhuddart parish from the 14th -16th centuries.

O'Dowling
Doolen, Doolin, Dooling, Dooly, Dowlan,
   Many of the name settled in Dublin City relatively early in time. Hence, we find Dowling more numerous in Dublin in 1890, than in either Kilkenny or Queens (Leix).
   (The above extracted from the 'Book of Irish Families, great & small').

Downs
Downes
   The most common spelling according to the 1890 index was 'Downes', which was given in Clare, Limerick and Dublin at that time.   (The above extracted from the 'Book of Irish Families, great & small').
   The Downes family is found seated at Donneybrook on the Donneybrook road in the 18th century. See introduction.

Dowse
Dousse
   Families of the name of Dowse are found in Ireland quite early. Many of the name are found in the city of Dublin, and some arrived during the Cromwellian settlement of Ireland. (The above extracted from the 'Book of Irish Families, great & small').

Doyle
Doil, Dooal, Dyle, Mcdoyle, O'doyle
   It is held by many that the Doyles are of old Norse origins in Ireland., One cannot find the name in any of the old Irish genealogies, like other Irish families have been. Doyle is among the top 20 names in all of Ireland, which points to other Irish origins as well. In Dublin, Doyle was the third most numerous name in the 1890 birth index.,
   Principal locations for the name in the last century were in Dublin, Wexford, Wicklow, Carlow, Kerry and Cork.
   John Doyle was a member of the Irish House of Commons in 1797.   (The above extracted from the 'Book of Irish Families, great & small').
   It is also a surname found in Quaker records in Dublin city in the 18th century.

Doyne
   Among the noted residents of Booterstown in the 18th century were included the names of Cooley; Doherty; Gough; O'Reilly; LaTouche; Doyne; Wight; Bradstreet; and Fitzgerald.

Drake
   The Drake family is also given as a principal one of Anglo-Norman descent, settling in Dublin City and County, according to Keatings 'History of Ireland'.

Drape
   One 'Mr. Drape' is found in Esker parish in the 17th century. See introduction.

Draycott
   Draycott's farm went to Arland Ussher in Glasnevin Parish. See introduction.

Dromgold
Drumgoole
   See appendix. Found in Dublin in the census of 1659. See also Drumgoole.

Drumgoole
Drumgool, Dromgoole, Drumgoold,
   The spelling of Drumgold is found in the 17th century in the city of Dublin. (The above extracted from the 'Book of Irish Families, great & small').

Drury, Drew
Drewery, Drew, Drewry, Druery.
   The name of Drury is cited in the census of 1659 as being of Dublin City, and appears as well in the Poll Money Ordinance survey.
   The name is also an English name, said to be taken from the French, meaning sweetheart. The Drew family of Drewscourt, Co. Cork is given in the Irish Book of Arms. (The above extracted from the 'Book of Irish Families, great & small').

Dryland
   Milesian Families finds the name in Dublin, of Saxon origins.

Duchamine
   One Mr. Duchamine is found in St. Catherine's parish in the Dublin City Pipe Water Accounts of 1680.

Ducker

It is a surname found in Quaker records in Dublin city in the early 18th century, where one of the name was listed as a merchant.

Dudly
Dudley

A family name found in the city of Dublin in the census of 1659.

Duff
Duffe

A family name found in Dublin in the census of 1659 and in the birth index of 1890.

At least five of the name from Dublin are given in the attainders of 1691 as given in King James Irish Army List. Patrick Duffe is given as of Westpalstown in Dublin at that time.

O'Hart gives the family as a principal one settling in Dublin from the 12th to the 18th century.

O'Duffy
Duhig, Doohey, Dowey, Duffey, Duffie,

The name ranks as one of the top 50 surnames in Ireland, and among the 700 most numerous families in America.

The Cross of Cong in the Dublin Museum was made by an O'Duffy (1123 a.d.) (The above extracted from the 'Book of Irish Families, great & small').

According to the works searched by O'Hart, the O'Duffy family was originally in Kildare and Carlow, but subsequently found in Dublin, and they are found migrating to several other areas in Ireland.

O'Duggan
O'duggan, Dugan, Doogan, Duggen,

Spelled as Duggan in the 1890 index, it was most popular then in Cork, Dublin, Tipperary and Waterford. (The above extracted from the 'Book of Irish Families, great & small').

Dulane
Dolane Dolan

Milesian Families finds the name in Dublin, of Saxon origins. (no documentation given).

Dundon

A family name in Dublin as found in the 1890 birth index.

Dundrum

A holding at Dalkey was given in 1320 to Alice, wife of John de Dundrum.

Dungan
Dongan

A family name found in Dublin in the census of 1659.

O'Dunne
Dunne, O'doyne, Dun, Dunn

The name has also been found in the kingdom of Meath as a chief in the district of Tara.

In 1890 the spelling of Dunne was found in several locations, including Dublin, Queens, Kilkenny, Kings, Kildare, Cork, Tipperary and Cavan. It was among the top ten most numerous surnames in Dublin County in the 1890 birth index.

In 1659 'Dunn' was found as a principal name in Dublin.

The Irish Book of Arms gives 'Dunne of Brittas'. (The above extracted from the 'Book of Irish Families, great & small').

Darby Dun is found in St. Audeon's parish in the Dublin City Pipe Water Accounts of 1680.

Around 1800 the Rev. James Dunn was lodging in the area of Killiney parish. See introduction.

Dunphy

Thé Dunphy family is found most numerous in Waterford and Dublin in the 19th century. (extracted from the 'Book of Irish Families, great & small').

Durdin

Milesian Families finds the name in Dublin, of English origins.

Durham

John Durham is found in St. Werburgh's parish in the Dublin City Pipe Water Accounts of 1680.

Dustin

Milesian Families finds the name in Dublin, of French origins.

Dutch

A family name found in Dublin city, given to be of Jewish heritage in at least one instance. (per 'OLochlainns journal of Irish Families').

Dutton

A family name found in Dublin in the census of 1659.

O'Dwyer
Dwire, Dwyre, Dwyar, Dwier

Spelled as Dwyer 155 births were recorded, found in Tipperary, Cork, Dublin, Kerry, Limerick etc... in 1890. (The above extracted from the 'Book of Irish Families, great & small').

Dyas

A family name found in Dublin at the time of the Birth Index of 1890.

Earhart

Milesian Families finds the name in Dublin, of German origins.

Early   Earley
Earley, Erley, D' Erley

Families of the Early name in Ireland are found in the city of Dublin in the 17th century, and subsequently they are found centered in Leitrim in the 19th century. The above family was of old Irish descent. (per the 'Book of Irish Families, great & small'). See appendix, 1659 census.

Eastwood

A family name found in the city of Dublin in the census of 1659. Alderman John Eastwood is found in St. Catherine's parish in the Dublin City Pipe Water Accounts of 1680.

Eccles

Eccles Mount was the country residence of Sir John Eccles, sometime Lord Mayor of Dublin.

Ecklin

One Mr. Ecklin is found in St. John's parish in the Dublin City Pipe Water Accounts of 1680.

Edkins

A name found in the city of Dublin in 1659. Joseph Edkins is found in St. Werburgh's parish in the Dublin City Pipe Water Accounts of 1680.

Edmonds
Edmounds

Milesian Families finds the name in Dublin, of Welch origins.

Edwards

Edwards is found in the birth index of 1890 in Co. Dublin. It is as well found in Dublin in the census of 1659. Richard Edwards is given as a landowner at Bullock. See introduction.

Egan
Eagan

A family name given in Dublin in the Birth Index of 1890.

Egerton

Thomas Egerton was a member of the Tatton family who died in 1756 at Glasnevin Parish.

Egyr
Agar Egar Eager

John Egyr is found in Dublin in 1502. (see substantial entry on the name in 'Families of Co. Kerry, Ireland'.)

Ekin
Egan Egin

A family name found in the city of Dublin in the census of 1659.

Elias

Early names at Newcastle parish after the 12th century invasions included Elias of Winchester.

Elkin

A family name found in Dublin city, given to be of Jewish heritage in at least one instance. (per 'OLochlainns journal of Irish Families').

Ellard

Milesian Families finds the name in Dublin, of English origins. (no documentation given).

Elliott
Elliot, Eliott Ellot

The census of 1659 finds the name in Dublin presumably spelled as 'Ellott', and in 1890, when spelled as Elliot the name is given to be of Fermanagh, Antrim, Dublin and Donegal. (The above extracted from the 'Book of Irish Families, great & small').

Ellis

A family name of Dublin in both the 1890 and 1659 index lists. Anthony Ellis is found in St. Werburgh's parish in the Dublin City Pipe Water Accounts of 1680.

In 'King James's Irish Army List, 1689' we find listed as a Dublin assessor, one Sir William Ellis.

In 1664 Abraham Ellis was rated for four hearths, near Howth.

Ellison
Elison, Ellis

The name Ellis is found centered in Dublin and Antrim in the 19th century. (The above extracted from the 'Book of Irish Families, great & small').

Elliston

Christopher Elliston is found in St. Catherine's parish in the Dublin City Pipe Water Accounts of 1680.

Ellott   Elliott

Ellott is a family name found in Dublin in the census of 1659. See also Elliott

Elrington
Ellrington

Robert Elrington was a west Indian merchant, said to be a descendant of Dublin actor, Thomas Elrington. Note also the work of Elrington Ball, author of The History of County Dublin.

Elward
Aylward

A family name found in the city of Dublin in the census of 1659.

Emery
Amery

Milesian Families finds the name in Dublin, of Norman origins.

Emmett

At the close of the 18th century at Robuck, the following were noted in connection with villas built in that era: John Exshaw; James Potts; Alexander Jaffray; Dr. Robert Emmett; and Henry Jackson.

Empson

Charles Empson is found in St. John's parish in the Dublin City Pipe Water Accounts of 1680.

William Empson is noted in Finglas Parish. See introduction.

England

In the 17th century we find John England, the village inn owner at Finglas.

English
L'englys, L'angleys, Lenglas, Englonde,

Several of the name are on record as property owners in Dublin and Louth.

The census of 1659 finds English as a principal name of Tipperary, and also in Dublin. The birth index of 1890 shows the name in Tipperary, Antrim and Dublin. The Irish variant of 'Mac Gallogly' is also associated with the name. (The above extracted from the 'Book of Irish Families, great & small').

Ennis
Ennes, Enniss, Ennoss, Enos

The 17th century finds the name of Ennis as a principal one of Dublin, and the possible variant spelling of Ennos was also a principal name of Dublin at that time.

The Ennis family is found most numerous in Dublin and Kildare in the 19th century as well. (per the 'Book of Irish Families, great & small').

In 1780 a 'Mr. Reilly' occupied the castle at Drimnagh, and it is said that Mr. Ennis was the grandfather of the owner before him.

Enos
Ennis'

James Enos occupied a house at Diswellstown in Castleknock parish.

Epstein

A family name found in Dublin city, given to be of Jewish heritage in at least one instance. (per 'OLochlainns journal of Irish Families').

Erlich

A family name found in Dublin city, given to be of Jewish heritage in at least one instance. (per 'OLochlainns journal of Irish Families').

Errill
Eirill Earl

The Errill family of Dublin was earlier located in Westmeath (before the Commonwealth period), and they were subsequently dispersed. One branch is found settled in Dublin. (see the works of O'Hart).

Erskine
Erskin

One noted family of the name can be found in Dublin, descended from John Erskin, who served as Earl of Mar, in the early 17th century. (The above extracted from the 'Book of Irish Families, great & small').

Espinasse

Due to the penal laws Mr. William Espinasse (d.1740) is given residing in a house built by George Ussher at Kill of the Grange parish. He arrived from France after the revocation of the Edict of Nantes at a time when many Huguenot families came to Ireland. Of this line was a Sheriff of Dublin. See introduction.

Eton
Eaton

Eton is a family name found in the city of Dublin in the census of 1659. Be aware of the variant spelling as Eaton.

Subsequent to the 17th century rebellions we find the names of Wharton; Chambers; Willion; Barry; Robinson; Moses; Reyly; Lovelace; Eaton; Murphy; Lawlor; Leedom; and Walsh in Rathcoole parish, Co. Dublin.

Euleston

One family of the name, of the House of Euleston in Lancashire settled in Ireland and provided us with Tristram Euleston, of Drumshallum, Co. Louth, who also served as Constable of Dublin Castle in the early part of the 17th century. (extracted from the 'Book of Irish Families, great & small').

Eustace
Eustace, Ustace, Eustice, Eustis,

Eustace belongs to an Anglo-Norman family in Ireland centered near the pale, (the area near Dublin.). Often found in alliance with the native Irish of the land, this led to the fall of the families' power. Sir Maurice Eustace held many lands in Dublin and Kildare, but they were confiscated as a result of his strong support for King James, whose troops he commanded.

James Eustace came to be seated at Monkstown Castle in Dublin subsequent to Sir John Travers. Thomas Cusack was leased the lands of Cabinteely, which were subsequently held by Sir John Travers in 1545, and then by Eustace. Eustace of Harristown is given at Kilgobbin as well. In Kilmactalway parish we find Eustace of Milltown.

Lt.-Col. Richard Eustace of Barretsown, Co. Dublin, is noted in King James' Irish Army List.

Perhaps more numerous in earlier times, the 1890 birth index finds only 9 births of the name, which may have come from "Eustacius", meaning "fruitful". Over 30 listings of the name are given in O'Harts' work. The Eustace families of Kilcock, Co. Kildare and of Newtown, Co. Carlow are given in the Irish Book of Arms.

Individuals of the name:
Maurice Eustace- (1590-1665) Speaker Of The House of Commons and 'Lord Chancellor'. (Some of the above is extracted from the 'Book of Irish Families, great & small').

The family is also given as a principal one of Anglo-Norman descent, settling in Dublin City and County, according to Keatings 'History of Ireland'.

Evans

The birth index of 1890 finds the family centered in Dublin, Londonderry and Antrim. (per the 'Book of Irish Families, great & small').

Although not listed in some sources, Evans is given in the works of O'Hart as one of the primary settler families subsequent to the 12th century.

Evers

A family name given in Dublin in the census of 1659, and which remained there at the time of the 1890 birth index.

In 1631 one Timothy Evers is given as Mayor of Dublin in the entry concerning Lt. Gerald Evers.

Eves
Eaves

It is a surname found in Quaker records in Dublin city in the 18th century.

Mac Evoy
Macveagh, Mac Elwee, Macgilloway,

In the 1890 birth index McEvoy is found concentrated in Dublin, Louth, Armagh and Queens counties. (The above extracted from the 'Book of Irish Families, great & small').

Ewing
Ewings, Ewin, Ewen

Some prominent members of this family name are found in Dublin, and they may be of traditional Ulster origins for the name. (per the 'Book of Irish Families, great & small').

Exham

Among houses noted at Ballyfermot were those of: Verveer; Styles; Carden; Ryves; Exham; and Talbot of Templeogue.

Exshaw

At the close of the 18th century at Robuck, the following were noted in connection with villas built in that era: John Exshaw; James Potts; Alexander Jaffray; Dr. Robert Emmett; and Henry Jackson.

Fade

It is a surname found in Quaker records in Dublin city in the late 17th century.

Fagan Fagon
Fegan, Hagan, Feehan, Fagin, Feagan,

The families of Fegan etc...are traditionally linked with Dublin and nearby areas into modern times. Some dispute remains as to their origins.

The name may stem from Norman origins, and in some cases may be a form of the Irish O'Hagan, or from O'Faodhagain of County Louth. Woulfe mentions possible origins as a branch of O'Hagan, while others disagree. Some believe Fagan to be a completely separate Irish family of the ancient territory of Oriel.

The first of the name we have found is one 'William Fagan' who in 1200 a.d., held property in Dublin. He may be of the family seated near Feltrim, Co. Dublin in that era. This family developed branches in both Kerry and Cork counties.

Keating gives the O'Fagans as numerous in Meath and Westmeath, the head of which was titled of Baron of Feltrim in Fingal (Dublin).

Keatings also says that Fagan 'some of whom have been called O'Fagan and Mac Fagan, are considered by some to be of Irish origin, but according to others they were English or Danish in descent, and the name is still numerous in Meath, Westmeath and Dublin'. Perhaps both origins may hold true, adding to the confusion.

The 1890 birth index finds the name mainly in Dublin and Leitrim.

The Fagan family of Feltrim descends from Thomas Fagan of Dublin, who married Amy Nangle in the year of 1524. Christopher Ffagan of Feltrim is listed among those transplanted from Dublin in the works of O'Hart. In the 16th century the Fagan family also held the lands and Castle at Bullock.

Several of the name are given as high sheriffs in Meath and Dublin from the 13th to the 15th century according to D'Alton.

See also the "Fagans of Feltrim" as found in the periodical "Reportorium Novum" 2 (1), 1958.

The Seven farms in Glasnevin parish, went to Thomas Lockwood and Richard Fagan. See introduction.

Faile

It is a surname found in Quaker records in Dublin city in the early 18th century.

Fairbrother

It is a surname found in Quaker records in Dublin city in the 18th century.

Samuel Fairbrother was a publisher from Glasnevin Parish who died in 1758.

Fairview

(Not a surname entry) In 1718 a Jewish burying ground had been made at Fairview in Clonturk Parish.

Falconer
Faulkner Falkiner

See "The Falkiners of Abbotstown, Co. Dublin", in the "Journal of the Kildare Archeological and Historical Society", 8 (1915-17).

Milesian Families also finds the name in Dublin, of English origins. (no documentation given in that source). See variant spellings.

Falk
Fallek

We find this family name in Dublin City, given to be of Jewish heritage. (per 'OLochlainns Journal of Irish Families').

Falkiner
Faulkiner Falkner Falconer

Mount Jerome in the early 18th century was occupied by Mr. Daniel Falkiner, the father of John Falkiner of Nangor Castle in Clondalkin. The Falkiners of Abbotstown descend from this line as well.

The Falkiner family became seated at Abbotstown, and the first of the name there was Frederick Falkiner, a leading Dublin banker. His grandfather was the first to settle in Ireland, and the family was early on identified with Leeds.

See "The Falkiners of Abbotstown, Co. Dublin", in the "Journal of the Kildare Archeological and Historical Society", 8 (1915-17).

Fallard

A family name found in the city of Dublin in the census of 1659.

Mc Farland

'Milesian Families' finds the names of McFarland and McFarlane in Dublin, of likely Scottish origins.

Farley

A family name of Dublin in the census of 1659. Modern day studies show nearly 30% of the name in Dublin today, with 8% of the name in Cork.

Farmer

John Farmer is found in St. Werburgh's parish in the Dublin City Pipe Water Accounts of 1680.

O' Farrell
Farral, Farel, Ferrall, Farrel

At the end of the 1800's only 19 births were recorded under the spelling of O'Ferrell, and 311 were spelled as Farrell primarily in Dublin, Meath, Longford, Louth and Westmeath. In 1890 Farrell and its variant spellings combined to form one of the top twenty most numerous surnames in the county of Dublin.

In 1659 Farrall was a principal name in Dublin. (The above extracted from the 'Book of Irish Families, great & small').

In 1623 William Wolverston, the owner of Stillorgan, held the lands of Tipperstown, and in 1645 they were held by Richard Swinfield of Murphystown, and in 1724 Christopher Ussher of Booterstown leased these lands. In the times of the Union they were held by Councillor O'Farrell and were farmed with great skill.

O' Farrelly
Farely, Farelly, Ferrely, Ferly, Farley

Traditionally considered a family of Cavan and Meath,(a Breffny clan), the name has remained most popular in those counties, as well as in Dublin, into modern times.

The 1890 birth index records some 69 births of the Farrelly name, mainly in Cavan, Meath and Dublin.

The Irish Book of Arms gives families of the name as "O'Farrell of Dalyston, Co. Galway". (The above extracted from the 'Book of Irish Families, great & small').

Farris

Milesian Families finds the name in Dublin. (no documentation given).

Faulkner
Falconer Falkiner

Milesian Families finds the name in Dublin, of Norman origins. See variant spellings.

Fawcett
Faucett

After the rebellion of 1641 the lands of Killiney parish were held by Gilbert Wye of Belfast; the Mossoms; the Fawcetts; the Pocklingtons; and the Domviles. See introduction.

Fay
Du Fay, Faye, Fey, Fee, Foy, De Fae, De

A name of Anglo-Norman origins in Ireland, found settled early in Co. Westmeath, and in modern times in Dublin. The Irish Book of Arms gives Fay of Faybrook, Co. Cavan. Other sources tell that the name of Fay has been found in records of the Pale from the time of King John. (The above extracted from the 'Book of Irish Families, great & small').

Fearnely
Ferenely   Fernelly

A family name found in Dublin in the census of 1659.

Fegan
Feghan, Fagan

The Fegan name is linked with counties Dublin, Armagh and Louth, and sometimes confused with O'Hagan. (per the 'Book of Irish Families, great & small'). See Fagan.

Fenelon
Finnellan, Fenlon, Fenlon

Families of the name of Fenlon are found centered in Carlow, Dublin and Wexford in the 19th century. (per the 'Book of Irish Families, great & small').

Fenlon
Fenelon

A family name found in Dublin at the time of the Birth Index of 1890. See Fenelon

Fennell
Fennelly, Fyenell, Fenell

The census of 1659 finds the family in Dublin, Kilkenny, Queens and Cork counties. The 19th century birth index gives them centered in Clare and Dublin. (The above extracted from the 'Book of Irish Families, great & small').

Ferguson

Milesian Families finds the name in Dublin, of Scottish origins. (no documentation given).

Ferneley
Fearnely

In the 17th century we find Lt. Col. Ferneley at Drimnagh Castle and subsequently the Archer family in 1735.

Phineas Ferneley is noted in Finglas Parish. See introduction. See also Fearnely in 1659 census in the appendix.

Ferris

Gilbert Ferris occupied Paslicktown in the 17th century.

Ferriter
Feritter, Ferreter

A name given to be of Dublin and Kerry quite early in Irish History, and originally this family was of Anglo-Norman origins. (The above extracted from the 'Book of Irish Families, great & small').

Ferry

Milesian Families finds the name in Dublin, of English origins.

Fetherston
Featherston

A family name given in Dublin in the Birth Index of 1890. One Mr. Fetherston is found residing at Killiney around the end of the 18th century.

Ffolliott
Foley

In the 15th century the Ffolliot family was granted property in Saggart parish.

Fians
Fyans, Fyan, Feighan, Foynes

The 'Fians' family name is most likely taken as a variant spelling of the name Fyans, which has been found in Dublin since the 1400's. Some of the name served as mayors of Dublin. The name has also been changed to Faghan. (The above extracted from the 'Book of Irish Families, great & small').

Field
Feild, Delafield, Delafeld, O Fihelly

The family name of Field is traditionally linked to Dublin, and they were originally a settler family of Anglo-Norman extraction. The family name is as well cited as being a main settler family in Co. Cork.

In more modern times the 1890 birth index finds the family centered in Dublin and Cork.

According to "Keatings History" the name of O'Fihelly was Anglicized to Field, and they were given by O'Brien as chiefs in west Barryroe. (The above extracted from the 'Book of Irish Families, great & small').

The de la Fields are given at Corduff in the 14th century. See introduction.

Fieragh

The Fieragh name is noted in Knocklyon, in the parish of Tallaght.

Figgis

Seemingly a very rare name found only in recent times in the city of Dublin in our records. (per the 'Book of Irish Families, great & small').

Finglas

According to "Keatings History" the name is that of a principal family of Dublin, and of Anglo-Norman descent. Note also the placename of 'Finglas'.

The old Finglas family of Westpalstown held over 1500 acres in 17th century Dublin. (The above extracted from the 'Book of Irish Families, great & small').

In the 13th century we find Butler, Wallis, Finglas, and Fitzgerald at Killakee.

In Clonsilla parish at the east end of the Clonsilla church was the 18th century burial place for a branch of the Slingsby family, one of whom was given as 'alias Finglas'.

Finlay

In the 18th century we find the Finlay family settled at Corkagh in Clondalkin parish.

O'Finn
Macfinn, Macfhinn, Maginn, Magphinn

Surprisingly, Finn is most common in Co. Cork in modern times, but most numerous in Mayo, Dublin and Roscommon in the 1890 birth index. (The above extracted from the 'Book of Irish Families, great & small').

Finucane
Finnucane Mac Finnucane

Several of the Finucane family of Drumcliffe, Co. Clare in the 18th century, are said to have settled in Dublin.

Fisher

A family name we find in Dublin in the census of 1659. Widow Fisher is found in St. Michael's parish in the Dublin City Pipe Water Accounts of 1680.

Fitz Rery
Fitzrory Fitzrury

See "The Fitz Rerys, Welsh Lords of Cloghran, Co. Dublin.", in the "Journal of the the Louth Archeological Society." 5 (1921).

At least one 'Fitzrury' family is found holding lands in 1640 in County Dublin.

Fitzgerald

Fitzgerrald Fitzgerrold

In 1255 we find Maurice Fitzgerald at Baggotrath in Dublin. Fitzgerald is found in Dublin in the 17th and 19th century records, though common in the west of Ireland as well. Fitzgerrold is one spelling found in Dublin in 1659.

The Irish Book of Arms (IGF edition) gives one James Fitzgerald of Kildare House, Dublin.

Among the residents of Booterstown in the 18th century were included the names of Bradstreet and Fitzgerald.

In the 13th century we find Butler, Wallis, Finglas, and Fitzgerald at Killakee.

Among the names noted at Rathcoole parish from the 16th century onwards are the Fitzgeralds.

The Fitzgeralds held the castle at Lucan until the 16th century.
(See major entry in 'The Families of Co. Kerry').

Fitzgibbon

Kilrock, near Howth, was the residence of Lord Justice FitzGibbon.

Fitzharris

Fitzharry, Fitzhenry

We find the family in Carlow and Dublin. (The above extracted from the 'Book of Irish Families, great & small').

Fitzpatrick

Macgilpatrick, Fitz, Patrick, Fitch,

Fitzpatrick is the exception to the rule. It is the only 'Fitz' name of ancient Irish origins, and not of Norman heritage. In the 1890 birth index this name is found in Dublin, Queens, Cork, Tipperary and Cavan.

(The above extracted from the 'Book of Irish Families, great & small').

Fitzrichard

In 1320 Andrew Fitzrichard received a holding at Dalkey. See introduction.

Fitzsimmons

Fitzsimon, Fitzsimmon, Fitz, Fitzsymon,

The 'Fitz' prefix is of Norman origin. In the 14th century the name arrived from Cornwall, England and settled in Dublin. One Thomas Fitzsimons of Calliaghstown is given as a substantial landowner in 17th century Co. Dublin.

Fitzsimons seems to be the most common spelling in the 1800's, although many variants exist such as Fitzsimon, Fits, Fitz, Symons etc..

Fitzsimmons is given in Dublin, Down and Cavan in the 1890 birth index of Ireland. (The above extracted from the 'Book of Irish Families, great & small').

O'Hart lists the family as a principal one between the 12th and the 18th centuries in Dublin.

The family is also given residing in a house built by George Ussher at Kill of the Grange parish. See introduction.

The lands of Glencullen are given as falling into the hands of the Fitzsimons family as well.

In 16th century in Glasnevin Parish leases are found held by Thomas and Oliver Stephens, Alson FitzSimon, and James and John Bathe.

St. Doulough's Well.

Fitzwilliam
Fitzwilliams

One family of the name of Fitzwilliam is found by O'Hart as of Merrion, Co. Dublin. This was the line of Sir Richard Fitzwilliam (d.1595). Of the same line, it is said that Richard Fitzwilliam became governor of the Bahama Islands in the early 18th century.

They are one of the few early settler families to 'retain all their property' through all the troubles of history into modern time. The first of the line was said to have arrived with King John. They claimed to be of the same line as Earl Fitzwilliam and it is of some note that they ceased using a separate coat of arms in the 17th century, adopting the arms of Earl Fitzwilliam. See introduction.

Thomas Fitzwilliam made the castle at Baggottrath his home in the 16th c..

The spelling of Fitzwilliams is also given in Dublin in the 17th century, at which time several of the name are found with estates in Co. Dublin.

The family is given as a principal one of Anglo-Norman descent, settling in Dublin City and County, according to Keatings 'History'. The family is also listed as part of the 'more recent nobility' by O'Hart where they are given as 'viscount Merrion' in Dublin.

They were firmly established in the south of Dublin in the 14th century and by the 15th century those lands were controlled by a branch of the family seated at Dundrum. At Dundrum by the 14th century, they erected a castle there. They also came to hold lands at Booterstown and elsewhere.

See also the article entitled " The Fitzwilliams of Merrion (Dublin)", as found in Reportorium Novum, 2 (1), 1958. See also introduction.

Richard Aubry held the lands of Jobstown or Rathmintin until 1326 when they were acquired by Richard Fitzwilliam.

The Fitzwilliams of Merrion were also given as holding the lands of Kiltiernan parish in 1577. Around 1600 in the House of Howth we find Peter Wynne and William Fitzwilliam.

Fitzwilliam

Readers will also note that Fitzwilliam Street Upper and Lower is an upscale residential street in Dublin.

Member Donal MacNamara notes that Fitzwilliam is also 'memorialized' in the poem-song "Follow Me Up To Carlow" to wit:

Lift Mac Cahir Og your face
Brooding o'er that old disgrace
That **Black Fitzwilliam** stormed your place
And drove you to the fern.

Grey thought victory was sure
Soon the Firebrand he'd secure
'Til he met at Glenmalure
Feagh Mac Hugh **O'Beirne**

Curse and Swear Lord Kildare
Feagh will to what Feagh will dare
Now **Fitzwilliam** have a care
Fallen is your star low

White is sick and **Lane** is fled
Now for Black **Fitzwilliam's** head
We'll send it over dripping red
To Liza and her ladies.

Flamstead
See introduction p. 19, for the name.

O' Flanagan
Flanagan, Flang, Flanigan,

The 69th most popular name in all of Ireland, several unrelated families of this surname are found. By 1890 principal locations for the family were in Roscommon, Dublin, Mayo, Clare, Galway and Fermanagh.

(The above extracted from the 'Book of Irish Families, great & small').

Fleming

Flemon, Flemming, Flemmyng,

Families of the name of Fleming in Ireland were originally from Flanders. They have arrived in Ireland at different times, and may descend from several families of the name in Flanders. They arrived in Ireland near the time of the Norman invasions, as well as during the time of the Plantation of Ulster.

In Keatings 'History of Ireland' the name is also cited as a principal one of Anglo-Norman descent in the city and county of Dublin. The De Flemmings, barons of Slane, are also cited here as a chief Anglo-Norman family settled in Louth.

In the 17th century 'Flemming' was a principal name of Limerick, and in Waterford and Dublin city.

At the end of the last century the name was most populous in Antrim, Dublin, Galway, Londonderry, Cork and Mayo. (The above extracted from the 'Book of Irish Families, great & small').

The Flemings are given by Ball to be one of the families located in Mulhuddart parish from the 14th -16th centuries.

Fletcher

A family name we find in Dublin in the census of 1659 and in the 1890 birth index.

It is also a surname found in Quaker records in Dublin city in the late 17th century.

Laurence and James Fletcher are found in St. John's parish in the Dublin City Pipe Water Accounts of 1680.

Flood

Floyd, Mactully, Macatilla

In the birth index the name is found primarily in Dublin in 1890, but was given in Wexford and Longford in the 1659 census in Ireland. The Irish Book of Arms gives Solly-Flood of Ballynaslaney House. (The above extracted from the 'Book of Irish Families, great & small').

Flower

A family name found in the city of Dublin in the census of 1659. It is also a surname found in Quaker records in Dublin city in the late 17th century.

Floyd

Flood

Our records find the family name in Kerry, Westmeath, Dublin, and Kilkenny in the 17th century. Flood has also been officially reported as a synonym of Floyd. (extracted from the 'Book of Irish Families, great & small').

Flynn

Flinn

A family name found in Dublin at the time of the Birth Index of 1890.

Foester

Foster

A family name found in Dublin in the census of 1659. It could possibly be 'Foster' misspelled.

O'Fogarty

Fogerty, Gogarty

Most of the name have dropped the 'O' prefix long ago, and 61 births of the name were recorded in the 1890 birth index, primarily located in Tipperary and Dublin. (The above extracted from the 'Book of Irish Families, great & small').

Mac Fogarty of South Bregia is given as such by the Four Masters in the 10th century.

O'Foley

Fowloo, Foli, Fooley, Fooluiah, Fowly,

One of the 100 most numerous names in Ireland, the Foleys descend from the O'Foghladha sept of Waterford., in one case. Some sources give the name as of Norman origin as well as Irish.

In modern times the name was found most often in Kerry, Cork, Waterford and Dublin in the 1890's birth index.

Most commonly found in the province of Munster, MacSharry (MacSearraigh) is a completely separate name which has been translated into Foley. (The above extracted from the 'Book of Irish Families, great & small').

Fookes

A family name found in the city of Dublin in the census of 1659.

Foot

Noted families at Killakee were those of Henry Joy; Guinness; St. Michael; and Mr. Lundy Foot.

Hollypark in Whitechurch parish was built by Jeffrey Foot.

Foran
O'forhane, O'foran, Forhan, Forane

As the 1890 birth index shows, the name is found in Dublin.

(The above extracted from the 'Book of Irish Families, great & small').

Forbes, George. Earl

Some of the name are found seated at Newtown Castle & Forbes in Longford, and at Symon's Court in Co. Dublin.

It is a surname found in Quaker records in Dublin city in the late 17th and 18th centuries, where several of the name are found as merchants.

Forde
Foran, Mackinnawe, Foorde, Foord, Foard

Many Fords here are of English extraction, arriving as settlers and merchants at various times in history.

One noted English family which settled in Meath, came from Devonshire in England, in the 14th century.

'Forde' rather than 'Ford' was the most common spelling of the name in 1890, when the name came primarily from Galway, Cork, Mayo and Dublin. There were 154 births of 'Forde' at that time, and only 39 births of 'Ford' .

In 1659 Ford was found in Dublin City. (The above extracted from the 'Book of Irish Families, great & small').

At Island Bridge we find the names of: Crowe in 1720; Curtis in 1724; Cox in 1736; Ford in 1738; and Trail in 1799.

Forester
Forster

Milesian Families finds the name in Dublin, of English origins. (no documentation given). See also Forster found in the census of 1659.

Forrest

A family name found in the city of Dublin in the census of 1659.

Forster
Forester

A family name found in Dublin in the census of 1659. It is a surname found in Quaker records in Dublin city in the early 18th century.

The Forsters are noted at Esker parish in the 17th century. Ballydowd served as home to the Fortser family there. See introduction.

Braghall's farm, in Glasnevin Parish, went to John Quartermas and later to John Forster.

Forth

A family name found in the city of Dublin in the census of 1659. At the end of the Elizabethan era we find Sir Ambrose Forth noted as the most notable resident in the parish of Finglas.

Fortick

Sir Wm. Fortick died at Coldblow in 1789, in Donneybrook.

Tristam Fortick, the founder of Fortick's alms house, held Clonlife or the Grange in the first half of the 18th century as noted in the introduction of this work at St. George parish. These lands later were known as Fortick's Grove.

Fossett

It is a surname found in Quaker records in Dublin city in the early 18th century.

Foster

A name we find in Dublin in the birth index of 1890. George Foster is found seated at Ballydowd in the 17th century.

Foster is given as among the few names of importance in Taney parish in the mid 18th century.

O'Hart lists the family among the principal settlers subsequent to the 12th century invasions.

Foules

A family name found in the city of Dublin in the census of 1659.

Founbaine

A family name found in the city of Dublin in the census of 1659.

Fount
Font Fant

In the 15th century we note the Fount family at Saggart parish.

Fountaine

A name found in the city of Dublin in 1659. Names connected to Rathfarnham parish in the 18th century were Palliser; O'Callaghan; Cramer; Coghill; Stannard; Fountain; Ward; Geering; How; Boyle; and Blackburn.

Fownes

The Fownes family is noted in Kilmainham in the 18th century.

Fox
Shinnock, Macashinah, Shanahy,

Most are assumed to be of Irish origins. In most instances, the name of 'Fox' arose as a nickname.

In 1890 the name was mainly in Dublin, Longford, Tyrone and Leitrim.

The Irish book of Arms finds Fox of Kilcoursey. (The above extracted from the 'Book of Irish Families, great & small').

Several of the name are found in earlier times in Irishtown, Co. Dublin. At least some of these descend from the Fox family of Tully, Co. Leitrim.

The principal resident at Booterstown in 1641 was Thomas Fox, a gentleman farmer. Sir Patrick Fox is found at Crumlin parish. See introduction.

Foxall

A family name found in the city of Dublin in the census of 1659.

Foxwich

A family name found in the city of Dublin in the census of 1659.

Foy
Fee, Fey, Fye, Fay, Hunt, Foye

The Foy name has been changed to several similar sounding forms, and has been translated into Hunt in earlier days.

In the census of 1659 the name of Foy is found in Dublin, as is the variant spelling of Foye. The more recent 1890 index places the name in Mayo, Cavan and Dublin. (The above extracted from the 'Book of Irish Families, great & small').

Foyle
Foyll

Families of the Foyle name are found rather sparingly in Ireland. We find the name from time to time in Dublin, and in Queens Co. in Ireland. (per the 'Book of Irish Families, great & small').

Frail
Freal

Milesian Families finds the name in Dublin, of Norman origins.

Frain
Freyn, Freyne, Frane, Frein, De Freyne

The similar sounding name of Freeney, Freny or Frainy is sometimes given as a variant spelling of Frain, and can sometimes be found in Dublin. (The above extracted from the 'Book of Irish Families, great & small').

Frame

A rare surname in Ireland, our records show scattered locations for the name including Dublin. (extracted from the 'Book of Irish Families, great & small').

Frampton

Milesian Families finds the name in Dublin, of Saxon origins.

Francis
Francis, Frances, Frank, Franks,

Families of the name of Francis, Frances, etc.. in Ireland are given to be of Norman heritage, and are not an old Gaelic family. The name carries with it the obvious meaning of "the Frenchman". The 1659 census finds the name in the city of Dublin, and the 19th century index finds 13 births of the name recorded in 1890 as Francis in scattered locations.

The Franks family of Westfield, Queens Co., and of Garrettstown and Dromrahane, Co. Cork, are given in the Irish Book of Arms. (The above extracted from the 'Book of Irish Families, great & small').

It is also a surname found in Quaker records in Dublin city in the late 17th century ('Francis').

The family of Thomas Franks, Esq. of Dublin, is given in "Families of Co. Kerry, Ireland" in the 'Day' family estates.

Frankel

A family name found in Dublin city, given to be of Jewish heritage in at least one instance. (per 'OLochlainns journal of Irish Families').

Franklin

A family name we find in Dublin in the census of 1659, sometimes given to be of Scottish origins.

Franks

In 'Families of Co. Kerry, Ireland' the family of Thomas Franks, Esq., of Dublin are given as descending from the Rev. John Day.

Fraser
Frazer, Frazier

Fraser families are found most numerous in counties Dublin, Antrim and Down in the 19th century. (The above extracted from the 'Book of Irish Families, great & small').

Freeman

Woulfe, in his *Irish Names and Surnames* gives Freeman as a mistranslation of the earlier Gaelic form of MacEntire etc.. outside of the Dublin area. (In Dublin he found the name was translated as Carpenter.).

The census of 1659 finds the name in Londonderry, Tipperary, Carlow and Dublin.

Four Freeman families are found in *The Families of Co. Kerry*. Accounts of this name are also found in v3 & v10 of OLochlainns journal of Irish Families. (The above extracted from the 'Book of Irish Families, great & small').

Freeme

In the 17th century Powerstown is noted as belonging to William Freeme.

French

Mathew French is found in St. Michael's parish in the Dublin City Pipe Water Accounts of 1680.

Johnstown was found in the occupation of Robert French, the ancestor of Lord de Freyne. See introduction under Finglas Parish. (See also major entry in 'The Families of Co. Galway').

Frend

At Newcastle in 1614 among the first city officials were: Parsons; Rolles; Kenny; Frend; Davies; White; Burton; Grible; Bridges; Rutledge; and Lushe.

Frieudman

A family name found in Dublin city, given to be of Jewish heritage in at least one instance. (per 'OLochlainns journal of Irish Families').

Fry

A family name we find in Dublin in the census of 1659, sometimes given to be of Scottish origins. It is also found in Dublin in 19th century. The name is to be traditionally linked to the Union of Strabane in Ireland.

Some give the name of Scottish origins.

Fryer

A family name found in the city of Dublin in the census of 1659.

Fullam
De Fullam, Fulham

The family of Fullam is traditionally linked to Swords in Co. Dublin, where they are on record for several centuries. In the 17th century the name is a principal one of the city of Dublin, as well as being found in Meath at that time.

The name of Fulham was also a principal name of Dublin and found in Dublin city in the 17th century. Two centuries later Fulham is found centered in Dublin and Kings Co. (Offaly). Some interchanging between these two names is reported. (The above extracted from the 'Book of Irish Families, great & small').

Patrick Fullam is found in St. Nicholas Parish 'Without the Walls', in the Dublin City Pipe Water Accounts of 1680.

Fullard

It is a surname found in Quaker records in Dublin city in the 18th century.

Fuller

It is a surname found in Quaker records in Dublin city in the late 17th and 18th centuries. (See major entry in 'The Families of Co. Kerry').

Fullerton
Milesian Families finds the name in Dublin, of Norman origins.

Fulton
A family name found in Dublin city in the census of 1659.

Fyan
Fyans Fian Feehan Fynes
The Fyan surname is found in the city of Dublin, where several are found as officials quite early. (The above extracted from the 'Book of Irish Families, great & small').
O'Hart lists the family among the principal settlers subsequent to the 12th century invasions.

Fyne
Feehan Fyan
See Fyan.

Gaban
John Gaban is mentioned as a tenant at Bullock who paid rent in fish. See introduction.

O' Gaffney
Gaughney, Keveny, Caulfield, Gaffey,
In the 1890's index 68 'Gaffney' births were recorded primarily in Cavan, Dublin and Roscommon. (The above extracted from the 'Book of Irish Families, great & small').

Gage
Milesian Families finds the name in Dublin, of English origins. (no documentation given).

Gaisford
The fourth Earl of Howth (d.1909) was buried at Howth in the tomb of his ancestors. On his death the barony and earldom of Howth lapsed. The estates passed to his nephew Julian Gaisford of Offington, who assumed the name of St. Lawrence.

Galagher
Gallaher
A family name found in Dublin at the time of the Birth Index of 1890. See Gallagher

Galbelly
A family name found in the city of Dublin in the census of 1659.

Gall
Milesian Families finds the name in Dublin, of French origins.

O' Gallagher
Gallougher, Gallagher, Gallaher,
The Gallagher family name has always been associated with Co. Donegal. One interesting source for further information on the family is the book 'Irish Chiefs and Leaders' published in Dublin, 1960.
The variant spellings of this families name are numerous, so be aware of possible changes here. (The above extracted from the 'Book of Irish Families, great & small').

Galvey
Names connected to Rathfarnham parish in the 14th and 15th centuries were Galvey; Hall; Cornwalsh; and Loftus.

Mac Gannon
Cannon Cannan Mcgann Gann Kennon
In 1890 the most common location of the name was in Co. Mayo, although the family is found in Dublin and Leitrim then. (The above extracted from the 'Book of Irish Families, great & small').
The name of 'Gannon' is sometimes of separate origins.

Gardiner
Milesian Families finds the name in Dublin, of English origins. (no documentation given), and also found there in the birth index of 1890.

Garland
Garlan, Gernon, Gartland, Mcgarland
Families of the name of Garland are found centered in Dublin and Monaghan in the 19th century. The name of Gernon has been used as a synonym. (extracted from the 'Book of Irish Families, great & small').

Garner
A family name found in the city of Dublin in the census of 1659.

Garnet

Although not given in several other sources, O'Hart gives the 'Garnet' family as a principal one settling in Dublin from the 12th to the 18th century.

In the mid 18th century New Park was the residence of George Garnett. See introduction under Ward Parish.)

Garrett

The Garrett family of Kilgaran of Co. Carlow is given in the Irish Book of Arms. The birth index of 1890 finds the family centered in Down, Antrim and Dublin. (The above extracted from the 'Book of Irish Families, great & small').

Mac Garry

Garrie, Garrihy, Garry, Garrey

With the "Mac" prefix Antrim, Dublin, Roscommon and Leitrim were centers for the name in the 1890 birth index. (The above extracted from the 'Book of Irish Families, great & small').

Garvey

Among the holders of land in Killiney parish in the 14th century and later were given: William Walsh alias McHowell; James Garvey; and the Goodman family.

Gaskin

A family name given in Dublin in the Birth Index of 1890.

Gavan

In 1761 in St. George Parish there was a house called Mountjoy which was occupied by Henry Gavan.

Gay

A family name found in the city of Dublin in the census of 1659.

Gaynor

Gainor, Gayner

A name traditionally linked to Co. Westmeath. The family is found most numerous in counties Dublin, Westmeath and Cavan in the 19th century. (per the 'Book of Irish Families, great & small').

Mac Gee, Magee

Magee, Mcghee, Ghee

Mac Gee and Magee are names traditionally associated with the province of Ulster.

Some of the name are of Scottish origins. They arrived during the plantations of the 17th century. One line of this strain was said earlier to have come from Ireland to Scotland, then migrating back to Ireland at the time of the plantations.

The book " The Magees of Belfast and Dublin" by F. J. Bigger was published in Belfast in 1916. ˙ (extracted from the 'Book of Irish Families, great & small').

Geering

Names connected to Rathfarnham parish in the 18th century were Palliser; O'Callaghan; Cramer; Coghill; Stannard; Fountain; Ward; Geering; How; Boyle; and Blackburn.

O' Gelbroin

Gilbroin

According to "Keatings History" the name is found as a chief of Clar Life, and is cited as near the Kildare and Dublin border, on the plains of Liffey. (The above extracted from the 'Book of Irish Families, great & small').

Genese

A family name found in Dublin city, given to be of Jewish heritage in at least one instance. (per 'OLochlainns journal of Irish Families').

Gennitt

Milesian Families finds the name in Dublin, of Norman origins.

Mac Geoghegan

Gegan, Gehegan, Gahagan, Geoghan

In the 17th century Geoghegan is found as a principal name of Kings County (Offaly), and in Westmeath, but the 1890's index gives the family mainly in Dublin and Galway.

(The above extracted from the 'Book of Irish Families, great & small').

George

Milesian Families finds the name in Dublin, of Norman origins. (no documentation given). Coldblow, at Donneybrook, was the home of Denis George who was Recorder of Dublin.

Mac Geraghty
Gerty, Jerety, Gerity, Gerrity, Garrity
By the 1890's the name was centered in Galway, Mayo and Dublin. (The above extracted from the 'Book of Irish Families, great & small').

Gernon
Gernan
Nicholas Gernon is found in St. Audeon's parish in the Dublin City Pipe Water Accounts of 1680.
Ball gives the names of Hanstede; Pippard; de Nottingham and Gernan at Lucan Parish in County Dublin.

Gerrard
Milesian Families finds the name in Dublin, of Norman origins.

Gerry
A family name found in the city of Dublin in the census of 1659.

Gibbons
The castle at Kilbride parish was leased to John Gibbons in 1537.

Gibbs
Milesian Families finds the name in Dublin, of English origins.

Gibner
Milesian Families finds the name in Dublin, of Welch origins. (no documentation given).

Gibney
Givney, Gibny
The 1890 birth index of Ireland finds the name centered in Dublin and Cavan at that time. (extracted from the 'Book of Irish Families, great & small').

Gibson
Gibsen, Giblin, Gipsey
Gibson is found in Dublin circa 1659. The majority of the Gibson name in Ireland are of Scottish descent. (The above extracted from the 'Book of Irish Families, great & small').
Thomas Gibson is found in St. Werburgh's parish in the Dublin City Pipe Water Accounts of 1680.

Giffard
Gifford
Mr. John Giffard was resident at Dundrum in Taney parish at the end of the 18th century.

Gilbert
Gilbert is a name given in Dublin city of Jewish heritage in at least one instance. The name is as well found in Dublin in the census of 1659 and in the 1890 birth index.
William Gilbert was tenant in Kill of the Grange parish in 1623. See introduction.

O' Gilbroin
O'Gilbroin is given on the borders of Dublin and Kildare in more ancient times.

Gilcolm
O'Hart gives the Donohoe and Gilcolm families as ancient chiefs of Dublin at Feltrim.

Mac Gilfoyle
Guilfoyle, Gilfoil, Powell
In modern times "Guilfoyle" etc.. is not a numerous name. It is given only in Dublin, with a total of 11 births in the 1890 index. The Mac prefix before the name had largely fallen into disuse by that time as well. (extracted from the 'Book of Irish Families, great & small').

Mc Gill
Gill, Macgill
The name of McGill is most often found in the province of Ulster in Ireland, and represents the shortened form of several different "Gil" names.
Gill is found most numerous in counties Dublin, Galway, Mayo and Longford in the 19th century. (extracted from the 'Book of Irish Families, great & small').
'Gill' is a surname found in Quaker records in Dublin city in the 18th century, assigned to one of the name who was an 'apothecary'.

Mac Gillamocholmog

Mac Gillamocholmog was the Irish chieftain who held so much of County Dublin before the coming of the 12th century Norman invasions. He is given as holding all of Fingal (the lands north of the River Liffey), as well as lands to the south. Kiltiernan and Glencullen were among his lands.

Mac Gillamocholmog held Newcastle parish as chief into the 13th century. This Irish chieftain was also granted lands at Esker parish after helping the Anglo-Norman forces rout the Danes.

Mac Gilligan
Magilligan, Galligan, Gillen

Note the place name of 'Magilligan's Strand' by Lough Foyle in northern Co. Derry. The 1890 index gives Gilligan a total of 32 births, coming primarily from Dublin. Some 26 of these births were from the provinces of Leinster and Connaught at that time. (The above extracted from the 'Book of Irish Families, great & small').

Gilpin

It is a surname found in Quaker records in Dublin city in the 18th century.

Giltrap
Gilthorpe, Gilstrap

A name not found in our older records to date, several families of the name are found in Dublin and surrounds in modern times. (extracted from the 'Book of Irish Families, great & small').

Gitt Elson

A family name found in Dublin city, given to be of Jewish heritage in at least one instance. (per 'OLochlainns journal of Irish Families').

Glascord

A family name found in the city of Dublin in the census of 1659.

O'Gleeson
Gleason, Glissane, O'glissane,

The family is found in Limerick, Dublin, Kilkenny and Cork. They held some lands in Tipperary, descending from the same ancestors as the O'Donegans, but they were subsequently lost with the coming of Cromwell. (The above extracted from the 'Book of Irish Families, great & small').

Mc Glory
Glorney, Mcgloyre, Mcclory

McGloyre was a principal name of the city of Dublin in the 17th century, and that name is taken to be a likely variant of McGlory. (extracted from the 'Book of Irish Families, great & small').

Glover

A family name found in the city of Dublin in the census of 1659. George Glover held lands in Kingstown in the 18th century. See introduction.

Glynn
Mcglynn, O'glynn, Glenn, Glenny,

When spelled with a "y" instead of an "e", as in Glynn, the name is most often located on the west coast of Ireland. (In Galway, Mayo, Clare and in Dublin). (The above extracted from the 'Book of Irish Families, great & small').

Godd

A family name found in Dublin city, given to be of Jewish heritage in at least one instance. (per 'OLochlainns journal of Irish Families').

Godiman
Goodiman Goodman

Early names at Newcastle parish after the 12th century invasions included Godiman; Carrick; and Russell.

Goff

The Goff family of Carrowroe Park, Co. Roscommon descend from early settlers of the name in Co. Dublin. (The above extracted from the 'Book of Irish Families, great & small').

It is a surname found in Quaker records in Dublin city in the 18th century.

Gold

Thomas Gold is found in St. Audeon's parish in the Dublin City Pipe Water Accounts of 1680.

Golding

The Golding family of Raheny, Co. Dublin, is noted among the minor gentry of the 17th century.

Goodman

An English family found settled in Dublin by at least the 17th century, where they held noted lands at that time.

Among the holders of land in Killiney parish in the 14th century and later were given: William Walsh alias McHowell; James Garvey; and the Goodman family. In the middle ages the lands of Loughlinstown belonged to the Talbots, being held under them by the Goodmans.

James Goodman is given at Rochestown in the middle of the 16th century. He was apparently the son of the owner of Loughlinstown. See introduction.

Goodrich

Milesian Families finds the name in Dublin, of English origins.

Goodwin

A family name given in Dublin in the Birth Index of 1890.

Goragh

A family name found in the city of Dublin in the census of 1659.

Gordon
Gorden

The name of Gordon is that of a settler family in Ulster, often of Scottish origins. The 1890 birth index finds the family most numerous in counties Antrim, Dublin and Down. (per the 'Book of Irish Families, great & small').

Gore

It is a surname found in Quaker records in Dublin city in the early 18th century.

Gorer

A family name found in Dublin city, given to be of Jewish heritage in at least one instance. (per 'OLochlainns journal of Irish Families').

O'Gorman
Mac Gorman, Bloomer, Gormon

The place name of Gormanstown or Gormanston, is common, for it can be found in Meath, Westmeath, Wicklow, Limerick, Tipperary and Dublin.

In the 17th century Gorman was a principal name in Clare, and found in Dublin. (The above extracted from the 'Book of Irish Families, great & small'). (See entry in 'The Families of Co. Clare').

O'Gormley
Gormaly, Gormooly, Gorman, Grimes

The O'Gormley family is found most anciently in Co. Donegal.

'Gormley' was a principal name of Dublin in 1659. Gormly and Gormely are also found in Dublin city at that time. (The above extracted from the 'Book of Irish Families, great & small').

Gothimer

A family name found in Dublin city, given to be of Jewish heritage in at least one instance. (per 'OLochlainns journal of Irish Families').

Gotler

A family name found in Dublin city, given to be of Jewish heritage in at least one instance. (per 'OLochlainns journal of Irish Families').

Gouge
Gough

A family name found in the city of Dublin in the census of 1659. (See Gough).

Gough
Goch Mac Geogh Goff Coch Mc Gue Gouge

Many of the name of Gough in Ireland are actually of Welsh origin. The name is found in Ireland as early as the 1200's, settled in Waterford and Dublin. In 1890 it is found in Dublin and Wexford. (The above extracted from the 'Book of Irish Families, great & small'). Note the spelling of Gouge found on the 1659 census, perhaps Gough in disguise.

O'Hart lists the 'Gough' family among the principal families to settle in Dublin subsequent to the 12th century invasions of Ireland.

Among the noted residents of Booterstown in the 18th century were included the names of Cooley; Doherty; Gough; O'Reilly; LaTouche; Doyne; Wight; Bradstreet; and Fitzgerald.

Before the Commonwealth the lands of Sutton were held by William Gough.

Goulbee
It is a surname found in Quaker records in Dublin city in the 18th century, where at least one of the name served as a 'weaver'.

Goulborne
A family name found in the city of Dublin in the census of 1659.

Gould
A family name found in Dublin City in the census of 1659.

Goulding
A family name found in Dublin in the birth index of 1890 as well as being listed in Milesian Families.

We find Walter Goulding with the lands of Kiltiernan parish. See introduction.

Gowen
Thomas Gowen is found in St. Werburgh's parish in the Dublin City Pipe Water Accounts of 1680.

Grace
A family name found in Dublin in the birth index of 1890. The family is also given as a principal one of Anglo-Norman descent, settling in Dublin City and County, according to Keatings 'History of Ireland'.

William Grace is found in St. Werburgh's parish in the Dublin City Pipe Water Accounts of 1680.

O' Grady
Graddy, Brady, Gready

The 1890 birth index gives O'Grady in Clare, Limerick, Dublin and Roscommon. (Extracted from the 'Book of Irish Families, great & small'). (See entry in 'The Families of Co. Clare').

Grafton
Milesian Families finds the name in Dublin, of English origins. (no documentation given).

Graham
Grahams

The name of Graham is generally assumed to be a Scottish name which settled in Ulster earlier than most. In more recent times the 1890 index finds the name in Antrim, Down and Dublin.

In the Irish Book of Arms the family of Graham of Drumgoon, of Ballinakill, Letterfrack, Co. Galway is given. (The above extracted from the 'Book of Irish Families, great & small').

Sir George Graham is found in St. John's parish in the Dublin City Pipe Water Accounts of 1680.

In the 17th century village at Rathfarnham we find: Burgoyne; Bishop; Wilks; and Graham.

At Saggart parish residents named Graham are noted in the History of County Dublin by Ball.

Mc Grane
A family name found in Dublin at the time of the Birth Index of 1890.

Grange
A family name found in Dublin at the time of the Birth Index of 1890.

Grattan
Gratan, Gratten, Macgretten

Our records show the name of Grattan in Tipperary, Dublin and Ulster. It is generally accepted as the name of settler origins in Ireland. Henry Grattan (d. 1820) was a noted politician in Ireland, and member of the Irish House of Lords in 1797.

According to "Keatings History" the name is that of a principal family of Dublin city or county, and of Anglo-Norman descent. (The above extracted from the 'Book of Irish Families, great & small').

The family is also found on the lands of Sutton, near Howth.

Graves
The family of Graves is found earliest in Offaly, Limerick and Dublin in Ireland. The census of 1659 finds the name in Dublin, Meath and Louth. (The above extracted from the 'Book of Irish Families, great & small').

Gray
Milesian Families finds the name in Dublin, of Scottish origins.

Graydon
A family name given in Dublin in the census of 1659..

Greeley
Milesian Families finds the name in Dublin, of English origins.

Green, Houneen
Huneen, O'houneen, Greene, O'honeen

By the end of the 19th century Green was the preferred spelling of the name with 105 births in Dublin, Antrim and Galway. 'Greene' had 47 births in Tipperary and Clare, and this family is most likely of older Irish origins.

In the 17th century 'Green' was found in Tipperary and Dublin, while 'Greene' was in Cork, Kildare, Kilkenny and Dublin.

Richard Greene of Cruagh is given in the introduction to this book.

The Irish Book of Arms gives several of the name. (extracted in part from the 'Book of Irish Families, great & small').

It is also a surname found in Quaker records in Dublin city in the late 18th century.

At Island Bridge we find the names of: Green in 1764; Pennefather in 1768; Keightly 1768; and Trail in 1799.

Greenhow
It is a surname found in Quaker records in Dublin city in the 18th century.

Gregory
Gregry, Gregorie

The Gregory name is found early in Dublin, but it is historically most often associated with Co. Kerry. In more modern times the name is found in Galway, and of that line was the famous Lady Gregory (d.1932). (The above extracted from the 'Book of Irish Families, great & small').

Grennan
De Grenan, O'grennan, Greenan

Families of the name of Grennan are found centered in Mayo and Dublin in the 19th century. The old Irish family of the name is to be found in Mayo, and those of County Dublin may be of Norman descent. (extracted from the 'Book of Irish Families, great & small').

Gressingham
One 'Mr. Gressingham' is found in St. Werburgh's parish in the Dublin City Pipe Water Accounts of 1680.

Grible

At Newcastle in 1614 among the first city officials were: Parsons; Rolles; Kenny; Frend; Davies; White; Burton; Grible; Bridges; Rutledge; and Lushe.

Grierson

See article in the "Irish Genealogist" entitled "King's Printers, Notes on the family of Grierson of Dublin." 2 (1953)

One George Grierson is given in Castlekelly townland in the 19th century. Grierson of Baldonell, Co. Dublin, is given in the Irish Book of Arms, (IGF edition).

Griffon
Griffen Grffin

Thomas Griffon is found in St. Werburgh's parish in the Dublin City Pipe Water Accounts of 1680. One Murtagh Griffin is found as a clerk of the common pleas in Dublin in 1700., and held lands in Kerry. See also 'Families of Co. Kerry, Ireland'.

Grogan
Grogane, Groggan, Grugane, Grugan,

By the time of the 19th century birth index Grogan is found centered in Dublin, Tipperary, Mayo and Clare. (The above extracted from the 'Book of Irish Families, great & small').

Thomas Grogan is found in St. Catherine's parish in the Dublin City Pipe Water Accounts of 1680.

Grolliax

A family name found in the city of Dublin in the census of 1659.

De Groot

A family name found in Dublin city, given to be of Jewish heritage in at least one instance. (per 'OLochlainns journal of Irish Families').

Grumby

It is a surname found in Quaker records in Dublin city in the late 17th century.

Gryffith   Griffith

Gryffith is a family name found in Dublin in the census of 1659. Note also spellings of Griffith, Griffitts, and Grifiths, etc..

It is a surname spelled as Griffitts found in Quaker records in Dublin city, in the 18th century.

Guilfoyle
Gilfoyle

A family name found in Dublin at the time of the Birth Index of 1890. It has been traditionally linked to the Union of Tulla in Ireland.

Mc Guinness
Magennis, Guinness, Mac Genis,

In more modern times "McGuinness" is given in 1890 in the counties of Dublin, Monaghan and Louth.   (Extracted from the 'Book of Irish Families').

Noted families at Killakee were those of Henry Joy; Guinness; St. Michael; and Mr. Lundy Foot.

(See major entry in 'The Families of Co. Kerry' as Genis, Ginnis, etc..)

Mac Guire
Maguire, Mcgwyer

One of the top 40 names in Ireland, MacGuire or Maguire is associated with Ulster and Fermanagh. The most prominent spelling of the name was Maguire in the 1890 index, found mainly in Fermanagh, Dublin, Cavan and Donegal. More on the name can be found in "Irish Chiefs and Leaders", by Rev. Paul Walsh. 1960. Dublin. (The above extracted from the 'Book of Irish Families, great & small').

Mc Guirk
Maguirke, Mcgurke,m'quirk,gurk

The 1890 birth index of Ireland gives the spelling of "McGuirk" with 17 recorded births of the name, mainly in Dublin. The name is traditionally associated with Ulster. (The above extracted from the 'Book of Irish Families, great & small').

Guiy
Guy

A family name found in the city of Dublin in the census of 1659. Note also the possible spelling as 'Guy' as found listed in Milesian Families as being in Dublin of English origins.

Gurling

Thomas Gurling is found in St. Werburgh's parish in the Dublin City Pipe Water Accounts of 1680.

Gutch

A family name found in the city of Dublin in the census of 1659.

Guthrie

Milesian Families finds the name in Dublin, of Scottish origins. (no documentation given).

Guy
Guiy

Milesian Families finds the name in Dublin, of English origins. (no documentation given). (see also Guiy as found in the census of 1659).

Gyles
Giles

A family name found in Dublin in the census of 1659.

Hackett
Machackett, Haket, Hakett

The Hackett family name is one which arrived with the Norman invasions in the latter half of the 12th century in Ireland.

The place names of Hacketstown, Hackettsland, and Ballyhackett are numerous, being found in Carlow, Derry, Dublin, Antrim, Cork and Waterford. Hackettsland in Dublin is named for the family so prominent in the 14th century in the south of Dublin.

In 'King James's Irish Army List, 1689' we find listed as a Dublin assessor, one Sir Thomas Hackett.

Despite the widespread areas the name has been found in earlier days, the 1890 birth index shows the name only in Tyrone, Dublin and Kilkenny.

In the Irish Book of Arms is given Hackett of Riverstown, Co. Tipperary, descended from Robert Hackett of English, Kings County (Offaly) (The above extracted from the 'Book of Irish Families, great & small').

Among the tenants at Tipperstown in the 13th and 14th centuries were the families of Whyte, Hacket, Wythir, Harold and Lagthenan. See introduction.

Among the early tenants of Taney parish were Edmund Hacket, Richard Chamberlain and John Locumbe in the 14th century. They are as well noted in Kilgobbin parish.

Ball gives that a castle stood on the lands of Sutton and it was held by the Hacket family near Howth (not Howth Castle however.)

Hadsor

Milesian Families finds the name in Dublin, of Norman origins. (no documentation given).

Hagan
Hagen

Thomas O'Hagan of Dublin was the Lord Chancellor of Ireland under Gladstone and was in 1870 in the peerage of the United Kingdom, and was created 'Baron O'Hagan'.

Haines
Haynes

Milesian Families finds the name in Dublin, of English origins.

McHale

Milesian Families finds the name in Dublin, of Norman origins.

Haliday
Halliday Holiday Aliday

Milesian Families finds the name in Dublin, of Norman origins.

Hall

Milesian Families finds the name in Dublin, of English origins. Names connected to Rathfarnham parish in the 14th and 15th centuries were Galvey; Hall; Cornwalsh; and Loftus.

Halley

Michael Halley is found in St. John's parish in the Dublin City Pipe Water Accounts of 1680.

Halligan
Hallighan, Hallaghan

A name traditionally linked to Armagh and Louth. The 1890 birth index finds the family most numerous in Roscommon, Dublin, Louth, Armagh and Mayo. (extracted from the 'Book of Irish Families, great & small').

Hallowel

Milesian Families finds the name in Dublin, of English origins.

Halpin
Halfpenny, Halpenny, Halpen

A name often linked to Dublin, the 1890 birth index finds the family name of Halpin most numerous in counties Dublin and Clare. Halfpenny is given in Co. Louth in that index. (per the 'Book of Irish Families, great & small').

Hamilton

Milesian Families finds the name in Dublin, of Scottish origins.

Although neglected in several other sources, O'Hart gives the family as a principal one settling in Dublin from the 12th to the 18th century.

Abbotstown was the home of the Hamilton family that held the title of HolmPatrick.

Hand

A family name found in Dublin at the time of the Birth Index of 1890.

Handcock
Hancock, Hand

The birth index of 1890 finds families of the separate name of Hand centered in Co. Dublin. (extracted from the 'Book of Irish Families, great & small').

Handcock is a surname found in Quaker records in Dublin city in the 18th century.

Among the owners of Knocklyon in the parish of Tallaght we find Handcock.

In the 15th century the Handcock family of Saggart parish, Co. Dublin is noted.

Handy

Milesian Families finds the name in Dublin, of English origins.

Hanes

Milesian Families finds the name in Dublin, of English origins. (no documentation given).

Hankes

It is a surname found in Quaker records in Dublin city in the late 17th century.

Hankshaw

A family name found in the city of Dublin in the census of 1659.

O'Hanlon
Hanlan, Hanlin, Handion, Hanlen

In the 1890 birth index "O'Hanlon" had 22 recorded births in its homeland of Armagh and in Co. Dublin. Hanlon, without the "O", had 95 births in Dublin, Kerry, Louth and Wexford. (The above extracted from the 'Book of Irish Families, great & small').

Hannigan
Hennigan, Hannagan

The 1890 birth index finds the family most numerous in counties Dublin, Waterford and Tyrone. (per the 'Book of Irish Families, great & small').

O'Hanraghty
Hanratty

In the 1890 index "Hanratty" was the preferred spelling of the name with some 30 births recorded in Louth, Armagh, Monaghan and Dublin. (The above extracted from the 'Book of Irish Families, great & small').

Hanstede

Ball gives the names of Hanstede; Pippard; de Nottingham; Gernan; Rokeby; and Fitzgerald at Lucan Parish in County Dublin.

Hanway

A family name found in the city of Dublin in the census of 1659.

O'Hara
Harah

By the time of the 1890 index, 105 O'Haras are found in Sligo, Dublin, and Antrim, and only 5 "Haras", all from Galway. (The above extracted from the 'Book of Irish Families, great & small').

Harborne
Harburne

A family name found in the city of Dublin in the census of 1659. William Harburne is found in St. Audeon's parish in the Dublin City Pipe Water Accounts of 1680.

One 'Mr. Harbourne' is found at Esker parish in the 17th century. See introduction.

Hard

Milesian Families finds the name in Dublin, of English origins. (no documentation given).

Harding

Milesian Families finds the name in Dublin, of English origins. The family is also centered in Dublin in the 1890 birth index. One 'Dr. Harding' is given at Kilgobbin. See introduction.

Hardy
Harty, Hardiman, Hard
We find families of the name in Dublin in 1659, and in Louth, Dublin and Tyrone in the 19th century. (The above extracted from the 'Book of Irish Families, great & small').

Harford
Hereford, Hertford
We find the name of Harford as a principal one of Dublin in the 17th century, and it is still centered there in the 19th century records at our disposal. The name is said by some to be of likely English origins, perhaps coming from the place name of Hereford etc..

Ball gives the name as one of Norse origins, and gives them as tall, fair complected, with bright blue eyes.

The 1890 birth index finds the family most numerous in Co. Dublin. (The above extracted from the 'Book of Irish Families, great & small').

Harington
Harrington
A family name found in the city of Dublin in the census of 1659.

Harkins
Harkin
While Harkin is sometimes found in England, in Ireland the name may stem from the older spelling of OhEarcain. In Milesian families the name is given in Dublin and Cork, arriving in 1171 from Wales. The family is more traditionally noted in Donegal as well. (The above extracted from the 'Book of Irish Families, great & small').

Harknett
Milesian Families finds the name in Dublin, of English origins.

Harman
Harmon
The Harman family is listed as part of the 'more recent nobility' by O'Hart where they are given as viscounts of Oxmantown or Ostmanstown in the city of Dublin.

Harmel
A family name found in Dublin city, given to be of Jewish heritage in at least one instance. (per 'OLochlainns journal of Irish Families').

Harnet
A family name found in the city of Dublin in the census of 1659.

Harold
Harrold, Haroid
Harold families in Ireland may trace their ancestry back to Dublin, where "Harolds Cross" is to be found. The Harold family of Harolds Grange were noted gentry in Co. Dublin into the 17th century at least. The children of one Walter Harold came to hold Kill Abbey some time after 1595, in Kill of the Grange parish. They were early owners of many lands, including those at Kilgobbin, Co. Dublin.

In the 14th and 15th century the Harold family is of note as Rathfarnham parish as well. The family is identified with many areas in Dublin, including Whitechurch parish. See introduction.

Among the tenants at Tipperstown in the 13th and 14th centuries were the families of Whyte, Hacket, Wythir, Harold and Lagthenan. The Harold clan is also found early at Templeogue.

An older form of the name is given to be Haroid, and is given as such in O'Harts work.

The Irish Book of Arms gives the family of Harold-Barry of Ballyvonare, Co. Cork. They were originally of Harolds Cross, Dublin and subsequently of Singland and Pennywell in Co. Limerick. (extracted from the 'Book of Irish Families, great & small').

Harper
Harpur, Harp, Harpor.
The Norman name of 'le Harpur', (the Harper), is found early in Irish records, dating from the 13th century or earlier in the province of Leinster. Harper was also the name of a ships captain sailing from Philadelphia to Dublin in 1752. (extracted from the 'Book of Irish Families, great & small').

Harpur
Harper
Mrs. Harpur is noted as resident at Castleknock parish. See introduction.

Harrington
Harroughten, Harington, Heraghty

The name of Harrington is of both English and Irish origins when found in Ireland. The family is found in Dublin for several centuries now, with the census of 1659 locating the family there at that time. Many of these are said to be of English origin.

Also given is one Sir Henry Harrington, who was knighted at Christ Church, Dublin, in 1574. (extracted from the 'Book of Irish Families, great & small').

Sir Henry Harrington is found at Grangegorman Parish. See introduction.

Harris
Harrihy

Families of the name of Harris are usually of foreign extraction in Ireland. Most were planter families of English heritage. The census of 1659 finds the name in Limerick, Dublin, Antrim and Cork. In more modern times the 1890 index finds the name in Dublin, Cork and Antrim. Harrihy has been given as a related spelling on occasion. (The above extracted from the 'Book of Irish Families, great & small').

One family of the name in Dublin City was of Jewish heritage, given in some sources as 'Harris of Germany'.

It is a surname found in Quaker records in Dublin city in the late 17th and 18th centuries, where the family is found as 'merchants'.

One 'Walter Harris' is found in St. Nicholas Parish 'Within the Walls', in the Dublin City Pipe Water Accounts of 1680.

Harrison
Harrison, Harisson, Harrisen, Harson

One of the top 30 most numerous names in England. The 1890 birth index finds the family most numerous in Antrim, Dublin and Down. (per the 'Book of Irish Families, great & small').

Harson
Harrison

A family name found in the city of Dublin in the census of 1659.

O'Hart
Harte, Hairt, Hart Hert

The O'Hart family is one of the noted "Four Tribes of Tara", along with O'Regan, O'Kelly and O'Connolly. These tribes of Tara are also described as princes of Bregia, and appear to have possessed territories near Tara in Meath, along with areas in Co. Dublin. They were known as "Lords of Teffia". (per Keatings 'History of Ireland' IGF edition).

"Hart" which had 64 births in Antrim, Dublin and Cork, in the 1890 index.

John O'Hart (1824-1870), wrote "Irish Pedigrees, the origin and stem of the Irish Nation", a tremendous genealogical compilation. (The above extracted from the 'Book of Irish Families, great & small').

John Hart is given in 1703 as of Blundelstown, Co. Dublin, as his forfeited estates were sold, according to a biography in King James' Irish Army List. The variant spelling of Hert is given therein as well.

Harte

In Kilmactalway parish we find the Harte family at Jordanstown.

O'Hartley
Hartley, Hartly

The Hartley family of Beech Park, Co. Dublin, is given in the Irish Book of Arms and may be of foreign origins. At least one undocumented source finds the family name in Dublin of English origins. (The above extracted from the 'Book of Irish Families, great & small').

William Hartley is found in St. Werburgh's parish in the Dublin City Pipe Water Accounts of 1680.

Hartney

A family name found in the city of Dublin in the census of 1659.

Hartpole

Sir T. Hartpole of Carlow is noted in the entry on Leixlip parish in the introduction to this book.

Harvey
Harvy, Hervey, Hervie, Harvey,
The Harvey family is given as settling in Ireland from England originally. The family is said to have joined Strongbow upon arrival here. The birth index of 1890 finds the family centered in Antrim, Dublin, Down and Donegal when spelled as Harvey. (The above extracted from the 'Book of Irish Families, great & small').

The census of 1659 finds the family in Dublin City spelled as 'Harvy'. Arthur Harvey is found in St. Audeon's parish in the Dublin City Pipe Water Accounts of 1680.

Haslam
Hasselham
A family name found in Dublin at the time of the Birth Index of 1890. (Note than 'Haslam' could appear in some records as a shortened form of 'Hasselham' which is found in the census of 1659.

Hasler
Hassler
At the close of the 18th century the principal families of Dalkey Parish were those of Sir John Hasler; Wm. Macartney; John Patrickson; and Charlotte Brooke.

Hasselham
A family name found in the city of Dublin in the census of 1659.

Hast
A family name found in the city of Dublin in the census of 1659.

Hatchell
John Hatchell was resident at Fortfield House on the lands of Kimmage in 1858. He was the grandfather of Mr. Louis Perrin-Hatchell who was resident in the early 20th century.

Hate
Milesian Families finds the name in Dublin, of Norman origins.

Hatfield
A family name found in the city of Dublin in the census of 1659.

Hatter
A family name found in the city of Dublin in the census of 1659.

Hatton
Haughton
Milesian Families finds the name in Dublin, of Norman origins. (no documentation given).

It is a surname found in Quaker records in Dublin city in the 18th century.

Haubois
Andrew Haubois is noted as an owner of a celebrated nursery near Island Bridge.

Haughton
Houghton Haghan Hotten Hatton
Most of the name of Haughton and Houghton in Ireland are of likely English extraction.

We find record of some of the name in Dublin and Cork in the 18th century, of English extraction. In the 17th century the family is found centered in Dublin and Wexford. (extracted from the 'Book of Irish Families, great & small').

In 1690-91 one Thomas Haghton is given in King James Irish Army List as clerk of the Crown and Peace of the County of Dublin.

It is also a surname found in Quaker records in Dublin city in the first half of the 18th century.

Haven
Milesian Families finds the name in Dublin, of English origins.

Haward
Howard Hayward
A family name found in Dublin in the census of 1659. (Note also the possible variant spellings of Hayward and Howard).

Hawkins

John and Joseph Hawkins appear in the rolls of the military in Ireland in the mid 17th century, and are listed as receiving lands in Ireland for their services.

John Hawkins, the Ulster King of Arms, is found at Ballydowd castle in the 18th century.

The Hawkins family of St. Fenton's, Co. Dublin are found in the Irish Book of Arms (IGF edition).

(The above extracted from the 'Book of Irish Families, great & small').

St. Fintans, near Howth, is given as the property of the Hawkings family. See introduction.

At Kilnamanagh the Talbot; Belgard; Parsons; Fitzwilliam; and Hawkins family are given of note.

Hawkshaw

John Hawkshaw is found in St. Michael's parish in the Dublin City Pipe Water Accounts of 1680.

Hayden
Haydon

The 1890 birth index finds the family most numerous in Dublin, Carlow and Tipperary. (extracted from the 'Book of Irish Families, great & small').

At least one undocumented source finds the family of English origins. Spelled as Haydon the family name is found in Dublin city in the 1659 census.

Hayes
O'hea, Heys, Hoy, Heas, O'hugh, Hays

There are several unrelated families of the Hayes name found in Ireland. Hayes is a common English name, and de la Haye is a Norman name found early in Ireland.

The 1890 birth index shows "Hay" as a name of Ulster, but as "Hayes" the name is more often found in Cork, Limerick, Tipperary, and Dublin, among others. (The above extracted from the 'Book of Irish Families, great & small').

It is a surname found in Quaker records in Dublin city in the 18th century as well.

O'Healy
O'hely, O'haly, O'healihy, Hally,

"Healy" was the preferred spelling of the name in the 1890's index, with some 291 births in Cork, Kerry, Dublin, Galway, Roscommon and Mayo. The name ranks among the top 50 most numerous in all of the country.

The Wallis-Healy family of Dublin is noted in O'Harts work. (The above extracted from the 'Book of Irish Families, great & small').

Heath

Robert Heath is found in St. Werburgh's parish in the Dublin City Pipe Water Accounts of 1680.

Heavisid

Noted names in 18th century Milltown, Co. Dublin, included: Mr. Heavisid; Classon; Burr; Hugh Johnson; Randall; Dogherty; Tomlinson; King; and Walcot.

Hellen

In 1777 Robert Hellen took residence at Barry House on the main road to Dublin. See introduction.

Hemphill

The Hemphill family of Springhill have been most associated with the city of Dublin in our records. (The above extracted from the 'Book of Irish Families, great & small').

Hemsworth

Henry Hemsworth is found in St. Werburgh's parish in the Dublin City Pipe Water Accounts of 1680.

Henderson

Milesian Families finds the name in Dublin, of Scottish origins. (no documentation given).

It is a surname found in Quaker records in Dublin city in the 18th century as well.

Hendrick
Mchendrick, Henrick

Hendrick or McHendrick is of Norse origins, meaning 'Henry'. In modern times the name has been found in Dublin. (The above extracted from the 'Book of Irish Families, great & small').

Henebry
Hynebry, Hanebry, Henneberry

Researchers have found reference to the family quite early in Dublin, and subsequently in Kilkenny and Waterford.

One original spelling of the name was found to be as de Hynteberge in Co. Dublin. Some of the name of Henneberry may have shortened the name to Henebry as well. (The above extracted from the 'Book of Irish Families, great & small').

O'Hennessy
Hensey, Henchy, Henesy, Hennesy,

O'Dugan mentions O'Hennesey, chief of "Galena Beg", now the parish of Gallen, in the barony of Gerrycastle, near the river Liffey on the Meath/ Dublin border. This branch apparently declines with the Norman invasions of the 12th century.

By the time of the 1890 birth index "Hennessy" is found in Cork, Limerick, Tipperary and Dublin.

(The above extracted from the 'Book of Irish Families, great & small').

McHenry, Mceniry
Maceninry, Mac Henry, O'henry,

Most of the above surname have changed the name to 'Henry' by now.

Some 'Henrys' may be of more recent arrival in Ireland, arriving with the Scottish and English settlers from the 17th century. These are assumed to be concentrated in Ulster and Dublin. (The above extracted from the 'Book of Irish Families, great & small').

Herbert
A Huguenot family of Ireland as given in some instances. The birth index of 1890 finds the family name centered in Dublin and Limerick. (The above extracted from the 'Book of Irish Families, great & small'). (See major entry in 'The Families of Co. Kerry').

Herman
A family name found in Dublin city, given to be of Jewish heritage in at least one instance. (per 'OLochlainns journal of Irish Families').

Hesse
A family name found in Dublin city, given to be of Jewish heritage in at least one instance. (per 'OLochlainns journal of Irish Families').

Hetherington
In 1641 Rathcoole was a stronghold of the Irish, supported by the Scurlocks and the Hetheringtons.

Hewetson
James Hewetson is found in St. Werburgh's parish in the Dublin City Pipe Water Accounts of 1680.

Hewitt Hewett
Hewet, Hewett, Hewetson, Hewison,

Hewitt families are generally assumed to be of English extraction when found in Ireland. Early records often find the family in Co. Cork in the 17th century, and subsequently in Dublin. (The above extracted from the 'Book of Irish Families, great & small').

Hewson
Col. John Hewson, once Governor of Dublin and past shoemaker in Westminster is found at Clonsilla parish in the 17th century.

Heynham
A family name found in the city of Dublin in the census of 1659.

Hiatt
Hyatt

Johnstown House at Cabinteely was occupied in 1778 by Mr. Love Hiatt and then by Mr. Williams.

O'Hickey
Hickie, Hicky

The Hickey family is given Dublin in the 1890 birth index (and elsewhere). (The above extracted from the 'Book of Irish Families, great & small').

Hicks
Milesian Families finds the name in Dublin, of English origins. (no documentation given).

Hickson
A family name found in Dublin City in the census of 1659.

Higby
Milesian Families finds the name in Dublin, of Welch origins. (no documentation given).

O'Higgin
Higgins, Hagans, Higgens, Higins,
Higgens may be of either Irish or English origins. The Irish likely descend from OhUigin.

By the close of the last century Higgins is given in Mayo, Galway, Dublin, and elsewhere. (The above extracted from the 'Book of Irish Families, great & small').

'Higgins' is also a surname found in Quaker records in Dublin city in the 18th century.

Hill
Hull
Families of the name of Hill in Ireland are often of English extraction. As expected the family is often found in Ulster and in Dublin, where so many settler families are found.

In 1641 George Hill occupied the lands of Simmonscourt. See introduction.

The 1890 birth index finds the family most numerous in Antrim, Dublin and Down. (The above extracted from the 'Book of Irish Families, great & small').

It is a surname found in Quaker records in Dublin city in the late 17th century.

Hilliard   Hylliard
Hillard, Hillyard, Hilyard
Most families of the name are found in Co. Dublin in more modern times, but official records also give the name in Co. Kerry at the turn of this century.

The 1890 birth index finds the family most numerous in Co. Dublin. (The above extracted from the 'Book of Irish Families, great & small').

Widow Hylliard, distiller, is found in St. Audeon's parish in the Dublin City Pipe Water Accounts of 1680.

Hilton
Milesian Families finds the name in Dublin, of English origins.

Hoadly
Milesian Families finds the name in Dublin, of Saxon origins.

Hoagman
A family name found in Dublin city, given to be of Jewish heritage in at least one instance. (per 'OLochlainns journal of Irish Families').

Hoare
Hore
A family name found in Dublin in the 1890 birth index. Philip Hore held an estate at Killsallaghan of some 1500 acres. See also Hore.

Hoban
Milesian Families finds the name in Dublin, of German origins. (no documentation given).

Hobson
It is a surname found in Quaker records in Dublin city in the early 18th century.

Hodges
A family name found in the city of Dublin in the census of 1659.

Hodgkins
A family name found in the city of Dublin in the census of 1659.

Hodser
A family name found in the city of Dublin in the census of 1659.

Hoey
O'heoghy
The 1890 birth index finds the family most numerous in counties Dublin and Louth. (The above extracted from the 'Book of Irish Families, great & small').

O'Hogan
Ogan, Hogin, Hogen, Hogane, Hogain
By the time of the 1890 index, Hogan was given in Tipperary, Dublin, Limerick, Clare, and Cork. (The above extracted from the 'Book of Irish Families, great & small').

Holden
A family name found in Dublin at the time of the Birth Index of 1890.

Holder
Patrick Holder is given at Kilmahuddrick parish in 1539.

Holford
A family name found in the city of Dublin in the census of 1659.

Holland
Hollande, Holohan, Mulholland

Moving into more modern times, the 1890 index shows the spelling of Holland found in Cork, Galway and Dublin. The name is also found in the index to Keatings History of Ireland.

John P. Holland was the inventor of the 'Submarine Torpedo Boat' and his obituary and portrait can be found in the Journal of the American Irish Historical Society, vol. 14. (extracted from the 'Book of Irish Families, great & small').

Hollaway
A name found in Dublin in the census of 1659. Note also the name of Alloway belonging to a Quaker, given as a merchant in Dublin in the 18th century.

Holliday
Haliday Holiday Alliday

Milesian Families finds the name in Dublin, of Norman origins. (no documentation given).

Hollywood
According to "Keatings History" the name is that of a principal family of Dublin city or county, and of Anglo-Norman descent. (The above extracted from the 'Book of Irish Families, great & small').

The census of 1659 finds the family name in Dublin as well. The Hollywoods of Artane held over 1,300 acres in the 17th century. Note the article on the "Hollywoods of Artane", in the "Reportorium Novum" 1 (2). 1956.

Holmes
Holme, Homes, Mac Combs, Mac

The name of Holmes and its various forms, may be of English or Scottish origin. It is usually assumed to be of Scots heritage in Ireland. This is confirmed by the 1890 birth index which gives Antrim as the principal location of the name, along with Dublin. (The above extracted from the 'Book of Irish Families, great & small').

Sampson Holmes is given at St. James and St. Jude parish. See introduction.

Holmpatrick
See introduction.

Holt
Not a common name in our records, 'Hoult' is found in Dublin City in the census of 1659, and is said to be of English origins.

Hone
We find Stephen Stock, Daniel Kinahan and Nathaniel Hone in the vicinity of Churchtown in Taney parish in the 18th century. See introduction.

Hood
Milesian Families finds the name in Dublin, of English origins. The lands of Robin Hood appear to have been the site of a well known house of entertainment in Drimnagh parish in the 18th century.

Hook
Hooke Hookes

The census of 1659 finds the family name in Dublin City. Some give the name as settling near that time in Dublin, being of English extraction.

The name of 'Hookes' is also found in Dublin city at that time.

Peter Hooke is found in St. Werburgh's parish in the Dublin City Pipe Water Accounts of 1680.

Hooker
A family name found in the city of Dublin in the census of 1659.

Hoop
It is a surname found in Quaker records in Dublin city in the first half of the 18th century.

Hopkins
Habbagan, Hobb, Hobkine

Hopkins is a well known English name, and some families in Ireland are descended from that line.

In the 17th century we find families of the name in Dublin, Westmeath and Kilkenny, and two centuries later the family is centered in Mayo and Dublin in the 1890 birth index. (The above extracted from the 'Book of Irish Families, great & small').

Hore

Hoar Hoare

Christopher Bassenet, John Brady, and John Hore, in 1561, are found leasing the lands of Kill of the Grange parish.

In 1561 we also find lands of Tipperstown leased to Bassenet, Brady and Hore. See introduction.

See also Hoar.

Horish

A family name given in Dublin in the census of 1659..

Horton

Horten

Of likely English origins, in Milesian families the name is found in Dublin and Wexford, arriving in 1666 from England. In the works of O'Brien published by the American Irish Historical Society, two of the name were found to be Irish. (extracted from the 'Book of Irish Families, great & small').

O' Houlihan

Holian, Holohan, Houlihan, Hulihan,

William Oullahan was a merchant in Dublin, (1781), and from his line, John in 1877 was living in Baltimore, Md.. The firm "Oullahan and Co." miners, in Stockton, California, stems from this line also. Family members were noted in O'Hart as having settled in New York and Washington D. C. as well. (The above extracted from the 'Book of Irish Families, great & small').

Hoult

Holt

Found in Dublin in 1659. See index.

How

Names connected to Rathfarnham parish in the 18th century were Palliser; O'Callaghan; Cramer; Coghill; Stannard; Fountain; Ward; Geering; How; Boyle; and Blackburn.

Howard

O'hure, O'hawrde, Hogart.

The census of 1659 shows the name in Tipperary, Cork and Dublin. In more modern times the name remains in Dublin and Cork, as evidenced by the 1890 birth index. (extracted from the 'Book of Irish Families, great & small').

McHowell

Among the holders of land in Killiney parish in the 14th century and later was given one William Walsh 'alias McHowell.'. In 1326 Peter Howell held lands at Murphystown. See introduction.

Names associated with the settlement of Balally in Taney parish were: de Walhope; Othyr; Howell; Taunton; Walsh in 1407 and Borr in the 17th century. It was given originally as a Danish settlement.

The Howell family are given as occupying the lands of Kilgobbin. See introduction.

Howlett

A family name found in Dublin at the time of the Birth Index of 1890.

Howse

Joseph Howse is found in St. Werburgh's parish in the Dublin City Pipe Water Accounts of 1680.

Howth

The name of Howth belongs to a principal family of Dublin city or county, and they are given in Keatings History as being of Anglo- Norman descent. Note also the place name of 'Howth'. (The above extracted from the 'Book of Irish Families, great & small').

Ball relates that William Howth slew John Gernon, the strongest man in Ulster in ancient times.

The fourth Earl of Howth (d.1909) was buried at Howth in the tomb of his ancestors. On his death the barony and earldom of Howth lapsed. The estates passed to his nephew Julian Gaisford of Offington, who assumed the name of St. Lawrence.

Huband

Milesian Families finds the name in Dublin, of Saxon origins.

Hudson

Hudson is a name of likely English origin when found in Ireland. It has been concentrated in two areas, namely that of Dublin, and in the province of Ulster.

In the census of 1659, the family is found in Carlow and Dublin, as well as in the Poll Money Ordinance Survey. The more modern 1890 birth index still found the name in Dublin. (The above extracted from the 'Book of Irish Families, great & small').

Hermitage, in Whitechurch parish, was home to the Hudson and Moore families.

At Damastown we find the Hudson family in the 1660's.

Huggard

Robert Huggard was 'Captain in Dublin' in 1674, as noted in 'Families of Co. Kerry, Ireland.'.

Hughes
Hughe, Hewson, Mackay, Maccoy,

By 1890 Hughes was in Armagh, Antrim and Dublin. (The above extracted from the 'Book of Irish Families, great & small').

Hughes is also given in Dublin in 1659, and Hughs is recorded in Dublin City at that time as well.

One source finds a family of the name settling here from Wales.

Humfrey
Humphry, Humphrey, Humphrys,

The birth index of 1890 finds the family centered in Armagh and Dublin. (The above extracted from the 'Book of Irish Families, great & small'). Note also the spelling of the name of Humphry, etc..).

Humphries
Humfrey Humphry

The census of 1659 finds the Humphries families in Dublin city. At least one family of the name is given to be of Jewish heritage there. Note also the spelling of the name of Humfrey.

Hunt
Le Hunt, Feeheny, Fey, Hunter, Hunte

Many of the name of Hunt settled in Ireland, coming from England originally. The census of 1659 finds the family in Limerick, Dublin and Kildare, and the 19th century birth index gives the family as centered in Mayo, Roscommon, Dublin and Waterford. (The above extracted from the 'Book of Irish Families, great & small').

Hunt is given as among the few names of importance in Taney parish in the mid 18th century.

The Hunts are given by Ball to be one of the families located in Mulhuddart parish from the 14th -16th centuries.

Huntington

Milesian Families finds the name in Dublin, of English origins. (no documentation given).

O' Hurley
Herlihy, Murily, Murhila, Hurly, De

In the 1890 index there were 134 "Hurley" births and 42 Herlihy births recorded. Herlihy was of Cork and Kerry. Hurley was of Cork, Waterford, Dublin and Galway. (The above extracted from the 'Book of Irish Families, great & small').

Hussey, O'hosey
Hussy, De Hose, De Houssaye

The Husseys are cited as a principal family of Anglo-Norman descent in the county and city of Dublin, as found in Keatings 'History'. They are also given as an English family in Dublin in the 17th century, where they held noted lands at that time.

The arms of Hussey of Rathkenny, Co. Meath are shown in the Irish Book of Arms. This family was granted lands in Galtrim, barony of Deene, Co. Meath and between Grange Gorman and the Liffey in Dublin, around the year 1200. (The above extracted from the 'Book of Irish Families, great & small'). (See entry in 'The Families of Co. Kerry').

Hutchison

Hutchinson

Hutchison is found in Dublin in the 1890 Birth Index, and 'Hutchinson' is recorded in Dublin at that time and in the Census of 1659.

It is also a surname found in Quaker records in Dublin city in the last half of the 17th century.

The Hutchinson family is given at Palmerston subsequent to the 17th century.

Hyde

Hide

We find Nicholas Hyde in a house at Lucan parish. See introduction. (See entry in 'The Families of Co. Cork').

Hyland

Hylan, Hiland, Hilan

The 1890 birth index finds the family name spelled as Hyland most numerous in Mayo, Dublin and Queens. (extracted from the 'Book of Irish Families, great & small').

Hyndeberge

See introduction page 19.

Hynes

Hines

A family name found in Dublin at the time of the Birth Index of 1890, and given as traditionally linked to the Unions of Bawnboy, Enniskillen, and Cork in Ireland at large. (See major entry in 'The Families of Co. Galway').

Immaulouz

The name of Immaulouz is noted at Killininny.

Ince

Robert Ince is found in St. Audeon's parish in the Dublin City Pipe Water Accounts of 1680.

Inglefield

It is a surname found in Quaker records in Dublin city in the last half of the 17th century.

Irwin

An Irwin is found occupying the lands of Fortick. See St. George Parish in the introduction to this work.

Isaacs

'Isaacs' and 'Isaac' are both family names found in Dublin city, given to be of Jewish heritage in at least one instance. (per 'OLochlainns journal of Irish Families').

Israel

A family name found in Dublin city, given to be of Jewish heritage in at least one instance. (per 'OLochlainns journal of Irish Families').

Ivers

Ivors, Iver, Mcivor, Ievers

The name of McIvor may have given rise to the name today found in Dublin and Louth. (McIomhair?)

The 1890 birth index finds the family most numerous in Dublin and Louth. (The above extracted from the 'Book of Irish Families, great & small').

Peter Iver is found in St. Audeon's parish in the Dublin City Pipe Water Accounts of 1680.

Ivory

One family is found settling in Waterford in the 1600's, and the name is subsequently found in Dublin. (per the 'Book of Irish Families').

Jackson

Jackson is one of the top 30 most numerous English surnames, and several of the name have arrived in Ireland over the centuries.

The birth index of 1890 finds the family most numerous in Antrim, Armagh, Dublin, Cork and Mayo. (The above extracted from the 'Book of Irish Families, great & small').

It is a surname found in Quaker records in Dublin city in the 18th and 19th centuries. Several of the name are given as 'weavers'.

At the close of the 18th century at Robuck, the following were noted in connection with villas built in that era: John Exshaw; James Potts; Alexander Jaffray; Dr. Robert Emmett; and Henry Jackson.

At Saggart parish residents named Jackson are noted in the History of County Dublin by Ball.

Jacob

One Wm. Jacob, of Cambridgeshire (d.1532) was founder of the line of the Jacob family of Bromley, England, and of the Jacob families of Co. Wexford, Queens County and Co. Dublin in Ireland. They family held lands in Dublin County in 1640.

The 1890 birth index finds the family most numerous in Co. Dublin. (per the 'Book of Irish Families, great & small').

Both 'Jacob' and 'Jacobs' are found as names of Jewish origin in Dublin.

Jaffray
Jaffrey

At the close of the 18th century at Robuck, the following were noted in connection with villas built in that era: John Exshaw; James Potts; Alexander Jaffray; Dr. Robert Emmett; and Henry Jackson.

Jameson

In the 19th century Mr. Andrew Jameson built a modern house near the site of the old Sutton house, near Howth.

Jamison
Jameson, Jamisone, Jamieson

Jamison is a well known Scottish name which settled in Ireland on more than one occasion.

Jamison is found in the 1890 birth index in Antrim and Down, while Jameson is found in Dublin at this date. (The above extracted from the 'Book of Irish Families, great & small'). See Jameson.

Jans

King James' Irish Army List gives one Capt. Christopher Jans, and in his brief biography is given one James Jans, of the Ward, in County Dublin, who was attainted in 1642.

We also find one Robert Jans, a merchant of Dublin in 1547 described as 'of Baggotrath'.

Jarvis
Jervice

Milesian Families finds the name in Dublin, of Scots origins. The spelling of Jervice is found in the 1659 census.

Jeffery
Jeffry Jaffery

Jeffery is a family name found in Dublin City in the 1659 census. It can also be found spelled as Jeffrey and Jaffray.

Jaffray is a surname found in Quaker records in Dublin city in the 18th century.

Jefford

A family name found in the city of Dublin in the census of 1659.

Jenkins

A family name given in Dublin in the 1890 birth index of Ireland.

Jenkinson

A family name found in Dublin at the time of the Birth Index of 1890.

Jennings
Jenings

The Irish Book of Arms gives Jenings of Ironpool, Co. Galway, who was then J. P. for the county and city of Dublin. They claimed descent from de Burgo, and their pedigree is given in O'Ferrals' Line Antiqua', down to 1709.

(The above extracted from the 'Book of Irish Families, great & small').

Jephson

John Jephson is noted in Finglas Parish. See introduction.

Jervice
Jarvis

A family name found in the city of Dublin in the census of 1659.

Joakes
Juckes

A family name found in the city of Dublin in the census of 1659. Edward Juckes is found in St. Catherine's parish in the Dublin City Pipe Water Accounts of 1680.

Joanes

A family name found in Dublin in the census of 1659.

Jocelyn

In the 18th century we find the families of Twigg, Stoyte, Jocelyn, and Sterne at the manor at Donneybrook. See introduction.

Joel

A family name found in Dublin city, given to be of Jewish heritage in at least one instance. (per 'OLochlainns journal of Irish Families').

John
Johns

We find the name of 'John' given in Dublin City in the census of 1659. We have one report of the surname of 'Johns' of Scottish heritage in Dublin as well. Milesian Families gives the name of 'St. John' in Dublin and Limerick of English origins, without substantiation.

Mr. Isaack Johns house is found in St. Werburgh's parish in the Dublin City Pipe Water Accounts of 1680.

Johnson
Johnston, Johnstone

Most of the name of Johnson in Ireland are of English or Scottish extraction. .

The name of Johnston, a separate Scottish name, is often interchanged and confused with Johnson.

The birth index of 1890 finds the family centered in Cork, Dublin and Antrim. (The above extracted from the 'Book of Irish Families, great & small').

It is a surname found in Quaker records in Dublin city in the 18th century.

Noted names in 18th century Milltown, Co. Dublin, included: Mr. Heavisid; Classon; Burr; Hugh Johnson; Randall; Dogherty; Tomlinson; King; and Walcot.

Kiltiernan is given as having fallen to the Johnson family as well.

Johnston
Johnstone

The Johnston family of Kilmore, Co. Armagh and of Blackhall, Co. Dublin are given to be of the same descent. Their common ancestor was William Johnston, an architect sent from Scotland to rebuild the destruction caused during the "rebellion of 1641".

The birth index of 1890 finds the family in Antrim, Down, Fermanagh, Armagh and Dublin when spelled as Johnston. (extracted from the 'Book of Irish Families, great & small').

It is a surname found in Quaker records in Dublin city in the late 17th century.

Jolley Jolly
Jolley, Joley, July, Joly, Jolliff

More than one family is said to have arrived from England here over time. In the 19th century we find the family centered in Dublin under the spellings of Jolley and Jolly. (extracted from the 'Book of Irish Families, great & small').

Jolliff

Milesian Families finds the name in Dublin, of English origins. (no documentation given).

Bloody Bridge.

Jones

The name is found in every county in Ireland in our records, and is often found in the city of Dublin.

With a grand total of 152 births being recorded in 1890, over half of the name are found in Dublin at that time.

The Jones family of Moolum, Co. Kilkenny are found in the IGF edition of the Irish Book of Arms. The latter family descends from Bryan Jones of Dublin, said to have come from an ancient family in Wales. He received a grant of lands from King James I in 1622.

John Jones was given as principal resident of the village of Tallaght in 1650.

After the Commonwealth, the lands of the Walsh family in Old Connaught parish passed to Henry Jones and then to John Baxter.

A publication for possible further research is "The Jones in Ireland", by Robert Leach, published in Yonkers, New York, in 1866. (The above extracted in part from the 'Book of Irish Families, great & small').

Mr. Owen Jones is found in St. Audeon's parish in the Dublin City Pipe Water Accounts of 1680.

We also find Scurlock and McDaniel at Newcastle parish giving place to Scarborough and Jones. See introduction.

In 1798 Arthur Orde and Thomas Jones kept a boarding school at Crumlin.

A publication for possible further research is "The Jones in Ireland", by Robert Leach, published in Yonkers, New York, in 1866.

At Island Bridge we find the names of: Jones in 1749; Green in 1764; Pennefather in 1768; Keightly 1768; and Trail in 1799.

Mac Jordan
Macjordan, Macsiurtan, Macshurton,

By the time of the 1890 birth index 'Jordan' was the main spelling of the name, with births recorded in Dublin, Mayo, Antrim and Galway. (The above extracted from the 'Book of Irish Families, great & small').

Jordan is as well recorded in Dublin and elsewhere in the census of 1659.

John Jordan occupied Tyrellstown in the 17th century.

Joy
Noted families at Killakee were those of Henry Joy; Guinness; St. Michael; and Mr. Lundy Foot.

Judah
A family name found in Dublin city, given to be of Jewish heritage in at least one instance. (per 'OLochlainns journal of Irish Families').

Judd
It is a surname found in Quaker records in Dublin city in the 18th century.

Judge
The 1890 birth index finds the family most numerous in Mayo, Dublin and Tyrone. (The above extracted from the 'Book of Irish Families, great & small').

Kane
Kain, Cain, Cahan, Cahane, Kaine,

'Kane' is listed in the 1890 birth index as being a name of Antrim, Londonderry and Dublin. (extracted from the 'Book of Irish Families, great & small').

Kaplan
A family name found in Dublin city, given to be of Jewish heritage in at least one instance. (per 'OLochlainns journal of Irish Families').

Kavanagh
Keevan, Cavanagh, Kavanaugh

The Kavanagh surname is the 53rd most popular name in Ireland. In 1890 O'Brien ranked among the top ten most numerous names in Dublin county. The family descends from the MacMurrough line, the first of the name being Donal Kavanagh, son of Dermot Mac - Murrough. Donals father, King of the Leinster, helped start the Norman invasions of the 12th century. (Through his daughter and Strongbow).

Dublin, Wexford and Wicklow were centers for the name in the 1890 index. (The above extracted from the 'Book of Irish Families, great & small').

Kay
A family name found in the city of Dublin in the census of 1659.

Keane   Kane   Cain
Kane, Cane, Cain, Kain, Cahan, Kean,

Among the 100 most numerous names in Ireland, 'Keane', 'Kane', 'Cahan', etc.. has several separate origins and these names have often been used interchangeably.

Spelled as 'Kane' the name is found centered in Antrim, Londonderry and Dublin in 1890.

The Keanes' of Beech Park, Co. Clare, descend from the family of Co. Derry. One of the name settled at Ballyvoe, near Ennis in the 1600's.

Keane is the most numerous spelling of all these names today. (The above extracted from the 'Book of Irish Families, great & small').

O' Kearney   Carney
Carney, Keherney, Mccarney,

In the 1890 index 'Kearney' was given in Dublin, Cork and Antrim with 3 times the population of 'Carney'. (The above extracted from the 'Book of Irish Families, great & small').

Richard Carney is found in St. Werburgh's parish in the Dublin City Pipe Water Accounts of 1680.

Kearns
A family name found in Dublin at the time of the Birth Index of 1890.

Kearogan
A family name found in Dublin as a principal name in the census of 1659.

Kearovan
A family name found as a principal name in Dublin in the census of 1659.

Keating
O'keating, Mackeating, Keeting

By the time of the 1890 birth index, 130 births were recorded in Cork, Kerry, Tipperary and Dublin.

The 'Keatinge' family is also given in 17th century Palmerston, and they were buried in the Palmerston churchyard.

Individuals of the name;
1777-maurice, Bath. (public Records Office, Dublin)
1765. Nicholas, Dublin.
1813. Patrick. Dublin.(p.r.o.). Starch Manufacturer
Keating Passengers:
John And Mary. Dublin To N. Y.,ship 'huntress', June 24, 1811.

(The above extracted from the 'Book of Irish Families, great & small').

Keavanagh
Cavanaugh Kavanaugh

A family name found as a principal name in Dublin in the census of 1659. See also various spellings.

O' Keefe
O'keeffe, Keefe, Keife, Kiefe

The O'Keefe family has always been identified with Cork. (see major entry in 'Families of Co. Cork, Ireland). 'O'Keeffe' was found in Limerick and Dublin in the 1890 index.   (The above extracted from the 'Book of Irish Families, great & small'). (See major entry in 'The Families of Co. Cork').

Keegan
Egan, Eagan, Eagen, Macegan,

The 1890 birth index finds the family most numerous in counties Dublin, Roscommon, Wicklow and Leitrim. (The above extracted from the 'Book of Irish Families, great & small').

Keeley
Keily Kealey Kelly Kellie Kealy

Both Keeley and Keely are found in Dublin in the 1890 Birth Index. These names may also be found spelled as Kelly, etc...

O' Keenan
Keon, Kinane, Kennan, Mackeenan,
'Keenan' is found in the 1890 birth index in Antrim, Monaghan, Dublin and Down.

A representative of the Keenans, chiefs of Fermanagh, Sir Patrick Joseph Keenan, of Delville, Glasnevin, Dublin, was born in 1826, and was the son of John Keenan, of Phibsborough, Dublin. (The above extracted from the 'Book of Irish Families, great & small').

Keightly
At Island Bridge we find the names of: Green in 1764; Pennefather in 1768; Keightly 1768; and Trail in 1799.

Kellett
A family name found in Dublin at the time of the Birth Index of 1890.

Kellie
We find Lt. John Kellie in Taney parish in 1757. See introduction.

O' Kelly
Keely, Queally, Keily, Kellye, Kehily,
Kelly is the 2nd most popular name in Ireland, and among the top 60 names in America. Several unrelated families of O'Kelly are found in Ireland, accounting for its great popularity. It was the 2nd most numerous name in Dublin County in the 1890 birth index.

One O'Kelly sept was found in Breagh (Meath and Dublin). (From the 'Book of Irish Families, great & small').

The O'Kelly family is one of the noted "Four Tribes of Tara", along with O'Hart, O'Regan and O'Connolly. These tribes of Tara are also described as princes of Bregia, and appear to have possessed territories near Tara in Meath, along with areas in Co. Dublin. They were known as "Lords of Teffia". (per Keatings 'History of Ireland' IGF edition).

It is also a surname found in Quaker records in Dublin city in the 18th century, where one of the name is given as a merchant. (See major entry in 'The Families of Co. Galway').

Mac Ken
Mackin
A family name found in Dublin at the time of the Birth Index of 1890.

Kendal
In 1326 John Kendal was tenant at the Priory at Dalkey.

Mac Kenna
Kennagh, Kenah, Ginnaw
The MacKenna surname is among the 100 most numerous names in Ireland. In ancient times, as well as today, the Mac Kennas are a family of the province of Ulster, in the north of Ireland.

Only 21 births of the name are given as 'Kenna' in the 1890 index, mainly in Dublin and Tipperary. (The above extracted from the 'Book of Irish Families, great & small').

Kennan
The Kennan family long held Diswellstown with the coming of the 18th century. See introduction.

O' Kennedy
Quenedy, Kenneday, Kenedie, Kenedy
Kennedy is one of the 20 most numerous surnames in Ireland, and among the 25 top surnames of Dublin County in the 1890 birth index.

By the time of the 1890 index we find Kennedy with some 446 births, mainly in Tipperary, Dublin and Antrim. (The above extracted from the 'Book of Irish Families, great & small').

Several of the name are given in King James's Irish Army List, including John, Thomas and Darby Kennedy of Dublin; William Kennedy of Finnstown, Co. Dublin (whose houses included that of Kennedy Lane in Dublin City).

Several estates are tied to the family name in 17th century Dublin. In the 18th century Belgard castle was held by the Dillion family, and subsequently by Dominick Trant and then Dr. Kennedy.

Sir John C. Kennedy is found seated at Johnstown House at Rathcoole parish. Sir Robert Kennedy was a much noted character at Esker parish.

O'Kenny, Kenney
Keaney, Keany, Kinney, Kinnie,

O'Kenny families may claim any one of several origins in Ireland. Most of the name are considered to be of true Irish origins. (See major entry in 'The Families of Co. Galway').

Among the 80 most numerous names in all of Ireland, most originally hailed from Galway, Roscommon (and Dublin city). It remains so to this day. (The above extracted from the 'Book of Irish Families, great & small').

At Newcastle in 1614 among the first city officials were: Parsons; Rolles; Kenny; Frend; Davies; White; Burton; Grible; Bridges; Rutledge; and Lushe.

Kent

Early reference to the name is found near Dublin, where Kent of Daneston was a prominent force. (The above extracted from the 'Book of Irish Families, great & small').

Mc Kenzie
Mc Kenzy

Found in Dublin in the birth index of 1890, of likely Scottish origins.

Mac Keogh
Kehoe, Keoghe, Keogh, M'keo, Keough

The MacKeoghs are found in various locations in Ireland today. By the time of the 1890 index three areas are identified with three spellings of the name. McKeough had 13 births in Westmeath, Keogh had 96 births mainly in Dublin, and Kehoe had 51 births in Wexford.

The most noted family is found in Leinster. The MacKeoghs as chief bards were present at the inauguration of the MacMurrough as Kings of Leinster. (The above extracted from the 'Book of Irish Families, great & small').

In 1784 Mt. Jerome was purchased by John Keogh (d.1817), who was an early leader of Catholic emancipation.

Kerdiff

Walter Kerdiff is noted in the 14th century at Castleknock parish. In the 16th century another Walter Kerdiff is given as the chief resident of Finglas parish.

Kerke
Kirke Kirk

A family name found in the city of Dublin in the census of 1659.

Mc Kernan
Kernahan, Kiernan, Mc Kern

In the 17th century, 'Kernan' was a principal name in Dublin city, also found in Longford and Westmeath. The 1890 birth index records 12 births, all in Ulster. (The above extracted from the 'Book of Irish Families, great & small').

Kerris

A family name found in Dublin in the census of 1659.

Kett

A family name found in the city of Dublin in the census of 1659.

Kettle

A name we have found in Dublin and Louth.

Mac Key
Mackie Mac Kie Mackee

A family name found in Dublin at the time of the Birth Index of 1890.

Mc Kibbons
Mc Kibben, Mckibbin, O'kibbon

One family of the name given in Dublin was said to be of Scots origins. (The above extracted from the 'Book of Irish Families, great & small').

Kickham

Some of the Kickam family name are found in Dublin City in the census of 1659. (The above extracted from the 'Book of Irish Families, great & small').

Kidd
Kid

Families of the name of Kidd in Ireland are generally assumed to be of Scottish or English extraction. As would be expected, the name is one of Ulster and the surrounds of Dublin. The 1890 birth index finds the family most numerous in counties Antrim, Armagh and Dublin. (The above extracted from the 'Book of Irish Families, great & small').

Kiely
Keily, Kieley, Keely, Kealey, Kealy,
The spelling of Keeley, in 1890, is found in Dublin, Wicklow and Galway. (The above extracted from the 'Book of Irish Families, great & small').

O' Kieran
Kearon, Kerrane, Kearns, Kerin, Keerin,
The 1890 birth index finds the family name of Kearns most numerous in Dublin and Mayo. (extracted from the 'Book of Irish Families, great & small').

McKiernan
Mac Ternan, Tiernan, Mackiernan,
Several unrelated families adopted this Irish name in days past.
Both O'Kernan and Mac Kernan were principal names of Fermanagh in 1659, and the Kernan spelling was prominent in the city of Dublin at that date.
(The above extracted from the 'Book of Irish Families, great & small').

Kilmore
In the 14th century we find John Mynagh, Robert Serjeant, and Roger Kilmore at Simmonscourt. See introduction.

Kinahan
Kinahane Kinaghan
A family name found in Dublin at the time of the Birth Index of 1890. We find Stephen Stock, Daniel Kinahan and Nathaniel Hone in the vicinity of Churchtown in Taney parish in the 18th century. See introduction.

King
Conry, Conroy, Mcaree, Gilroy,
It is one of the 100 most popular names found in Ireland. Many of the name are of foreign origins. Several old Irish families translated their old Gaelic names into "King" as well.
'George King' is given in King James Irish Army List, proprietor of the town and manor of Clontarf.
The King family is found in Dublin, Galway, Antrim, Mayo and Limerick in the 1890 birth index, with 203 births of the name at that time. (The above extracted from the 'Book of Irish Families, great & small').
It is a surname found in Quaker records in Dublin city in the first half of the 18th century.
Noted names in 18th century Milltown, Co. Dublin, included: Mr. Heavisid; Classon; Burr; Hugh Johnson; Randall; Dogherty; Tomlinson; King; and Walcot.
The lands of Tynon in Tallaght parish were anciently held by O'Mothan and we find Loftus and one Barnaby Relly there in the 17th century.

Kingsbury
One member reports that the family tree for the Kingsbury family of Dublin is given in the "Swanzy Notebooks" in the Library of the Representative Church Body, in Dublin.

Kingsmill
The Kingsmill family of Hermitage Park, Co. Dublin are given in the Irish Book of Arms. (extracted from the 'Book of Irish Families, great & small').

Kingston
Kingstone
The name, as it sounds, is of English extraction. The 1890 birth index finds the family most numerous in Cork with 37 recorded births, and in Dublin, with 3 recorded births. (per the 'Book of Irish Families, great & small').

Kinsella
Kinsellagh, Kinsela, Kinchella,

Kinsella families descend from the noted Dermot MacMurrough, the 12th century King of Leinster who helped initiate the Anglo-Norman invasions of Ireland. The Kavanaghs who descend from the same line, along with Kinsella, represent two Irish surnames which do not have the 'O' or 'Mac' prefix in front of their names. This is rare, inasmuch most Irish family names were preceded by those prefix's early in history.

By the time of the 1890 birth index "Kinsella" is found with 81 births in Dublin, Wexford, Wicklow and Kildare. (The above extracted from the 'Book of Irish Families, great & small').

Kirkpatrick

About 1773 Drumcondra House in Clonturk Parish, was leased to Alexander Kirkpatrick, a leading citizen of Dublin.

O' Kirwan
Kerovan, Kyrvan, Kerwan, Kirwin

By the time of the 1890 birth index of Ireland, 59 births were recorded in Dublin, Wexford and Tipperary. It is strange to note that the name was not found in Galway in that index. (The above extracted from the 'Book of Irish Families, great & small'). (See major entry in 'The Families of Co. Galway').

Kithinyman

A family name found in the city of Dublin in the census of 1659.

McKnight
Mckneight, Mac Aveely, Fitzsimons,

Families of the name of Knight may be of Scots, English or Irish origins.

The 1890 birth index finds McKnight centered in Antrim and Down, and Knight is found in scattered locations at that time. In the 17th century we find the name in Roscommon, Dublin and Kerry. (The above extracted from the 'Book of Irish Families, great & small').

Nicholas Knight is found in St. Nicholas Parish 'Within the Walls', in the Dublin City Pipe Water Accounts of 1680.

Knott
Nott, Knot

"Knot" families are found in the city of Dublin in the 17th century, others of the name are found from time to time in scattered locations in Ireland. Originally the name of Nott was believed to have come from separate origins, and both are believed to have arrived in Ireland after the 12th century Norman invasions. (The above extracted from the 'Book of Irish Families, great & small').

Knowles
Newell, Knowls, Knowels, Knowle,

The name of Knowles is most likely of English extraction when found in Ireland. Spelled as Knowles the name is found in County Cork in the 1659 Census, and in Dublin and Antrim in the more modern 1890 index. (The above extracted from the 'Book of Irish Families, great & small').

Knox

Knox is the name of a settler family from Scotland often found concentrated in Ulster and Dublin. (The above extracted from the 'Book of Irish Families, great & small').

It is also a surname found in Quaker records in Dublin city in the late 17th century.

La Touche

Although not listed in several other sources, O'Hart gives the family as a principal one settling in Dublin from the 12th to the 18th century.

Among the noted residents of Booterstown in the 18th century were included the names of Cooley; Doherty; Gough; O'Reilly; LaTouche; Doyne; Wight; Bradstreet; and Fitzgerald.

Marlay House, in Whitechurch Parish, was the seat of the La Touche family, later owned by R. Tedcastle. The family is also noted in Whitechurch parish.

Lacey, De Lacy
Lacy, Leash, De Lees, Lacie, O'lacy, Lacye

With the coming of the 12th century invasion of Ireland, De Lacy and his followers came to hold title to most of the county of Dublin.

The name is early associated with Donneybrook in the person of Walter de Lacy, the brother of the Earl of Ulster.

In the 1890 birth index both "Lacy" and "Lacey" are found in Wexford, Dublin and Galway.

"The Roll of the House of Lacy" by E. de Lacy-Bellingarri, was published in Baltimore in 1928. (The above extracted from the 'Book of Irish Families, great & small').

Lagthenan
Among the tenants at Tipperstown in the 13th and 14th centuries were the families of Whyte, Hacket, Wythir, Harold and Lagthenan. See introduction.

Lahiff
A family name found in Dublin at the time of the Birth Index of 1890.

Laird
Milesian Families finds the name in Dublin, of Scottish origins. (no documentation given).

O'Lalor
Lalor, O'lalor, Lawler, Lawlor

In ancient times they held extensive lands in Leix. One principal seat of the family name was at Disert, near the rock of Dunamase. From here a branch of the family settled in Tipperary. A branch of this line is found in the Irish Book of Arms.

In more modern times the name is found in Dublin, Leix, Wicklow and Wexford in the 1890 index. (The above extracted from the 'Book of Irish Families, great & small').

Lawler is found in Dublin in both the 1659 and 1890 records, and is spelled as Lawlor and Lalor. (see also Lalor)

One of the name at Kingstown was noted for frequently swimming from Dunleary to Howth in 1760.

Subsequent to the 17th century rebellions we find the names of Lawlor; Leedom; and Walsh in Rathcoole parish, Co. Dublin.

Lamb
The names of Lamb and Lambe are found in Dublin in the 1890 Birth Index. At least some of the name are of English extraction.

Lambert
Lambart, Lamberton

Lambert is considered traditionally to be a name of English extraction when found in Ireland. The census of 1659 finds the name in Dublin City and county spelled as Lambart.

John Lambert is found in Killiney parish occupying the former house of the Goodman family there. See introduction.

In the 19th century the name is found centered in Wexford and Dublin. (The above extracted from the 'Book of Irish Families, great & small').

Landy
Landa, Landers, Lawndy, Laundy, De

The Landy family is traditionally linked to counties Kilkenny and Tipperary earliest in Ireland. At the time of the census of 1659 we find the name under various spellings, including that of Laundy, centered in the barony of Balrothy in County Dublin. (The above extracted from the 'Book of Irish Families, great & small').

Lane

A family name found in Dublin in the census of 1659, and fairly widespread in Ireland as a whole. Generally given to be a name of English origins in Ireland. (See major entry in 'The Families of Co. Cork').

Langdale

A family name found in the city of Dublin in the census of 1659.

Langham

John Langham is found in St. Nicholas Parish 'Within the Walls', in the Dublin City Pipe Water Accounts of 1680.

Langtry

Milesian Families finds the name in Dublin, of Norman origins. (no documentation given).

Lapham

It is a surname found in Quaker records in Dublin city in the 18th century.

Larkin

O'lorcain, O'lorcan, Lorkan

In the 1890 index Larkin is found with 85 births in Dublin, Armagh, Galway and Tipperary. In the 1659 census "Larkin" was found in Kings (Co. Offaly), and "Larkan" was a principal name of Louth among other areas, and that spelling was found in Dublin, too. (The above extracted from the 'Book of Irish Families, great & small').

Lasch

A family name found in Dublin city, given to be of Jewish heritage in at least one instance. (per 'OLochlainns journal of Irish Families').

Latimer

Lattimer

Milesian Families finds the name in Dublin, of Norman origins. (no documentation given). Also found in the birth index of 1890 in Dublin.

Mac Laughlin

Macloughlin, Macgloughlin, Melaghlin,

McLaughlin was the preferred spelling of the name in 1891, with some 191 births recorded mainly in Antrim, Donegal, Londonderry, Tyrone and Dublin. McLoughlin had 170 births recorded in various locations.

"The MacLaughlins or Clan Owen", was published by T. P. Brown in Boston, in 1879. (The above extracted from the 'Book of Irish Families, great & small').

Laundy

A family name found in Dublin as a principal name in the census of 1659.

Laurence

Lawrence

A family name given in Dublin in the Birth Index of 1890. See St. Lawrence.

Lavelle

Milesian Families finds the name in Dublin, of Norman origins. (no documentation given).

Law

Note the family tree of the Law family of Dublin as given in the "Journal of the Association for the Preservation of Memorials for the Dead", 11, (1921+).

Lawces

A family name found in Dublin as a principal name in the census of 1659.

Lawless
Lawles, Outlaw, Outlawe, Laweles, Labhles

Families of the name of Lawless in Ireland are said to have taken their name from the English word of 'laghles' or Outlawe. In 1312 Richard Lawless was Mayor of Dublin and at about that time one Hugh Lawless is found negotiating with the 'Irishry' of the Pale, according to King James Irish Army List, under the entry of Capt. Walter Lawless which runs several pages.

The name is found several times after the 12th century Norman invasions of Ireland in Dublin, Galway and Mayo.

The Archbolds are in Bray in the 14th century, and along with the Lawless family were quite prominent.

The lands of Rochestown may have been transferred to Matthew Birsell and Thomas Lawless in 1563. The Lawless family was replaced by the Walsh family at Rathmichael in the 15th century.

The census of 1659 finds the family in Kilkenny and Dublin, and it is in Dublin where the name is most prominent today. Among the spellings of the name at that time are Lawles and Lawlis, both found in Dublin.

"Honest Jack" Lawless, b. 1772, was a noted politician of the Dublin family of the name. John Lawless was of Shank Hill, Co. Dublin. (Much of the above is extracted from the 'Book of Irish Families, great & small').

The family is given as a principal one of Anglo-Norman descent, settling in Dublin City and County, according to Keatings 'History'. Note the article on the "Lawless Family" as found in the "Reportorium Novum", 1 (2), 1956.

John Lawless and the Ussher family are given as farming the lands of Irishtown prior to 1642.

Lawrence
Lawrance Laurance
See 'St. Lawrence'.

Lawrenson
See introduction.

Lawson
A family name given in Dublin in the Birth Index of 1890. It is also a surname found in Quaker records in Dublin city in the 18th century, where one of the name is found as a 'cooper'.

Layfield
Lewis Layfield, the Dublin actor, is noted in Finglas Parish. See introduction.

Lazarus
The family names of Lazarus and Lazarus of Birmingham are given in Dublin city of Jewish heritage.

Le Brun
Basset, of the great Norman family, and le Brun, were two of the families noted in the 13th century at Roebuck, Co. Dublin. See introduction.

Le Fevre
Nicholas Le Fevre is found at Stillorgan House after 1789. See introduction.

Lea
Lee
A family name found in Dublin in the census of 1659. In the town of Howth we find Thomas Lea as a tituladoe.

Leacy
Lacy Lucy
A family name given in Dublin in the 1890 birth index of Ireland, also found in Wexford and Galway at that time, given to be a traditional family name of the Union of New Ross in Ireland at large.

Leake
A family name found in Dublin in the census of 1659. Nathanial Leeke occupied a house at Diswellstown in Castleknock parish. See introduction.

Lecch
Leech
A family name found in the city of Dublin in the census of 1659.

Lecchfield
Leechfield
A family name found in the city of Dublin in the census of 1659.

Lecora

A family name found in the city of Dublin in the census of 1659.

Ledwidge

Ledwich, Ledwith

Families of the name are generally given as settling in Meath around the time of the 12th century Norman invasions of Ireland, and subsequently they were prominent in Westmeath in the 14th century. William Ledwidge, lending some strength to the argument for German origins perhaps, was an opera singer born in Dublin who changed his name to Ludwig!

Ledwich is a variant spelling of the name and visitors to Dublin will note the Ledwich Medical School, named after Thomas Ledwich (d.1858).

The 1890 birth index finds the name of Ledwith most numerous in Co. Dublin. (The above extracted from the 'Book of Irish Families, great & small').

Ledwith

Ledwidge Ledwitch

A family name found in Dublin at the time of the Birth Index of 1890. Note also the name of 'Ledwidge'.

O' Lee

Lea, Maclee, Macalea, Mclee, O'lee, Lea

Families of the surname of "Lee" in Ireland may stem from one of several origins. A common name in England, some are originally from there. Lee is also an old Irish family name, stemming from families of O'Lee and MacLee. In Dublin City the name of Lee is also on record as a settler name of Jewish origins.

In the 1890 index "Lee" is found mainly in Antrim, Dublin, Galway and Limerick with some 120 births given.

In 1659 the spelling of "Lea" was common, found in Dublin and elsewhere. (The above extracted from the 'Book of Irish Families, great & small').

Leech

Leach, Mac An Leagha

Families of the name of Leech in Ireland are generally of Scottish origins.

We read of Richard Leech who was murdered at Churchtown in Taney parish during the 17th century rebellion.

The birth index of 1890 finds the family centered in Dublin. (per the 'Book of Irish Families, great & small').

Leedom

Subsequent to the 17th century rebellions we find the names of Wharton; Chambers; Willion; Barry; Robinson; Moses; Reyly; Lovelace; Eaton; Murphy; Lawlor; Leedom; and Walsh in Rathcoole parish, Co. Dublin.

Leeson

Leason

A fairly rare name in Ireland, some Leeson families had arrived in Ireland in the 17th century, coming from England. Others may be more properly of the "Gleason" or "O'Lyshane" families of old Ireland. In modern times the name is often connected to the city of Dublin. Leeson Street in Dublin was named after the Earl of Milltown. (The above extracted from the 'Book of Irish Families, great & small').

Note that Joseph Leeson of Stephens Green, Dublin is given in the Irish Book of Arms.

Thomas Leeson is found in St. John's parish in the Dublin City Pipe Water Accounts of 1680.

The Leeson family held Milltown, Co. Dublin in the 18th century.

The family is listed as part of the 'more recent nobility' by O'Hart where they are given as earls of Milltown, Co. Dublin.

At the time of the Commonwealth survey we find Mr. Munn in possession of a stone house subsequently held by Mr. Leeson.

Lefroy

Milesian Families finds the name in Dublin, of Flemmish origins. (no documentation given).

St Leger
Milesian Families finds the name in Dublin, of Norman origins.

Lehman
A family name found in Dublin city, given to be of Jewish heritage in at least one instance. (per 'OLochlainns journal of Irish Families').

Leischman
A family name found in Dublin city, given to be of Jewish heritage in at least one instance. (per 'OLochlainns journal of Irish Families').

Lely
Lally
Edward Lely is given in Finglas parish. See introduction.

Lemon
Milesian Families finds the name in Dublin, of English origins. (no documentation given). The name of 'Lemond' is found in the census of 1659 however, and it is possible that these names have been mistakenly used for each other in the past. Note also the spelling of Lehman, of presumably separate origins.

Lemond
A family name found in the city of Dublin in the census of 1659.

O' Lennon
Linnane, O'lennan
The history of the name can be difficult to trace because several families have changed their name to Lennon. This is further complicated by English settlers of the name found in Ireland.
Lennane or Linane is one Irish family that has been changed into Lennon.
In 1890, 103 births of Lennon were given in Dublin and Armagh.
In 1659 Lennan was a principal name of Dublin and in Louth. (The above extracted from the 'Book of Irish Families, great & small').

Lentaigne
Lentaigne of Tallaght is given in the Irish Book of Arms (IGF edition), and the name is found of 'ancient Norman descent'.
Milesian Families finds the name in Dublin, also of Norman origins.

Leonard
Lenard
Most of the name in Ireland are surely of English origins.
The 1890 birth index finds the family most numerous in Dublin, Sligo and Cork. (The above extracted from the 'Book of Irish Families, great & small').

Lesaw
A family name found in the city of Dublin in the census of 1659.

Leuett   Levitt
Levett
Leuett is a family name found in the city of Dublin in the census of 1659. It may likely be a misspelling of Levitt, etc..

Levenston
A family name found in Dublin city, given to be of Jewish heritage in at least one instance. (per 'OLochlainns journal of Irish Families').

Levi
A family name found in Dublin city, given to be of Jewish heritage in at least one instance. (per 'OLochlainns journal of Irish Families').

Levingston
A family name found in Dublin city, given to be of Jewish heritage in at least one instance. (per 'OLochlainns journal of Irish Families').

Lewis
Louis
The Lewis family of Inniskeen, Co. Monaghan and of Seatown, Co. Dublin are of the same descent and are given in the Irish Book of Arms.
The birth index of 1890 finds the family centered in Dublin, Antrim, Cork and Tipperary. (per the 'Book of Irish Families, great & small').
One settler family is also on record in Dublin, being of Jewish heritage.
Walter Lewis is found in St. Werburgh's parish in the Dublin City Pipe Water Accounts of 1680.

Lightburne
After the 17th century restoration we find one 'Dr. Lightburne' at Brennanstown. See introduction.

Lightfoot
In 1664 Thomas Lightfoot was rated for two hearths near Howth.

Lincoln
Michael Lincoln is found in St. Michael's parish in the Dublin City Pipe Water Accounts of 1680.

Lindley
It is a surname found in Quaker records in Dublin city in the early 18th century, where one of the name is listed as a 'smith' (occupation).

Linegar
At the beginning of the 18th century Dunbro was occupied by John Linegar, a citizen of Dublin.

Linkfield
John Linkfield, a distiller, is found in St. Catherine's parish in the Dublin City Pipe Water Accounts of 1680.

Linton
Milesian Families finds the name in Dublin, of Scottish origins. (no documentation given).

Little
Lyttle Littell
The 1890 birth index finds the family most numerous in counties Antrim, Dublin and Fermanagh. (per the 'Book of Irish Families, great & small').

The name is found centered in Dublin City in the census of 1659 spelled as Little. Families of the name of Littell are also found in Dublin, said to be of Scots heritage in one instance.

Litton
Litten
The Litton Family of Ardavilling, Co. Cork, descend from Thomas Litton of Dublin, b. 1657, and they are given in the Irish Book of Arms. (The above extracted from the 'Book of Irish Families, great & small').

In 1760 we find the obituary of Mr. William Litton, a silk weaver, at Dundrum.

Livinglyhurst
One of the principal residents at Bullock at the time of the 17th century Restoration was Mr. Kenelm Livinglyhurst (d.1685).

Livingston
Livingstone, Levingston
Several of the name are found settled in Dublin as well as in Ulster. The name is said to sometimes be found as Levingston(e). The 1890 birth index finds the family most numerous in Armagh, Antrim and Dublin. (per the 'Book of Irish Families, great & small').

Lloyd
Found in the census of 1659 in Dublin. Rees Lloyd is found in St. Werburgh's parish in the Dublin City Pipe Water Accounts of 1680..

Lockard
Lockhart
A family name found in the city of Dublin in the census of 1659.

Locke
Lock
A family name found in the city of Dublin in the census of 1659. The Locke family of Colmanstown and Athgoe were of some note in Dublin county at that time. They were of note at Newcastle parish from the 16th century.

Lockwood
The Seven farms in Glasnevin parish, went to Thomas Lockwood and Richard Fagan. See introduction.

Locumbe
Richard Locumbe, an Englishman, is given as tenant in Stillorgan parish in the 15th century. See introduction.

Among the early tenants of Taney parish were Edmund Hacket, Richard Chamberlain and John Locumbe in the 14th century.

Loftus
Loftis, Loughnane

At the beginning of the 13th century, we read in King James Irish Army List of one Ulfran de Barneville, who obtained estates in 'the Vale of Dublin', which were held by the family until the reign of James I, when they were granted to James Loftus.

Milltown, Co. Dublin was held by the Brigg family in the 14th century, and by the Loftus family in 1641, and at that time John Bacon was principal resident there. Adam Loftus also came to hold lands in 1641 at Kilgobbin.

Names connected to Rathfarnham parish in the 14th and 15th centuries were Galvey; Hall; Cornwalsh; and Loftus.

The lands of Tymon in Tallaght parish were anciently held by O'Mothan and we find Loftus and one Barnaby Relly there in the 17th century.

The census of 1659 shows Dublin and Wexford as principal locations. (The above extracted from the 'Book of Irish Families, great & small').

The family is listed as part of the 'more recent nobility' by O'Hart where they are given as earls of Rathfarnham and viscount Ely, Co. Dublin.

Lord Loftus disposed of Loftus hill prior to 1778 when it was occupied by Mr. Medlicott and then by Mr. Minchin.

Among the owners of Knocklyon in the parish of Tallaght we find Loftus.

Loghenan
Loughnan ?

In the 15th century John Loghenan was principal tenant of a manor house at Stillorgan parish. See introduction.

Loghlin
O' Loughlin Mc Loughlin

This spelling, a variant of O'Loghlin or McLoghlin etc.. is found as a principal name in Dublin in the census of 1659 and remained there at the time of the 1890 birth index. The spelling of Loughlin was found in the latter index as well. See various spellings. (See major entry in 'The Families of Co. Clare').

Lombard

Milesian Families finds the name in Dublin, of Lombardy origins. (no documentation given).

Long
Maclongahan Longan De Long

The 1890 birth index finds the family name of Long most numerous in counties Cork, Dublin, Limerick, Kerry and Donegal. (The above extracted from the 'Book of Irish Families, great & small'). (See major entry in 'The Families of Co. Cork').

The census of 1659 also finds the name of Long in Dublin. Nicholas Corr and Gerald Long in 1564 leased the lands of Newtownpark and in that century the Wolverston family occupied a good slated house there. See introduction.

Longervile

Robert Longervile is found in St. Werburgh's parish in the Dublin City Pipe Water Accounts of 1680.

Longley

Milesian Families finds the name in Dublin, of English origins.

Lord
Lorde

Milesian Families finds the name in Dublin, of English origins. (no documentation given). Found in Dublin City in the census of 1659.

Losse

One English family of the name is found settled in Dublin in the early 17th century in our records. (per the 'Book of Irish Families, great & small').

The descend from Sir Hugh Losse, of Canons, in Middlesex England and are found in Dublin in the first half of the 17th century, according to the works of O'Hart.

Mc Loughlin
Loughlin Mac Loughlin

A family name given in Dublin in the Birth Index of 1890. One Michael Loughlin is found in Castlekelly townland in the 19th century.

O'Loughlin

O'loghlen, O'lochalinn, O'laughlin,

One family used the name anciently, they were near Dublin, and are cited as Kings of Ireland, but soon changed the name to MacLoughlin. (The above extracted from the 'Book of Irish Families, great & small').

O'Loughlin remained in Dublin at the time of the 1890 birth index, though it has always been a name of Co. Clare. (see 'Families of Co. Clare, Ireland'.

Louis

Lewis

A family name found in Dublin city, given to be of Jewish heritage in at least one instance. (per 'OLochlainns journal of Irish Families').

Lovelace

Paul Lovelace is found in St. Werburgh's parish in the Dublin City Pipe Water Accounts of 1680.

Subsequent to the 17th century rebellions we find the names of Wharton; Chambers; Willion; Barry; Robinson; Moses; Reyly; Lovelace; Eaton; Murphy; Lawlor; Leedom; and Walsh in Rathcoole parish, Co. Dublin.

Lovell

Milesian Families finds the name in Dublin, of Norman origins. (no documentation given).

Lowe

Low

The birth index of 1890 finds the family centered in Dublin. (per the 'Book of Irish Families, great & small').

Lowry

Lowery Loughery

A family name given in Dublin in the Birth Index of 1890.

Lowther

A family name found in the city of Dublin in the census of 1659. Alderman Luke Lowther is found in St. Catherine's parish in the Dublin City Pipe Water Accounts of 1680.

Ludlow

Lodlowe

The names of Lodlowe and Ludlow are both given in the census of 1659 in Dublin. The noted General Edmund Ludlow came to assume the Castle at Monkstown subsequent to Henry Cheevers, the former owner.

Lupton

Searjant William Lupton is found in St. John's parish in the Dublin City Pipe Water Accounts of 1680.

Lushe

At Newcastle in 1614 among the first city officials were: Parsons; Rolles; Kenny; Frend; Davies; White; Burton; Grible; Bridges; Rutledge; and Lushe.

Birthplace of Burke.

Luttrell
Lutterell Lutrell

According to "Keatings History" the name is that of a principal family of Dublin city or county, and of Anglo-Norman descent. The family is listed as part of the 'more recent nobility' by O'Hart where they are given as 'earls of Carhampton', Co. Dublin.

The first of the name to come to Ireland is given as Sir Geoffrey Luttrell who arrived in 1204. From him descends the noble family of Luttrell of Dunster Castle in Sumersetshire, England.

Note the place name of Luttrellstown, near Lucan, Co. Dublin, where the family is on record from the 17th century. Luttrellstown was from the middle ages to the 19th century the home of the Luttrell family, and its lands served as the county boundary on its Meath and Kildare borders. (The above extracted in part from the 'Book of Irish Families, great & small').

In 'King James's Irish Army List, 1689' we find listed as an assessor in Dublin, one Simon Luttrell, Esq. Governor of the city. One Thomas Lutrell of Lutrellstown is also given in that work, in the chapter on Luttrell's Horse. Several thousand acres of lands in Dublin were also confiscated from the family according to the biography in King James Irish Army List.

Widow Luttrell is found in St. Audeon's parish in the Dublin City Pipe Water Accounts of 1680.

In the 16th century Tallaght Hills was granted to the Luttrell family and the Talbots of Belgard. At the time of the 17th century Restoration the Luttrell family are given as owners of Baldonan.

Lynacar

A family name found in the city of Dublin in the census of 1659.

Lynam
Lynagh, Leynagh, Lynan

The birth index of 1890 finds Lynam families centered in Dublin and Kings counties. References to this family are found early in Wexford and Carlow, and subsequently in Dublin. (The above extracted from the 'Book of Irish Families, great & small').

Lynch
Lynchy

A principal name of Dublin in the census of 1659. Note also a major entry for the name in "Families of Co. Galway" where Lynch is one of the noted tribes.

Lynchy
Lynch Lynsey

A family name given in Dublin in the census of 1659. (also spelled as Lynsey). See also Lynch

Lynsey
Lynchy Lynch

A family name found in Dublin in the census of 1659. (also spelled as Lynchy).

Lyons

A family name found in Dublin city, given to be of Jewish heritage in at least one instance. (per 'OLochlainns journal of Irish Families').

Lysle
Lisle

William Lysle is found in St. Werburgh's parish in the Dublin City Pipe Water Accounts of 1680.

Lyttle
Little

A family name found in Dublin at the time of the Birth Index of 1890.

Macartney
Mac Cartney

At the close of the 18th century the principal families of Dalkey Parish were those of Sir John Hasler; Wm. Macartney; John Patrickson; and Charlotte Brooke.

Mackey
Mckey, Mac Key, Macky, Mackay, Mackee
The 1890 birth index of Ireland finds the name of Mac Key in Dublin, Cork, Tipperary and Antrim. (The above extracted from the 'Book of Irish Families, great & small').

Macklean
Johnny Macklean is given to have run a pretty thatched inn not far from the sea at Sandymount.

Maconchy
Maconchie
The family of Maconchy of Rathmore, Co. Longford and of Raheny, Co. Dublin are of the same line. George Maconchy of Dublin, had his arms registered in Ulsters Office, during the reign of George the II. (extracted from the 'Book of Irish Families, great & small').

O' Madden
Madigan, Macavaddy, Madagane,
The Madden family of Balbriggan, County Dublin, is given as a branch of the Hy Many (Ui Maine) Maddens, according to O'Donovan. (See major entry in 'The Families of Co. Galway').
Madden had some 107 births, in Galway, Cork, Dublin and Antrim as recorded in the 1890 index.

Maddox
Maddicks
It is a surname found in Quaker records in Dublin city in the late 17th century.

Magg
A family name found in the city of Dublin in the census of 1659.

Magill
Mac Gill
Capt. Arthur Magill is given in *King James' Irish Army List*, and in his biography is given one John Magill who in 1642 was attained and named as from Naptown, County Dublin. In that work the family name is given as having been introduced into Ireland with the Plantations of Ulster.

Magrane
Mac Grane
A family name found in Dublin at the time of the Birth Index of 1890.

Maguire
Macguire, Macgwyer
The Maguire family is traditionally associated with Co. Fermanagh, and it has been prominent there since the 15th century.
As the 39th most popular name in all of Ireland, it was also found in counties Dublin, Cavan and Donegal in the 1890 index. (The above extracted from the 'Book of Irish Families, great & small').

Maher   Meagher
Magher, Maheir, Mara, O'meachair,
Ranking among the top 90 surnames in Ireland, the most numerous spelling of the name is as "Maher", which had some 176 births recorded in the 1890 index, mainly located in Tipperary, Dublin and Kilkenny. (extracted from the 'Book of Irish Families, great & small').

Mac Mahon
Mahon, Maghan, Mann, Maughan
The 1890 birth index shows "Mahon" in Dublin and Galway, with McMahon in Clare, Monaghan, Limerick and Dublin. The name itself is said to come from the Irish word for 'bear'. (The above extracted from the 'Book of Irish Families, great & small'). (See major entry in 'The Families of Co. Clare').
The census of 1659 also finds 'Mahon' in Dublin. This shortened form of MacMahon, may also represent other Irish family origins as well.
Sir Wm. McMahon came to possess Fortfield House on the lands of Kimmage in 1811.

O' Mahowne
Mahoney, Mahowney, Mcmahoney,
In the 17th century (O) or (Mac) Mahowne was a principal name in Cork, Tipperary, Dublin, and found in Kerry as well. Most often spelled as Mahoney. (extracted from the 'Book of Irish Families, great & small').

Maine
Maynes
It is a surname found in Quaker records in Dublin city in the late 17th century.

Makagan
Maceagan Makeegan Keegan
In the 13th century we find P. Makagan at Old Connaught parish.

Maklelan
Mac Clellan
It is a surname found in Quaker records in Dublin city in the late 17th century.

O'Malone
Mallone, Malloone
By the time of the 1890 index "Malone", which had dropped its "O" prefix altogether, had 100 births given in the counties of Dublin, Wexford and Clare.

In the census of 1659 "Malone" is found in Dublin, Kildare, and Westmeath. "Mallone" was in Dublin city at that time as well. (The above extracted from the 'Book of Irish Families, great & small').

Elm Green, in Castleknock parish, is given as residence of Richard Malone.

Man
Mann
William Man is found in St. John's parish in the Dublin City Pipe Water Accounts of 1680.

O'Mangan
Mongan, Manghan, Mangin, Manion,
"Mangan" is the most popular spelling of this family name today, as it was in the 1890 birth index where it is given 52 births, coming from Dublin, Limerick, Kerry and Mayo.

They are listed as a principal family of Co. Dublin by O'Hart. (The above extracted from the 'Book of Irish Families, great & small').

Manly
Manley
Found in Dublin in the census of 1659.

Manney
A family name found in the city of Dublin in the census of 1659.

Manning
Mannin, Maning
The family name of Manning is considered to be a name of English origin in Ireland in most instances. The name is most common in Dublin and Cork counties in Ireland, as evidenced by the 1890 birth index. (extracted from the 'Book of Irish Families, great & small').

Thomas Manning held Rockfield subsequent to 1772. See introduction.

Mannion
Mannin, Manning, O'mannion,
Some 91 Mannion births were recorded in the 1890 index, primarily in Galway and Roscommon. Manning, which is also of English origins, had 54 births, in Cork and Dublin. (The above extracted from the 'Book of Irish Families, great & small'). (See major entry in 'The Families of Co. Galway').

Mapes
Mapas Malpas Mape
A family name found in the city of Dublin in the census of 1659. John and Christopher Mapas are given as of Rochestown, Co. Dublin in 1691, according to the writings in King James Irish Army List.

Mara
Maura Meara
One family of the name is found in Castlekelly townland in the 18th and 19th century.

Marcus
'Marcus' and 'Marcus of Prussia' are given in Dublin city as names of Jewish heritage.

Marienhoff
A family name found in Dublin city, given to be of Jewish heritage in at least one instance. (per 'OLochlainns journal of Irish Families').

Markam
Markham
Markam and Markham are on record in Dublin City in the census of 1659.

Marks
Mark

A family name found in Dublin city, given to be of Jewish heritage in at least one instance. (per 'OLochlainns journal of Irish Families').

'Mark' is a surname found in Quaker records in Dublin city in the first half of the 18th century.

O' Marky
Markey

They are found in older works in the old territory of Oriel in Ireland. In more modern times the family is found most numerous in Louth, Monaghan and in the city of Dublin. The 1890 birth index finds the family most numerous in Monaghan and Dublin. (The above extracted from the 'Book of Irish Families, great & small').

Marlow

A family name found in Dublin at the time of the Birth Index of 1890.

Marsden

Samuel Marsden is found in St. Werburgh's parish in the Dublin City Pipe Water Accounts of 1680.

Marshall
Marshal, Marshell

A family name of accepted English extraction in Ireland. The 1890 birth index finds the family most numerous in Antrim, Londonderry, Down and Dublin. (The above extracted from the 'Book of Irish Families, great & small').

Meldiric, Aubry, Marshall, and Rath families are given early in Rathcoole parish in the History of the County Dublin by Ball. The le Marshall name is also given at Aderrig in the 14th century.

Early names at Newcastle parish after the 12th century invasions included Carrick; Russell; and le Marshall.

Robert Marshall is given in the area of Seapoint and Templehill in the 18th century. See introduction.

Martell
Mardell

Milesian Families finds the name in Dublin, of Norman origins. (no documentation given).

Martin, Gilmartin
Martin, Martyn, Marten, Kilmartin,

Martin is one of the top 50 names in Ireland, Scotland and England. Hence, origins may stem from any of these countries. Several Irish origins for the name exist, including forms of Gilmartin, Kilmartin and O'Martin.

Martyn, was a principal name of Dublin in 1659. Martine, was a principal name of Down, and found in Cork and Dublin in 1659. (From the 'Book of Irish Families, great & small').

'Martin' is a surname found in Quaker records in Dublin city in the 18th century, where one of the name is listed as a 'weaver'. (See major entry in 'The Families of Co. Galway').

Marwards
Marward

According to "Keatings History" the name is that of a principal family of Dublin city or county, and of Anglo-Norman descent. (The above extracted from the 'Book of Irish Families, great & small').

Mason

A family name found in Dublin in the 1890 birth index, and also found there earlier in the census of 1659.

In the 17th century Thomas Mason was a tenant in Rathfarnham parish who was robbed by John Woodfin. See introduction.

It is a surname found in Quaker records in Dublin city in the 18th century. (See major entry in 'The Families of Co. Kerry').

Massey

In 'King James's Irish Army List, 1689' we find listed as a Dublin assessor, one Christopher Massey.

Masterson
Mcmaster

The 1890 birth index finds the family most numerous in Dublin, Longford and Cavan. (The above extracted from the 'Book of Irish Families, great & small').

Mathews
Mathewes, Matthews

By 1890 the name is given in Louth, Dublin, Antrim and Down. Spelled as Matthews in 1890 it was found in Louth, Dublin and Antrim. (The above extracted from the 'Book of Irish Families, great & small').

We find a Mathew family at Crumlin parish around the 17th or 18th century.

Maule
Malley

A family name found in the city of Dublin in the census of 1659.

Mautner

A family name found in Dublin city, given to be of Jewish heritage in at least one instance. (per 'OLochlainns journal of Irish Families').

Maxwell

The birth index of 1890 finds the family centered in Antrim, Down and Dublin. (The above extracted from the 'Book of Irish Families, great & small').

May

Milesian Families finds the name in Dublin, of English origins. (no documentation given).

Mayhugh

Milesian Families finds the name in Dublin, of English origins. (no documentation given).

Mayler
Meilor

Milesian Families finds the name in Dublin, of German origins. (no documentation given).

Maynes
Maine   Mayne

Christopher Maynes is found in St. Werburgh's parish in the Dublin City Pipe Water Accounts of 1680.

At Churchtown in Taney parish we find one Mr. Edward Mayne around the end of the 18th century.

Mayo

Milesian Families finds the name in Dublin, of English origins. (no documentation given). It is also a surname found in Quaker records in Dublin city in the 18th century.

Mayson

It is a surname found in Quaker records in Dublin city in the 18th century.

Meagher
Maher

A family name given in Dublin in the Birth Index of 1890.

O' Meara
Marra, Marah, O'meera O' Mara

Meara and O'Meara are found in about equal numbers in the 1890 birth index. "Meara" was a name of Tipperary and O'Meara of Dublin, Limerick and Tipperary. (extracted from the 'Book of Irish Families, great & small').

Meath

A family name found in the city of Dublin in the census of 1659.

Medlicott

Lord Loftus disposed of Loftus hill prior to 1778 when it was occupied by Mr. Medlicott and then by Mr. Minchin.

Mee

A family name found in the city of Dublin in the census of 1659.

O' Meehan
Meighan, Meegan, Mcmeekin, Mehegan,

The family remained in Clare at the turn of the last century, when they are also found in Galway, Sligo, Donegal and Dublin. (The above extracted from the 'Book of Irish Families, great & small').

Melaghlin
Mac Laughlin

The O'Melaghlins were kings of Meath and monarchs of Ireland, as well as being chiefs and princes of Tara and Bregia for centuries. In Keatings 'History of Ireland' it is remarked that the family had largely decayed, and that the name had reportedly been changed in some cases to MacLaughlin.

O'Connellan states the family changed the name of Melaghlin to MacLaghlin or McLaughlin since the reign of Queen Anne.

Meldiric

Mulderick

Meldiric, Aubry, Marshall, and Rath families are given in Rathcoole parish in the History of the County Dublin by Ball.

Meldon

Melden

One family of the name is found in Fore, Co. Westmeath, and subsequently of Casino, Miltown, in Dublin City. (The above extracted from the 'Book of Irish Families, great & small').

Melville

Milesian Families finds the name in Dublin, of Norman origins. (no documentation given).

Mercer

Mercier

A family name found in the city of Dublin in the census of 1659. Edward Mercer is found in St. John's parish in the Dublin City Pipe Water Accounts of 1680.

In 1795 Laughanstown was held by the Mercer family, who were the tenants of Brenanstown. See introduction.

Meredeth

Meredith

Meredith and Meredith families are on record in Dublin City in 1659.

Merrick

Merricke, meyrick, mayrick

In the 1890 birth index of Ireland only 7 births of the name are recorded. This in itself makes it a relatively rare surname. Going back to the census of 1659 we find only one listing of the family name, and that spelled as "Merricke". The individual in question was one Cornett Merricke, of Dublin City. (The above extracted from the 'Book of Irish Families, great & small').

Merrigan

Merrygan

A family name found in Dublin at the time of the Birth Index of 1890.

Merry

The widow of Christopher Merry, a Dublin baker, is given residing in a house built by George Ussher at Kill of the Grange parish. See introduction.

Mervin

Merwin Marvin

A family name found in the city of Dublin in the census of 1659.

Messit

Missit

Messit is given as among the few names of importance in Taney parish in the mid 18th century.

Metzenberg

A family name found in Dublin city, given to be of Jewish heritage in at least one instance. (per 'OLochlainns journal of Irish Families').

Mey

May

Among the names noted at Rathcoole parish from the 16th century onwards are: John Mey; James Bathe; the Fitzgeralds; and the Darlasses of Maynooth.

The name is also noted at Kilmactalway parish.

Michell

Mitchell

A family name found in the city of Dublin in the census of 1659.

Mickle

It is a surname found in Quaker records in Dublin city in the 18th century.

Middleton

It is a surname found in Quaker records in Dublin city in the late 17th and 18th century.

Thomas Middleton is found in St. Werburgh's parish in the Dublin City Pipe Water Accounts of 1680.

Mildmay

Milmo Milmay Milmoy

Milesian Families finds the name in Dublin, of foreign origins. (no documentation given). The spelling of Milmo is also found for this name.

Miller
Millar, Miler

The birth index of 1890 finds the family centered in Antrim with 50% of the name found in that county, and also in Londonderry and Dublin. (The above extracted from the 'Book of Irish Families, great & small').

The spelling of Millar, is of course, on record in Dublin as well. It is a surname found in Quaker records in Dublin city in the first half of the 19th century.

One 'Robert Miller' is found in St. Werburgh's parish in the Dublin City Pipe Water Accounts of 1680.

Millinton
Millington

A family name found in the city of Dublin in the census of 1659.

Mills
Mill   Milis

The family name is often found in the province of Ulster as would be expected, as well as in Dublin. (The above extracted from the 'Book of Irish Families, great & small').

'Mill' is also given as an English family name found settled in Dublin by at least the 17th century, where they held noted lands at that time.

One John 'Milis' is found occupying the lands of Killiney in the 14th century. See introduction.

Minchin

Lord Loftus disposed of Loftus hill prior to 1778 when it was occupied by Mr. Medlicott and then by Mr. Minchin. See introduction.

Miner

Milesian Families finds the name in Dublin, of English origins. (no documentation given).

Missett

Milesian Families finds the name in Dublin, of Norman origins. Walter de Lacy granted lands of Baggottrath to Walter Missett around the 13th century.
See introduction.

Mitchell
Mitchel, Michell

Mitchell ranks among the top 30 most numerous names of England, so it is not surprising to find the name fairly widespread in Ireland.

The 1890 birth index finds the family most numerous in Antrim, Galway and Dublin. (The above extracted from the 'Book of Irish Families, great & small').

Henry Mitchell succeeded John Putland in Glasnevin House. He was a banker and a man of great horticultural talent.

Moclare
Mockler

One Lt.-Col. Sir James Moclare is given in *King James Irish Army List* as having been outlawed in 1691 as 'of the City of Dublin, Knight'. This family is further given to have been of Tipperary.

Mocter

Milesian Families finds the name in Dublin, of German origins. (no documentation given).

Mocton

Ellena Mocton held lands at the Church of St. Stephen at Leperstown (Leopardstown) in the 14th century.

O Modarn
Modern

The O'Modarns, chiefs of Kinel Eochain, are mentioned by O'Dugan as chiefs of the Britons and Welsh, located near Dublin (per Keatings 'History of Ireland'. IGF edition.).

Moelet

Milesian Families finds the name in Dublin, of French origins. (no documentation given).

Moenes

See introduction page 28.

Moffat
Moffitt

A name given by some in Dublin, spelled as Moffat and Moffitt. More commonly found in the North of Ireland.

Molesworth

Richard Molesworth, Viscount, is found seated at Breckdenstown, Co. Dublin.

Mollenex

Molleneaux Molyneaux

A family name found in the city of Dublin in the census of 1659. We find the country house of the Molyneux family at Clondalkin in the 17th century. See Molyneaux.

O'Molloy

Mulloy, Molley, Molloy, Millea, Mullee,

"Molloy" was the preferred spelling of the name in the last century as it had 153 births in Dublin, Galway, Mayo, Kings, Donegal, etc... (The above extracted from the 'Book of Irish Families, great & small').

Molyneux

Mollenex

We find the country house of the Molyneux family at Clondalkin in the 17th century. See Mollenex.

O'Monaghan Monahan

Monaghan, Monnaughan, Monohan,

The family is anciently found in Co. Roscommon near Elphin and Jamestown, but by the time of the 1890 birth index the family is found most numerous in Galway, Mayo, Dublin and Fermanagh. (extracted from the 'Book of Irish Families, great & small').

Money

Mooney

A Johannes Money is given at Glenasmole in prior centuries. See also possible spelling of O'Mooney.

Monks

Muncks Munks Muonks Monck

Monks is a family name found in Dublin in the 1890 Birth Index. The possibly related name of Muncke is found in Dublin City in the census of 1659.

General Monk is noted at Kilgobbin.

In the early 18th century Grangegorman became the residence of Charles Monck (d.1751), who also possessed Charleville, in Co. Wicklow, through the family of his wife.

O'Mooney

Meeny, Meany, Mainey, Meaney

"Mooney" is the common spelling of the name, with 136 in Dublin, Antrim and Kings in the 1890 birth index. (The above extracted from the 'Book of Irish Families, great & small').

O'Moore Moor

More, Moor, Moir, Morey, O'more, Muir,

Being the 20th most popular name in Ireland and among the top 40 names in England, the name is well represented in Dublin, being among the 20 most numerous there in the 1890 index.

The Moore family is found in the 17th and 19th century in counties Antrim and Dublin. (extracted from the 'Book of Irish Families, great & small').

Robert Moore is found in St. Werburgh's parish in the Dublin City Pipe Water Accounts of 1680.

Hermitage, in Whitechurch parish, was home to the Hudson and Moore families.

Note the article on "Moore of Rutland Square, Dublin" found in the Library of the Representative Church Body in Dublin, as found in the "Swanzy Notebooks".

Thomas Moore, the poet, was of Kerry heritage, also noted in Dublin.

Moorhouse

See "A Moorhouse Family of Dublin, Carlow and Kildare." from the Irish Ancestor, 9(1) 1977. (periodical).

Moory

A family name found in the city of Dublin in the census of 1659.

Moran

Morran

A family name given in Dublin in the census of 1659, and it is found there in the 1890 birth index as well.

A small castle and house were held by John Moran at Newtown subsequent to 1539 (see introduction).

O' Morgan
Morgen, Morgin,morahan, Murrigan
The name of Morgan is quite common in Ireland, with some 132 births in the 1890 index in counties Antrim, Armagh, Down, Dublin and Louth. Morgan is a common English name, and many of the name in Ireland are originally of that stock.   (The above extracted from the 'Book of Irish Families, great & small').
In Tully parish obituaries we note the daughter of Thomas Morgan in 1761.

Moroly
A family name found in the city of Dublin in the census of 1659.

Morphy
Murphy
A family name found in Dublin in the census of 1659.

Morran
Moran
A family name found as a principal one in Dublin in the census of 1659. A different spelling of Moran.

Morris, Maurice
Mores, Morrison, Morres, Fits, Fitz,
The name is common in England and Wales, so this accounts for many of the name. (See major entry in 'The Families of Co. Kerry').
Fitzmaurice has remained a name of Co. Kerry. "Morris" was recorded in the 1890 index with some 115 births in Dublin, Mayo, Tyrone and Monaghan.
(The above extracted from the 'Book of Irish Families, great & small'). (See entry in ' Families of Co. Galway').
It is also a surname found in Quaker records in Dublin city in the last half of the 17th century.
In 1787 Thomas Morris advertised for stabling 60 horses in Chapelizod parish.

Morrison
Morrisson
A family name found in Dublin in the 1890 birth index of Ireland.

Morse
Morris
Milesian Families finds the name in Dublin, of Welch origins. (no documentation given).

Mortomer
Mortimer
A family name found in the city of Dublin in the census of 1659.

Morton
Milesian Families finds the name in Dublin, of Scottish origins. (no documentation given).

Morville
The name of Simmonscourt is given to have come from the Smothe family, who succeeded the Morville family there. See introduction.

Moseley
A family name found in Dublin city, given to be of Jewish heritage in at least one instance. (per 'OLochlainns journal of Irish Families').

Moses
A family name found in Dublin city, given to be of Jewish heritage in at least one instance. (per 'OLochlainns journal of Irish Families').
Subsequent to the 17th century rebellions we find the names of Wharton; Chambers; Willion; Barry; Robinson; Moses; Reyly; Lovelace; Eaton; Murphy; Lawlor; Leedom; and Walsh in Rathcoole parish, Co. Dublin.

Mossom
After the rebellion of 1641 the lands of Killiney parish were held by Gilbert Wye of Belfast; the Mossoms; the Fawcetts; the Pocklingtons; and the Domviles. See introduction.

O Mothan
The lands of Tymon in Tallaght parish were anciently held by O'Mothan and we find Loftus and one Barnaby Relly there in the 17th century.

Mould
A family name found in the city of Dublin in the census of 1659.   Moulds is given as among the few names of importance in Taney parish in the mid 18th century.

Moxon
Thomas Moxon is found in St. Nicholas Parish 'Within the Walls', in the Dublin City Pipe Water Accounts of 1680.

Moyle

John Moyle is found in St. Werburgh's parish in the Dublin City Pipe Water Accounts of 1680.

Moynes
Moenes

A family name found in the city of Dublin in the census of 1659.

Muckleborne

A family name found in the city of Dublin in the census of 1659.

Muir

Milesian Families finds the name in Dublin, of Scottish origins. (no documentation given).

Mulchinock

'Families of Co. Kerry, Ireland' finds the widow of Mulchinock of Tralee, Co. Kerry, at 53 Pembroke Road in Dublin.

Mulhall
Mulhal

The 1890 birth index finds the family most numerous in Dublin, Kilkenny, Carlow and Queens. (The above extracted from the 'Book of Irish Families, great & small').

O'Mullally
Lally, Mulally, Mullaly, Mullooly

The Mullaly family is considered to be one of Ui Maine. (see also 'Tribes and Customs of the Hy Many' by O'Donovan).

Passengers From Ireland:

Watt Mullally- (Male) From Dublin to New York. Aboard "Perseverance", May 18, 1846. (The above extracted from the 'Book of Irish Families, great & small').

Mullan, Mullen
Mullin, Mullen, Mullane, Mullins,

In Keatings History we find the O'Mullens given as one of the Leinster clans, numerous in Meath, Dublin and Kildare at that time. (The above extracted from the 'Book of Irish Families, great & small').

O'Mulligan
Milligen, Milliken, Mulgan, Mullagen,

O'Mulligan, or "O'Maelagain" is given in Keatings History as chief of Tir Mac Caerthain, a territory included in the baronies of Raphoe and Boylagh in Co. Donegal. With the disturbances of the 17th century this clan was dispossessed of its power there, until today they are primarily located in Mayo, Monaghan and Dublin. (extracted from the 'Book of Irish Families, great & small').

Munn

At the time of the Commonwealth survey we find Mr. Munn in possession of a stone house subsequently held by Mr. Leeson.

Munson

Milesian Families finds the name in Dublin, of English origins. (no documentation given).

O Murcain
Murcan

The O'Murcains were chiefs of Moy Liffey along with the Brackens. This area is apparently near Dublin, and given as meaning lands along the Liffey, near Dublin. (per Keatings 'History of Ireland', I.G. F. edition.)

Mac Muregain

MacMuregain was given as a chief of East Liffey, and is given in some battles with the Danes in the 10th century. (per Keatings 'History of Ireland' I.G.F. edition).

Murphy

A family name given in Dublin in the Birth Index of 1890, it ranked as the 4th most numerous name in Dublin at that time, which is not surprising considering the great number of the name found in Ireland. No doubt several unrelated families of the name sent members to the city of Dublin over time.

The O'Murphy family of Wexford is given as particularly numerous in Dublin and Meath, according to O'Hart.

Edward Murphy (d.1777), is given in the area of Seapoint and Templehill in the 18th century. See introduction.

In Tully Parish in 1780 obituaries we find Samuel Murphy, Doctor of Music.

Subsequent to the 17th century rebellions we find the names of Wharton; Chambers; Willion; Barry; Robinson; Moses; Reyly; Lovelace; Eaton; Murphy; Lawlor; Leedom; and Walsh in Rathcoole parish, Co. Dublin.

Murray

Murry, Kilmurray, Murrihy, Mcmurry,

The name of O'Murray, Murray etc.., ranks among the top 20 names in all of Ireland. It is also one of the top 25 most numerous surnames of Dublin in the 1890 birth index.

Locations for the name in the 17th century include 'Murry' and 'Murrey' in Dublin. (The above extracted from the 'Book of Irish Families, great & small').

Murtagh

Murtaugh, Murta, Murdock, Murdoch,

An old Irish family located near Kells, in County Meath, is said to be the origin of Irish Murtaghs. The O'Murtahs are mentioned by O'Dugan as chiefs of the Britons and Welsh, located near Dublin. They are given as chiefs of the tribe of O'Maine. (per Keatings 'History of Ireland'. IGF edition.)

By the time of the 1890 birth index, the name of Murtaugh was found primarily in Dublin and Sligo counties, with a total of 58 births given for the family name. (The above extracted from the 'Book of Irish Families, great & small').

'Murtagh' was the name of a ploughman at Glencullen, in the parish of Kiltiernan.

Muschamp

William Muschamp occupied Porterstown according to Ball. See introduction.

Mustian

Mustan

A family name found in Dublin in the census of 1659.

Myers

A family name found in Dublin city, given to be of Jewish heritage in at least one instance. (per 'OLochlainns journal of Irish Families').

Mynagh

Minnaugh

In the 14th century we find John Mynagh, Robert Serjeant, and Roger Kilmore at Simmonscourt. See introduction.

Nagle

Neagle, Nangle

The Nangles are cited in Keatings as a principal family of Anglo-Norman descent in the county and city of Dublin.

O'Hart says that Jocelin de Angulo, the first baron of Navans eldest son, was the ancestor of Nangle in Leinster and Nangle in Munster. (The above extracted from the 'Book of Irish Families, great & small'). (See major entry in 'The Families of Co. Cork').

MacNally
Mac Anally, Mcanelly, Knally, Mcnelly

The majority of the above families are to be found in the province of Ulster, and many are found in the two major cities of Dublin and Belfast in Ireland. (The above extracted from the 'Book of Irish Families, great & small').

Mr. William Nally is noted at Roebuck, Co. Dublin, in a house containing two hearths, and that was probably part of the castle there. See introduction. Mr. William Nally, of Roebuck, was given as a principal farmer at Kiltiernan parish.

McNamara
Mac Conmara,

The Mac Namaras held the office of hereditary marshals of Thomand, where they had numerous castles in Co. Clare. Mac Namara was a principal name of Limerick city in 1659.

In the 1890 birth index Clare, Limerick, Mayo, Dublin and Cork held families of the name. (The above extracted from the 'Book of Irish Families, great & small'). (See major entry in 'The Families of Co. Clare').

Nangle
Although not given in other sources, O'Hart gives the family as a principal one settling in Dublin from the 12th to the 18th century.

Naper
In Esker parish Hermitage was the residence of Maj. Gen. Robert Naper which passed to the Hon. Robert Butler in 1739.

Napier
Milesian Families finds the name in Dublin, of Scottish origins. (no documentation given).

Nary
Menarry, Mac Nary, Mac Neary,

The McNary families in Ireland hail from the old territory of Oriel. The early forms of 'Mac Naradhaigh' include Mac Nary and Mac Neary. In more modern times the spelling of 'Menarry' has become most common.

The name is also often found in Dublin. Rev. Cornelius Nary (1658 - 1738) of Co. Kildare. was author-parish priest of St. Michan's in Dublin. (The above extracted from the 'Book of Irish Families, great & small').

Nash
Ash, Neish, Naish, Nasse, Nashe

One English family of the name held lands in Worcester and is later found in Farrihy, Co. Cork in the 18th century and in Dublin in the 19th century.

The Nash family of Finnstown and Howth, Co. Dublin are of the same line, tracing their descent to Patrick Nash or Naish, of Kanturk, Co. Cork, in the 17th century. (The above extracted from the 'Book of Irish Families, great & small' and the 'Irish Book of Arms'.).

Nathan
A family name found in Dublin city, given to be of Jewish heritage in at least one instance. (per 'OLochlainns journal of Irish Families').

McNaul
Macnally, Mcnulty...

Several possibilities exist for the origins of the name. In Dublin the name may come from MacNally, and you may always find corrupt forms of names such as Naulty, which could have been further changed to McNaul. (The above extracted from the 'Book of Irish Families, great & small').

Navill
A family name found in the city of Dublin in the census of 1659.

Naylor
Nailor

A family name found in Dublin at the time of the Birth Index of 1890.

O'Neale
O' Neill Neale Neal Neil

A family name found in Dublin in the census of 1659. It was widespread in Ireland at that time, as well as today (see O'Neill).

'Neale' is a surname found in Quaker records in Dublin city in the late 17th century.

Mac Neale
MacNeale of Portrane, Co. Dublin, is given in the Irish Book of Arms (IGF edition).

Neary
A family name found in Dublin at the time of the Birth Index of 1890.

Mac Nebury
Macnebury

Among the occupants of Laughanstown from the 14th to the 17th century we find the Macnebury family of Ashpoll or Archbold.

O'Neill
Neel, Neil, Niel, Nihill, Neele, Nielson,

One of the top 12 most numerous surnames in all of Ireland, several unrelated families of the name exist in Ireland. In 1890 O'Neill ranked among the top ten most numerous names in Dublin county.

(The above extracted from the 'Book of Irish Families, great & small').

O'Neill and Neill are two spellings of the name in the 1890 Birth Index. Neale and O'Neale are a spellings found in Dublin in 1659. (see also O'Neale)

Backweston House in Aderrig parish, was given as the residence of Sir Bryan O'Neill, a descendant of the 'chiefs of Clanaboy'.

The Neills, from whom the townland in the parish of Clandalkin is named, were prominent in that area of Dublin.

Nelson
Neilson

Milesian Families finds the name in Dublin, of English origins. (no documentation given).

Nerwich
A family name found in Dublin city, given to be of Jewish heritage in at least one instance. (per 'OLochlainns journal of Irish Families').

Nesbitt
A family name found in Dublin in the birth index of 1890.

Netterville
Nutterville, Nettervill

According to "Keatings History" the name was that of a principal family of Dublin city or county, and of Anglo-Norman descent. (The above extracted from the 'Book of Irish Families, great & small').

Patrick Netterville is listed among those transplanted from Dublin in the works of O'Hart. Luke Netterville of Corballies, is found with over 1,000 acres of land in Dublin in the 17th century.

In the 17th century we find the Nettervilles at Finglas.

Neville
Nevill

The Neville family of Ahanure, Co. Kilkenny and of Rockfield, Co. Dublin is found in the Irish Book of Arms. (per the 'Book of Irish Families').

Newcomb
Newcom, Newcome

The name of Newcomb (Newcomen) in Ireland is found in Dublin in the 16th and 17th centuries. It is possibly a form of O'Niadh (O'Nee). Newcomen is found in the census of 1659 in Dublin. In 'Milesian Families' Newcomb listed as being of Saxon origin settling in Dublin in 1630. (The above extracted from the 'Book of Irish Families, great & small').

Newcomen
Robert Newcomen arrived in Ireland in in 1585 and resided at the castle at Ballyfermot, founding a family of note in Ireland for some 200 years. A family name found in Dublin in the census of 1659. Be also aware of the spelling of the name of Newcoment found in the 1659 census.

Newcomen is also noted at Killininny in Co. Dublin.

In 1664 Col. Newcomen was rated for six hearths.

Newcoment

A family name found in Dublin in the census of 1659. Be also aware of the spelling of the name of Newcomen, also found in 1659.

Newenham

Sir Edward Newenham (d.1814) is found in the Montpelier area. See introduction.

Sir Edward Newnham also came to live at a house on the site of Drumcondra Castle around 1780 in Clonturk Parish.

Newman

Newmen

The name of Newman is assumed to be of English extraction when found in Ireland, The name is also found in Dublin in our records. The birth index of 1890 finds the family centered in Cork, Meath and Dublin. (per the 'Book of Irish Families, great & small').

At least one family of the name in Dublin City however, is found in Ireland of Jewish heritage.

Nicholas

Nichlas

A family name found in the city of Dublin in the census of 1659.

Nicholls

A family name found in the city of Dublin in the census of 1659.

Nicholson

A family name found in Dublin in the birth index of 1890.

Nihill

One James Nihill of Limerick and Dublin is given on the attainders of 1691 according the the biographical entry of Lt. David Nihill, in *King James' Irish Army List*.

Nixon

It is a surname found in Quaker records in Dublin city in the 18th century. Capt. Nixon is given as resident in Castleknock parish. See introduction.

Noble

Nobel

The name of Noble is assumed to be of English extraction in Ireland. Many of the name are found in Fermanagh and Antrim, as well as in the city of Dublin. The birth index of 1890 finds the family centered in Antrim and Dublin. (per the 'Book of Irish Families, great & small').

O'Nolan

O'nowlan, Knowlan, Knowland,

One of the top 40 most numerous surnames in all of Ireland. The name is found in Dublin and Wicklow in the 1890 birth index. It was the 11th most numerous surname of Dublin County at that time.

In the census of 1659, spelled as Nowlane and Nowland, it is a principal name of Dublin. (The above extracted from the 'Book of Irish Families, great & small'). (see also Nowland)

Norecone

A Walter Norecone is given at Glenasmole in earlier times.

North

North is found in Dublin City in 1649, given to be of English extraction. John North is found in St. Michael's parish in the Dublin City Pipe Water Accounts of 1680.

Norton

The Norton family name is found in Dublin in the Birth Index of 1890. The widow of Alexander Norton is found in St. Catherine's parish in the Dublin City Pipe Water Accounts of 1680.

Nottingham

Lawrence Nottingham is found holding Ballyowen with some 832 acres in 17th century Co. Dublin, and he was noted as an Irish Catholic. We also find one 'Lamerick Nottingham' in Esker parish in the 17th century.

Ball gives the names of Hanstede; Pippard; and de Nottingham at Lucan Parish in County Dublin.

One Capt. Peasley is found with lands in Esker parish which would go to the Nottinghams after Restoration.

See also the "Nottinghams of Ballyowen" as found in the "Reportorium Novum", 1 (2), 1956.

Milesian Families finds the name in Dublin, of English origins.

Nowland
Knowland Nowlan Nowlin

Both Nowland and Nowlane are found as principal names of Dublin, and are assumed to be Noland, or Nolan in disguise. (see also Nolan)

Roger Nowland is found in St. Werburgh's parish in the Dublin City Pipe Water Accounts of 1680.

Noy

At Island Bridge we find the names of: Noy in 1746; Jones in 1749; Green in 1764; Pennefather in 1768; Keightly 1768; and Trail in 1799.

Noyce

Mr. Richard Noyce is found in St. Werburgh's parish in the Dublin City Pipe Water Accounts of 1680.

Nuel

A family name found in Dublin city, given to be of Jewish heritage in at least one instance. (per 'OLochlainns journal of Irish Families').

Nugent
Nughent, De Nugent, Nogent

Traditionally the name has been linked to Meath and Westmeath. In 1890, the name is given in Armagh, Dublin, Cork, Tipperary and Tyrone. (The above extracted from the 'Book of Irish Families, great & small').

Walter Nugent is found in St. Nicholas Parish 'Within the Walls', in the Dublin City Pipe Water Accounts of 1680. Several estates are tied to the family name in 17th century Dublin.

Among the owners of Knocklyon in the parish of Tallaght we find Nugent.

Ignatius Nugent is noted in Finglas Parish. See introduction.

McNulty
Nulty, Macanulty, Nolty, Nolte,

The MacNulty family is traditionally given to be a family of Co. Donegal. In the 17th century 'Nulty' is given as a name from the city of Dublin. (The above extracted from the 'Book of Irish Families, great & small').

Nutley

Nutley is given at Kilgobbin parish in County Dublin. See introduction.

Nuttall

Richard Nuttall is found in St. Werburgh's parish in the Dublin City Pipe Water Accounts of 1680.

Oakley

Milesian Families finds the name in Dublin, of Saxon origins. (no documentation given).

Ob

An apparent abbreviation of a family name found in the city of Dublin in the census of 1659.

Odlum

At Jamestown in Finglas parish we find one William Odlum. See introduction under Finglas parish.

Opolinser

A family name found in Dublin city, given to be of Jewish heritage in at least one instance. (per 'OLochlainns journal of Irish Families').

Orde

In 1798 Arthur Orde and Thomas Jones kept a boarding school at Crumlin.

Orr

A family name found in Dublin city in the census of 1659, where it is often found. It is also a name found in Cork and in Northern Ireland.

Orson

A family name found in the city of Dublin in the census of 1659.

Othyr

Names associated with the settlement of Balally in Taney parish were: de Walhope; Othyr; Howell; Taunton; Walsh in 1407 and Borr in the 17th century. It was given originally as a Danish settlement.

Owen(s)

Owens, Mcowen, Owenson

The name of Owen (or Owens) may stem from several sources. It is on record as often confused with Owenson, MacKeown, MacOwen and even Hinds. In 1890 the family is centered in Dublin, Roscommon and Cork. (The above extracted from the 'Book of Irish Families, great & small').

John Owen held Diswellstown in the 14th century.

Ownyan

A family name found in Dublin in the census of 1659.

Padmore

A family name found in the city of Dublin in the census of 1659.

Page

Milesian Families finds the name in Dublin, of English origins. (no documentation given). Found as well in Dublin in the 1890 birth index.

Paget

Milesian Families finds the name in Dublin, with Isle of Anglesey origins. (no documentation given).

Paine

Payne

A family name found in the census of 1659 in Dublin City.

Paisley

A family name found in Dublin at the time of the Birth Index of 1890.

Palfery

A family name found in the city of Dublin in the census of 1659.

Paling

Jonathan Paling is found in St. John's parish in the Dublin City Pipe Water Accounts of 1680.

Pallatio (del)

Milesian Families finds the name in Dublin, of 15th century Italian origins. (no documentation given).

Palles

Pallas Pallys Pallace

Capt. Christopher Pallas is given in King James' Irish Army List as a goldsmith in the City of Dublin, where the family had been from the time of Queen Elizabeth. The spellings of Pallys and Pallace are among the spelling of the family name given in that source.

Milesian Families finds the name in Dublin, of 15th century Italian origins.

Palliser

Milesian Families finds the name in Dublin, of Norman origins.

Names connected to Rathfarnham parish in the 18th centuries were Palliser; O'Callaghan; Cramer; Coghill; Stannard; Fountain; Ward; Geering; How; Boyle; and Blackburn.

Palmer

A family name found in Dublin in the census of 1659. The family is also given as a principal one of Anglo-Norman descent, settling in Dublin City and County, according to Keatings 'History of Ireland'. (See major entry in 'The Families of Co. Kerry').

Parker
Park, Parks

Several families of the name of Parker are to be found in Ireland. Most are of English extraction.

One William Parker of Dublin is of the line of a family which came to settle later in Philadelphia. (per the 'Book of Irish Families, great & small').

Under the entry for Col. John Parker in King James Irish Army List, we read of one Geoffrey Parker who was Mayor of the Staple in Dublin. Several others of the name were given therein.

A Stephen Parker is found in Castlekelly Townland in 1771 and in 1831 as well.

Parkinson
A family name given in Dublin in the Birth Index of 1890.

Parnall
Parnell

Parnall and Parnell are on record in Dublin City. The former spelling is found there in the 1659 census.

John Parnell is found in St. Werburgh's parish in the Dublin City Pipe Water Accounts of 1680.

In 1641 the lands of Cullenswood (Ranelagh and Sandford) were occupied by Yeoman Thomas Ward, who was taken captive along with a Mr. Parnell.

Parry
Henry Parry is found in St. Nicholas Parish 'Without the Walls', in the Dublin City Pipe Water Accounts of 1680.

Parsons
The family is listed as part of the 'more recent nobility' by O'Hart where they are given as earls of Rosse in King's County and as barons of Oxmanstown or Ostmanstown in Dublin city.

At Kilnamanagh the Talbot; Belgard; Parsons; Fitzwilliam; and Hawkins family are given of note. The Parsons are also found at Tallaght Hills.

In the 17th century Sir Wm. Parsons held many lands at Saggart parish in Dublin county.

At Newcastle in 1614 among the first city officials were: Parsons; Rolles; Kenny; Frend; Davies; White; Burton; Grible; Bridges; Rutledge; and Lushe.

Parvin
It is a surname found in Quaker records in Dublin city in the 18th century.

Pasco
Milesian Families finds the name in Dublin, of Scottish origins. (no documentation given).

Patrickson
At the close of the 18th century the principal families of Dalkey Parish were those of Sir John Hasler; Wm. Macartney; John Patrickson; and Charlotte Brooke.

Patton
Milesian Families finds the name in Dublin, of English origins. (no documentation given).

Payne
Paine

Milesian Families finds the name in Dublin, of English origins. (no documentation given). The family name is also given in Dublin in the 1890 birth index of Ireland.

In Tully parish obituaries we note in 1761, John Payne, an eminent livery lace weaver. See introduction.

Peachen
A family name found in the city of Dublin in the census of 1659.

Mac Peake
Peak, Peake
In the 17th century we find Mc Peake as a principal name in Londonderry, as well as being found in Dublin city and Meath. (The above extracted from the 'Book of Irish Families, great & small').
'Peake' is also found in Dublin city at that time. See Peake in 1659 census.

Pearson
Pierson
A family name given in Dublin in the Birth Index of 1890.

Peasley
Paisley
A family name we find in Dublin in the census of 1659. One Capt. Peasley is found with lands in Esker parish which would go to the Nottinghams after Restoration.

Peche
In 1204 the lands of Lucan parish, County Dublin, were granted to Wirris Peche, apparently a native of Hamshire. The name is found elsewhere at that time as well. Richard Peche is found in the reign of Richard II.

Pedelow
The Pedelow family is given in Aderrig parish in the 14th century.

Peepes
A family name found in the city of Dublin in the census of 1659.

Pemberton
It is a surname found in Quaker records in Dublin city in the 18th century.
See also the notes on "Pemberton of Dublin" as found in the "Irish Ancestor", 11 (1), 1979.

Pendergast
Walter Pendergast is found in St. Audeon's parish in the Dublin City Pipe Water Accounts of 1680.

Pennefather
At Island Bridge we find the names of: Green in 1764; Pennefather in 1768; Keightly 1768; and Trail in 1799.

Pennington
A family name found in the city of Dublin in the census of 1659. Widow Pennington is found in St. John's parish in the Dublin City Pipe Water Accounts of 1680.

Penny
A family name found in Dublin at the time of the Birth Index of 1890.

Penoyx
A family name found in Dublin in the census of 1659.

Penteny
A family name found in the city of Dublin in the census of 1659. Richard Penteny of Sugolstown is listed among those transplanted from Dublin, in the works of O'Hart.

Peppard
Pepper
The 1890 birth index finds the family name of Pepper, most numerous in Dublin and Antrim. Pepper is a known variant spelling. (extracted from the 'Book of Irish Families, great & small').
Robert Pepard is found in St. Werburgh's parish in the Dublin City Pipe Water Accounts of 1680.
Walter Peppard is given with lands in Kiltiernan parish. See introduction.
O'Hart gives the family as a principal one settling in Dublin from the 12th to the 18th century.
Walter Peppard was granted the lands of St. George Parish in 1539.

Pepper
Peppard
Capt. Charles Pepper obtained grants of land in Meath in 1666, The birth index of 1890 finds the family centered in Dublin and Antrim. (The above extracted from the 'Book of Irish Families, great & small').

Perkins
Perkens
In Milesian Families the family is said to have come from Wales in 1682 and settled in Dublin and Limerick. (The above extracted from the 'Book of Irish Families, great & small').

Perrier

Milesian Families finds the name in Dublin, of 17th century Brittany origins. (no documentation given).

Perry

A family name we find in Dublin in the birth index of 1890. This name is sometimes given of Welsh origins.

We find the wife of Anthony Perry at Dundrum (d.1756).

Petticrew

It is a surname found in Quaker records in Dublin city in the late 17th and 18th century.

Pettit

Milesian Families finds the name in Dublin, of English origins. (no documentation given).

Phepoes
Pheopoes

According to "Keatings History" the name is that of a principal family of Dublin city or county, and of Anglo-Norman descent. (The above extracted from the 'Book of Irish Families, great & small').

Subsequent to the 12th century invasions, the Phepoes received the lands of Santry and Clontarf.

McPhillip
Philips, Phillip, Phillips

Phillips is quite numerous in both England and Wales,

The 1890 birth index finds the family most numerous in Mayo, Antrim and Dublin. (The above extracted from the 'Book of Irish Families, great & small').

Phillipps is on record in Dublin City in the census of 1659. Phillips is also on record in Dublin City as a name of Jewish extraction.

One Phillip family is found in Aderrig parish in the 14th century.

Phillpot

A family name found in the city of Dublin in the census of 1659. Capt. Nathanial Philpott is found in St. Werburgh's parish in the Dublin City Pipe Water Accounts of 1680..

Phipps

One Charles Phipps, schoolteacher, is given as arriving in the U.S. from Dublin in 1729, in the "Journal of the American Irish Historical Society" v.6.

Picket

Milesian Families finds the name in Dublin, of Norman origins. (no documentation given).

Picknall

A family name found in the city of Dublin in the census of 1659.

Mac Pierce
Peirce, Pers, Pearce, Pearse, Piers

The names of Pierce, Pearce, Persse, etc.. are assumed to have belonged to English settler families in Ireland, The 1890 birth index finds the family most numerous in Dublin and Wexford. (The above e from the 'Book of Irish Families, great & small'). (See major entry in 'The Families of Co. Kerry' as Pierse).

Piggott
Pigott

The birth index of 1890 finds the family centered in Cork and Dublin. (The above extracted from the 'Book of Irish Families, great & small').

Pilson

Thomas Pilson is found in St. John's parish in the Dublin City Pipe Water Accounts of 1680.

Pim

It is a surname found in Quaker records in Dublin city in the 18th and 19th centuries.

Pin

A family name found in the city of Dublin in the census of 1659.

Pinson

A family name found in the city of Dublin in the census of 1659.

Pippard

Ball gives the names of Hanstede; Pippard; de Nottingham; Gernan; Rokeby; and Fitzgerald at Lucan Parish in County Dublin.

Pitts

A family name found in the city of Dublin in the census of 1659.

Playford

A family name found in the city of Dublin in the census of 1659.

Plunkett

Plunket, Plunkitt

The Plunketts are specifically singled out as being of Danish origin.

Linked with Meath, Louth, and the north of Dublin, they achieved rank as Lords of Killeen and Earls of Fingall.

The Plunkett family of Portmarnock House, Dublin, descend from Henry Plunkett who was the Mayor of Dublin in 1546. More on this line can be found in the "Reportorium Novum" 2 (1), 1958. (The above extracted in part from the 'Book of Irish Families, great & small').

King James Irish Army List gives George and William Plunkett of Portmarnock, Co. Dublin among several others of the name. We further find a Walter Plunkett of Portmarnock holding over 600 acres of land in the north of Dublin, and a James Plunkett of of Dunsoghly who held over 1,000. William Plunkett of Dublin in 1618 was granted lands in Co. Kerry.

The family is also given as a principal one of Anglo-Norman descent, settling in Dublin City and County, according to Keatings 'History of Ireland'. The works of O'Hart contain several stems of the family. The family is listed as part of the 'more recent nobility' by O'Hart where they are given as barons of Killeen and earls of Fingal.

The Plunketts are given by Ball to be one of the families located in Mulhuddart parish from the 14th -16th centuries. They are also noted in the area of Dunsoghly and Dunbro in the 16th and 17th centuries.

Pocklington

After the rebellion of 1641 the lands of Killiney parish were held by Gilbert Wye of Belfast; the Mossoms; the Fawcetts; the Pocklingtons; and the Domviles. See introduction.

Pockrich

A brewery was owned by Richard Pockrich at Island Bridge subsequent to 1704.

Polak Of Holland

Pollack Pollock

A family name found in Dublin city, given to be of Jewish heritage in at least one instance. (per 'OLochlainns journal of Irish Families').

Polexfield

A family name found in the city of Dublin in the census of 1659.

Pollard

A family name we find in Dublin in the 1890 Birth Index of Ireland.

Ponsonby

Ponsonby was a name of note at Newlands in Tallaght parish. (See also major entry in 'The Families of Co. Kerry').

Pontoney

A family name found in the city of Dublin in the census of 1659.

Pony

A family name found in the city of Dublin in the census of 1659.

Poole

A family name found in Dublin City in the census of 1659.

Pooley

Widow Honor Pooley is given at Rathcoole parish giving deposition in the 17th century. (see Pooly).

Pooly

A family name found in the city of Dublin in 1659. (see also Pooley).

Poope

Pope

A family name found in the city of Dublin in the census of 1659.

Porter
Le Porter

In modern times it may be considered a name of the province of Ulster. It is a fairly numerous name throughout Ireland today, and is found as both a Catholic and Protestant name.

Note the place name of Porterstown in Meath, Westmeath, Kildare and Dublin. (The above extracted from the 'Book of Irish Families, great & small').

The Porters of Porterstown are given in 14th century Dublin according to Ball.

Pott
A family name found in Dublin in the census of 1659.

Potter
Le Poter, Poter

We find record of the Potter family in Co. Kerry and in Dublin City in the 17th century. (extracted from the 'Book of Irish Families, great & small').

Peter Potter is found in St. Catherine's parish in the Dublin City Pipe Water Accounts of 1680.

Potts
At the close of the 18th century at Robuck, the following were noted in connection with villas built in that era: John Exshaw; James Potts; Alexander Jaffray; Dr. Robert Emmett; and Henry Jackson.

Poudyhard
A family name found in the city of Dublin in the census of 1659.

Povey
In the 17th century we find that Povey was in possession of Powerstown.

Powell
In 1683 the Powell family is found at the castle at Brennanstown.

Power
De Poher, Powre, Powers, Poor, Poors

One of the 60 most numerous names of Ireland, Power is spelled as Poher, le Poer, and Powre etc.. In the 1890 birth index Power is found in Waterford, Cork and Dublin. (extracted from the 'Book of Irish Families, great & small').

Prendergast
Pendergast, Pendergas, Pender, Pendy,

The Prendergas or Pendergass etc...family may trace their line of descent back to Maurice de Prendergast, who arrived with Strongbow in the Anglo-Norman invasions of the 12th century. He became one of the leading families to obtain large grants of land in Ireland as a result of his service in those invasions.

Prendergast became the preferred spelling of the name by the time of the 1890 index, when the family was centered in Mayo, Dublin and Waterford. (extracted from the 'Book of Irish Families, great & small').

Preston
De Preston

The name is first found in records as 'de Preston' in counties Dublin and Meath.

The family is found as Viscounts of Gormanstown, and are cited as Viscount Preston of Dublin. They are as well given in Dublin prior to the 15th century in Ireland.

Keatings History finds the name among the great families of English or Norman descent settled in Meath in early times, and as a principal family of Dublin of Anglo-Norman descent. The family is listed as part of the 'more recent nobility' by O'Hart where they are given as viscounts of Tara.

In the 15th century the Preston family of Saggart parish is noted.

The Preston family of Swainston, Co. Meath descend from John Preston of Dublin and of Ardsallagh, Co. Meath. Robert Preston of Balmadun is found holding over 1,000 acres in 17th century Dublin. (extracted in part from the 'Book of Irish Families, great & small').

Price
Aprice, Rhys, Rice

The birth index of 1890 finds the family centered in Dublin and Antrim. (The above extracted from the 'Book of Irish Families, great & small').

John Price is found in St. Werburgh's parish in the Dublin City Pipe Water Accounts of 1680.

After 1641 in the area of Killakee we find the 'British Protestants': Thomas Price; John Whyte; and William Thomas, all suffering damages.

Prigget
A family name found in the city of Dublin in the census of 1659.

Prinn
A family name found in Dublin in the census of 1659.

Pritchet
A family name found in the city of Dublin in the census of 1659.

Proby
Lord John Proby is found seated at Stillorgan, Co. Dublin in earlier times.

Proby is also noted at Damastown in the 1660's.

Prossor
At the close of the 18th century one 'Mr. Prossor' kept a school at the castle at Ballyfermot.

Purcell
Pursell, Purtill, Purcill, Purshell, Porcel

In 'King James's Irish Army List, 1689' we find listed as a Dublin assessor, one Ignatius Purcell, Esq.. They are also given as an English family found settled in Dublin by at least the 17th century, where they held noted lands at that time.

Kilkenny and Tipperary were still the main centers for the name in 1890, along with Dublin. (extracted from the 'Book of Irish Families, great & small').

At the close of the 16th century we find the Purcell family seated at Crumlin parish (known as Crum or Trum in early times). They remained so for several hundred years.

Purdon
The family so named in Co. Clare is said to have descended from the Purdons of Dublin several centuries ago. Several families of the name are found in the aftermath of the Cromwellian invasions of the 17th century. (The above extracted from the 'Book of Irish Families, great & small').

William Purdon is found in 18th century Glasnevin.

Purdy
Milesian Families finds the name in Dublin, of English origins. (no documentation given).

Purefoy
Milesian Families finds the name in Dublin, of Norman origins. (no documentation given).

Purfield
Milesian Families finds the name in Dublin, of Saxon origins. (no documentation given).

Putland
Although not listed in other major sources, O'Hart gives the 'Putland' family as a principal one settling in Dublin from the 12th to the 18th century.

Henry Mitchell succeeded John Putland in Glasnevin House. He was a banker and a man of great horticultural talent.

Pyn
Nicholas Pyn is found at Dalkey Parish in 1394. See introduction.

Pyne
Pine

Likely of several different origins in Ireland, some of the name are noted in Dublin in the 18th century. (see also 'Families of Co. Cork, Ireland'.).

Quane
Michael Quane of Dublin is found marrying E. Fitzgerald as given in 'Families of Co. Kerry, Ireland,')

Quartermas
Braghall's farm, in Glasnevin Parish, went to John 'Quartermas' and later to John Forster.

Mac Queale
Quail, Quayle, Queale
The name of a family of Manx origins. Most of the name are found in Dublin and Antrim. The pronunciation of the name has been as "Quail" in the past. (The above extracted from the 'Book of Irish Families, great & small').

O'Quigley
Twigley, Cogley, O'quigley, Kegley,
Quigley is listed in the birth index from the last century in the following counties: Londonderry, Dublin, Donegal, Galway, Louth and Sligo.
(The above extracted from the 'Book of Irish Families, great & small').

O'Quinn
Quin, Queen, Quen, O'cuinn, Quinne,
The Quinn name is one of the top 20 most numerous surnames in Ireland.
In the 17th century (O) Quinn was found in Dublin, Kings, Down and Tipperary. In the 1890 index, Quinn (with 2 n's), was the most numerous spelling of the name, being found in Dublin, Tyrone, Antrim and Roscommon. (extracted from the 'Book of Irish Families, great & small').

Radcliffe
Thomas Radcliffe is found under St. Peter Parish and is given involved in legal proceedings regarding Rathmines in 1668. Radcliffe is also given at Kilgobbin. See introduction.

Rafter
Rafter, O'ragher, O'raftery, Roarty,
The name of Rafter is found in Dublin, Queens and Mayo in the 1890 index. (The above extracted from the 'Book of Irish Families, great & small').
A Darby and Michael Rafter are given in Castlekelly townland in the first half of the 19th century.

Raftery
Rafter, O'raghter, O'raftery
In the 1890 index the name of Rafter is given in the counties of Dublin, Queens and Mayo. (extracted from the 'Book of Irish Families, great & small').

Rainllow
A family name found in the city of Dublin in the census of 1659.

Ram
Alderman Ram is found in St. John's parish in the Dublin City Pipe Water Accounts of 1680.

Ramsey
A family name found in Dublin City in the census of 1659.

Randall
Randell
Milesian Families finds the name in Dublin, of English origins.
Noted names in 18th century Milltown, Co. Dublin, included: Mr. Heavisid; Classon; Burr; Hugh Johnson; Randall; Dogherty; Tomlinson; King; and Walcot.

Ransford
Mark Ransford is found in St. Catherine's parish in the Dublin City Pipe Water Accounts of 1680.

Raphson
William Raphson is found in the Montpelier area. See introduction.

Rath
Meldiric, Aubry, Marshall, and Rath families are given in Rathcoole parish in the History of the County Dublin by Ball. Those who took the surname of 'Rath' were said to have done so by the 13th century.

Rathburne
Rathbourne Rathborne
A family name found in Dublin city, given to be of Jewish heritage in at least one instance. (per 'OLochlainns journal of Irish Families').
In another instance the Rathborne family is located at Scribblestown.
Elsewhere, in the 'Dublin Historical Record', we read an entry from a 1957 issue entitled "An Early Dublin Candlemaker: History of the family of Rathborne, Chandlers, Dublin.". (14)
Wm. Rathborne is given at Cardiffsbirdge in the parish of Finglas. See introduction.

Rawlings
Milesian Families finds the name in Dublin, of Welch origins. (no documentation given).

Rawlingson
Rawlinson

The names of Rawlingson and Rawlinson (likely the same name) are found in Dublin city and county in the census of 1659.

Rawson

The family is listed as part of the 'more recent nobility' by O'Hart where they are given as viscounts of Clontarf. O'Hart also gives the family as a principal one settling in Dublin from the 12th to the 18th century.

Raynor

A family name found in Dublin in the census of 1659.

Rea
Raw, Mac Crea, Reagh, Reavy, Wray,

The name of Rea is often of Scottish origin in Ireland, and is commonly found in Antrim and Down

Thomas Matthew Ray. (1801 - 1881) born in Dublin, was a prominent member of O'Connell's Repeal Association. (extracted from the 'Book of Irish Families, great & small').

Read
Reid

It is a surname found in Quaker records in Dublin city in the 18th century. See also Reid.

Readeinge

A family name found in Dublin in the census of 1659.

Reader

Alderman Enoch Reader is found in St. Werburgh's parish in the Dublin City Pipe Water Accounts of 1680.

Real
Reel, Really, O'really, Riall O'realy,

In the census of 1659 we find the family name of Realy as a principal one of Dublin. See also Riall. (The above extracted from the 'Book of Irish Families, great & small').

Realy
Riley Really

A family name found as a principal one in Dublin in the census of 1659.

O' Reddan
Rodan, Ruddan, Ruddanes, Reddin,

Separate families of long standing in the city of Dublin and Leix are on record. (The above extracted from the 'Book of Irish Families, great & small').

Reddy
Ready, Reddington Ruddy

The 1890 birth index finds the family most numerous in Dublin and Kilkenny. (extracted from the 'Book of Irish Families, great & small').

In 1776 we find a Dr. Richard Reddy at Chapelizod parish.

Redesdale

Redesdale House, in Kilmacud Parish, was occupied for a short time by Lord Redesdale in 1799, having passed from the ownership of the Smith family.

Redmond
Redmon, Redmont, Redmun, Radman,

The Redmond family is found to be an Anglo-Norman family in Keatings History. By the time of the 1890 birth index the name was listed in Wexford, Dublin and Wicklow with 79 births. (The above extracted from the 'Book of Irish Families, great & small').

Patrick Redmond is found in St. Audeon's parish in the Dublin City Pipe Water Accounts of 1680.

Reeues   Reeves

Reeues is a family name found in the city of Dublin in the census of 1659. It would appear likely that it is a misspelling of Reeves.

Joseph Reeves is found in St. Werburgh's parish in the Dublin City Pipe Water Accounts of 1680.

O'Regan
Reagan, Reegan, Ragan, Raygan,
Regan and O'Regan..etc. families rank among the top 100 most numerous names in Ireland. (The above extracted from the 'Book of Irish Families, great & small'). (See entry in 'The Families of Co. Cork' as Regane).

The O'Regan family is one of the noted "Four Tribes of Tara", along with O'Hart, O'Kelly and O'Connolly. These tribes of Tara are also described as princes of Bregia, and appear to have possessed territories near Tara in Meath, along with areas in Co. Dublin. They were known as "Lords of Teffia". (per Keatings 'History of Ireland' IGF).

Reid
Reed, Reede, Mulready, Reade,
The 81st most common surname of Ireland, the name ranks 13th in Scotland as well. The normal confusion exists when trying to determine its origin, due to the great number of Scottish and British families of the name in Ireland.

Spelled as Reid the name is found in Antrim, Dublin, Down, Tyrone and Armagh in the 1890 index. (The above extracted from the 'Book of Irish Families, great & small').

O'Reilly
Reily, O'relly, Riley, Reyley, Really,
One of the 12 most numerous names of Ireland, the O'Reillys are a family of the east Breffni. Counties Dublin, Meath and Mayo were prime locations for the name in the 1890 index. The spelling of O'Reilly was listed only in Dublin then. (The above extracted from the 'Book of Irish Families').

A brief line of one O'Reilly family of Dublin is given by O'Hart, with branches noted also in Cavan and Meath, from this same line. The O'Reillys are among the most numerous families of Dublin in 1890.

Among the noted residents of Booterstown in the 18th century were included the names of Cooley; Doherty; Gough; O'Reilly; and Fitzgerald.

In 1780 a 'Mr. Reilly' occupied the castle at Drimnagh, and it is said that Mr. Ennis was the grandfather of the owner before him.

Reis
Reese
A family name found in Dublin city, given to be of Jewish heritage in at least one instance. (per 'OLochlainns journal of Irish Families').

Relick
A family name found in the city of Dublin in the census of 1659.

Relly
Reilly
The lands of Tymon in Tallaght parish were anciently held by O'Mothan and we find Loftus and one Barnaby Relly, (a devout Catholic) there in the 17th century. Relly is also noted at Knocklyon nearby.

Renourd
Col. Peter Renourd who died in 1763 was from Glasnevin Parish.

Renville
The Renvilles at Renvelstown, Co. Dublin are given there in the 14th century according to Ball.

Revell
De Revell
Early names at Newcastle parish after the 12th century invasions included: St. John; de Revell; and le White.

Reyly
Riley   Reily   O'reyly O Reilly
A family name found in the city of Dublin in the census of 1659. Subsequent to the 17th century rebellions we find the names of Wharton; Chambers; Willion; Barry; Robinson; Moses; Reyly; Lovelace; Eaton; Murphy; Lawlor; Leedom; and Walsh in Rathcoole parish, Co. Dublin. See also variant spellings.

Reynolds
Mac Rannall, Grannell, Mcrannall,
  Mac Raghnaill, or Mac Rannall , is an Irish name, sometimes Anglicized to Reynolds.
  Reynolds is also found in Dublin, Antrim and Louth in the 1890 birth index, with a total of 113 births overall.
  (The above extracted from the 'Book of Irish Families, great & small').
  The Reynolds and Russells are noted at Newcastle beginning in the 16th century and in 1612 a 'Reynolds' was among the first city officials.
  O'Hart gives Reynolds of Dublin and mentions Thomas Reynolds, or the 'English MacRannall' who changed his name to Reynolds.

Reynor
  Thomas Reynor is found in St. Michael's parish in the Dublin City Pipe Water Accounts of 1680.

Riall
Real
  The family of Riall of Old Conna Hill, Co. Dublin, descend from one Charles Riall, of Heywood, Clonmel. Capt. Riall was resident there in the early part of the 20th century. See also Real. (The above extracted in part from the 'Book of Irish Families, great & small').

Rice
Roice, Rhys
  Families of the name of Rice may stem from ancient Welsh origins when found in Ireland.
  By the time of the 1890 birth index of Ireland we find some 99 births of the name concentrated in Ulster, found in the counties of Antrim, Armagh, Louth and also in Dublin.   (The above from the 'Book of Irish Families'). (See major entry in 'The Families of Co. Kerry').

Rich
  A family name found in the city of Dublin in the census of 1659.

Richard
Richards
  A family name found in the city of Dublin in the census of 1659. In the 16th century we find the lands of Rathgar held by James Richards and subsequently by Nicholas Segrave.

Richardson
Richardsen
  The families of Richardson in Ireland may be of either Scottish or English extraction originally.
  The birth index of 1890 finds the family centered in Dublin and Antrim.
  (The above extracted from the 'Book of Irish Families, great & small').
  It is a surname found in Quaker records in Dublin city in the 18th century.

Richt
  A family name found in the city of Dublin in the census of 1659.

Rickard
  Ball gives the name of Rickard as being of possible Norse descent in the area near Howth.

Rickard
  See introduction page 30.

Riddle
Riddell
  Milesian Families finds the name in Dublin, of 16th century Scottish origins. (no documentation given).

Rideleford
De Rideleford
  The lands of Kilmacud were granted to Walter de Rideleford, Lord of Bray, along with other lands. They are also found early at Booterstown, Knocklyon, and Donneybrook. Bray served as the seat of Manorial government for de Rideleford after the invasions. (See introduction)

Rider
Ryder
  A family name found in the city of Dublin in the census of 1659. Andrew Trench (d.1750) and John Rider (d.1762) both lived to be 100 years old and are noted in Crumlin parish.

Ridgate
  Hugh Ridgate is found in St. Werburgh's parish in the Dublin City Pipe Water Accounts of 1680.

Rielly
Riley Ryley O'reilly
  A family name found in Dublin at the time of the Birth Index of 1890. See also O'Reilly.

Rigg

A family name found in the city of Dublin in the census of 1659.

Rinkle

Rinkel

Rinkle is given as among the few names of importance in Taney parish in the mid 18th century.

Robert

Roberts

The 'Robert' family name is found in the census of 1659 in Dublin City. 'Roberts' is as well found in Dublin at that time.

'Roberts' is a surname found in Quaker records in Dublin city in the late 17th century.

The Roberts family is found in Old Connaught parish in the mid 18th century and they were given to be of ancient Welsh descent.

Roberts

Robert

Benjamin Roberts is found in St. John's parish in the Dublin City Pipe Water Accounts of 1680. Dr. Robert Roberts (d.1758) is given at Monkstown in the mid 18th century. See also Robert.

Robinson

Robinsen, Robenson

Families of the name of Robinson are found throughout Ireland. They are generally assumed to be of Scottish or English extraction.

Subsequent to the 17th century rebellions we find the names of Wharton; Chambers; Willion; Barry; Robinson; Moses; Reyly; Lovelace; Eaton; Murphy; Lawlor; Leedom; and Walsh in Rathcoole parish, Co. Dublin.

At Tully parish we note the wife of Anthony Robinson (1760) in the obituaries of the day.

The 1890 birth index finds the family most numerous in Antrim, Down, Dublin, Armagh and Tyrone. (The above extracted from the 'Book of Irish Families, great & small').

One family of the name is given to be of Jewish heritage in Dublin City.

It is a surname found in Quaker records in Dublin city in the 18th century.

Robotham

A family name found in the city of Dublin in the census of 1659.

Roche   Roach

De Rupe, De La Rupe, Roach, Roch

The "Roche" family name is fairly common, with the "Roach" spelling being most common in the 1890 index of births. At that time 183 births were recorded in Cork, Wexford, Dublin, Limerick and Mayo.

Place names incorporating this family name are common. . Rocheshill is in Co. Dublin. (The above extracted from the 'Book of Irish Families, great & small'). (See major entry in 'The Families of Co. Cork').

Rochford

Rocheford, Roachforde, Rochfort

The 1890 birth index finds the family most numerous in Dublin, spelled as Rochford. (extracted from the 'Book of Irish Families, great & small').

We find the family at Kilboggett being dispossessed for their part in the rebellion, their lands being subsequently granted to Wm. Domville. See introduction.

Rock

A family name given in Dublin in the Birth Index of 1890. Andrew Rock is found in St. Catherine's parish in the Dublin City Pipe Water Accounts of 1680.

Rogers

Rodgers O' Rory

The 1890 birth index finds the family numerous in Antrim, Down, Dublin and Roscommon. (extracted from the 'Book of Irish Families, great & small').

O'Rory was a name anglicized to Rogers and Rodgers. They are mentioned by O'Dugan as experienced chiefs, one 'of the men of Bregia'.

Rogers is given as among the few names of importance in Taney parish in the mid 18th century.

Rogerson

In the 18th century Dorothy Berkeley is found as the principal resident at Glasnevin Parish, but was shortly replaced by Sir John Rogerson.

Rohan

Roughan

Milesian Families finds the name in Dublin, of Norman origins. (no documentation given).

Rokeby

Ball gives the names of Hanstede; Rokeby; and Fitzgerald at Lucan Parish in County Dublin.

Rolles

At Newcastle in 1614 among the first city officials were: Parsons; Rolles; Kenny; Frend; Davies; White; Burton; Grible; Bridges; Rutledge; and Lushe.

O'Ronan

Roynane Ronane

Milesian Families finds the name in Dublin, of Hy Neil origins. (no documentation given).

Roney

Rooney

A family name found in the city of Dublin in the census of 1659.

Rooke

It is a surname found in Quaker records in Dublin city in the 18th century.

O'Rooney

Mulrooney, Runey, Roony, Roney,

The 1890 birth index indicates that there were some 119 births of 'Rooney' in Dublin, Leitrim, Down, Antrim and Mayo. Only 12 births of Mulrooney were recorded at that time. (The above extracted from the 'Book of Irish Families, great & small').

Roseingrave

Rosengrave

William Roseingrave is given in the village of Dunleary. See introduction.

Rosengrane

A family name found in the city of Dublin in the census of 1659.

Rosenstein Of Germany

A family name found in Dublin city, given to be of Jewish heritage in at least one instance. (per 'OLochlainns journal of Irish Families').

Rosenthal Of Hanover

A family name found in Dublin city, given to be of Jewish heritage in at least one instance. (per 'OLochlainns journal of Irish Families').

Ross

Rossiter, Rosswell...

Ross may have origins in Scotland or England. In Dublin the name is more likely of English extraction. (The above extracted from the 'Book of Irish Families, great & small').

Rothes

Milesian Families finds the name in Dublin, of Scottish origins. (no documentation given).

Rothwell

Rooth, Roth, Ruthe, Ruth, Rothwell

In 1890 we find the name of Rothwell centered in Wexford and Dublin. (The above extracted from the 'Book of Irish Families, great & small').

O'Rourke

Rorke, Roark, Roarke, Rorque, Mcrourke

The name of O'Rourke and its' variant spellings rank among the top 100 most numerous names in all of Ireland.

In the 1890 index 136 births were recorded as 'Rourke' in Dublin, Leitrim, Roscommon and Wexford. (The above extracted from the 'Book of Irish Families, great & small').

Rowlandson

Rolandson

Henry Rowlandson is found in St. Nicholas Parish 'Within the Walls', in the Dublin City Pipe Water Accounts of 1680.

Rowles

A family name found in Dublin in the census of 1659. In the early 16th century William Rowles was of Blanchardstown.

Rowley

Rowly, O'rowley, De Roley

The Rowley family of Marlay Grange, Rathfarnham, Co. Dublin are given in the Irish Book of Arms. (The above extracted from the 'Book of Irish Families, great & small').

The Hon. Clotworth Rowley is given in Finglas parish. See introduction.

Rubinstein

A family name found in Dublin city, given to be of Jewish heritage in at least one instance. (per 'OLochlainns journal of Irish Families').

Rudman

A family name found in Dublin city, given to be of Jewish heritage in at least one instance. (per 'OLochlainns journal of Irish Families').

Rueff

A family name found in Dublin city, given to be of Jewish heritage in at least one instance. (per 'OLochlainns journal of Irish Families').

Russell
Rusell, Russel

The 1890 birth index finds the family most numerous in Antrim, Dublin and Down. (The above extracted from the 'Book of Irish Families, great & small').

In 'King James's Irish Army List, 1689' we find listed as a Dublin assessor, one Capt. Robert Russell. Several others of the name are listed in the biography of Capt. Barholomew Russell in that work, of various places in County Dublin. Several of the name held lands in the 17th century.

Thomas Russell of Brownstown is listed among those transplanted from Dublin, in the works of O'Hart. The Brownstown family was of some note in the 17th century.

Early names at Newcastle parish after the 12th century invasions included: Russell; and le Marshall.

The Reynolds and Russells are noted at Newcastle beginning in the 16th century. The beginning of the 17th century saw the Russell family with many lands in Kilmactalway parish.

It is a surname found several times in Quaker records in Dublin city in the 18th century, found there as merchants and weavers.

Rutledge

At Newcastle in 1614 among the first city officials were: Parsons; Rolles; Kenny; Frend; Davies; White; Burton; Grible; Bridges; Rutledge; and Lushe.

Rutter

John Rutter is found in St. Werburgh's parish in the Dublin City Pipe Water Accounts of 1680.

Rutty
Ruddy

See J. Rutty as noted on page 29.

O'Ryan, Mulryan
O'mulryan, Royan, Ruan, Rouane,

Ryan families rank as one of the ten most numerous in Ireland, and as one of the twenty most numerous surnames of County Dublin. (extracted from the 'Book of Irish Families, great & small').

John Ryan was noted as an entertainer at Chapelizod parish in 1760.

Rynd
Rind

James Rynd (b.1748) of Dublin, is given in the 'Families of Co. Clare', and is given in Clare and Tipperary. This line was originally of Co. Fermanagh in the 1600's.

Rysback

Noted as the one who sculptured the monument for Thomas Wyndham. Thomas Wyndham was laid to rest in Salisbury Cathedral and was a noted resident at Finglas parish.

Ryves
Reeves   Reaves

Sir Richard Ryves is found in St. Michael's parish in the Dublin City Pipe Water Accounts of 1680.

Among houses noted at Ballyfermot were those of: Verveer; Styles; Carden; Ryves; Exham; and Talbot of Templeogue.

Sall
Saul, Sale, De La Salle

The name is rather widespread in older records, including being found in Meath, Dublin and Kilkenny. (The above extracted from the 'Book of Irish Families, great & small').

Salmon
Solomon Salaman
The census of 1659 finds the Salmon family in Dublin City.
Individuals of the name:
From the census of 1659;
John Salmon. Merchant. From the city of Dublin.
Other: Rev. George Salmon, D.D.. 1819-1904. Dublin University . (The above extracted from the 'Book of Irish Families, great & small').
The similar sounding name of Salaman belonged to a Jewish family in Dublin City. (see also Solomon)

Saltinsball
A family name found in the city of Dublin in the census of 1659.

Sampson
Samson
A family name found in Dublin city, given to be of Jewish heritage in at least one instance. (per 'OLochlainns journal of Irish Families').
In another instance we find that Hillbrook, near Abbotstown, was the home of Lt. Col. Robert Sampson (d.1764). He seems to descend from a Scots family identified with Co. Donegal, as stated by Ball.

Samuelson
A family name found in Dublin city, given to be of Jewish heritage in at least one instance. (per 'OLochlainns journal of Irish Families').

Sancky
Sanky Sanchy
A family name found in the city of Dublin in the census of 1659. Note also the spelling of Sankey in that same document.

Sanders, Saunders
Sanderson
The name is of both English and Scottish extraction. The birth index of 1890 finds the family name of Saunders centered in Dublin and Antrim. (The above extracted from the 'Book of Irish Families, great & small').

Sandford
Sanford
A family name found in the city of Dublin in the census of 1659.

Sandheim
A family name found in Dublin city, given to be of Jewish heritage in at least one instance. (per 'OLochlainns journal of Irish Families').

Sands
Sand, Sandes, Sandys
We find the Sands family in scattered locations in our records. In the 17th century families of the name are found in Kildare, Wexford, Kerry and Dublin to name some locations. (The above extracted from the 'Book of Irish Families, great & small').

Sandwith
It is a surname found in Quaker records in Dublin city in the 18th century, given there was a merchant of the name.

Sankey
Sancky Sanky
A family name found in Dublin in the census of 1659. Note also the spelling of Sancky also found in that document.

St. Michan's Church—Burial-place of Emmet.

Sarsfield
Archfield, Sarsefeld

Keatings History gives us reference to the Sarsfield family in Dublin.

The family was granted lands in the 14th century in Co. Cork, and some of this line are subsequently found in and near Lucan, Co. Dublin. (The above extracted from the 'Book of Irish Families, great & small'). The Lucan estates of the family were in excess of 1500 acres. They were received after an attainder of the Kildare Fitzgeralds in the 16th century.

The family is also given as a principal one of Anglo-Norman descent, settling in Dublin City and County, according to Keatings 'History of Ireland'.

In 'King James's Irish Army List, 1689' we find listed as a Dublin assessor, one Col. Patrick Sarsfield.

John Sarsfield is found in St. Werburgh's parish in the Dublin City Pipe Water Accounts of 1680.

The family is listed as part of the 'more recent nobility' by O'Hart where the noted Patrick Sarsfield, commander under James II, was 'Earl of Lucan', Co. Dublin.

The fortunes of the family suffered with the coming of Cromwell.

Sir William Sarsfield made Lucan Castle one of the principal houses in Co. Dublin.

Savage
Savauge Savadge

The Savage family is found in the 1890 birth index and under the spelling of Savadge we find the family name in Dublin City in 1659.

The Savage family is also noted in the 15th century in Saggart parish.

At Finglaswood House, in Finglas Parish, we find Thomas Savage, who established a tannery there.

Sawey

Milesian Families finds the name in Dublin, of English origins. (no documentation given).

Sayers
Sears. Say.

This English sounding name is most often found in the area around Dublin, in Co. Kerry, and in Ulster. (The above extracted from the 'Book of Irish Families, great & small').

Scally
Skelly, Mac Skally, O'skelly

We find Scally most numerous in counties Roscommon, Westmeath and Dublin in the 19th century. (The above extracted from the 'Book of Irish Families, great & small').

Scarborough

Scarborough and Scarborrough are both on record in Dublin in the census of 1659. We also find Scurlock and McDaniel at Newcastle parish giving place to Scarborough and Jones.

Robert Scarborough is given as a principal resident in the townland of Aderrig. See introduction.

Scott

The family name of Scott is the 10th most common name of Scotland, and among the 90th most numerous names in Ireland. It is generally assumed that the name is of Scottish origins in Ireland.

In the 1890 birth index of Ireland 196 births of the name were recorded mainly in Antrim, Down, Londonderry and Dublin. (The above extracted from the 'Book of Irish Families, great & small').

It is a surname found in Quaker records in Dublin city in the 18th century.

Scriven

William Scriven is found in St. John's parish in the Dublin City Pipe Water Accounts of 1680.

O'Scully
Skully, Scully, Scullion, Scullin, Sculy,

Both Scally and Scully families are found in Dublin in the last century.

One William O'Scully was found in possession of lands in Dublin in 1256. (The above extracted from the 'Book of Irish Families, great & small').

Scurlock
Scurlagh Scurlogh
The Scurlock family is found at Rathcoole from the 15th century.
In 1641 it was a stronghold of the Irish with the support of the Scurlocks and Hetheringtons.

We also find Scurlock and McDaniel at Newcastle parish giving place to Scarborough and Jones. (See intro).

See the notes on " The Scurlocks of Rathcredan" in "Reportorium Novum", 1 (1), 1955.

The Scurlaghs are given by Ball to be one of the families in Mulhuddart parish from the 14th -16th centuries.

Seagrave
Segrave
According to "Keatings History" the name is that of a principal family of Dublin city or county, and of Anglo-Norman descent.

One family of the name descends from Captain John Segrave, of Cabra, Co. Dublin, found there in the late 18th century. Of this line was the Segrave who died at the hands of the great Hugh O'Neill at the battle of Clontibret. This family supported the cause of King James II, until the fall of Limerick.   More on this line of the family is found in "Reportorium Novum" 1 (2), 1956. (The above extracted from the 'Book of Irish Families, great & small').

We also find Henry Seagrave, of Cabra, holding nearly 1,000 acres of land as an Irish Catholic in 17th century Dublin. They are found intermarried with prominent Protestant families, and were known for dealing fairly with the English.

In the 16th century we find the lands of Rathgar held by James Richards and subsequently by Nicholas Segrave.

Seaman
A family name found in the city of Dublin in the census of 1659.

Seden
A family name found in the city of Dublin in the census of 1659.

Sedgraue
Sedgrave
A family name found in Dublin in the census of 1659. Subsequent to his 15th century listings, we find the Sedgraves, of the Dublin mercantile family at Aderrig parish.

Sedgrave of Cabra is noted in the 17th century at Kilmahuddrick parish.

Seery
A family name found in Dublin at the time of the Birth Index of 1890.

Segerson
Sigerson
Chris Segerson of Dublin, held a grant of Ballinskelligs Abbey in 1615. The family is also given of Norse origins, serving as merchants at Dublin. (See also, 'Families of Co. Kerry, Ireland.')

Segrave
See Seagrave.

Semple
Simple
Milesian Families finds the name in Dublin, of Scottish origins. (no documentation given).

Sergeant
Sergent Seargent Serjeant
Sergeant and Sergent are both found in Dublin City in 1659.

In the 14th century we find John Mynagh, Robert Serjeant, and Roger Kilmore at Simmonscourt. See introduction.

Seward
A family name found in Dublin in the census of 1659.

Shackleford
Milesian Families finds the name in Dublin, of Saxon origins. (no documentation given).

Shakleton
John Shakleton is found in St. John's parish in the Dublin City Pipe Water Accounts of 1680.

Shane
A family name found in the city of Dublin in the census of 1659.

O' Sharkey
O'sharkey,o'serky,sharket, O'sherkott...
In the 1890 birth index of Ireland, 57 births of the name were recorded as "Sharkey", and most of the family was found in Roscommon, Donegal, Tyrone, Dublin and Louth. (extracted from the 'Book of Irish Families, great & small').

Sharp
It is a surname found in Quaker records in Dublin city in the latter 17th century.

Shaw
Shawe
The most noted family of the name hailed from Dublin. The 1890 birth index finds the family most numerous in Antrim, Down and Dublin. (The above extracted from the 'Book of Irish Families, great & small').

O'Hart gives the family as a principal one settling in Dublin from the 12th to the 18th century.

Mr. Robert Shaw occupied Terenure House in the latter 18th century. See introduction.

Shea
In 1771 we find the obituary of the wife of Mr. Shea, a linen draper, at Dundrum.

Sheapherd
Shepherd Sheaperd
Sheapherd and Sheapheard are both given in Dublin City in the Census of 1659.

Sheils
O' Shiel Shields
A family name found in Dublin at the time of the Birth Index of 1890. See also O'Shiel.

Shelly
Shelley, Shelloe, Shallowe, Shalloo
Some of the name of Shelly will be of English heritage. The 19th century birth index records indicate that the family of Shelly was centered in Tipperary and Dublin at that time. (The above extracted from the 'Book of Irish Families, great & small').

Shelton
A family name found in Dublin City in the census of 1659.

Sherding
A family name found in the city of Dublin in the census of 1659.

Shergoll
The Shergoll family is found around Howth in the 17th century.

O' Sheridan
Sherden, Sherdon, Sherdan, Sherodan,
The 1890 birth index gives the family in Cavan, Dublin and Mayo with 145 births around that time. (The above extracted from the 'Book of Irish Families, great & small').

Sherlock
Sherlog
According to "Keatings History" the name is among the chief families of English descent settling in Waterford and Tipperary. The birth index of 1890 finds the family centered in Dublin. (The above extracted from the 'Book of Irish Families, great & small').

Sherry
Sharry, O'sherry, Mac Sherry, Mcshery,
The 1890 birth index finds the family of Sherry centered in Monaghan, Dublin and Meath. (extracted from the 'Book of Irish Families, great & small').

Sherwin
Sharvin
Most of the name in our records hail from Dublin, and many are of English extraction here.
(see also 'Irish Names and Surnames' by Rev. P. Woulfe.) (extracted from the 'Book of Irish Families, great & small').

O' Shiel   Sheilds
Sheilds, Shield, Shiel, Sheil, Shiell
The O'Shiel or O'Sheil family of Ireland is most often found in Dublin, Donegal and Londonderry in the 1890 birth index of Ireland. (extracted from the 'Book of Irish Families, great & small').

Shillingford
In 1393 we find John Shillingford at Clondalkin parish.

Shipcott
Shipsea, Shippy, Shipward, Shipton, Shipcott
Shipcott is found in Dublin city in the 1659 census. (The above extracted from the 'Book of Irish Families, great & small'). Shippy is also a name found in rural Dublin.

Shiply
Shippy
Robert Shiply is found in St. John's parish in the Dublin City Pipe Water Accounts of 1680.

Shore
A family name found in Dublin in the census of 1659. Capt. Wm. Shore is found in St. Peters parish in Dublin and he is given connected to Co. Fermanagh as well.

Short
Shortall
The name of Short is generally assumed to be that of settler families in Ireland, coming from both Scotland and England. As would be expected many of the name are found in the province of Ulster and in Dublin. (The above extracted from the 'Book of Irish Families, great & small').

Shortall   Shortell
Short
The 1890 birth index finds the family most numerous in Dublin and Kilkenny. (extracted from the 'Book of Irish Families, great & small').

Shuldham
In 1703 Edmond Shuldham of Dublin, purchased lands in Co. Clare. (see (Families of Co. Clare, Ireland'.).

Shurlog
Sherlock Shurlock
A family name found in the city of Dublin in the census of 1659.

Siev
A family name found in Dublin city, given to be of Jewish heritage in at least one instance. (per 'OLochlainns journal of Irish Families').

Simons
Symons Simmons
A family name found in Dublin city, given to be of Jewish heritage in at least one instance. (per 'OLochlainns journal of Irish Families').

Simons and Simmons are surnames found in Quaker records in Dublin city in the 18th century.

Singleton
Harry Singleton is given at Clonturk Parish according to Ball.

Sinnot
Synott, Synot, Synnott, Sinnott
Spelled as Synnott the name is one of Dublin in the year 1890, with a total of 12 entries in the birth index. (The above extracted from the 'Book of Irish Families, great & small').

Sinton
It is a surname found in Quaker records in Dublin city in the first half of the 19th century.

Sirr
See the work entitled " A Genealogical History of the Family of Sirr of Dublin". London. 1903.

Sisk
Siske
Milesian Families finds the name in Dublin, of Danish origins. (no documentation given).

Skelly
A family name given in Dublin in the Birth Index of 1890.

Skelton
Skelten
Skelton is a name which we have found in Dublin in the 15th century. The census of 1659 finds the name in the city of Dublin as well. (extracted from the 'Book of Irish Families, great & small').

Under the biography for Lt. Thomas Skelton in King James' Irish Army List we find mention of John and Bevil Skelton of Dublin as appearing on the attainders of 1691. That source also gives that a genealogical manuscript in Trinity College, Dublin, gives five generations of Skeltons from Limerick.

Skiddy
Milesian Families finds the name in Dublin, of English origins. (no documentation given).

Skully
Skelly
A family name found in Dublin at the time of the Birth Index of 1890.

Slator
Slater
A family name found in Dublin at the time of the Birth Index of 1890.

Slingsby
In Clonsilla parish at the east end of the Clonsilla church was the 18th century burial place for a branch of the Slingsby family, one of whom was given as 'alias Finglas'.

Smallman
It is a surname found in Quaker records in Dublin city in the latter half of the 17th century.

Smidt
Schmidt
A family name found in Dublin city, given to be of Jewish heritage in at least one instance. (per 'OLochlainns journal of Irish Families').

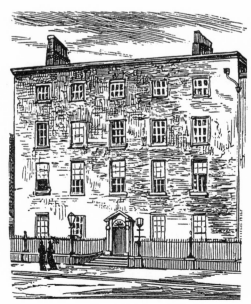

Mornington House.

Smith
Smythe, Smithe, Mac Gorhain, Going,
In Ireland the name ranks among the 10 most numerous surnames. The spellings of Smyth and Smythe are found commonly in Ireland as well.

The birth index of 1890 gives "Smith" as the most common spelling of the name with 471 births concentrated in Antrim, Cavan, Dublin and Kerry. Estate papers on the Smith family in Ireland are at the National Library of Ireland in Dublin. (The above extracted from the 'Book of Irish Families, great & small').

Thomas Smith, a fellow of Trinity College is noted at Laughanstown.

William Smith is given as a principal resident of Palmerston in the 17th century.

Smyth of Belmont House, Stillorgan, county Dublin, is found recorded in tombstone inscriptions at Irishtown, Co. Dublin in the 19th century.

Redesdale House in Kilmacud Parish, was occupied for a short time by Lord Redesdale in 1799, having passed from the ownership of the Smith family.

O'Hart gives the family as a principal one settling in Dublin from the 12th to the 18th century.

Smith ranked as the 5th most numerous surname in Dublin in 1890, coming right after 'Murphy'.

The school at Finglas had Williams, Teebay and Smith as licensed masters, around the end of the 17th century or shortly thereafter.

Smothe
The name of Simmonscourt is given to have come from the Smothe family, who succeeded the Morville family there. See introduction.

Smullen
A family name found in Dublin at the time of the Birth Index of 1890.

Solomon
Salmon Salaman
Solomon and Solomons are given as family names found in Dublin city of Jewish extraction. (see also Salaman / Salmon)

Somers

Sommers Summers

A family name of Dublin in the birth index of 1890.

Somerville

Somers Summerly

Families of the name of Somerville may have arrived from Scotland or England. The birth index of 1890 finds the family name of Somers centered in Wexford and Dublin. (from the 'Book of Irish Families, great & small').

Sommerford

It is a surname found in Quaker records in Dublin city in the 18th century.

Southwell

Thomas-George Southwell is found seated at Rathkeal, Co. Limerick, and at Clontarfe, Co. Dublin in earlier times. Glensouthwell in Whitechurch parish was built by the Southwells.

Southy

A family name found in the city of Dublin in the census of 1659.

Sowthick

George Sowthick is found in St. Werburgh's parish in the Dublin City Pipe Water Accounts of 1680.

Sparrow

The family of William Sparrow of Sandymount, Co. Dublin, is of record at Irishtown, Co. Dublin.

Speght

Thomas Speght is found in St. Werburgh's parish in the Dublin City Pipe Water Accounts of 1680.

Spence

A family name found in the city of Dublin in the census of 1659.

Spencer

Milesian Families finds the name in Dublin, of English origins. (no documentation given). Also given in Dublin in the 1890 birth index.

Spiers

Speers

A name sometimes found in Dublin city.

Spiro

A family name found in Dublin city, given to be of Jewish heritage in at least one instance. (per 'OLochlainns journal of Irish Families').

Spranger

Springer

A family name found in the city of Dublin in the census of 1659. Mrs. Spranger is found in St. Catherine's parish in the Dublin City Pipe Water Accounts of 1680.

Spring

Springham, Springe

Families of the name of Spring are found in counties Dublin and Kerry in the 17th century, and families of the name of Springham are found in Dublin and Londonderry at that time. (The above extracted from the 'Book of Irish Families, great & small'). (See major entry in 'The Families of Co. Kerry').

Springham

A family name found in Dublin in the census of 1659.

Sproule

Sprule

It is a surname found in Quaker records in Dublin city in the 19th century.

St. John

Early names at Newcastle parish after the 12th century invasions included St. John; de Revell; and le White.

St. Lawrence
Lawrence Laurence Lawrance Laurance

The St. Lawrence family held the lands of Howth from the 12th century into modern times. The seat of the family for over 700 years was at Howth Castle, not far from the isthmus on the northern shore of the peninsula.

Much information on the family can be found in The History of The County Dublin by Ball. Legend has it that the original name of the founder of the name in Ireland was 'Tristam'. It is further given that Howth was granted to him on the feast of St. Lawrence, hence the family adopted the name. See introduction under Howth.

The name of St. Lawrence is given in Dublin City in the 1659 census. The names of St. Lawrence and St. Lawrence are found in Dublin at that time as well. The spelling of Lawrence remained in Dublin at the time of the 1890 Birth Index.

It should be remembered that St. Lawrence can be shortened to Lawrence, but this is not always the case.

The family is also given as a principal one of Anglo-Norman descent, settling in Dublin City and County, according to Keatings 'History of Ireland'. (see also Laurence). The family is listed as part of the 'more recent nobility' by O'Hart where they are given as earls of Howth in Dublin. Arms for the Gaisford-St. Lawrence family of Howth are shown in the 'Irish Book of Arms'.

St. Michael
Michael

Noted families at Killakee were those of Henry Joy; Guinness; St. Michael; and Mr. Lundy Foot.

Stafford
Staford

The 1890 birth index finds the family most numerous in Wexford and Dublin. (The above extracted from the 'Book of Irish Families, great & small').

Stanford

A family name found in the city of Dublin in the census of 1659.

Stanihurt
Stanihurst Stanyhurst

According to "Keatings History" the name is that of a principal family of Dublin city or county, and of Anglo-Norman descent. (The above extracted from the 'Book of Irish Families, great & small'). In O'Harts list of principal families of Dublin is listed the 'Stanihurst' family.

James Stanyhurst is given in the area of Seapoint and Templehill in the 18th century. See introduction.

Stanley

We find the Stanley or Stanly family name in Dublin City in the census of 1659 and in the 1890 birth index.

John Stanley is found in St. Werburgh's parish in the Dublin City Pipe Water Accounts of 1680.

Stannard

Names connected to Rathfarnham parish in the 18th century were Palliser; O'Callaghan; Cramer; Coghill; Stannard; Fountain; Ward; Geering; How; Boyle; and Blackburn.

Stanton
Staunton

A family name of Dublin City as given in the census of 1659.

Stanyhurst
Stanihurst Stanyhurt

Given as an early settler name in Dublin. Be aware of spellings.

Stapleton
Gaul

Dublin and Limerick are also given as early areas of settlement by the family. (The above extracted from the 'Book of Irish Families, great & small').

Starky

It is a surname found in Quaker records in Dublin city in the 18th century.

Staughton
Staunton
Staughton was a family name found in the city of Dublin in the census of 1659. In the biography for Cornet Patrick Staunton found in King James' Irish Army List we find that in 1220 one Adam de Staunton was granted lands in Kilbrenin, with the mill and the church, and the tithes, to Christ Church Dublin, for the founding of a cell with resident canons.

Stavenhagen
A family name found in Dublin city, given to be of Jewish heritage in at least one instance. (per 'OLochlainns journal of Irish Families').

Steele
Steel, Steill, O'steille, O'steill
The surname of Steele is of probable English origin. Looking exclusively at the 'Steele' spelling, we find the name listed in Dublin city on the census of 1659. (The above extracted from the 'Book of Irish Families, great & small').

Stellman
A family name found in Dublin city, given to be of Jewish heritage in at least one instance. (per 'OLochlainns journal of Irish Families').

Stephens
Stephen, Stephenson, Fitzstephen.
It is today considered a name of Dublin and County Mayo.
'Stephenson', a name which can be shortened to Stephens on occasion, is found in 1659 as a name of Dublin city. (The above extracted from the 'Book of Irish Families, great & small').
'Stephens' is a surname found in Quaker records in Dublin city in the 18th century.
John Stephens, an eminent tanner and weaver, died in 1761. (see St. James and St. Jude parish- introduction).
In 16th century Glasnevin Parish leases are found held by Thomas and Oliver Stephens, Alson FitzSimon, and James and John Bathe.

Stephenson
Stevenson
A family name found in the city of Dublin in the census of 1659.

Sterling
A family name found in Dublin in the census of 1659..

Sterne
In the 18th century we find the families of Twigg, Stoyte, Jocelyn, and Sterne at the manor at Donneybrook. See introduction.

Steward
Stewart
A family name found in the city of Dublin in the census of 1659. Also found spelled as Stewart.

Stewart
Stuart, Steuart, Steward
Families of the name of Stewart, etc.. in Ireland are assumed to be of Scottish origins unless known otherwise.
Families are found as well in Summerhill, Co. Dublin in the 'Irish Book of Arms.' (The above extracted from the 'Book of Irish Families, great & small'). Also found spelled as Steward.

Stibbe
A family name found in Dublin city, given to be of Jewish heritage in at least one instance. (per 'OLochlainns journal of Irish Families').

Stiles
A family name found in the city of Dublin in the census of 1659.

Stock
We find Stephen Stock, Daniel Kinahan and Nathaniel Hone in the vicinity of Churchtown in Taney parish in the 18th century. See introduction.

Stokes
Stoke
The family name is cited in Co. Dublin and Co. Down in the 15th century or prior, in the works of O'Hart. (The above extracted from the 'Book of Irish Families, great & small').
The spelling as Stoakes is found in Dublin City in the 1659 census.
Carrig Breac was long the home of physician Wm. Stokes, near Howth.

Stopford
A family name found in the city of Dublin in the census of 1659.

Storey

William Storey is found in St. Werburgh's parish in the Dublin City Pipe Water Accounts of 1680.

Storton

A family name found in the city of Dublin in the census of 1659.

Stoughton

A family name found in the city of Dublin in the census of 1659. (Note also the name of 'Straughton' found at that time.)

George Stoughton is found in St. Werburgh's parish in the Dublin City Pipe Water Accounts of 1680.

Stowell

George Stowell is found in St. Werburgh's parish in the Dublin City Pipe Water Accounts of 1680.

Stoyte

Richard Stoyte is found in St. Werburgh's parish in the Dublin City Pipe Water Accounts of 1680.

In the 18th century we find the families of Twigg, Stoyte, Jocelyn, and Sterne at the manor at Donneybrook. See introduction.

Strabane

A family name found in Dublin in the census of 1659.

Strange

Milesian Families finds the name in Dublin, of English origins. (no documentation given).

Strangman

It is a surname found in Quaker records in Dublin city in the 18th century.

Straughton

A family name found in Dublin in the census of 1659. Note also the name of 'Stoughton' at that time.

Strettle

It is a surname found in Quaker records in Dublin city in the latter 17th and 18th centuries. Several are found as merchants.

Strickland

Milesian Families finds the name in Dublin, of English origins. (no documentation given).

Strieley

Milesian Families finds the name in Dublin, of English origins. (no documentation given).

Strong

Milesian Families finds the name in Dublin, of English origins. (no documentation given).

Stryny

A family name found in the city of Dublin in the census of 1659.

Styles

Among houses noted at Ballyfermot were those of: Verveer; Styles; Carden; Ryves; Exham; and Talbot of Templeogue.

Sueterby

Two of the earliest tenants noted at 'St. Catherines and St. Nicholas Without' are Wm. Moenes of Rathmines and Nicholas Sueterby.

O'Sullivan
Sulliban, Sulivan, Soolivan

The O'Sullivan name is the third most numerous name in all of Ireland . Sullivan was the preferred spelling of the name in 1890, with 839 recorded births throughout Ireland and in Dublin. (From the 'Book of Irish Families, great & small'). (See major entry in 'The Families of Co. Cork'). (See major entry in 'The Families of Co. Kerry').

Sulyvant
Sullivan

John Sulyvant is found in St. Werburgh's parish in the Dublin City Pipe Water Accounts of 1680.

Summer Summars
Somers

Summer and Summars are both names of Dublin City in the census of 1659.

Supple Suppels
Suppels, Suppel, Soople

Supple is another family name which arrived in Ireland along with the invasion by Strongbow around 1171. (The above extracted from the 'Book of Irish Families, great & small').

Surdeville

Widow Surdeville is found in St. Michael's parish in the Dublin City Pipe Water Accounts of 1680.

Sutton
De Sutun

The 1890 birth index gives the name in Dublin, Wexford and Cork.

(The above extracted from the 'Book of Irish Families, great & small').

It is a surname found in Quaker records in Dublin city in the 18th century.

Ball gives the Sutton family as likely residing on the southern lands near Howth.

Swan

A family name found in Dublin in both the 1659 census and in the 1890 birth index of Ireland.

Wm. Swan is given at the Parish of Finglas. See introduction.

Swanton
Swan

Swanton families are assumed to be of English settler origins. The 1890 index finds 5 of the name in Cork and 2 of the name in Dublin. "Swan" is found in Dublin and Antrim then. (The above extracted from the 'Book of Irish Families, great & small').

Sweetman
Sweteman

Families of the name in Ireland are given to be of Norse origins.

They are given in the county and city of Dublin as among the principle families of foreign descent from the 12th to the 18th centuries according to the works of O'Hart, and Keatings 'History'.

Both the census of 1659 and the 1890 birth index find the name in Cork and Dublin. (The above extracted from the 'Book of Irish Families, great & small').

Swift
Swifte, Tappy, Fodey, O'tapa

One Swift family is recorded in Dublin, and subsequently in Kilkenny. (The above extracted from the 'Book of Irish Families, great & small').

Godwin Swift is found in St. Werburgh's parish in the Dublin City Pipe Water Accounts of 1680.

See also "Notes on the Cooke, Ashe and Swift Families" (Dublin), in the "Journal of the Association for the Preservation of Memorials for the Dead." 9, 1912+.

The family is also found near the lands of Sutton, near Howth.

Swinfeild

A family name found in Dublin in the census of 1659. At Dean's Grange the chief house was occupied by Ralph and Nathanial Swinfield. See introduction.

In 1623 William Wolverston, the owner of Stillorgan, held the lands of Tipperstown, and in 1645 they were held by Richard Swinfield of Murphystown.

Swords

A family name found in Dublin at the time of the Birth Index of 1890.

Symons
Simons

A family name found in Dublin city, given to be of Jewish heritage in at least one instance. (per 'OLochlainns journal of Irish Families').

Synge

John M. Synge (1871 - 1909) was the noted author and playwright of the name, of Dublin roots.

(The above extracted from the 'Book of Irish Families, great & small').

Synnott
Synott, Sinnott

The name is found in early records of Dublin city and in Wexford. Note also the spelling of Sinnot. (The above extracted from the 'Book of Irish Families, great & small').

Synyres

A family name found in the city of Dublin in the census of 1659.

Taaffe

Taa, Taff, Taafe, Taffe

Those of the Taafee family name in Ireland are given to be of Welsh descent. They are found in Ireland around the time of the Norman invasions of the 12th century. They can subsequently be found in Dublin and Louth. (The above extracted from the 'Book of Irish Families, great & small').

Tacker

A family name found in the city of Dublin in the census of 1659.

Talant

Tallent

A family name found in the city of Dublin in the census of 1659. (see also Tallon)

Swift's Birthplace.

Talbot

One family of the name arrived in England with William the Conqueror. Richard Talbot settled at Malahide, Co. Dublin and the name is of long standing there, holding over 1,600 acres of land in the 17th century there. One Henry Talbot of Templeogue is also found as a substantial landowner at that time. Peter Talbot came to hold Bullock Castle, and may have been killed by a party of kerns (Irish mercenaries) in 1555.

In the middle ages the lands of Loughlinstown belonged to the Talbots, being held under them by the Goodmans.

The Talbot family of Mt. Talbot, Co. Roscommon, descends from Richard Talbot of Templeoge, Co. Dublin in the 16th century. (The above extracted in part from the 'Book of Irish Families, great & small'). Capt. James Talbot of "Templeogue" is given in King James' Irish Army List. In Dublin and Galway he suffered confiscation's.

John Talbott of Malahide is listed among those transplanted from Dublin in the works of O'Hart. See also "Talbot de Malahide" in the "Reportorium Novum" 2 (1) 1958. Talbott is found in Dublin in the census of 1659 as well.

In 'King James's Irish Army List, 1689' we find listed as a Dublin assessor, one John Talbot of Belgard.

The family is also given as a principal one of Anglo-Norman descent, settling in Dublin City and County, according to Keatings 'History'. The family is listed as part of the 'recent nobility' by O'Hart and are given as earls of Shrewsbury, centered at Malahide and Belgard in Dublin. (see introduction). The Belgard branch also held lands at Rochestown.

See also the work entitled "The Genealogical Memoir of the Family of Talbot of Malahide, Co. Dublin." 1829.

At Belgard in the 15th century the Talbots of Feltrim are found at the castle. At Kilnamanagh the Talbot; Belgard; Parsons; Fitzwilliam; and Hawkins families are given of note.

Talbot

(cont'd.) The Talbot families, who were Roman Catholic, are found at Templeogue in the parish of Tallaght.

Among houses noted at Ballyfermot were those of: Ververeer; Styles; Carden; and Talbot of Templeogue.

Tallon

The Tallon family is given as settling early in areas around Dublin. Our 19th century records show the family centered in Dublin as well. (extracted from the 'Book of Irish Families, great & small'). (see also Talant)

Tally
Mactully, Mac Atilla, O'tully, Flood

Families of the name of Tally in Ireland may spring from one of several unrelated families.

A century ago the name was most common in Galway, Dublin and Cavan.

(The above extracted from the 'Book of Irish Families, great & small').

Tansy
Tansey

Milesian Families finds the name in Dublin, of Norman origins. (no documentation given).

Tasker

James Tasker is found in St. Werburgh's parish in the Dublin City Pipe Water Accounts of 1680.

Tate
Taite Tayte

Milesian Families finds the name in Dublin, of English origins. (no documentation given).

Tatton

Thomas Egerton was a member of the Tatton family who died in 1756 at Glasnevin Parish.

Taunton

Names associated with the settlement of Balally in Taney parish were: de Walhope; Othyr; Howell; Taunton; Walsh in 1407 and Borr in the 17th century. It was given originally as a Danish settlement.

Taylor
Tailor, Tayler, Tailer

Taylor is traditionally linked with the province of Ulster. One family of the name came from Yorkshire in England and subsequently settled at Swords, in Co. Dublin. They were among the minor gentry in 17th century Dublin.

Other families of the name of note are those of Taylor of Old Court, Harolds Cross in Dublin, and Taylour of Dublin City. Sir James Taylor was Lord Mayor of Dublin in 1765 and held lands at Kingstown as well. See introduction.

The Taylor family of Ardgillan Castle, Co. Dublin, is given in the Irish Book of Arms. (The above extracted from the 'Book of Irish Families, great & small').

Thomas Taylor of Prospect, Dublin is given in the Irish Book of Arms (IGF Edition). George Taylor is given as Recorder of Dublin in the 16th century, according to the biography of Capt. John Taylor given in King James Irish Army List.

It is a surname found in Quaker records in Dublin city in the 18th century.

Samuel Taylor is found in St. Werburgh's parish in the Dublin City Pipe Water Accounts of 1680.

Christopher Taylor is found at Esker parish in the 17th century.

One of the Taylor name is also found occupying the land of Fortick's Grove, as given in the entry under St. George Parish in the introduction to this book.

Tedcastle

Marlay House, in Whitechurch Parish, was the seat of the La Touche family, later owned by R. Tedcastle.

Teebay

The school at Finglas had Williams, Teebay and Smith as licensed masters, around the end of the 17th century or shortly thereafter.

Teeling
Telyng

We find the name in Co. Westmeath in the census of 1659, and centered in Dublin in the 19th century. (The above extracted from the 'Book of Irish Families, great & small').

Temple

The census of 1659 finds the Temple family name in Dublin city, and it is also found in the Poll Money Ordnance records of that era. Henry Temple is found at Palmerstown, Co. Dublin in the Irish Book of Arms (IGF edition).

The Temple family, holding the title of Palmerston, came to possess Rathmines in the 18th century. See introduction.

The family is listed as part of the 'more recent nobility' by O'Hart where they are given as 'viscount Palmerston or Palmerstown", Co. Dublin.

Terrell
Tyrell

Milesian Families finds the name in Dublin, of Norman origins. (no documentation given).

Terry

Milesian Families finds the name in Dublin, of English origins. (no documentation given).

Tew

Although not given in several other sources, O'Hart gives the family as a principal one settling in Dublin from the 12th to the 18th century.

Thackerly

It is a surname found in Quaker records in Dublin city in the late 17th century, where we find one Ezra Thackerly.

Theswell

A family name found in the city of Dublin in the census of 1659.

Thomas

Milesian Families finds the name in Dublin, of Welch origins. (no documentation given).

It is a surname found in Quaker records in Dublin city in the latter 17th and 18th centuries.

After 1641 in the area of Killakee we find the 'British Protestants': Thomas Price; John Whyte; and William Thomas, all suffering damages.

Thompson   Thomson
Mcavish, Mctavish, Tomson, Thomson,

Thompson ranks among the top 50 names in Ireland, Scotland and England. The 1890 birth index finds 317 births of the name, mainly in Antrim, Down, Armagh, Londonderry, Dublin, Fermanagh and Longford.

(The above extracted from the 'Book of Irish Families, great & small').

Searjant Thomson is found in St. John's parish in the Dublin City Pipe Water Accounts of 1680.

Thornhill

Edward Badham Thornhill is given as holding Rockfield at some time after 1772.

Thornton
Thorton

Thornton is considered to be a name of English origin, The census of 1659 finds the name in Dublin city and Kildare. The birth index of 1890 finds the family centered in Galway, Dublin and Mayo. (The above extracted from the 'Book of Irish Families, great & small').

Thunder

The Thunder family of Ballaly of Dublin is found in the Irish Book of Arms. The birth index of 1890 finds the family centered in Dublin.

We find the Thunder family at Grange in Kilmactalway parish.

Patrick Thunder is given at Kilmahuddrick parish in 1666.

Ball gives 'Thunder' as a name of possible Norse descent in the area of Howth.

(The above extracted in part from the 'Book of Irish Families, great & small').

Thurgood

One 'Mr. Thurgood' is found in St. Nicholas Parish 'Without the Walls', in the Dublin City Pipe Water Accounts of 1680.

Thwaits

A family name found in the city of Dublin in the census of 1659.

Thwaites is given as among the few names of importance in Taney parish in the mid 18th century. They are also noted at Crumlin in that century.

Tichborne
A family name found in the city of Dublin in the census of 1659. Dunsoghly Castle came under the possession of Tichborne before being transferred to John Avery in 1672.

Tickell
Thomas Tickell's house and lands were sold in the late 18th century by his grandson to the Dublin Society and made the nucleus of the Botanic Gardens there.

O' Tierney
Teirney, Tierny, Tiernan
In the census of 1659 "Tierny" was a principal name of Tipperary, and "Tierney" was given in Dublin, Tipperary and Galway in the 1890 birth index. (The above extracted from the 'Book of Irish Families, great & small').

Mac Tighe   Mc Teague
Teige, Tiege, Tighe, Mc Teague, Mctague
The Tighe family of Woodstock, Co. Kilkenny, settled in Ireland, where one of the family became Mayor of Dublin in 1651. (The above extracted from the 'Book of Irish Families, great & small').
Stearne Tighe is given as resident at Castleknock parish.

Timmins
Timmons, Timon, Timmin, Tomin,
The Timmins family is found centered in counties Dublin, Kildare and Wicklow in the 19th century.   (The above extracted from the 'Book of Irish Families, great & small').

Tingham
In Lord Valentia's time, a great artificer by the name of Edmond Tingham resided at Chapelizod parish.

Tisdall
Tisdall, Teesdale
The birth index of 1890 finds the family centered in Dublin. (extracted from the 'Book of Irish Families, great & small').
Michael Tisdall is found in St. Michael's parish in the Dublin City Pipe Water Accounts of 1680.

Tobias
A family name found in Dublin city, given to be of Jewish heritage in at least one instance. (per 'OLochlainns journal of Irish Families').

Tobin
Tobyn, Tobbine, Tobynn, Tobine, Tobynn
In modern time the name is found simply as Tobin, and in the 1890 birth index 98 births of the name were recorded in Waterford, Cork, Tipperary, Limerick, Dublin and Kilkenny. (The above extracted from the 'Book of Irish Families, great & small').

Tomey
Twomey Toomey
Tomey is a surname found in Quaker records in Dublin city in the 18th century, where two of the name are found as 'carpenters'. See also 'O'Twomey'.

Tomlins
A family name found in the city of Dublin in the census of 1659.
Noted names in 18th century Milltown, Co. Dublin, included: Mr. Heavisid; Classon; Burr; Hugh Johnson; Randall; Dogherty; Tomlinson; King; and Walcot.

Tone
The Tone family name is a rare one in Ireland. The most noted of the name was Theobald Wolfe Tone (1763 - 1798) of noted historical importance. Of his line were some coach builders in Dublin by trade. (The above extracted from the 'Book of Irish Families, great & small').

Tonge
Tong, Tongue
The family of the name in Ireland is most often found in connection with Co. Wexford and the city of Dublin in our records. The family is generally given to be of English origins when found in Ireland. (The above extracted from the 'Book of Irish Families, great & small').

Tonstall
A family name found in the city of Dublin in the census of 1659.

Toogood
A family name found in the city of Dublin in the census of 1659.

O'Toole
Toal, Tuhill, O'tool
Toole was the most common spelling in 1890, found located in Dublin, Galway, Mayo and Wicklow etc..
(The above extracted from the 'Book of Irish Families, great & small').
The O'Tooles and the O'Byrnes were two of the leading Irish chieftains to wage war in Dublin for centuries after the 12th century Norman invasion. They were feared by their opponents, and at times ravaged the entire countryside.
In 1313 they burned Bray, and those lands were considered 'wild territory' by the settlers.

Tooley
A family name given in Dublin in the Birth Index of 1890.

Toomey
Twomey Toumey
A family name found in Dublin at the time of the Birth Index of 1890. See also O'Twomey.

Topham
Doctor John Topham is found in St. Nicholas Parish 'Within the Walls', in the Dublin City Pipe Water Accounts of 1680.

Totten
Milesian Families finds the name in Dublin, of English origins. (no documentation given).

Tottenham
Milesian Families finds the name in Dublin, of English origins. (no documentation given).

Tottericke
A family name found in the city of Dublin in the census of 1659.

Touche
La Touche
See introduction page 22.

Toulson
A family name found in the city of Dublin in the census of 1659.

Towers
A family name found in Dublin in the census of 1659. Thomas Towers is given in Finglas parish. See introduction.

Townshend
Townsend
Rockfield was held by Lord Townshend around 1772.

Towson
In the 18th century the Towson family is found at Hackettsland in Co. Dublin. See also introduction.

Toye
A family name found in Dublin in the census of 1659.

O'Tracy
Treacy, Tressy, Tracey, Trasey,
There are several likely unrelated families of the name of Tracey, Treacy..etc.. found in Ireland. In 1890 the 'Tracey' had 31 births in Dublin, and 'Tracy' had 16 births in Dublin.
Although the name was found mainly in Dublin, Tipperary and Galway under three spellings in 1890, older records show a wider scope for the name. (The above extracted from the 'Book of Irish Families, great & small').
The 'Treacy' family is listed as part of the 'more recent nobility' by O'Hart where they are given as viscounts of Rathcoole, Co. Dublin.

Trail
At Island Bridge we find the names of: Pennefather in 1768; Keightly 1768; and Trail in 1799.

Trant
According to "Keatings History" the name is that of a principal family of Dublin city or county, and of Anglo-Norman descent. (The above extracted from the 'Book of Irish Families, great & small'). (See major entry in 'The Families of Co. Kerry').
In the 18th century Belgard castle was held by the Dillion family, and subsequently to Dominick Trant and then Dr. Kennedy in Dublin.

Travers
Traverse

The 1890 birth index finds the family most numerous in Donegal, Dublin and Leitrim. (The above extracted from the 'Book of Irish Families, great & small').

Robert, Luke and William Travers are given in 1642 as of Ballykea, Co. Dublin, according to King James Irish Army List. Also mentioned are some lands of the family in the parish of Lusk, Dublin. One family of the name is noted in 1640 as landowners.

Sir John Travers was Master of the Ordnance in Ireland under King Henry VIII, sometime after 1539. He was a noted 'adventurer' in 16th century Ireland. He was seated at the Castle at Monkstown in Ireland.

Thomas Cusack was leased the lands of Cabinteely, which were subsequently held by Sir John Travers in 1545, and then by the Eustace, Cheevers and O'Bynre families. See introduction.

Mac Traynor, Trainor
Treanor, Trainor, Trainer, Mc Trenor

Traynor, Treanor, or Trainor families may take their name from the original "Mac Threinfhir" in Gaelic. The Mac prefix had generally been dropped by the time of the 1890 birth index. At that time "Traynor" was the preferred spelling with 35 births listed in Dublin.

(The above extracted from the 'Book of Irish Families, great & small').

Trench

Andrew Trench (d.1750) and John Rider (d.1762) both lived to be 100 years old and are noted in Crumlin parish.

Triar

A family name found in Dublin in the census of 1659.

Trulock
Truelock Trulocke

At the end of the 18th century Counsellor Whittingham and Mr. Trulock are given as chief residents at Simmonscourt. See introduction.

Tuinon

A family name found in the city of Dublin in the census of 1659.

Tuite

The Tuite family is also given as a principal one of Anglo-Norman descent, settling in Dublin City and County, according to Keatings 'History of Ireland'.

Tullamore

See page 34 in the introduction.

Tully

A family name given in Dublin in the Birth Index of 1890.

Turner

The name of Turner may be of English, Scottish or Welsh origins. The 1890 birth index finds the family most numerous in Dublin, Antrim, and Cork. (The above extracted from the 'Book of Irish Families, great & small').

It is a surname found in Quaker records in Dublin city in the latter 17th century.

John Turner is found in St. Werburgh's parish in the Dublin City Pipe Water Accounts of 1680.

Robert Turner, a traveling clothier, was robbed on the road in Taney parish by Donagh Cahere of Dundrum.

Tweddell

Gregory Tweddell, yeoman and soldier, is given at Ballydowd in Esker parish in the mid 16th century.

Tweedy

See "The Dublin Tweedys: The Story of an Irish Family 1650 - 1882" London. 1956, written by Owen Tweedy.

Twigg

In the 18th century we find the families of Twigg, Stoyte, Jocelyn, and Sterne at the manor at Donneybrook. See introduction.

O' Twomey   Toomey
Toomey, Toomy, Twomy

In 1890 Twomey is found in Cork and Kerry, while Toomey was found in Dublin and Limerick. (The above extracted from the 'Book of Irish Families, great & small'). (See major entry in 'The Families of Co. Cork').

Tynte

Milesian Families finds the name in Dublin, of English origins. Several of the Tynte family are found at Old Bawn in the 18th century or later.

Tyrell
Tyrrell, Tirell

Tyrell is an Anglo-Norman family noted for settling in areas around Dublin, Kildare and in Westmeath.

Several branches of the name are found on record in Ireland, including Tirrell of Westmeath and Dublin. Hugh Tyrell got the land around Castleknock in the 12th century. His descendants held the land as barons of Castleknock. The townland of Murphystown was also likely held by the family in the 13th century.

In 1890 the family is most numerous in Dublin, Kildare and Wicklow. (The above extracted from the 'Book of Irish Families, great & small').

The family is also given as a principal one of Anglo-Norman descent, settling in Dublin City and County, according to Keatings 'History of Ireland'.

Thomas Tyrrell is found in St. Werburgh's parish in the Dublin City Pipe Water Accounts of 1680.

See also the book entitled "The Genealogical History of the Tyrrells of Castleknock in Co. Dublin......", London. 1904, by J. H. Tyrrell.

The Tyrells of Powerstown are given by Ball to be one of the families located in Mulhuddart parish from the 14th -16th centuries.

Tyth

A family name found in the city of Dublin in the census of 1659.

Uniack

James Uniack is found in St. Nicholas Parish 'Within the Walls', in the Dublin City Pipe Water Accounts of 1680.

Ussher
Usher

The family is found most prominent in the county and city of Dublin in early records. The Ussher family of Eastwell, Co. Galway descend from Arland Ussher, Bailiff of Dublin in 1460.

Christopher Ussher was twice the Mayor of Dublin city. The family is given in O'Harts work as one of the chief families settling in Waterford and Dublin. (The above extracted from the 'Book of Irish Families, great & small').

The 'Usher' family is also found in Dublin city and county in the census of 1659. Several of the name held considerable lands in the 17th century.

In 1623 William Wolverston, the owner of Stillorgan, held the lands of Tipperstown, and in 1645 they were held by Richard Swinfield of Murphystown, and in 1724 Christopher Ussher of Booterstown leased these lands. In 1524 the lands of Donneybrook passed to the Ussher family. The Usshers of Donneybrook also came to hold the lands of Cullenswood in the 17th century.

The family is also given as a principal one of Anglo-Norman descent, settling in Dublin City and County, according to Keatings 'History of Ireland'.

George Ussher, a wealthy Dublin merchant, in 1595 built 'Kill Abbey' in Kill of the Grange Parish. See introduction.

Draycott's farm went to Arland Ussher in Glasnevin Parish. See introduction.

Ustace
Eustace

The family names of Ustace and UUstice are found in Dublin City in the census of 1659. The name may be found as Eustice, etc...today. (see Eustace)

Valentine

A family name found in Dublin at the time of the Birth Index of 1890.

Vance

The family is found in Rutlandsquare, Dublin as well as Ulster, said to be of English extraction. (per the 'Book of Irish Families, great & small').

Vancoulster

Dymon Vancoulster is found in St. John's parish in the Dublin City Pipe Water Accounts of 1680.

Vanderpuer

A family name found in Dublin in the census of 1659.

Vaughan

A family name given in Dublin in the census of 1659..

Vavasor

Vavasour

One family of the name is found in burial grounds at Irishtown, Co. Dublin, from the late 18th century.

Verneuil

See introduction page 19.

Vernon

We find one family of the name coming from England and settling near Clontarf, Co. Dublin and at Ballyhugh Co. Cavan.

The Vernon family of Erne Hill, Co. Cavan descends from a family found earliest at Clontarf Castle in Co. Dublin. The Vernon family of Clontarf Castle are given in the Irish Book of Arms. ... (The above extracted from the 'Book of Irish Families, great & small').

The above family is also given in the works of O'Hart as a principal one settling in Dublin from the 12th to the 18th century. One of the name was among the forfeiting proprietors in Co. Louth during the Cromwellian confiscation's.

Vernor

Milesian Families finds the name in Dublin, of Norman origins. (no documentation given).

Verschoyle

The family of Verschoyle of Kilberry, Co. Kildare came from Holland in the 16th century as a result of religious persecution, settling in Dublin in the 17th century. (extracted from the 'Book of Irish Families, great & small').

The family name is on record in Dublin in the Census of 1659.

Verveer

Among houses noted at Ballyfermot were those of: Verveer; Styles; Carden; Ryves; Exham; and Talbot of Templeogue.

Vesey

Milesian Families finds the name in Dublin, of Norman origins. In Lucan Parish in the old parish church was a burial place of the Vesey family. The old castle was home to the Vesey family until 1772 when a new house was erected.

Vincent

A family name found in Dublin in the census of 1659. Thomas Vincent is given as a 'wealthy' Englishman in 17th century Palmerston.

Vipoint

We find Charles Vipoint at Finglasbridge. See introduction under Finglas parish.

Vizard

A family name found in the city of Dublin in the census of 1659.

Voyzin

Abraham Voyzin is found in St. Werburgh's parish in the Dublin City Pipe Water Accounts of 1680.

Wade

Quade, Mcquade

Families of the name of Wade in Ireland are generally considered to be of English extraction. The name is found concentrated in Dublin for several centuries. (extracted from the 'Book of Irish Families, great & small').

Wadsworth

Milesian Families finds the name in Dublin, of English origins. (no documentation given).

Waight

Wayte Waite

A family name found in the city of Dublin in the census of 1659. Thomas Wayte is found in St. Catherine's parish in the Dublin City Pipe Water Accounts of 1680.

Wainman

A family name found in the city of Dublin in the census of 1659.

Wakefield

A family name found in Dublin in the census of 1659.

Walcot
Walcott

Noted names in 18th century Milltown, Co. Dublin, included: Mr. Heavisid; Classon; Burr; Hugh Johnson; Randall; Dogherty; Tomlinson; King; and Walcot.

Waldron
Waldren

It is most often given that the name of Waldron in Ireland is of English extraction. The 1890 birth index finds the family most numerous in Mayo, Roscommon and Dublin.

Ball gives the name of 'Waldron' as one of possible Norse origins when connected with the area surrounding Howth. (The above extracted from the 'Book of Irish Families, great & small').

Walker

The name is found most commonly in Dublin and in Ulster in Ireland. The 1890 index gives the name in Counties Antrim and Dublin, much the same as it remains today.

(The above extracted from the 'Book of Irish Families, great & small').

Wall
Walls, Wale

The Wall family, believed to be of Norman origins, first spelled the name as "de Valle" etc... Some of the name are found in 12th century Dublin records.

Wall, with 58 births of the name in 1890 was found in Dublin, Waterford, Cork, Limerick and Tipperary etc.. Keatings History also found the name in Waterford, Tipperary and Dublin more anciently. (The above extracted from the 'Book of Irish Families, great & small').

The family is also given as a principal one of Anglo-Norman descent, settling in Dublin City and County, according to Keatings 'History of Ireland'.

One family of the name is found in the graveyard at Irishtown, Co. Dublin, including one Rev. Richard Henry Wall, D.D., whose coat-of-arms was inscribed therein.

Wallace   Wallis
Wallis, Walis, Walsh

One Wallis family is found centered at Killeny, in Queens Co., in the late 17th century. Subsequently the family is also found at Portrane, Co. Dublin. (The above extracted from the 'Book of Irish Families, great & small').

The Wallis family, including one Ralfe Wallis of the City of Dublin, is given in the works of O'Hart. Crest, arms and motto of the 'ancient' family are given therein.

The 1659 census gives 'Wallis' in Dublin, and Wallas is another variant spelling in our records.

In the 13th century we find Butler, Wallis, Finglas, and Fitzgerald at Killakee.

Walse
Walsh

Walse was a family name noted at Kilmactalway Parish. See introduction.

Ogham Stone, in Trinity College.

Walsh   Welsh
Welch, Walshe

Walsh is the 4th most popular name in Ireland, following only Murphy, Kelly and Sullivan. It ranked among the top 20 most numerous names of County Dublin in 1890.

Phillip the Welshman, (i.e. Phillip Walsh) settled after the 12th century invasions, and his line is found settled in Dublin around Bray and Carrickmines.

Carrickmines Castle was garrisoned by the Walsh family who came to be expert in both military and farming endeavors there. Several of the name are given by Ball in his History of County Dublin. They built a castle at Balally in 1407.

Among the holders of land in Killiney parish in the 14th century and later were: William Walsh alias McHowell; James Garvey; and the Goodman family.

The Walsh family probably held Brennanstown from the 14th century onwards. See introduction.

In the 1890 index the spelling as "Walshe" was most common in Galway, Dublin and Wexford. (The above extracted from the 'Book of Irish Families, great & small').

Several pages are devoted to Walsh families in King James' Irish Army List. Here it is stated that a little manuscript in Trinity College ties the Walsh family of Shanaganagh, Co. Dublin, to those of Wicklow.

John Walsh is found with 900 some acres of land in Co. Dublin in the 17th century. In the same century we also find reference to a Henry Walsh, farmer, at Butterfield. (see introduction).

The family is also given as a principal one of Anglo-Norman descent, settling in Dublin City and County, according to Keatings 'History of Ireland'.

A branch of the Walsh family of Carrickmines, who were the comrades in arms of the Harold family in protecting the Pale, are noted as settling at Kilgobbin. We also find the Lawless family being replaced by the Walsh family at Rathmichael in the

Walsh   Welsh
15th century.

After the Commonwealth, the lands of the Walsh family in Old Connaught parish passed to Henry Jones and then to John Baxter. (See major entry in 'The Families of Co. Cork').

Walshman
Walsh

A family name found in Dublin in the census of 1659. See also Walsh.

Mac Walter
Qualter, Walters, Walter

The name of MacWalter was used by a branch of the Burke family of Connaught and by other Norman families. (extracted from the 'Book of Irish Families, great & small').

Walton

A family name found in the city of Dublin in the census of 1659. Samuel Walton is found in St. Werburgh's parish in the Dublin City Pipe Water Accounts of 1680.

Wamought

A family name found in the city of Dublin in the census of 1659.

Wandesford

Wandesford is noted at Kilgobbin parish.

Mac Ward
Ward, Macanward, Mac Award

A century ago the name of Ward was most common in Donegal and Galway, a traditional homeland for the family. The name was also concentrated in Dublin at that time . (extracted from the 'Book of Irish Families, great & small').

Keep in mind that 'Ward' may be a family name of settler or of native Irish origins, particularly in Dublin.

In 1641 the lands of Cullenswood (Ranelagh and Sandford) were occupied by Yeoman Thomas Ward, who was taken captive along with a Mr. Parnell.

Names connected to Rathfarnham parish in the 18th century were Palliser; O'Callaghan; Cramer; Coghill; Stannard; Fountain; Ward; Geering; How; Boyle; and Blackburn.

Ware

A family name found in Dublin county and city in the census of 1659. Ware is also mentioned in Ward Parish. See introduction.

Warren

The birth index of 1890 finds the family centered in Kerry, Cork and Dublin. (The above extracted from the 'Book of Irish Families, great & small').

The family is also given as a principal one of Anglo-Norman descent, settling in Dublin City and County, according to Keatings 'History of Ireland'. At least one family of the name is found holding lands in 1640 in Dublin.

King James' Irish Army List gives several of the name in the biography of Capt. Thomas Warren, including Edward Warren 'late of Dublin'. The family is given as having extended to all the counties of the Pale in that work.

The Warrens resided at Corduff in the first half of the 18th century.

Mr. Robert Warren, of Killiney Castle, helped develop the neighborhood of Rochestown in the 19th century. See introduction.

In the parish of Old Connaught, Garret Warren is given as schoolteacher for the Catholic residents.

A branch of the Warren family is given to have held the lands of Harristown around the 17th century.

The castle at Drumcondra was the residence of Sir William Warren at Clonturk Parish.

Wasbery

A family name found in the city of Dublin in the census of 1659.

Waterhouse

A family name found in the city of Dublin in the census of 1659.

Watson

A family name of Dublin as found in the census of 1659. It is also a surname found in Quaker records in Dublin city in the 18th century.

Watts

A family name found in the city of Dublin in the census of 1659.

Waybrent

A family name found in the city of Dublin in the census of 1659.

Wayman

A family name found in the city of Dublin in the census of 1659.

Weatherhead

Milesian Families finds the name in Dublin, of Saxon origins. (no documentation given).

Weaver

Weever, Weafer, Wafer

Some give the Weaver family as English, settling in 1640 in Dublin and Limerick.   (extracted from the 'Book of Irish Families, great & small').

Webb

Webber

Not unexpectedly, the family is found in Dublin records, and the name is often found outside Dublin as well.

The birth index of 1890 finds the family centered in Dublin and Antrim. (The above extracted from the 'Book of Irish Families, great & small').

It is a surname found in Quaker records in Dublin city in the latter 17th century.

Webber

A family name found in Dublin in the census of 1659.

Webster

A family name we find in Dublin in the 1890 birth index of Ireland.

Weld

The Weld family was at Harolds Cross for many years. See introduction.

Weldon

Widow Weldon is found in St. Werburgh's parish in the Dublin City Pipe Water Accounts of 1680.

Wellesley

Milesian Families finds the name in Dublin, of Norman origins. (no documentation given).

Wells

The family names of Welles and Wells are given in Dublin, of English extraction, according to Milesian Families.

Wenman

The family is listed as part of the 'more recent nobility' by O'Hart where they are given as ' barons of Kilmainham', Co. Dublin.

Wenwell

A family name found in the city of Dublin in the census of 1659.

Werthheim

A family name found in Dublin city, given to be of Jewish heritage in at least one instance. (per 'OLochlainns journal of Irish Families').

Wesley

Richard Colley, who later assumed the name of Wesley, was made Lord Mornington. He is found at Booterstown in the 18th century. See introduction.

Wespey

In 1578 we find Richard Wespey at Ballyfermot.

Westbury

Mr. Robert Westbury is found in St. Catherine's parish in the Dublin City Pipe Water Accounts of 1680.

Westby

The Westby family of Roebuck Castle, Co. Dublin and Kilballyowen and Rosroe in Co. Clare are given to be of the same line, as found in the Irish Book of Arms. (The above extracted from the 'Book of Irish Families, great & small').

The census of 1659 finds the family name of Wesby in Dublin City as well.

Westenra

Westinra

Westinra and Westenra are given in the census of 1659 in Dublin City. Peter Westenra is found in St. Audeon's parish in the Dublin City Pipe Water Accounts of 1680.

Weston

Westen   Westenra

Milesian Families finds the name in Dublin, of English origins. (no documentation given). The family is further given in Dublin in the census of 1659.

It is also a surname found in Quaker records in Dublin city in the latter 17th and 18th centuries.

Wetherall

A family name found in the city of Dublin in the census of 1659.

Whaly

A family name found in the city of Dublin in the census of 1659.

Wharton

Subsequent to the 17th century rebellions we find the names of Wharton; Chambers; Willion; Barry; Robinson; Moses; Reyly; Lovelace; Eaton; Murphy; Lawlor; Leedom; and Walsh in Rathcoole parish, Co. Dublin.

Whately

Archbishop Redesdale occupied Redesdale House at one time, in the parish of Kilmacud. See introduction.

Whatton

John Whatton, dyer, is found in St. Catherine's parish in the Dublin City Pipe Water Accounts of 1680.

Wheeler

A family name we find in Dublin in the birth index of 1890.

Whelen, Phelan

Felan, Whalan, Phellane, Phalen,

The family names of Whelan and Phelan stem from the same Irish name of O'Faolain.

Whelan is mainly found in Dublin, Wexford, Waterford, Tipperary and Carlow in the 1890 birth index. It was among the top 25 most numerous names in Dublin at that time.

Passengers from Ireland: Thomas Whalen, Aboard Dublin Packet, April 3, 1816, Dublin To New York.

(The above extracted in part from the 'Book of Irish Families, great & small').

Whetlock

A family name found in the city of Dublin in the census of 1659.

Whitchurch
Whitechurch
A family name found in the city of Dublin in the census of 1659.

White
Whyte, Whight, Bane, Bawn
White is among the 100 most numerous names in Ireland, and most are of original English stock.

The preferred spelling is "White", which had 269 births recorded mainly in Antrim, Cork, Dublin and Wexford, in the 1890 index. (The above extracted from the 'Book of Irish Families, great & small').

'Whyte' is the preferred spelling found in Dublin at the time of the 1890 Index.

The family is also given as a principal one of Anglo-Norman descent, settling in Dublin City and County, according to Keatings 'History of Ireland'. They are also given as an English family found in Dublin in the 17th century, where they held noted lands at that time.

'Nicholas White' is found in St. Nicholas Parish 'Within the Walls', in the Dublin City Pipe Water Accounts of 1680. Sir Nicholas White came to control St. Catherines Park in Leixlip parish in the 16th century. He appears to be the son of James White, steward of the household of James, ninth Earl of Ormonde. The Whytes of Lough-brickland descend from Sir Nicholas White.

Early names at Newcastle parish after the 12th century invasions included: St. John; de Revell; and le White.

Luke White of Woodlands is noted in the introduction to the book you are currently reading.

At Newcastle in 1614 among the first city officials were: Parsons; Rolles; Kenny; Frend; White; and Lushe. We find the Whites and the Allens once more owning land at Aderrig parish after the 17th century Restoration.

In the 16th century Corr Castle was held by the White family.

Whitefield
Whitfield
A family name found in Dublin in the census of 1659.

Whitehead
Whithead
In 'King James's Irish Army List, 1689' we find listed as a Dublin assessor, one Thomas Whitehead.

Whitehead is also a surname found in Quaker records in Dublin city in the 18th century.

Whiteside
Whitside
Milesian Families finds the name in Dublin, of English origins. (no documentation given).

Whitgrove
Whitegrove
A family name found in the city of Dublin in the census of 1659.

Whitihell
A family name found in the city of Dublin in the census of 1659.

Whitmore
A family name found in the city of Dublin in the census of 1659.

Whitshed
In the 17th century the Archbold family held the lands of Jobstown and subsequently the Whitshed families are found there. See introduction.

Whittingham
At the end of the 18th century Counsellor Whittingham and Mr. Trulock are given as chief residents at Simmonscourt. See introduction.

Whitwell
Sir N. Whitwell is noted in Finglas Parish. See introduction.

Whyte
White
See also White.

Among the tenants at Tipperstown in the 13th and 14th centuries were the families of Whyte, Hacket, Wythir, Harold and Lagthenan.

After 1641 in the area of Killakee we find the 'British Protestants': Thomas Price; John Whyte; and William Thomas, all suffering damages. See introduction.

Wickombe
Wicombe

A family name found in Dublin in the census of 1659. Peter Wicombe of 'the Lyons' is listed among those transplanted from Dublin, in the works of O'Hart.

Wiggstead

One 'Richard Wiggstead' is found in St. Nicholas Parish 'Without the Walls', in the Dublin City Pipe Water Accounts of 1680.

Wight
Whyte Wighte White

Among the noted residents of Booterstown in the 18th century were included the names of Cooley; Doherty; Gough; O'Reilly; LaTouche; Doyne; Wight; Bradstreet; and Fitzgerald.

Wilcox
Wilcocks

A family name found in the city of Dublin in the census of 1659.

It is a surname found in Quaker records in Dublin city in the latter 17th and 18th centuries, where several of the name are given as merchants.

The Wilcocks family is found at Palmerston parish subsequent to the 17th century.

Wild

Joseph Wild is found in St. Werburgh's parish in the Dublin City Pipe Water Accounts of 1680.

Wiley
Wyly

It is a surname found in Quaker records in Dublin city in the 18th century.

Wilkinson

The Wilkinson family was at Mt. Jerome in the mid 18th century. See introduction.

Wilks

In the 17th century village at Rathfarnham we find: Burgoyne; Bishop; Wilks; and Graham.

Willan

It is a surname found in Quaker records in Dublin city in the 18th century.
(could this also stand for the Irish name of Whelan?).

Willes
Wiles Wyles

Edward Willes is given in the area of Seapoint and Templehill in 1757. See introduction.

McWilliam
Williams

Milesian Families finds the name in Dublin, of Norman origins. (no documentation given).

Williams

The family name is also found in Dublin in the census of 1659, and in the birth index of 1890.

Johnstown House at Cabinteely was occupied in 1778 by Mr. Love Hiatt and then by Mr. Williams.

It is also a surname found in Quaker records in Dublin city in the 18th century.

The school at Finglas had Williams, Teebay and Smith as licensed masters, around the end of the 17th century or shortly thereafter.

Williamson

Mr. Williamson is found in St. John's parish in the Dublin City Pipe Water Accounts of 1680.

Willion

Subsequent to the 17th century rebellions we find the names of Wharton; Chambers; Willion; Barry; Robinson; Moses; Reyly; Lovelace; Eaton; Murphy; Lawlor; Leedom; and Walsh in Rathcoole parish, Co. Dublin.

Willis

John Willis, given in 'Families of Co. Kerry, Ireland', was given as master of Manchester and Dublin Art Schools.

Milesian Families also finds the name in Dublin, of English origins.

Willmore
Willmer, Wellmore
A scarce name in Ireland, we find some of the family in Dublin. The name is likely of English origins. (The above extracted from the 'Book of Irish Families, great & small').

Willoughby
Willouby
A family name found in Dublin in the census of 1659. At Dunbro we find Col. F. Willouby, a poor cavalier of a well known family.

Wills
A family name found in Dublin city, given to be of Jewish heritage in at least one instance. (per 'OLochlainns journal of Irish Families').

Wilson
Willison, Willson
Wilson is one of the more popular names the nearby countries of Scotland and England.

The 1890 birth index finds 366 births of the name recorded mainly in Antrim, Armagh, Down, Tyrone, Dublin, Londonderry and Fermanagh. (The above extracted from the 'Book of Irish Families, great & small').

Towards the end of the 18th century Peter Wilson built a lodge in Killiney parish. He came there from Dalkey.

Wimsey
Milesian Families finds the name in Dublin, of English origins. (no documentation given).

Wingfield
We find the Wolverston family at the end of the 16th century granting a lease to the Right Hon. Jacques Wingfield in Stillorgan Parish. They had ties to the Travers family. See introduction.

Winslow
Milesian Families finds the name in Dublin, of English origins. (no documentation given).

Winstanley
Richard Winstanley and Robert Woodward were farmers who were depositioned concerning the rebellion of 1641.

Withams
A family name found in the city of Dublin in the census of 1659.

Withington
John Withington is found in St. Audeon's parish in the Dublin City Pipe Water Accounts of 1680.

Wizard
A family name found in the city of Dublin in the census of 1659.

Woder
Although not given in several other sources, O'Hart gives the family as a principal one settling in Dublin from the 12th to the 18th century.

Wogan
Wogane
According to "Keatings History" the name is that of a principal family of Dublin city or county, and of Anglo-Norman descent.

(The above extracted from the 'Book of Irish Families, great & small').

Wolf
Woulfe Wolfe
A family name found in Dublin city, given to be of Jewish heritage in at least one instance. (per 'OLochlainns journal of Irish Families').

In another instance we find Arthur Wolfe was a name of note at Newlands in Tallaght parish.

Wolverston
Woolverston   Wolferston

The census of 1659 finds the Wolverston family name in Dublin and an account of "The Wolverstons of Stillorgan" can be found in the "Reportorium Novum", 2 (2), 1960.

The Wolverstons or Woolverstons of Stillorgan held some 500+ acres of land in 17th century Dublin. They were originally of a Suffolk family of the name. In Ireland they were also found to be Catholic, as were their neighbors, the Cheevers, the Goodmans and the Walshes.

In 1623 Christopher Wolverston was tenant in Kill of the Grange Parish. In 1623 William Wolverston, the owner of Stillorgan, held the lands of Tipperstown. In that century they also owned the lands of Hackettsland. Nicholas Wolverston is found at Kilmahuddrick parish in 1650.

Nicholas Corr and Gerald Long in 1564 leased the lands of Newtownpark and in that century the Wolverston family occupied a good slated house.

Wood

A family name found in Dublin in the census of 1659.

Woodcock

John Woodcock is found in St. Catherine's parish in the Dublin City Pipe Water Accounts of 1680.

Woodfin

In the 17th century Thomas Mason was a tenant in Rathfarnham parish who was robbed by John Woodfin. See introduction.

Woodlock

According to "Keatings History" the name is that of a principal Anglo-Norman family of Dublin city or county, and of Anglo-Norman descent. (The above extracted from the 'Book of Irish Families, great & small').

The Woodlocks are given at Cappoge in the 14th century.

Woodruff

Milesian Families finds the name in Dublin, of English origins. (no documentation given).

Woods
Wood, Quill, Quilly

One Woods family is given as English, settling in Dublin in 1640.   Note the names of Quill and Quilty also used, coming from the Gaelic for 'Wood' etc..

One 'Mr. Woods' is found in St. Werburgh's parish in the Dublin City Pipe Water Accounts of 1680.

Woodside

A fairly rare name in Irish records, the birth index of 1890 finds the family in the counties of Antrim and Dublin. (The above extracted from the 'Book of Irish Families, great & small').

Woodward

Richard Winstanley and Robert Woodward were farmers who were depositioned concerning the rebellion of 1641.

Workman

A family name found in the city of Dublin in the census of 1659.

Wormington

Hugh Wormington is found in St. Nicholas Parish 'Within the Walls', in the Dublin City Pipe Water Accounts of 1680.

Worship

A family name found in the city of Dublin in the census of 1659.

Worth

Milesian Families finds the name in Dublin, of English origins. Judge Worth (d.1721) is found at Old Bawn.

Worthington

A Worthington family burial place was found at Irishtown, Co. Dublin, with stones dating from the late 18th century into the mid-19th century.

Wright
Right

The 1890 birth index finds the family most numerous in Antrim, Down, Dublin and Armagh. (The above extracted from the 'Book of Irish Families, great & small').

In Tully parish obituaries in 1773 we find the Rev. Henry Wright.

Wybrants

One family of the name is found originally as a merchant from Antwerp, settling in Ireland in the city of Dublin in the early 17th century. (The above extracted from the 'Book of Irish Families, great & small').

The census of 1659 finds the name in Dublin City as Wybrant.

Wyburne

A family name found in Dublin in the census of 1659.

Wye

After the rebellion of 1641 the lands of Killiney parish were held by Gilbert Wye of Belfast; the Mossoms; the Fawcetts; the Pocklingtons; and the Domviles. See introduction.

Wylder
Wyld, Wilde, Wylie, Wilders, De Wylde

"de Wylde" is given to be in Ireland subsequent to the Norman invasions and has been found quite early in Dublin and Limerick.(per the 'Book of Irish Families, great & small').

Wyly
Wiley

Wyly is a surname found in Quaker records in Dublin city in the 18th century.

Wyndham

Thomas Wyndham was laid to rest in Salisbury Cathedral and was a noted resident at Finglas parish in the 18th century.

Wynn
Wynne

The 1890 birth index finds the family most numerous in Dublin and Sligo. (The above extracted from the 'Book of Irish Families, great & small').

'Wynne' is given in Dublin in the 1659 census as well.

Around 1600 in the House of Howth we find Peter Wynne and William Fitzwilliam.

Wythir

Among the tenants at Tipperstown in the 13th and 14th centuries were the families of Whyte, Hacket, Wythir, Harold and Lagthenan. See introduction.

Yates
Yeats

A family name found in the city of Dublin in the census of 1659.

Yeats
Yeates, Yeats, Yates

The Yeats or Yates..etc.. family is traditionally linked to Dublin when found in Ireland. William Butler Yeats (1865-1957) was the noted poet of the name in modern times.

At Booterstown in the 18th century we find an extremely successful farmer by the name of Isaiah Yeates.

The 1890 birth index finds the family most numerous in Antrim and Dublin when spelled as Yeates. (The above extracted from the 'Book of Irish Families, great & small').

Yelverton

We find Mr. Caldbeck and Barry Yelverton at Clondalkin in the 17th century or later.

Yerwood
Yearwood

Early names at Newcastle parish after the 12th century invasions included: le White; and Yerward the Welshman.

Young

Milesian Families finds the name in Dublin, of Scottish origins. Alderman Gerald Young of Dublin leased the lands of Kilboggett at the close of the 16th century. See introduction.

Appendix

page 212 - Family Names of Co. Dublin found In
The Master Book of Irish Surnames

page 218 - Surnames of Jewish Families in Dublin.

page 219- Place Names of Co. Dublin taken from
The Master Book of Irish Placenames.

Surname Extract from
page 223 - The Census of 1659 for the City of Dublin.
page 227 - The Census of 1659 for the County Dublin.

page 231- Family Name Index to this volume.

Surnames in County Dublin, Ireland

Names connected in some way with Co. Dublin, as given in the
Master Book of Irish Surnames.   (O'Laughlin. IGF. ©1999)
Names listed twice appear twice in the source book above.

Abbecaces	Ashbrook	Bather	Blackburn	Brandon	Bulkeley
Abbott	Ashley	Bathripp	Blackhall	Branham	Bulkley
Abbott	Ashly	Bathurst	Blackwell	O'Brannigan	Burgess
Ackley	Ashton	Battersby	Blackwell	Braun	Burgess
McAdam	Assin	Baulman	Bladen	Bray	Burgoyne
McAdams	Aston	Baxter	Blanchfield	Bray	Burke
Adrian	Audley	Baxter	Bligh	Brayne	Burke
Adryan	Aungier	Bayley	Bligh	Brazil	Burne
Aghwell	Aungier	Bayly, Bayley	Blum	Breen	Burnett
Aghwell	Austin	Bealing	Blundell	Brennan	Burrowes
Ahlborn	Austin	Beame	Boas	Brereton	Burt
Alan	Avery	Beatty	Bodley	Brerton	Burton
Albert	Avory	Becket	Bollard	Brett	Busby
Albun	O'B	Beggs	Bollard	Brett	Bush
Alding	Babbitt	Behan	Bolton	Brice	Bushell
Alding	Bacon	Behan	Bolton	Bridges	Buston
Aldworth	Bagworth	Bell	Bond	Brien	Butler
Alexander	Bailey	Bell	Bonole	O'Brien	Butterfield
Allan	Bain	Bellingham	Bonorly	Brighness	Butterly
Allen	Baird	Bender	Boorke	Bright	Byrne
MacAllen	Baker	Benmohel	Booth	Brimingham	O'Byrne
McAllen	Baker	Bennell	Booth	Brin	Byron
Allen,	Baldwin	Bennett	Borden	Briscoe	Byron
Allexander	Bale	Bennett	Borr	Briscoe	MacCabe
Allison	Ball	Benson	Boudler	Brocas	McCabe
Allison	Ball	Beresford	Bould	Broderick	Caddell
Allsworth	Banks	Berford	Boulton	Broe	Cadmore
Alpine	Banks	Berg	Bourne	Bromagen	Cadwell
Altman	Banning	Bergin	Bowes	Brooke	Cady
Alwoodhouse	Barber	Bermingham	Bowman	Brookes	Caffrey
Amansham	Barber,	Berry	Bowyer	Brooking	Cahill
Amery	Barlowe	Berstow	Bowyer	Brooks	Calbs
McAnally	Barnes	Bertram	Boyd	Brooks, Brooke	Callaghan
Anderson	Barnewall	Best	Boyd	Brophy	Callan
Anderson	Barnewall,	Bettin	Boylan	Brophy	Callan
Anger	Barnwall	Betzold	Boyle	Broughall	Callen
Anger	DeBarnwall	Beuchamp	Boyne	Broughall	MacCallery
Anketel	Barret	Bickford	Boyne	Broun	Callin
Anthony	Barrett	Bicknell	Brabazon	Broune	Callisher
Archbold	Barrington	Bilder	Brabzon	Browne	MacCan
Archbould	Barrow	Billings	O'Bracken	Bruister	Candit
Archer	Barrytt	Billinsley	Bradley	Bruton	McCann
Archer	Barton	Bird	Bradshaw	Bryan	Cantrel
Ardough	Bary	Birford	Bradshaw	Bryscoe	Cantwell
Arnold	Basill	Birmingham	Brady	Buck	Cantwell
Arnop	Basnett	Bishop	Bragg	Buckarton	Carbery
Arthur	Bateman	Bishopp	Braham	Buckingham	Cardyff
Arundall	Bateman	Bisse	Brampton	Buckley	Carey
Arundel	Bates	Black	Branagan	Buggle	Carley
Asbury	Bath	Blackand		Buggle	Carlis

Carnett	Clinton	Corrigan	Daniel	Doly	Elkin
Carpenter	Clinton	Corscadden	Mc Daniell	Domville	Ellard
Carr	Clotworthy	Cosgrave	Dannaher	Domville	Elliot
Carre	Mc Cloud	Costello	Darcy	McDonald	Ellis
Carricke	Mc Cluskey	Costigan	Dardes	Donell	Ellott
Carroll	Coan	Costleloe	Dardis	McDonell	Elward
Carruthers	Cobbe	Cottle	Dargan	Donn	Emery
Carson	Cobbe	Cotton	Dargan	McDonnell	English
Cart	Coddington	Coulter	Darin	Donnellan	English
Carter	Coffey	Coultry	Darling	Donnelly	Ennis
Carton	Coghlan	Courtney	Dason	Donohoe	Ennis
Caruthers	Cohen	Cowell	Daton	Doolan	Ennos
Casement	Cohen	Cowman	Dauson	Dooley	Epstein
Casey	Colby	Cowse	Davidson Of	Doolin	Erlich
O'Casey	Cole	Cox	Davieson	Dore	Erskine
Caskin	Cole	Cox,	Davis	Dorland	Eton
Cassidy	Coleman	Coyle	Davis	Dowd	Eustace
Cassilly	O'Coleman	Coyle	Dawkins	Dowdall	Eustace
Cassy	Colgan	Crabb	De Long	Dowdall	Evans
Casy	Collett	Crafton	Dean	Dowling	Evers
Caulfield	Collier	Cramby	Deane	Downes	McEvoy
Cavan	Collier	Cranwell	Debart	Dowse	Ewing
Cavanagh	Collis	Crary	Dee	Doyle	Fagan
Cavenagh	Colvin	Creamer	Deegan	Drury	Fagan
Cavenah	Combes	Creamer	Delahoyd	Drury, Drew	Fagon
Cecil	Comerford	Creighton	Delahoyde	Dryland	Falconer
Chabner	Compton	Crofton	Delaney	Dudly	Falk
Chaffee	Condron	Crosbie	Delany	Duff	Fallard
Chamberlain	Conley	Cross	Delasale	Duffy	Fallek
Chamberlyn	Conly	Crostenton	Dempsey	Duggan	McFarland
Chambers	O'Connell	Cruise	Den	Dulane	McFarlane
Chambers	Connolly	Cruse	Dent	Dundon	Farley
Champines	Connor	Cuff	Derbon	Dungan	Farrall
Chandler	O'Connor	Cullan	Dermott	Dunn	Farrell
Chapman	Conroy	Cullen	McDermott	Dunne	O'Farrell
Charlton	Conway	O'Cullen	Derry	Dunphy	Farrelly
Chetten	Coogan	Cullin	Desmineer	Dunphy	Farris
Chichester	Cooke	Cumming	Desmineers	Durdin	Faulkner
Christian	Cooke	Cummins	Devery	Dustin	Fay
Clapham	Cooney	Cunningham	Devine	Dutch	Fay
Clare	Cooper	Curley	Devitt	Dutton	Fearnely
De Clare	Cooper	Curragh	Devlin	Dwyer	Fegan
Clarke	Coote	Curran	Diamond	Dyas	Fegan
Clay	Coote	Currid	Diamont	Earhart	Fenelon
Claypoole	Copeland	Cusack	Diggs	Earley	Fenlon
Clayton	Corballis	Cuthbert	Dillon	Early	Fennell
Cleabear	Corbally	Cutter	Dillon, Dillior	Early	Ferguson
Cleary	Corbett	Cyrch	Dixon	Eastwood	Ferriter
Cleburne	Corcoran	Dagg	Dixson	Edkins	Ferry
Clemens	Corey	Dalton	Doane	Edmonds	Fetherston
Clere	Mac Cormack	Daly	Dobson	Edwards	Fians
Cliff	McCormick	Danaher	Dockrell	Edwards	Field
Clinch	Corr	Dancer	Dodson	Egan	Field
Clinch	Corr, Corry	Dandridge	Dolan	Ekin	Figgis

Surnames in Dublin in The Master Book of Irish Surnames

Finglas	Frankel	Glascord	Gutch	Harvy	Hollaway
Finglas	Franklin	Gleeson	Guthrie	Haslam	Holliday
Finn	Fraser	O'Gleeson	Guy	Hasselham	Hollywood
Fisher	Fraser	McGlory	Gyles	Hast	Hollywood
Fitzgerald	Frazer	Glover	Hackett	Hate	Holmes
Fitzgerald	Freeman	McGloyre	Hackett	Hatfield	Holmes
Fitzgerald	Freeman	Glynn	Hadsor	Hatter	Holt
Fitzgerrold	Frieudman	Godd	Haines	Hatton	Holywood
Fitzharris	Fry	Goff	McHale	Haughton	Hood
Fitzpatrick	Fryer	Goodrich	Haliday	Haughton	Hook
Fitzsimmons	Fulham	Goodwin	Hall	Haven	Hooke
Fitzsimons	Fullam	Goragh	Halligan	Haward	Hooker
Fitzwilliam	Fullam	Gordon	Hallowel	Hawkins	Hookes
Fitzwilliam,	Fullerton	Gordon	Halpin	Hawkins	Hopkins
Fitzwilliams	Fulton	Gorer	Halpin	Hayden	Hopkins
Flanagan	Fyan	Gorman	Hamilton	Haydon	Horish
Fleming	Gaffney	Gormely	Hand	Hayes	Horton
Fleming	Gage	Gormly	Handy	Healy	Horton
Flemming	Galagher	Gothimer	Hanes	Hemphill	Hoult
Fletcher	Galbelly	Gotler	Hankshaw	Henderson	Howard
Flood	Gall	Gouge	Hanlon	Hendrick	Howard
Flower	Gannon	Gough	Hannigan	Hendrick	Howlett
Floyd	MacGannon	Gough	Hannigan	Henebry	Howth
Floyd	Gardiner	Goulborne	Hanratty	Hennessy	Howth
Flynn	Garland	Gould	Hanway	McHenry,	Huband
Foester	Garland	Goulding	O'Hara	Herbert	Hudson
Fogarty	Garner	Grace	O'Hara	Herbert	Hudson
O'Fogarty	Garrett	O'Grady	Harborne	Herman	Hughes
Foley	McGarry	Grafton	Hard	Hesse	Hughs
Fookes	Gaskin	Graham	Harding	Hewett	Humphries
Foran	Gay	Graham	Hardy	Heynham	Humphries
Forbes,	Gaynor	McGrane	Hardy	Hickey	Hunt
Ford	Gaynor	Grange	Harford	O'Hickey	Hunt
Forde	Genese	Grattan	Harford	Hicks	Huntington
Forester	Gennitt	Graves	Harington	Hickson	Hurley
Forrest	Geoghegan	Graves	Harkins	Higby	Hussey
Forster	George	Gray	Harknett	Higgins	Hussey
Forth	Geraghty	Graydon	Harmel	Hill	Hutchinson
Foster	MacGeraghty	Greeley	Harnet	Hill	Hutchison
Foules	Gerrard	Green	Harold	Hilliard	Hyland
Founbaine	Gerry	Green,	Harrington	Hilliard	Hyland
Fountaine	Gibbs	Greene	Harrington	Hilton	Hynes
Fox	Gibner	Gregory	Harris	Hoadly	Isaac
Foxall	Gibney	Grennan	Harris	Hoagman	Isaacs
Foxwich	Gibney	Grennan	Harris	Hoare	Israel
Foy	Gibson	Grogan	Harris	Hoban	Ivers
Foy	Gibson	Grogan	Harrison	Hodges	Ivers
Foye	Gilbert	Grolliax	Harrison	Hodgkins	Ivory
Foyle	Gilbert	DeGroot	Harson	Hodser	Jackson
Frail	McGill	Gryffith	Hart	Hoey	Jacob
Frame	Gilligan	Guilfoyle	Hartley	Hogan	Jacob
Frampton	MacGilligan	McGuinness	O'Hartley	Holden	Jacob
Francis	Giltrap	McGuirk	Hartney	Holford	Jacobs
Francis,	Gitt Elson	Guiy	Harvey	Holland	Jameson

 ©1999 IGF. Box 7575, Kansas City, Missouri 64116 USA - .

Surnames in Dublin in The Master Book of Irish Surnames

Jarvis	Kettle	Leacy	Ludlow	Maxwell	Mould
Jeffery	MacKey	Leake	Lutrell	May	Moynes
Jefford	McKibbin	Lecch	Lutterell	Mayhugh	Muckleborne
Jeffrey	Kickham	Lecchfield	Luttrell	Mayler	Muir
Jenkins	Kickham	Lecora	Lynacar	Mayo	Mulhall
Jenkinson	Kidd	Ledwith	Lynam	Meagher	Mulligan
Jennings	Kiernan	Lee	Lynam	O'Meara	Muncke
Jervice	Kinahan	Lee	Lynch	Meath	Munson
Joakes	King	Leech	Lynchy	Mee	Murphy
Joanes	Kingsmill	Leeson	Lynsey	Meehan	Murray
Joel	Kingston	Leeson	Lyons	Meldon	Murrey
John	Kingston	Leeson,	Lyttle	Melville	Mustian
St. John	Kinsella	Lefroy	Mackey	Mercer	Myers
Johns	Kirwan	StLeger	Maconchy	Meredeth	Nagle, Nangle
Johnson	Kithinyman	Lehman	Madden	Meredith	McNally
Johnston	Knight	Leischman	Magg	Merrick	McNamara
Jolley	Knot	Lemon	Magrane	Merricke	Napier
Jolliff	Knowles	Lemond	Maguire	Merrigan	Nash
Jolly	Knowles	Lennan	Maher	Mervin	Nathan
Jones	Knox	Lennon	Maher,	Metzenberg	Navill
Jones	Lacey	O'Lennon,	Mahon	Michell	Naylor
Jordan	Lacy	Lentaigne	McMahon	Mildmay	Neale
Judah	Lahiff	Lesaw	Mahowne	Millar	O'Neale
Judge	Laird	Leuett	Mallone	Miller	Neary
Kane	Lalor	Levenston	Malone	Millinton	Neill
Kaplan	Lamb	Levi	O'Malone	Mills	O'Neill
Kavanagh	Lambart	Levingston	Mangan	Miner	Nelson
Kay	Lambe	Lewis	O'Mangan	Missett	Nerwich
Kearney	Lambert	Lewis	Manly	Mitchell	Nesbitt
Kearns	Lane	Linton	Manney	Mitchell	Netterville
Kearogan	Lane	Littell	Manning	Mocter	Neville
Kearovan	Langdale	Little	Manning	Moelet	Newcomb
Keavanagh	Langtry	Litton	Mapes	Moffat	Newcomb
O'Keefe	Larkan	Livingston	Marcus	Moffitt	Newcomen
O'Keeffe	Larkin	Livingston	Marcus Of	Molesworth,	Newcoment
Keegan	Lasch	Lloyd	Marienhoff	Mollenex	Newman
Keeley	Latimer	Lockard	Markam	Monaghan	Newman
Keely	Laundy	Locke	Markey	O'Monaghan	Newman
Keenan	Laurence	Lodlowe	Markham	Monahan	Nicholas
Kellett	Lavelle	Loftus	Marks	Monks	Nicholls
Kelly	Lawces	Loghlin	Marlow	Mooney	Nicholson
O'Kelly	Lawler	Lombard	Marshall	Moore	Noble
MacKen	Lawles	Long	Marshall	Moory	Noble
Kenna	Lawless	Longley	Martell	Moran	Nolan
Kennedy	Lawless	Lord	Martin	Moroly	O'Nolan
Kenny	Lawlis	Losse	Martine	Morphy	North
McKenzie	Lawlor	Loughlin	Martyn	Morran	North
Keogh	StLawrance	McLoughlin	Marwards	Morris	Norton
MacKeogh	Lawrence	O'Loughlin	Mason	Morrison	Norton
Kerke	StLawrence	Louis	Masterson	Morse	Nottingham
Kernan	Lawson	Lovell	Mathews	Mortomer	O'Nowlan
McKernan	Lazarus	Lowe	Matthews	Morton	Nowland
Kerris	Lazarus Of	Lowry	Maule	Moseley	Nowlane
Kett	Lea	Lowther	Mautner	Moses	Nuel

Surnames in Dublin in The Master Book of Irish Surnames

Nugent	Pin	Reddy	Sandheim	Skiddy	Summars
Nulty	Pinson	Redmond	Sands	Skully	Summer
Oakley	Pitts	Reeues	Sands	Slator	Suppels
Ob	Playford	Reid	Sankey	Smidt	Sutton
Opolinser	Plunket	Reilly	Saunders	Smith	Swan
Orr	Plunkett	O'Reilly	Savadge	Smullen	Swanton
Orson	Plunkett	Reis	Savage	Smyth	Swanton
Owens	Polak	Relick	Sawey	Solomon	Sweetman
Ownyan	Polexfield	Reyly	Sayers	Solomons	Sweetman
Padmore	Pollack	Reynolds	Sayers	Somers	Swift
Page	Pollard	Riall	Scally	Southwell,	Swinfeild
Paget	Pontoney	Riall	Scarborough	Southy	Swords
Paine	Pony	Rich	Scarborrough	Spence	Symons
Paisley	Poole	Richard	Seagrave	Spencer	Synge
Palfery	Pooly	Richardson	Seagrave	Spiers	Synnott
Pallatio Del	Poope	Richt	Seaman	Spiro	Synnott
Palles	Porter	Riddle	Seden	Spranger	Synyres
Palliser	Pott	Rider	Sedgraue	Spring	Taaffe
Palmer	Potter	Rielly	Seery	Spring	Tacker
Parker	Potter	Rigg	Semple	Springham	Talant
Parkinson	Poudyhard	Robert	Sergeant	St. Lawrence	Talbot
Parnall	Power	Roberts	Sergent	St. Lawrence,	Talbot
Parnell	Powers	Robinson	Seward	Stafford	Talbott
Pasco	Prendergast	Robotham	Shackleford	Stanford	Tallon
Patton	Preston	Roche	Shane	Stanihurt	Tallon
Payne	Preston	Roche, Roach	Shaw	Stanley	Tansy
Peachen	Price	Rochford	Shaw	Stanly	Tate
Peake	Prigget	Rock	Sheapheard	Stanton	Taylor
MacPeake	Prinn	Rodgers	Sheapherd	Stapleton	Taylor
Pearson	Pritchet	Rogers	Sheils	Stapleton	Taylor,
Peasley	Proby,	Rohan	Shelly	Staughton	Teeling
Peepes	Purcell	O'Ronan	Shelly	Stavenhagen	Temple
Pennington	Purcell	Roney	Shelton	Steele	Temple,
Penny	Purdy	Rooney	Sherding	Steele	Terrell
Penoyx	Purefoy	Rosengrane	Sheridan	Stellman	Terry
Penteny	Purfield	Rosenstein	Sherlock	Stephens	Theswell
Perkins	MacQueale	Rosenthal	Sherry	Stephenson	Thomas
Perkins	Quigley	Ross	Sherry	Sterling	Thornton
Perrier	Quin	Rothes	Sherwin	Steward	Thornton
Perry	Quinn	Rothwell	Shiels	Stibbe	Thunder
Persse	Quinne	Rourke	Shipcott	Stiles	Thunder
Pettit	Rafter	Rowles	Shore	Stoakes	Thwaits
Phepoes	Rainllow	Rubinstein	Short	Stokes	Tichborne
McPhillip,	Ramsey	Rudman	Short	Stopford	Tierney
Phillipps	Randall	Rueff	Shortall	Storton	MacTighe,
Phillips	Rathburne	Russell	Shortell	Stoughton	Timmins
Phillips	Rawlings	Salaman	Shurlog	Strabane	Tisdall
Phillpot	Rawlingson	Sall	Siev	Strange	Tobias
Picket	Rawlinson	Salmon	Simons	Straughton	Tobin
Picknall	Raynor	Saltinsball	Sinnot	Strickland	Tobin
Pierce	Readeinge	Sampson	Sisk	Strieley	Tomlins
MacPierce	Realy	Samuelson	Skelly	Strong	Tone
Piercie	O'Reddan	Sancky	Skelton	Stryny	Tonge
Pigott	Reddy	Sandford	Skelton	Sullivan	Tonstall

Toogood	Wallace	Willoughby
Toole	Wallas	Wills
O'Toole	Wallis	Wimsey
Tooley	Walsh, Welsh	Winslow
Toomey	Walshe	Withams
Totten	Walshman	Wizard
Tottenham	Walton	Wogan
Tottericke	Wamought	Wolf
Toulson	Ward	Wolverston
Towers	Ware	Wolverston
Toye	Warren	Wood
Tracey	Wasbery	Woodlock
Tracy	Waterhouse	Woodruff
Trant	Watson	Woods
Travers	Watts	Woods
Traynor	Waybrent	Woodside
MacTraynor	Wayman	Woodside
Triar	Weatherhead	Workman
Tuinon	Weaver	Worship
Tully	Weaver	Worth
Turner	Webb	Wright
Turner	Webb	Wright
O'Twomey	Webber	Wybrant
Tynte	Webster	Wybrants
Tyrell	Welles	Wyburne
Tyrrell	Wellesley	Wylder
Tyth	Wells	Wynn
Usher	Wenwell	Wynne
Ussher	Werthheim	Yates
Ussher	Wesby	Yeates
Ustace	Westby	Yeats
Uustice	Westenra	Young
Valentine	Westinra	
Vance	Weston	
Vanderpuer	Wetherall	
Vaughan	Whaly	
Vernon	Wheeler	
Vernor	Whelan	
Verscoyle	Whelen,	
Vesey	Whetlock	
Vincent	Whitchurch	
Vizard	White	
Wade	Whitefield	
Wade	Whiteside	
Wadsworth	Whitgrove	
Waight	Whitihell	
Wainman	Whitmore	
Wakefield	Whyte	
Waldron	Wickombe	
Waldron	Wilcox	
Walker	McWilliam	
Walker	Williams	
Wall	Willis	
Wall	Willmore	

Names of Jewish Families Found Primarily in Dublin

Abbecaces of	Genese	Lewis	Sampson
Ahlborn	Gilbert	Louis	Samuelson
Albun	Gitt Elson	Lyons	Sandheim
Altman	Godd	Marcus	Siev
Bender	Gorer	Marienhoff	Simons
Benmohel	Gothimer	Marks	Smidt
Berg	Gotler	Mautner	Solomon
Betzold	Groot	Metzenberg	Spiro
Blum	Harmel	Moseley	Stavenhagen
Boas	Harris	Moses	Stellman
Braham	Herman	Myers	Stibbe
Braun	Hesse	Nathan	Symons
Calbs	Hoagman	Nerwich	Tobias
Callisher	Humphries	Newman	Werthheim
COAN	Isaacs	Nuel	Wills
Cohen	Israel	Opolinser	Wolf
Crabb	Jacob	Phillip, Phillips	
Davidson of Poland	Joel	Polak of Holland	
Davieson	Judah	Pollack	
Davis	Kaplan	Rathburne	
Diamond Diamont	Lasch	Reis	
Dutch	Lazarus	Robinson	
Elkin	Lee	Rosenstein of	
Epstein	Lehman	Rosenthal of	
Erlich	Leischman	Rubinstein	
Falk Fallek	Levenston	Rudman	
Frankel	Levi	Rueff	
Frieudman	Levingston	Salmon	

Some Dublin Placenames

A selection of placenames found in 17th - 20th Century Records
including Modern Parishes, Unions & Registrars Districts.

Shown are counties/district where placename is found. Counties may
be abbreviated thus; Dub = *Dublin.* This is a partial listing taken from the
larger collection found in The Master (Atlas &) Book of Irish Placenames. (I.G.F.)

Key: Tl = townland   Pl = place   pm = modern parish:
par = parish   * = given as a registrars district in the union of....
Some placenames may have multiple locations. (Placename / County)

Abbottstowne, Pl. *Dub.*
Abby, The *Dub. cty.*
Aderrig pm *Dub.*
Ardgillam, Pl. *Dub.*
Ardinoade, Pl. *Dub.*
Ardlawe,pl. *Dub.*
Artaine pm *Dub.*
Athgoe, Pl. *Dub.*
Back Lane, *Dub. cty.*
Backestowne, Pl. *Dub.*
Baggatroth, *Dub. cty.*
Balacoly, Pl. *Dub.*
Balbriggan, Pl. *Dub.*
Balconnye, Pl. *Dub.*
Balcurtry, Pl. *Dub.*
Baldergane, Pl. *Dub.*
Baldonane, Pl. *Dub.*
Baldongan, *Dub.*
Baldongan pm *Dub.*
Baldoyle pm *Dub.*
Baldoyle, Pl. *Dub.*
Baldwinstowne, Pl. *Dub.*
Balgaddy, Pl. *Dub.*
Balgeath, Pl. *Dub.*
Balgriffen, Pl. *Dub.*
Balgriffin, *Dub.*
Balgriffin pm *Dub.*
Balhary, Pl. *Dub.*
Balhodge, Pl. *Dub.*
Ballakerstowne, Pl. *Dub.*
Ballawlye, Pl. *Dub.*
Ballemadd, Pl. *Dub.*
Balleruris, Pl. *Dub.*
Ballileas, Pl. *Dub.*
Ballimon, Pl. *Dub.*
Ballincley, Pl. *Dub.*
Ballintlea, Tl Pl *Cla Kilk*
Wex Dub
Que
Balliske, *Dub.*
Ballistroan, Pl. *Dub.*
Ballogh, Pl. *Dub.*
Ballybane, Tl *Ker Wex*
Ros Dub
Ballyboghill pm *Dub.*
Ballyboughall, *Dub.*
Ballybought, Pl. *Tip. Dub.*

Ballycheevers, Pl. *Dub.*
Ballycolan, Pl. *Dub.*
Ballycoolan, Pl. *Dub.*
Ballydowde, Pl. *Dub.*
Ballyfarmott, Pl. *Dub.*
Ballyfermot pm *Dub.*
Ballyforeish, Pl. *Dub.*
Ballygaats, Pl. *Dub.*
Ballykea, Pl. *Dub.*
Ballymadun pm *Dub.*
Ballymon, Pl. *Dub.*
Ballymore Eustace, Pl. *Dub.*
Ballymount, Pl. *Dub.*
Ballynescorney, Pl. *Dub.*
Ballyowen, *Lond.*
Lim. Tip.
Dub.
King.
Ballytoudine, Pl. *Dub.*
Balmadraught, Pl. *Dub.*
Balmadune, *Dub.*
Balmadunn, Pl. *Dub.*
Balmagwire, Pl. *Dub.*
Balmaston, Pl. *Dub.*
Balrickard, Pl. *Dub.*
Balrodery, *Dub.*
Balromyn, Pl. *Dub.*
Balrothery, *Dub.*
Balrothery pm *Dub.*
Balscaddan, *Dub.*
Balscaddan pm *Dub.*
Balseskin, Pl. *Dub.*
Balstibbocke, Pl. *Dub.*
Baltra, Pl. *Dub.*
Baltreslon, Pl. *Dub.*
Barbistowne Pl Tl *Dub Kild.*
Barrettstowne, Pl. *Dub.*
Bascaddan, Pl. *Dub.*
Baskine, Pl. *Dub.*
Bay, The, Pl. *Dub.*
Bealing Towne, Little, *Dub.*
Pl.
Bealings Towne, Great, *Dub.*
Pl.
Bealingstowne, Pl. *Dub.*
Belcamye, Pl. *Dub.*
Belgard, Pl Tl *Dub Kild.*
Benshee, Pl. *Dub.*

Beverstowne, Pl. *Dub.*
Black Stahenny, Pl. *Dub.*
Blanchardstowne, Pl. *Dub.*
Blundelstowne, Pl. *Dub.*
Bolyhouse, Pl. *Dub.*
Booterstown pm *Dub.*
Booterstowne, Pl. *Dub.*
Borranstowne, Pl. *Dub.*
Braghan, Pl. *Dub.*
Braspott, Pl. *Dub.*
Bray, Little, Pl. *Dub.*
Brazeele, Pl. *Dub.*
Brecknanstowne, Pl. *Dub.*
Bremoore, Pl. *Dub.*
Brenanstowne, *Dub. West.*
Bridge St, *Dub. cty.*
Brownestowne, Tl *Wat. Kilk.*
Lou. Dub.
Brownstowne, *Cor. Kild.*
Mea. Tip.
Dub.
Bull Lane, *Dub. cty.*
Bullocke, *Arm. Dub.*
Burchersheas, Pl. *Dub.*
Burnt House, Pl. *Dub.*
Butterfield, Pl. *Dub.*
Butterlane, Pl. *Dub.*
Buzzards Towne, Pl. *Dub.*
Cabragh, *Arm.*
Dow.
Lond.
Mea. Sli.
Tip. Dub.
Cabragh, Great, *Dub.*
Cacnadye, Pl. *Dub.*
Calliaghtowne, Pl. *Dub.*
Carranstowne, Pl. *Dub.*
Carrickhenhead, Pl. *Dub.*
Carrickhill, Pl. *Dub.*
Carrickmayne, Pl. *Dub.*
Carrstowne, Pl. *Dub.*
Castigobb, *Dub.*
Castle Farme Of *Dub.*
Castleknocke, Pl.
Castle Street, *Dub. cty.*
Castleknock, *Dub.*
Castleknock pm *Dub.*
Castleknocke, *Dub.*
Chapelizod pm *Dub.*

Chapple Izod, Pl. *Dub.*
Charlstowne, Pl. *Dub.*
Chequer Lane, *Dub. cty.*
Christ Church pm *Dub C.*
Christs Church Ln. *Dub c.*
Church Street *Dub. cty.*
Churchtowne, *Dub. Kild.*
Wex.
Churchtowne Of *Dub.*
Castleknocke, Pl.
Clandalkan, *Dub.*
Clandalkin, Pl. *Dub.*
Clantarfe, *Dub.*
Clanturke, *Dub.*
Cloghlan Swords, *Dub.*
Cloghran, *Dub. West.*
Cloghran pm *Dub.*
Cloghran Swords, *Dub.*
Cloghrodery, Pl. *Dub.*
Clondalkin pm *Dub.*
Clonmeathan, Pl. *Dub.*
Clonmedane, *Dub.*
Clonmethan pm *Dub.*
Clonshogh, *Dub.*
Clonsilla pm *Dub.*
Clonsillagh, *Dub.*
Clontarf pm *Dub.*
Clonturk pm *Dub.*
Clunamuck, Pl. *Dub.*
Clutterland, Pl. *Dub.*
Colcott, Pl. *Dub.*
Cold Winters, Pl. *Dub.*
Colemanstowne, *Cla. Dub.*
Colemyne, Pl. *Dub.*
Colganstowne, Pl. *Dub.*
Collatrath, Pl. *Dub.*
Colledge Greene, *Dub. cty.*
Collenstowne, Pl. *Dub.*
Collinstowne, *Dub.*
Kild.
West.
Commons Of Santry, Pl. *Dub.*
Connagh, *Cork, Dub.*
Connyborrow Of *Dub.*
Portmarnock, Pl.
Cooke Street, *Dub. cty.*
Cookestowne, *Dub. Lou.*
Mea.

Cooleduffe, Tl. *Cork, Dub.*
Coolock pm *Dub.*
Copper Alley, *Dub. cty.*
Copper Ally, *Dub. cty.*
Corballis, *Dub. Kild.*
    Lou. Mea.
    West.
Corballyes, *Dub. Mea.*
Cordanstowne, Pl. *Dub.*
Corduffe, Pl. *Dub.*
Cork Hill, *Dub. cty.*
Corkath, Pl. *Dub.*
Corke Hill, *Dub. cty.*
Corn Markett, *Dub. cty.*
Cornelstowne, Pl. *Dub.*
Corrstowne, Pl. *Dub.*
Cottrelstowne, Pl. *Dub.*
Cottresktowne, Pl. *Dub.*
Coultry, Pl. *Dub.*
Court Duff, Pl. *Dub.*
Cowlock, *Dub.*
Cowlocke, *Dub.*
Cowlocke = Coolick *Dub.*
Crevah, *Dub.*
Cromlyn, *Dub.*
Cruagh pm *Dub.*
Cruise Rath, Pl. *Dub.*
Crumlin pm *Dub.*
Curragh, East, Pl. *Dub.*
Curragh, Little, Pl. *Dub.*
Curtlagh, Pl. *Dub.*
Dalkey, *Dub.*
Dalkey pm *Dub.*
Damalstowne, Pl. *Dub.*
Damaske Street, *Dub. cty.*
Damastowne, Pl. *Dub.*
Davistowne, Pl. *Dub.*
Deane Rath, Pl. *Dub.*
Deans Graunge, Pl. *Dub.*
Denbroe, Pl. *Dub.*
Dermottstowne, Pl. *Dub.*
Dernedall, Pl. *Dub.*
Diswillstowne, Pl. *Dub.*
Dolphins Barn, Pl. *Dub.*
Donabate pm *Dub.*
Dondrom, Pl. *Dub.*
Donebate, *Dub.*
Donekernye, Pl. *Dub.*
Donibrooke, *Dub. cty.*
Donlovan, *Dub.*
Donnaghs, Pl. *Dub.*
Donnybrook pm *Dub.*
Donower, *Dub.*
Donshoghly, *Dub.*
Dowdenstowne, Pl. *Dub.*
Dowlaght, Pl. *Dub.*
Drimnagh pm *Dub.*
Drishoye, Pl. *Dub.*

Dromconcagh, Pl. *Dub.*
Dromnagh, Pl. *Dub.*
Dryneham, Pl. *Dub.*
Dubber, Pl. *Dub.*
Dublin, *Dub cty.*
    PMO.
Dublin diocese *Dublin*
Dublin City pm *Dub.*
Dublin, Co., *Dub.*
Duinstowne, Pl. *Dub.*
Dunmuskye, Pl. *Dub.*
Dunsincke, Pl. *Dub.*
Edmondstowne, *Dub. West.*
Effelstowne, Pl. *Dub.*
Ellistowne, Pl. *Dub.*
Elverstowne, Pl. *Dub.*
Esker, *Mon Dub*
    King Leit
Esker pm *Dub.*
Feildstowne, Pl. *Dub.*
Festryne, Pl. *Dub.*
Finglas pm *Dub.*
Finglas, Pl. *Dub.*
Finglass, *Dub.*
Finglasse, Pl. *Dub.*
Fishamble Street *Dub c.*
Flemingtowne, *Dub. Meath*
Forsterstowne, Pl. *Dub.*
Fowkestowne, Pl. *Dub.*
Fowkstowne, Pl. *Dub.*
Fox And Geese, Pl. *Dub.*
Francis Street *Dub. c.*
Frierstown, Pl. *Dub.*
Furrowes, Pl. *Dub.*
Gaberagh, *Dub. cty.*
Gallenstowne, Pl. *Dub.*
Galroestowne, Pl. *Dub.*
Garistowne, *Dub.*
Garristown pm *Dub.*
Gerrardstowne, Pl. *Dub.*
Gilianstowne, *Dub Kilk*
    Mea
Gittons, Pl. *Dub.*
Glancullan, Pl. *Dub.*
Glasnamuckye, Pl. *Dub.*
Glasnevin pm *Dub.*
Globe Ally, *Dub. cty.*
Golden Lane, *Dub. cty.*
Gracediewe, Pl. *Dub.*
Grainge Of   *Dub.*
Portmarnock, Pl.
Grallagh, *Tip. Dub.*
    Ros.
Grallagh pm *Dub.*
Grange, *Tip. Dub.*
    Que.
    West.
Grange Of   *Dub.*
Baldoyle, Pl.
Grangegorman pm *Dub.*

Graunge, *Dub.*
Graunge Of Ballycolan, *Dub.*
Pl.
Graunge Of Bascaddan, *Dub.*
Pl.
Graunge, Pl. *Ant. Tip.*
    Dub .
Grawngh Clanliffe, Pl. *Dub.*
Grazeele, Pl. *Dub.*
Greene, *Dub. cty.*
Hacketstowne, *Car. Dub.*
Hangmans Lane *Dub. c.*
Harandstowne, Pl. *Dub.*
Harristowne, *Dub Que*
    Kilk Wex
Harrolds Grang, *Dub.*
Hasill Hast, Pl. *Dub.*
Haynestowne, *Dub. Louth*
Haystowne, Pl. *Dub.*
Heggistowne, Pl. *Dub.*
High Street *Dub cty.*
    Kilk
Holly Wood Rath, Pl. *Dub.*
Hollywood, *Dow. Dub.*
Hollywood pm *Dub.*
Hollywood, great, *Dub.*
Holme Patricke, *Dub.*
Holmpatrick pm *Dub.*
Howth, *Dub.*
Howth pm *Dub.*
Hunstowne, Pl. *Dub.*
Huntstowne, *Dub. Kilk.*
Inchiguore, Pl. *Dub.*
Irishtowne, *Cor Kild*
    Lou Mea
    Dub
Irishtowne, *Dub.*
    Dub c.
Island Bridge, Pl. *Dub.*
Izod, *Dub.*
Jamesland, Pl. *Dub.*
Jamestowne, *Lim Leit*
    Tip Dub
Jobstowne, Pl. *Dub.*
Johnstowne, *Car Dub*
    Que Kild
    Mea West
Jordanstowne, Tl. *Cork Dub.*
Keppocke, *Dub. Kild.*
Kilbarrack pm *Dub.*
Kilbarrocke, Pl. *Dub.*
Kilbobban, Pl. *Dub.*
Kilbride pm *Dub.*
Kilcoskan, Pl. *Dub.*
Kilcreagh, Pl. *Dub.*
Kildonan, Pl. *Dub.*
Kilgobbin pm *Dub.*
Kill pm *Dub.*
Kill Of Grange, Pl *Dub.*
Killakee, Pl. *Dub.*

Killbride, *Dub Kilk*
    Ros King
Killeek pm *Dub.*
Killeene, *Long Lou*
    Cor Tip
    Dub King
    Que
Killeigh, *Dub.*
Killelane, Pl. *Dub.*
Killenardar, Pl. *Dub.*
Killenenny, *Dub.*
Killeninge, *Dub.*
Killester *Wat Dub*
Killester pm *Dub.*
Killiney pm *Dub.*
Killmalumme, Pl. *Dub.*
Killogher, Pl. *Dub.*
Killossery pm *Dub.*
Kilmacheoge, Pl. *Dub.*
Kilmactalway pm *Dub.*
Kilmacud pm *Dub.*
Kilmahuddrick pm *Dub.*
Kilmalway, *Dub.*
Kilmanham, Pl. *Dub.*
Kilmarcadd, Pl. *Dub.*
Kilmartin, Pl. *Dub. Que.*
Kilmatalway, Pl. *Dub.*
Kilmayneham, *Dub.*
Kilmoore, Pl. *Dub. Wex.*
Kilossery, *Dub.*
Kilreeske, Pl. *Dub.*
Kilsallaghan pm *Dub.*
Kilshawe, Pl. *Dub.*
Kilsolachan, *Dub.*
Kiltallonen, Pl. *Dub.*
Kilternan, Pl. *Dub.*
Kiltiernan pm *Dub.*
Kiltome, Pl. *Dub.*
Kinaude, Pl. *Dub.*
Kingstowne, Pl. *Dub.*
Kinnure, Pl. *Dub.*
Kinsaley pm *Dub.*
Kinsaley, Pl. *Dub.*
Kishocke, Pl. *Dub.*
Kittanstowne, Pl. *Dub.*
Knightstowne, Pl. *Dub.*
Knock, *Dow. Ros.*
    Cor. Dub.
Knockdromyn, Pl. *Dub.*
Knockingen, Pl. *Dub.*
Knocklyne, Pl. *Dub.*
Knockoeddan, Pl. *Dub.*
Kylnemanagh, Pl. *Dub.*
Kysars Lane, *Dub. cty.*
Laine, Pl. *Dub.*
Lambay, Pl. *Dub.*
Larecorr, Pl. *Dub.*
Laundistowne, Pl. *Dub.*
Lazy Hill, *Dub. cty.*

Some Dublin Placenames

Leas, *Dub.*
Leas, Pl. *Dub.*
Leatowne, Pl. *Dub.*
Lecklnstowne, Pl. *Dub.*
Leestowne, Pl. *Dub.*
Leffenhall, Great, *Dub.*
Leixlip pm *Dub.*
Lenthrops Ally *Dub cty.*
Liapardstowne, Pl. *Dub.*
Lispopell, Pl. *Dub.*
Logattinigh, Pl. *Dub.*
Loghbragh, Pl. *Dub.*
Loghshinigh, Pl. *Dub.*
Loghtowne, Pl. *Dub. Que.*
Long House, *Dub.*
Loughanstowne, *Dub.*
Loughlinstowne, *Dub.*
Lucan, *Dub. Que.*
Lucan pm *Dub.*
Lusk pm *Dub.*
Luske, *Dub.*
Luske, East, *Dub.*
Luttrellstowne, *Dub.*
Mabestowne, Pl. *Dub.*
Magilstowne, Pl. *Dub.*
Malahiddart, *Dub.*
Malahide, *Dub.*
Malahide pm *Dub.*
Malahowe, *Dub.*
Malt, *Dub.*
Marshallstowne, *Dub. Wex.*
Mayme, Pl. *Dub.*
Mayne, Little, Pl. *Dub.*
Mayock, Pl. *Dub.*
Merchants Key *Dub. cty.*
Milltowne, *West. Tip.*
Dub.
Miltowne, *Cor. Dub.*
King.
Que. Kild.
Kilk. Lou.
Milverstowne, *Dub.*
Molhyanstowne, Pl. *Dub.*
Monkstown pm *Dub.*
Moorestowne, Pl. *Dub.*
Mooretowne, *Dub. Kild.*
Morganstowne, *Dub.*
Morrough, Pl. *Dub.*
Mounk Towne, Pl. *Dub.*
Mulhuddart pm *Dub.*
Mullenestillan, *Dub.*
Murderye, Pl. *Dub.*
Naall, *Dub.*
Nangor, Pl. *Dub.*
Naptowne, *Dub.*
Naul pm *Dub.*
Nealstowne, Pl. *Dub.*
Neithercross, *Dub.*
Neithercrosse, *Dub.*

Nespelstowne, Pl. *Dub.*
Nevenstowne, Pl. *Dub.*
Newcastle, *Lim. Tip.*
Wat. Dub.
Newcastle pm *Dub.*
Newcastle & *Dub.*
Uppercrosse
Newcastle & *Dub.*
Uppercrosse
Newell, Pl. *Dub.*
Newhaggard, *Dub. Meath*
Newhall, *Dub. Kild.*
Newhaven, Pl. *Dub.*
Newimings, Pl. *Dub.*
Newland, *Dub. Kild.*
Newminges, Pl. *Dub.*
Newstreet Ward, Pl. *Dub.*
Newtown, Little, *Dub.*
Newtowne, *Dub. King.*
Newtowne, Great, Pl. *Dub.*
Newtowne, Little, *Dub.*
Newtowne Of *Dub.*
Balscaddan, pl.
Newtowne Of *Dub.*
Cowlocke, pl.
Newtowne Of *Dub.*
Donshoghly, pl
Newtowne Of *Dub.*
Garistowne, Pl.
Newtowne One *Dub.*
The Strand,
Nottstowne, Pl. *Dub.*
Obriestowne, Pl. *Dub.*
Old Orchard, The, *Dub.*
Old Towne, *Lim. Kilk.*
Car. Dub.
Oldconnaught pm *Dub.*
Ould Court, *Dub. Kild.*
Wex.
Ould Towne, *Dub. Kild.*
West.
Owenstowne, *Dub.*
Pace, Little, Pl. *Dub.*
Palmerstown pm *Dub.*
Palmerstowne, *Dub.*
Palstowne, *Dub.*
Parnellstowne, *Dub.*
Parsonage, Pl. *Dub.*
Pasloestowne, *Dub.*
Pedanstowne, Pl. *Dub.*
Pelletstowne, *Dub.*
Pheblestowne, Pl. *Dub.*
Pheopostowne, Pl. *Dub.*
Phillippstowne, *Dub. Lou.*
Phipps Parke, *Dub. cty.*
Poocestowne, *Dub.*
Porterstowne, *Dub. West.*
Portmarnock, *Dub.*
Portmarnock pm *Dub.*
Portmarnocke, *Dub.*
Portraine pm *Dub.*

Portrarne, *Dub.*
Promstowne, Pl. *Dub.*
Rabeale, Pl. *Dub.*
Rabucke, Pl. *Dub.*
Rahany, Pl. *Dub.*
Raheny pm *Dub.*
Raholke, Pl. *Dub.*
Rainconey, Pl. *Dub.*
Rascall, *Dub.*
Ratchedan, *Dub.*
Rath, *Wex. Car.*
Dub.
Rath Of Kilossery, *Dub.*
Rathartan, *Dub.*
Rathcoole, *Tip. Dub.*
Kilk. Lou.
Rathcoole pm *Dub.*
Rathcoole, Portreue, *Dub.*
Rathdowne, *Dub.*
Rathenny, *Dub.*
Rathfarnham pm *Dub.*
Rathfarnum, *Dub.*
Rathfarnum, *Dub.*
Whitechurch And
Rathgarr, Pl. *Dub.*
Rathmichael pm *Dub.*
Rathmichall, Pl. *Dub.*
Rathmynes, Pl. *Dub.*
Read Chymny, Pl. *Dub.*
Reckinhead, Pl. *Dub.*
Reinoldstowne, Pl. *Dub.*
Rickenhoare, Pl. *Dub.*
Ringe, *Dub. Wex.*
Ringsend, *Dub. cty.*
Roans, *Dub.*
Robinhood, Pl. *Dub.*
Robs Walls, Pl. *Dub.*
Rochestowne, *Tip. Dub.*
Kild. Kilk.
Wex.
Roganston, *Dub.*
Roganstowne, pl. *Dub.*
Rogerstowne, *Dub. Kilk.*
Lou. Mea.
West.
Rose Mary Lane *Dub. cty.*
Roulestowne, *Dub. Meath*
Rowlagh, *Dub.*
Rush, Pl. *Dub.*
Sagard, *Dub.*
Saggart pm *Dub.*
Santry, *Dub.*
Santry pm *Dub.*
Saucerstowne, Pl. *Dub.*
Schellerstowne, Pl. *Dub.*
Scoole House Lane *Dub cty.*
Seatowne, Pl. *Dub.*
Sencier, Pl. *Dub.*
Shallon, *Dub. Meath*

Shangannagh, *Dub.*
Shankill, *Fer. Mon.*
Dub. Wat.
Ros.
Sheeps Street, *Dub. cty.*
Sherryes, Pl. *Dub.*
Silloge, Pl. *Dub.*
Silverhill, Pl. *Dub.*
Simonscourt *Dub. cty.*
Sippers Lane, *Dub. cty.*
Skesuble, Pl. *Dub.*
Skiddowe, Pl. *Dub.*
Skillinglass, *Dub.*
Skinner Row, *Dub. cty.*
Skippers Lane, *Dub. cty.*
Slafferstowne, Pl. *Dub.*
Sprecklestowne, Pl. *Dub.*
St. Andrew's pm *Dub. City*
St Andrewes, *Dub. cty.*
St Andrews, *Dub. cty.*
St. Anne's pm *Dub. City*
St Audians, *Dub. cty.*
St. Audoen's pm *Dub. City*
St. Bartholomews pm *Dub C.*
St Brides, *Dub. cty.*
St. Bridget's pm *Dub. City*
St. Catherine's pm *Dub C.*
St Dowlaght, Pl. *Dub.*
St. George's pm *Dub C.*
St Georges Lane *Dub c.*
St. James' pm *Dub. City*
St John Hoys Ally *Dub c.*
St. John's pm *Dub. City*
St Johns, *Cor c Dub*
c Kild Ros
St Katherins, Pl. *Dub.*
St Kathrines *Dub. cty.*
St Keavans, *Dub.*
St. Luke's pm *Dub. City*
St. Margaret's pm *Dub.*
St Margretts, *Dub.*
St. Mark's pm *Dub. City*
St. Mary's pm *Dub. C.*
St. Michael's pm *Dub. City*
St. Michan's pm *Dub. City*
St Michans, *Dub. cty.*
St Michells, *Dub. cty.*
St Nicholas, *Dub. cty.*
St. Nicholas pm *Dub C.*
Within
St. Nicholas pm *Dub C.*
Without
St Patrick, *Dub. cty.*
St. Patrick's pm *Dub. City*
St Patricks, *Lim. cty.*
Dub. cty.
St Patricks Close, *Dub.*
St. Paul's pm *Dub. City*
St. Peter's pm *Dub.*

Some Dublin Placenames

St. Peter's pm *Dub. City*
St. Thomas' pm *Dub City*
St Warbroug, Par *Dub c.*
St Warbrough, Par *Dub c.*
St Warbroughs *Dub c.*
St. Werburghs pm *Dub C.*
Stacoole, Pl. *Dub.*
Stapolin, *Dub.*
Staughtons Fram, Pl. *Dub.*
Stephentowne, *Dub.*
Stephephenstowne, Pl. *Dub.*
Sterminstowne, Pl. *Dub.*
Stevens Street *Dub. cty.*
Stillorgan pm *Dub.*
Stillorgan, Pl. *Dub.*
Stradbally, *Ker. Wat.*
  Lim. cty.
  Dub. Que.
Strand, *Dub.*
Surgolls Towne, Pl. *Dub.*
Sutton, *Dub.*
Swanally, *Dub. cty.*
Swords, *Dub.*
Swords pm *Dub.*
Symonscourt, Pl. *Dub.*
Tallaght, *Dub.*
Tallaght pm *Dub.*
Taney pm *Dub.*
Tankardstowne, *Lim. Kilk.*
  Dub. Que.
Tartayne, Pl. *Dub.*
Teddanstowne, Pl. *Dub.*
Temploge, *Dub.*
Terrellstowne, Pl. *Dub.*
Terrelstowne, *Dub.*
Texmercgin, *Dub.*
Thomastowne, *Cor. Dub.*
  Wat. Kild.
  Kilk. Lou.
Thomond, Pl. *Dub.*
Tibrodan, *Dub.*
Tick Mickie, Pl. *Dub.*
Tinstowne, Pl. *Dub.*
Tipperkeavan, *Dub.*
Tipperkeavin, *Dub.*
Tirenure, *Dub.*
Tirrenure, *Dub.*
Titnocke, Pl. *Dub.*
Tobbar Bride, Pl. *Dub.*
Tobberbarr, Pl. *Dub.*
Tobbergregan, Pl. *Dub.*
Tobberlonny, *Dub.*
Tobbersoole, Pl. *Dub.*
Tobbertowne, Pl. *Dub.*
Tobrelstowne, Pl. *Dub.*
Tomingtowne, Pl. *Dub.*
Tonleged, *Dub.*
Tonlegeeth, *Dub.*
Tornaat, Pl. *Dub.*

Trolly, Pl. *Dub.*
Trynity Lane *Dub. cty.*
Tubber, *Dub Long*
Tubberskeakin, Pl. *Dub.*
Tully pm *Dub.*
Turvey, Pl. *Dub.*
Tymen, Pl. *Dub.*
Uppercross & Newcastle *Dub.*
Uppercrosse & *Dub.*
Newcastle
Walls, *Dub.*
Walshtowne, Pl. *Dub.*
Ward, *Dub.*
Ward pm *Dub.*
Warde, *Dub.*
Westowne, *Dub.*
Westpalstown pm *Dub.*
Whitechurch, *Cor c. Wat*
  Dub Wex
Whitechurch pm *Dub.*
Whitestowne, *Dub. Wex.*
Wimbleton, *Dub.*
Wine Taverne Street *Dub.c.*
Wisetowne, Pl. *Dub.*
Wood Key, *Dub. cty.*
Woodtowne, *Dub. Lou.*
  Wex.
Worganstowne, *Dub.*
Wyanstowne, Pl. *Dub.*

From *The Master Book of Irish Placenames.* ©1994 I.G.F., Box 7575, K.C., MO. 64116

The Census of 1659 - City of Dublin

Location	Individuals	Location	Individuals
Skinner Row	Ridyly Hatfield, John Preston, Esqrs ; Thomas Kickham, John Pitts, Nicholas Wilcox, Ralph Allen, Francis Harris, James Kelly, gentlemen ; Robert Kenedy, Phillipp Harris, Esqrs ; William Evers, James Steward gent, Sr Thomas Shurlog Knt, James his sonn gent Esqr, Theophilus Eton Esqr, Edmond Ramsey, John White, gentlemen ; Richard Kenny Esqr, Leut Henry Wade, Nicholas Knight gent, Thomas Broune, Ralph King, John Pin, Esqrs ; Thomas Floyd gent, Roger Bishopp Esqr, Thomas Storton ; Alderman Tho : Hookes, Esqrs, Thomas Hookes gent, Nathainell Boyle Esqr, James Edkins, Edward Penteny gentle, Silvester Waight, John Bettin, and James Webb, M'chants.	Francis Street	Thomas Whitgrove Esqr, Robert Arundall gent, William Taylor Esqr, Capt. Phillpot Esqr, Alderman John Cranwell Esq, Captn Derbon.
		St Brides &c	Leut Coll Warren, Captn Francis Shane, Thomas Foules Esqrs, Cornett Jefford, Isaack Collier, John Pinson, Mr Debart gentlemen, Coll Barrow Esqr, Captn Thomas Poope, Mr Richard, John Archer gentlemen John Browne M'chant, Richard Ward gent, Mr Dauson Esqr, John his sonn gent, Marshall Peake Esqr, Captn Early, Capt. Shaw Esqr, Mr Richt gent, Mr Markham Esq, Leut Wm Dason Inkeeper, Robert Seaman gent/George Maxwell, Josias Debart, Capt. Potter, Walter Potter his sonn gentlemen, James Moroly Esq, Mr Clarke, Leut Lecora.
Swanally	John Paine, Capt. Robert Hughs gent, Capt Claypoole, Christopher Palmer gent.	Sheeps Street	Salt' Corey, Captn Playford, Robert Broune gentlemen, The Lady Phillipps, Robert hir son, Roger Glascord, Gryffen Borden, gentle-, men ; Henry Sancky Esqr, George King, James Founbaine, Leut Wright, Arthur Padmore, Silvanus Stryny, Arthur Padmore, John Joakes, gentlemen ; Robert Hughs, William Seden, John Staughton, Robert Bealing, gentlemen ; Mr Barnes lodger, The Lord Anger, James Cuff Esqr.
Damaske Street	John Kithinyman, Robert Candit, Thomas Haydon gent, Mr Samuell Jones lodgr, Captn Burt Lodger, The Lord Rainllow, Captn John Franklin, John Dodson, Stephen Buston gent, Sr John Temple Knt, John Temple Esqr, Henry Temple gent, Maior John Bligh Esqr, William Bligh gent, Capt. Graves, Samuell Drury, Thomas Pooly, John Walsh, William Wesby gentlemen ; Sr George Wenwell Knt, Sir Morris Uustice Knt, Mr Elward gent, Tho : Buckarton.		
St Georges Lane	Peter Synyres, Anthony Roe, Ralph Manney, John Crych, gentlemen ; Thomas Maule Esqr, Abraham Muckleborne, Cha : Lemond gent	Golden Lane	Capt. Rob't Newman, Patricke Talant gent, Ralph Coleman Bruer, Cornet Roney, Nicholas Combes, gentlemen ; Captn Able Warren Esqr, Leut Robert Newman, Phillipp Alding, Mr Moynes, Captn Pritchet, & Mr Benson, gentlemen.
Trynity lane			
Colledge Greene	William Jones, Jeremy Watts, Francis Little Esqr, Pierce Hast Capt, William Jones, John Boudler, Christopher Blackand, Doctr Robert Mould, Henry Jones, Richard Edwards, Cornett Merricke, Quartermasr Lloyd, Mr Cox, Capt Glover, Edward Gutch, gentlemen.	Stevens Street	Thomas Ob, Mr Bridges, Thomas Warren, John Warren his son, Thomas Walton, John Thornton, Edmond Gouge, Mr Jeffery, John Guiy gentlemen, John Moore, Esqr, John Avery gent, Thomas Tacker Esqr, Leut Cotton, Richard Bennett gent, Edward Roberts Esqr, Cornett Burton, John Assin gent, Leut Coll. Arnop Esqr.
Lazy Hill	Capt Rich, Capt John Nicholls gent.	Chequer Lane	Thomas Holford, William Holford, George Dixson, William Dores, Samuell Foxwich, John Harington, John Bryan, John Cliff,

223

The Census of 1659 - City of Dublin

Location	Individuals	Location	Individuals
	Richard Stanton and Robert Hall, gentlemen.		Esq[r], William North gent, Rigmould Wamought gent, Gregory Lambart gent, John Tonstall gent, Horatio Bonorly gent, Joseph Stoakes gent, Tobias Wetherall gent, Andrew Moory gent, Samuell Peepes Esq, John Hughs Esq, Edward Swan gent, S[r] James Ware Kn[t], James Ware Esq, Robert Ware gent, John Brampton gent,/ Richard Phillipps Esqr, Thomas Caulfield gent, John Broun gent, Nicholas Ware gent, John Bushell gent, Robert Bathripp gent, Richard Martin gent, Esq[r] Robert Woods gent, Doct[r] Gerry Esq, Coll Long Esq, Doct[r] Waterhouse Esq, John Bisse Esq[r], William Tichborne Esq, Samuell Bathurst gentle, Even Vaughan gent, Richard Wilson gent, Robert Cooke Esqr, Robert Symons gent, Richard Butler gent, John Pony Esq.
Ringsend	—		
Irishtowne	Oliver Lord Fitzwilliams, William Fitzwilliams Esq,		
Simonscourt	—		
Donibrooke	—		
Baggatroth	—		
Fishamble Street parte	John Sheapheard gent, James Barlowe M'chant, Richard Blundell gent, Arthur Usher Merchant, Edmond Duff Esq[r] Lodger, The Lady Crosby, Alderman Weston.		
Wine Taverne Streete	Andrew Lord M'chant, Richard Palfery gent, Jeremiah Berstow Merchant, William Taylor Merchant, John Fitzgerald gent, Adam Gould Merchant, James Gould gent, Alderman Daniell Hutchinson, Mathew Farley gent, Leut Coll Hookes Esq[r], William Harrison gent, Robert Marshall gent, Henry Markam gent, Francis Dudly gent, Joseph Banks gent, Humphry Withams gent, Tobias Bennell gent a lodger, John Boulton Merchant, Leut Pontoney a lodger.		
		Pte of Copper Alley	Thomas Bale gent, Samuell Kett gent, Richard Picknall gent, John Wallis gent, Charles Wainman Esq, Robert Ekin gent, Charles Butler gent, John Flemming gent, Robert Yates gent.
Wood Key Ward	Thomas Summars gent, Thomas Howard Merchant, Nicholas Amansham gent, John Maddin Esq[r], William Martin Bruar, William Hill merchant, Vallentine Cooke gent, Alderman William Smyth, Thomas Poole gent, Thomas Fulton Merchant, John Hanway gent, Thomas Kay gent, Thomas Robotham gent, Robert Wade bruar, Doct[r] Dudly Loftus Esq[r], Thomas Boyd Merchant, Henry Lewis gent, Jeffery Toulson gent, Samuell Bonole gent, William Harborne gent, Christopher Leuett Merchant, Joseph Whitchurch Merchant, Einor Tuinon Merchant, Humphry Jervice Merchant, Edward Aghwell gent, John Price Sheryff, Ezeckell Larkan Merchant.	Part of S[t] Warbroughs Streete	Thomas Sheapherd gent, Thomas Haughton gent, Nicholas Harman gent, Cornet Stanley gent, John Hooker gent, Coll Knight Esq, Thomas Lewis gent, Mathew Forth gent, John Gay gent, James Polexfield Esq, James Polexfield gent, John Polexfield gent, William Robert gent, James Yates gent, Robert Shipcott Esq,/Thomas Harnet gent, Henry Herbert Esq, Wadhine Sands gent, Henry Rawlingson gent, S[r] Tho : Herbert Knt, — Alexander Junior gent, Chidly Coote Esq, John Harson gent.
Castle Street	Alderman Daniell Bellingham, John Fletcher gent, Samuell Doughty gent, William Shelton gent, John North gent, Anthony Derry gent, George Stoughton gent, Richard Harvy Esq[r], Edward Wallis Esq[r], Christophert Hart gent, George S[t] George	Lenthrops Ally	William Kenedy gent
		S[t] John Hoys Ally	Jerome Allexander Esq
		Fishamble Street Pte	Mathew Nulty gent, Jn Barker gent.
		Phipps Parke Bull Lane	Geo : Charlton Esq, Capt Edmond Tomlins Esqr.
		Little Gaberagh	S[r] Jeremiah Sankey Knt, Mr Herbert Esq.

The Census of 1659 - City of Dublin

Location	Individuals
St Warbroughs Street	Quartermastr Stanly gent, Ralph Whetlock gent, Richard Webb gent, William Lane gent, Edward Burrowes gent, Jonas Lee gent, Richard Crofton gent, Henry Keating gent, William Hill gent, Robert Johnson gent, William Dixson Esq, Doctr Alwoodhouse Esq, Enoch Rider gent, Pp Hasselham gent, Corporall Stiles gent, Jn Norton gent, Sr Charles Coote Kt & Bart, William Sherding gent, Hen : Bollard Esq, Roger Bould gent, Rich : Young gent, Tho : Hooke gent, Isaack John gent, Tho : Reynolds gents, Jn Thornton gent, Sampson Toogood gent, Robert Cadwell gent, Samuel Cotton gent, Nathaniell Fookes gent, Robert Thornton gent, Thomas Parnall gent, Hugh Price Esqr, Robert Theswell gent, John Bush gent, Sr Oliver St George Knt William Hill gent, Cary Dillon Esq, William Bladen Esq, Humphry Poudyhard gent, Hugh Clotworthy Esq, Lewis Fallard Esq, William Stephenson gent, Samuell Nicholas gent, John Branham gent, Richard Haydon gent, Mathew Langdale.
pte of Corke Hill	Garrott Weldon gent
Part of Copper Ally	Edward Wayman gent, Nicholas Fountaine Esqr, Thomas Dent gent, William Diggs gent.
Globe Ally	William Butler gent, Dudly Loftus gent, Timothy Grolliax gent, Richard Reeues Esq.
Bridge St	Alderman John Forrest, Patrick Arthur gent, Thomas Springham M'chant, Alderman George Gilbert, Peter Lesaw gent, Francis Stanford M'chant, Nathaniell Palmer distiller, Symon Caricke Merchant, James Cleare Merchant, John Cooke Merchant, Peter Travers Merchant, Alderman John Desmineers M'chant Esqr, Thomas Freeman Merchant, William Barrow Merchant, Alderman Peter Waybrent Merchant, Lewis Desmineer Merchant, James Ashly Merchant, Sr Wm Usher Usher Kt, Mathew Magg gent, David Conly M'chant, Derrick Westinra Marchant, Geo : Dowdall M'chant, Paul

Location	Individuals
	Cadmore gent, William Deane gent, Waren Westenra Mct, Robert Goulborne gent, Albertus Crostenton gent, Audly Mervin Esq, Mr Morgan Lawyer, John Sergeant M'chant, Robert Dee Esqr, Mayor William Summer gent, Allen Jones gent.
Sippers lane Cooke Street	Nicholas Gorman Merchant, Abraham Clemens Merchant, William Hopkins gent, Robert Ardogh gent, Patrick Mapes gent, James White gent, John Hodges gent, John Cardyff gent, William Bragg gent, William Plunket gent, Valentine Savadge gent.
Corn Markett	William Plunkett gent, Richard Ward Distiller, James Ustace gent, Edmond Clere Mchant, John Dutton Mercht, William Fulham Mcht, Paul Delasale Mcht, William Harvy gent, Dominick White Mct, Samll Saltinsball Merct, Richard Berford Esq, John Salmon Merct, Jn Bollard Apothicary.
Pte of High Stret	Tho : Johnson Merct, Mr Browne gent, Doctor Robert Talbot, Rich : Clarke Apothicary
Back Lane Pt	Rich : Muncke gent
More of High Street	Dot Morgan Smyth, William Kerke Merchant, John Champines Mchant, Philipp Costleloe Shop Keeper, William Cramby Mct.
Kysars lane	Regnell Ball gent Ephram Hardy gent
High Streete	Mynard Christian Mctt, William Whitihell Mctt, Doctr Fennell lodgur, William Brooking Mctt, James Wade Apothicary, John Knot clothier, Samuell Chandler Mctt, Capt Robert Locke, Thomas Whitmore gent, Sr Robert Ford Knt, John Smyth Merchant, Thomas Kenedy gent, Joshua Rawlinson Mctt, Mathew French merchant, Stephen Butler Esq, Alderman Marke Quinn, Geo : Fisher Shopkeeper, Francis Harvy Esq, Alderman Kenedy, Thomas Brett gent, Alderman Cooke, Henry Reynolds gent, Rich : Millinton Merchant, Coll Owens, (more tituladoes names), Judge Whaly, Capt Chambers, Capt Chambers, Barnard Wizard, John Foxall Merchant.

The Census of 1659 - City of Dublin

Location	Individuals
St Michells lane	Thomas Hutchinson gent, Mr Mortomer Esq, Henry Martin Attorny
Cork Hill pte	— — —
Christs Church Lane	James Galbelly gent James Jones gent
Scoole house lane	Thomas Richardson Esq
Cooke Street	Mr Young gent, William Howard M'chant, Edward Barrytt Grocer, Richard Price gent.
Rose Mary lane	John Sergent Merchant
Merchants Key	John Hankshaw Merchant, Mathew Barry Esq, Gerrald Fay gent, Daniell Wybrant Merchant, John Beuchamp Merchant, Maior Brighness gent, Mr Lecch Merchant.
Skippers Lane	Mr Bruister gent, Timothy Miller gent, John Kelly gent, John Bygins Phis'.
St Kathrines Parish	Luke Lowther gent, Richard Heynham gent, Owen Jones gent, Ralph Wallis gent, Tobias Creamer gent, John Fryer gent, Tho : Worship Esq, Tristram Thornton gent, Ralph Rosengrane gent, John Workman gent, Ralph Vizard Esq, Edward Earle of Meath, Richard Green gent, Doctr Smyth Esq, Peter Lockard gent, Giles Mee gent, John Eastwood gent, Christopher Bennett gent, William Lecchfield gent, Tho : Clarke gent, Jer Skelton Esqr, Wm Phillipps gent, Aldermant Hunt, Robt Ludlow Esq, Robt Harding Esq, Edw : Brabzon Esq, Jn Hughs Secretary, Tho : Dungan Esq, John Cole gent, Tho : Shaw gent, his sonn Henry, his sonn Thomas, Theophilus Sandford Esq,/Rich : Tyth Esq, Joshua Allen gent, James Mollenex Esq, Patrick Allen gent, Robert Allen his sonn gent, Thomas Powell gent, Thomas Butler gent, William Goragh gent, Henry Spranger gent, Thomas Quirke gent, James Relick gent, Richard Stiles gent, John Pennington Esq, Marke Cheswright gent, Thomas Cooke gent, Thomas Waterhouse Esq, Hugh Roberts gent, Tho : Hoult gent, Robert Wasbery gent, Robert Archer gent, Tho : Dromgold gent, Edward Chambers gent, Tho :

Location	Individuals
	Navill gent, John Kelly gent, Sr Robt Newcoment Knt and Bart, Robert Wade gent, James Browne gent, Joseph Dobson gent, Hen : Verscoyle gent, Abram Rigg gent.
(folio 20). St Michans Parish	John Kelly Merchant, Thomas Cole M'chant, Robert Mercer Merchant, Robert Reeues clarke, Ralph Hartney gent, James Stopford Esq, Randall Becket Esq, William Sands Esq, Sr James Barry Kt, Rich : Barry Esq, Stephen Butler Esq, Coll Hen : Flower, Edward Short Esq, William Blackwell Esq, John Southy Esq, William Sands gent.
Church Street	Maior William Meredeth Esq, John Brookes Vintner, Tho : Orr Shopkeeper, Henry Orson shopkeeper, Edward Michell Shopkeeper, Tho : Dowding Merchant, William Allen Shopkeeper, Bartholomew Hodser Shop Kr, Robert his sonn, Obediah Bradshaw Shop Keeper, Will' Peachen Merchant, James Boyle Merchant, Rich : Cleabear Merchant, George Clapham gent, Adam Darling, Doctr Garner, Mr Francis gent, Geo : Prigget Esq, Capt Francis Spence gent.
Hangmans Lane	Alderman Will : Cuff, Felix Birne gent, Bartholomew Lynacar Maulster, Daniell Doyle Merchant, Charles Coote Esq, Charles Meredith Esq, Tho : Doude gent, Wm Thwaits Malster, Wm Hodgkins gent, Ralph Barker gent, Rich : Barret Esqr, Richard Owens gent, Sr Paul Davis Knt, Edward Temple Esq, Sr Robert Meredith Knt, Geo : Carr Esq, Tho : Carre gent, William Carr gent, Tho : Seagrave Esq, Lawrence Thornton gent.
The Abby	Christopher Curren gent, Danll Hickson gent, James Barnwall gent, Arthur Chichester Esq, Thomas Taylor gent, William Hatter gent, Edmond Tottericke gent, William Lawles Maulstr, John Bridges Esq, Jo : Doughty Esq, Sr Arthur Morgan Kt, Sr Hen : Tichborne Kt, John Cole Esq, Edmond Lucas gent, Geo : Crosby Esq, Henry Steele Maulster, Markes Mould Esq.
The Greene	Thomas Mason Esq

226

Francis Parsons Esq   Thomas Toye gent
Rowland Bulkley gent
—
Gabriell Briscoe gent   Charles Cottle gent

Nicholas Kealy gent
John Denn gent

Robert Hawkins gent

Joseph Avory Esqr
Robert Pott gent
Darby Burgoyne gent   Roger Brerton Esq

Samuell Browne gent

Moses Reyly gent   John Robinson gent   James Wilson Portreue
Richard Harvey gent   Symon Harvey his sonn
Hermon Miller gent a Foreigner

Francis Carbery gent

John Foye gent

William Greene gent

Sr Adam Loftus Knt   Adam Loftus Esq   Robert Loftus gent   Mathew Penoyx gent George Hopkins Esq

Robert Scarborrough gent Morgan Jones gent
John Smyth gent

William Clinch gent

Arthur Usher Esq   Sr Theophylus Jones Knt
Edward Harrington gent

Henry Burton Esq
Francis Peasley Esq   Francis Vaughan gent
Edward Cooke gent

Nathaniell Stoughton gent

Thomas Vincent Esq

Huibart Adryan Ald^r

John Blackwell Esq   Richard Cowse gent   Allexander Usher gent   William Purcell gent Ignatius his sonn
Captn Roger Beame Esq

Richard Raynor gent

Capt Richard Newcomen Esq

Daniell Readeinge gent
Edward Gryffith gent
Robert Cusack Esq   John Cusack gent
Maior Ellott Esq

Lawrence Hudson gent

Phillipp Fearnely Esq
John Borr Marchant Esq, Begnet Borr gent, Jacob Borr gent Forrenner, Cornelius Borr D^r of Physick Esq, Walter Brice gent, Davie Williams gent, Vallentine Dawkins gent, William Williams gent.

William Shore Esq
Captn John Smyth Esq, Owen Ellis gent, Walter Clay marshall gent, Edmond Bradshaw Merc, John Hughes gent, Jaques Vanderpuer Merchant and Forrenner, Maior Joseph Dean Esq, Robert Brady gent, John Prinn Merchant, Thomas Chabner gent, Adam Foester Merchant, Francis Spring Bruer, Doct^r John Foy Esq, Edward Bryscoe Merchant, John Wyburne gent, Maior Edward Warren Esq.
Thomas Talbott gentl, Edward Bather gent, James Lynsey gent, Peter Ward gent, William Hollaway, John Webber gent, John Rawlinson Marchant, John King gent, John Watson M'chant.
William Sterling gent   Captn William Cox Esq.

John Graydon gent

Richard Buckley Esq

The Census of 1659 - Tituladoes in 'The County of Dublin'

BARONY OF RATHDOWNE	BARONY OF NEITHERCROSS	BARONY OF BALROTHERY
Evan Vaughan gent	Oliver Barnewall gent	John Caddle gent
Edward Billinsley gent	Peter Russell gent Thomas White gent	
Henry Burnett gent		John Coddington gent Francis Walsh gent John Aston gent
	John Arthur gent	Thomas Clarke gent
Valentine Wood gent Doc⟨r⟩ John Harding Esq		
		John Flower gent Jeffery Russell gent
James Woolverston gent	Walter Plunkett Esq John Wakefield gent	Francis Travers gent William Gibson gent
Isaac Dobson Esq	Andrew Delahoyd gent	
		Nicholas Lord Viscount Barnewall, Henry Barnewall Esq, Francis Barnewall Esq, Mathew Barnewall Esq, Lawrence Dowdall gent
William Manly gent	Clement Daniell gent, Robert Haward gent, John Locke gent, William Horish gent, Robert Smyth gent, Thomas Dancer Esq.	
Henry Joanes Esq Owen Joanes	James Donnellan Esq John Forth Esq	Thomas Burton Esq
Edmond Lodlowe Esq	James Woods gent Nicholas Brimingham gent	George Forster gent Ald⟨r⟩ John Carbery Esq
		James Wickombe gent
William Morgan gent Raphell Swinfeild gent	Thomas S⟨t⟩ Lawrence gent John Smyth gent	Samuell Hall gent
		William Talbot gent
John Lambart gent	Samuell Walshman gent Richard Triar gent	
		Richard Talbott gent Robert Whitefield gent Stephen Scarborough gent
	Thomas Jones gent	Nicholas Coddington Esq
	Thomas Springham gent Thomas Taylor gent Nicholas Luttrell gent Thomas Richardson Esq	John Gyles gent
	John Sedgraue Esq Patrick Sedgraue gent	Christopher Barnewall gent
Anthony Straughton gent William Straughton his sonn		Christopher S⟨t⟩ Lawrence gent

228

The Census of 1659 - Tituladoes in 'The County of Dublin'

BARONY OF COWLOCKE

BARONY OF CASTLEKNOCKE

Robert Barnewall gent

Nicholas Bolton Esq
James Penteny gent

Luke Dillon gent Bona-
venture Dillon gent
Barthol' Dillon gent
Jerome Russell gent

George Lord Barron of
Strabane Christopher
Fagon Esq

John Hollywood gent
Thomas Towers gent

Lewit' Coll George Smyth
Esq
Arthur Smyth gent
Edward Bary gent
Beniamin Bolton gent

Miles Corbett Esq Richard
Cotton Esq Miles Cor-
bett Junior gent
Roger Bishopp Esq George
Usher gent

John Barker gent

Richard Browne gent
Michall St Lawrence
gent
— Mustian Esq Mr Seward
gent
Charles Earl of Cavan
Oliver Lambert Esq
Walter Lambert Esq
Edward Taylor gent
Coll Chidley Coote Esq
John Baxter Esq Henry
Taylor gent
Henry Porter Esq

William Lord Barron of
Howth, Peter Wynne
gent, William Fitz-
Williams gent
Thomas Lea gent Richard
St Lawrance gent
Thomas Ownyan gent
Robert Chamberlyn gent
Thomas Chamberlyn his
sonn
William Basill Esq Peter
Vaughan gent
John Smyth gent

Richard Forster gent
Richard Gibson gent

Michell Jones Esq

Coll Francis Willoughby
Esq
————

Mathew Barnewall gent

Nathaniell Leake gent

John Connell gent

James Dillon gent James Barne-
wall gent
Henry Rowles Esq, Robert Ball
gent, Richard Birford gent,
Christopher Plunkett gent,
Patricke Plunkett his sonn
Bennet Arthur gent
William Warren gent
Coll. Richard Lawrence Esq

James Sweetman gent

David Edwards gent, John
Mason gent, Rouse Davis
gent.

Thomas Lutterell Esq

John Jordan gent

Nicholas Cart : gent

Gilbert Kerris gent

Thomas Bagworth gent

John Gibson gent

Richard Broughall gent
Sr William Berry Knt

James Russell gent

Taylor
of Ardgillan

Nash of Finnstown

Lentaigne of Tallaght

Hawkins of St. Finton's

Stewart of Summerhill

E. of Dublin

Dublin

230

Index

Names arranged alphabetically, ignoring the Mac, Mc, or O' prefix, (i.e. for O'Flaherty see Flaherty,.. O'Leary see Leary.). For a more complete listing of all family names in Ireland, see <u>The</u> <u>Master</u> <u>Book</u> <u>of</u> <u>Irish</u> <u>Surnames,</u> containing 100,000 listings, arranged in variant spelling groups, with source and/or location given for each name.

Be aware of variant spellings. Note that a person may be found with his name spelled in several different ways.

Abbecaces 218
Abbecace 53
Abbott 53
Abot 53
Ackley 53
Acton 53
Adair 23, 53
Adam 53
McAdam, Etc.. 37-40
Adam Family 26
Adams 53
McAdams 53
Address List 47
Aderrig (pl) 26
Adley 57
Adrain 53
Adrien 53
Adryan 53, 227
Agar 105
Agard 33, 53
Aghwell 53, 224
Ahlborn 53, 218
Aiken 53
Aikens 53
Ailmer 58
Aitken 53
Alan 53
Albert 53
Albun 53, 218
Aldercorn 53
Aldercron 53
Aldercron, J. 13
Alding 53, 223
Aldworth 53
MacAlea 149
Alexander 22,54,224

Aliday 126
Allen 38-40
Allen 9,10,22
Allen 24,55, 223, 226
MacAllen 54
McAllen 37
Allen, J. 226
Allen, John 16
Allen Of 27
Allen, Patrick 226
Allens 26
Alexander 54, 224
Alliday 134
Allison 55
Alloway 55
Allsworth 55
Alpine 55
Altman 55,218
Alton 95
Alwoodhouse 55,225
Amansham 55,224
Ambrose 55
Amery 55, 106
MacAnally 165
McAnally 55
Andersen 55
Anderson 23,55
McAnelly 165
Anger 55
Anger, Lord 223
Angier 55,58
Anketel 55
MacAnleagha 149
MacAnna 79
Anncham 55

Annesley 29,55
Anthony 56
MacAnulty 168
MacAnward 203
Appendix 211
Aprice 175
Arabin 16,56
Archbald 56
Archbold 9,10,16, 22,56
Archbold, G. 27
Archbold, W. 27
Archbould 38-40
Archdall 33,56
Archer 9,10,28,56. 223, 226
le Archer 56
Archfield 184
Archibald 56
de Arcy 96
Ardagh 56
Ardogh 56,225
Ardough 56
McAree 144
Arms 52,230
Arms- King 13
Arnold 56
Arnop 56,223
Arthur 22,26,57, 225, 228
MacArthur 57, 81
Arthur, J. 228
Arthure 57
Arthurs 31,57
Arundall 57, 223
Asbury 57
Ash 57, 165

Ashbourne 22, 57
Ashbrook 57
Ashe 46,57
MacAshinah 116
Ashley 57
Ashly 57,225
Ashton 57
Askin 81
Askins 57
Assin 57,223
Aston 57,228
Aston, John 228
MacAtilla 195
Atkinson, J. 13
Attwood 57
Atwood 57
Aubry 22, 24, 57
Audley 57
Aungier 55, 58
Aurthur 57
Austen 33
Austin 58
MacAveely 145
Avery 58, 223
Avery, John 32
McAvish 196
Avory 58, 227
Avory, Joe. 227
MacAward 203
Aylercorn 16, 58
Aylmer 9, 10, 58
Aylmer, Capt. 29
Aylmer, Sir G. 11
Aylward 106
O'B 58
Babbitt 58

Bacon 58
Bacon, John 20
Badham 13, 58
Baggotrath (pl) 18
Bagod 59
Bagod, Sir R. 19
Bagot 9,10,27,59
Bagster 63
Bagworth 59, 229
Bailey 59, 63
Baily 59
Baily, Wm. 32
Bain 59
Baird 59
Baker 59
le Bakere 59
Baldwin 59
Bale 59, 224
Ball 9,10,60,
   225,229
Ball, John 33
Ball, Robert 31,32,229
Ball, Walter 32
Bamford 60
Bane 206
le Bank 32,60
Banks 60,224
Banning 60
Baptist Records 44
Barber, Barbour 60
Barclay 60
Barcly 60
Barcroft 60
Bargerett 60
Barker 224-26-29
Barker, John 229
Barkerxx 226
Barkley 60
Barlowe 60,224
Barnard 60
Barnes 60,223
Barneville 61
Barnewall 38-40
Barnewall 20,23,61,
   228-9
Barnewall Of 28
Barnewall, R. 229
Barnewalls 27
Barnwall 9-11,226

de Barnwall 61
Barony List 34
Barony Map iv
Barret 10,226
Barrets 9
Barrett 226
Barrett Barrytt 61
Barrington 61
Barron, Lord 229
Barrow 61,223-25
Barry 9-11,19, 38-
   40,62,226
Barry, James 226
Barry, Paul 32
Barrytt 226
Barton 62
Bary 62,229
Bary, Ed. 229
Basill 62,229
Basnett 62
Bassenet 13,14
   23,27,62
Basset 20,62
Bateman 62
Bates 62
Bath 62
de Bath 62
Bathe 22,24,34,
   45,62
de Bathe 9
Bathe, J. 33
Bathe, Thomas 27
Bather 62,227
Bathripp 62,224
Bathurst 63,224
Battersby 63
Baulman 63
Bawn 206
Baxter 23,63,229
Mac Baxter 63
Baxter, John 23
Bayley 59
Bayly, Bayley 63
Beaghan 63
Beahan 64
Bealing 63,223
Beame 63,227
Bearsford 65
Beattie 63

Beatty 63
Beaumont 11,63
Becket 63,226
Beckford 64
Beebe 63
Began 63
Begg 15
Begg Beggs 63
Beggan 63
Beghan 64
Behan 63-4
O Beirnes 75
Bekeford 28,64
Belgard 22,64
Belinges 64
de Belinges 23
Bell 64
Bellew 9,10,64
Bellew, Col. 27
Bellingham 64,224
Bellings 31,64
Bellon 64
Bellon, Dr. 29
Bellow 64
Bender 64,218
Benison 32,64
Benmohel 64,218
Bennell 64,224
Benner 65
Bennet 229
Bennett 10,65, 223,226
Bennett, H. 23
Benson 65,223
Bereford 65
Beresford 11,65
Berford 65,225
Berg 65,218
Bergin 65
Berkeley 33,65
Bermingham 9,13,
   65,66
Bernard 60,65
Berrill 10,65
Berry 65, 229
Berstow 65,224
Bertram 65
Beryl 65
Best 66

Betham 66
Betham, W. 13
Bettin 66,223
Bettsworth 66
Betzold 66,218
Beuchamp 66,226
Bevan 66
Bewley 66
Bickford 66
Bicknell 66
Bierne 75,77
Bigg 63
Bigge 63
Biggens 76
Biggins 76
Bilder 66
Billings 66
Billingsly 66
Billingsly, Ed 23
Billington 66
Billinsley 66, 228
Bingham 11,66
Birford 66,229
Birford, R. 229
Birmingham 10,65-6
Birne 38-40,226
Birne, Felix 226
O Birnes 34
Birsell 14,67
Bishop 20
Bishop Bishopp 67
Bishopp 223-9
Bisse 67,224
Black 67
Blackall 67
Blackand 67,223
Blackbourne 67
Blackburn 67
Blackburne 20
Blacken 67
Blacker 67
Blackhall 67
Blackney 67
Blackwell 67,226-27
Bladen 67,225
Blake 9,10,67
Blanchfield 31,67

Blanchfort *31,67*

Bleigh *67*

Bligh *45,67, 223*

Blondell *67*

Bloody Bridge *139*

Bloomer *122*

Blum *67,218*

Blume *67*

Blundell *28,67,224*

Boales *68*

Boas *68,218*

Bodley *68*

Boe *68*

Bohelly *74*

Boid *69*

Bold *68*

Boles *68*

Bollard *68,225*

Bolten *68*

Bolton *68,229*

Bolton, N. *229*

Bond *68*

Bonole *68,224*

Bonorly *68,224*

Boorke *38-40,68*

Booterstown *18*

Booth *68*

Borden *68,223*

Borr *68,227*

Borr, John *19*

Boston *41*

Boudler *68,223*

O Bough *68*

Boughla *74*

Bould *68,225*

Boulton *68,224*

Bourke *38-40,75*

Bourne *68*

Bowe *68*

Bowes *68*

Bowker *68*

Bowman *68*

Bowye *69*

Bowyer *69*

Bowyr *69*

Boyd *69,224*

Boylan *38-40,69*

Boyland *69*

Boyle *38-40,20,69, 223,226*

Boyn *69*

Boyne *69*

Brabazon *9-11,69*

Brabzon *69,226*

O Bracken *10,69*

Bradbury *69*

Braddock *69*

Bradey *70*

Bradley *69*

Bradly *69*

Bradshaw *70,226-7*

Bradstreet *18,29,70*

Brady *14,72, 123,227*

Mac Brady *70*

Brady, John *13*

Bragg *70,225*

Braghall *33,70*

Braham *70,218*

Braken *69*

Brampton *70,224*

O'Branagan *70*

Branam *70*

Brandon *70*

Branham *70,225*

Branigan *70*

Brannan *71*

Brannigin *70*

Brassil *71*

Braun *70,218*

Brawne *71*

Bray *70*

de Bray, Robt. *23*

Brayne *38-40,71*

Brazil *71*

O Brazzil *71*

di Bre *70*

O Bree *70*

Breen *71-2*

Breerton *71*

O Brein *72*

Bremigan *66*

O Brennan *71*

Brennanstown *15*

Brenon *71*

Brereton *26,28,71*

Brerton *71,227*

O Bressyl *71*

le Bret *71*

Brett *9,10,71,225*

Breviter *71*

Brew *72*

Brewster *71,73*

de Bri *70*

Brian *74*

Briane *71*

Brice *71,227*

Bridges *24,71, 223-26*

Brien *71*

O Brien *22,72-74*

Briene *71*

Brigg *72*

Brigg Of *20*

Briggs *72*

Brighness *72,226*

Bright *72*

Brimingham *38-40, 72,228*

Brin *38-40,72*

Briody *70*

O'Briody *72*

Briscoe *22,72,74, 227*

Britons *viii*

Brocas *72*

Broderick *72*

Brody *72*

Mac Brody *72*

Broe *72*

Broghe *72*

Brohel *73*

Brokas *72*

O Brolchain *69*

Bromagen *72*

Broo *72*

Brook *73*

Brooke *20,72*

Brooke, Miss *14*

Brookes *73,226*

Brookfield *72*

Brooking *73,225*

Brooks *72,73*

Brophy *73*

Brothell *73*

Broughall *73,229*

Broughill *73*

Broun *73,224*

Broune *73,223*

Brown *9,11*

Brown, Saml. *22*

Browne *73, 223...29*

Browne (eng *38-40*

Browne Of *27*

Browne, Pat. *27*

Browne, R. *229*

Bruar *224*

Bruen *71*

Bruer *223*

Bruister *74,226*

le Brun *20*

Bruton *74*

Bryan *38-40,72,74, 223*

O Bryan *74*

Bryan, John *223*

Bryscoe *74,227*

Buck *74*

Buckarton *74,223*

Buckeley *74*

Buckingham *74*

Buckley *74,227*

Buckley, R. *227*

Budd *74*

Budd, Wm. *29*

Buggle *74*

Bugle *74*

O Buhilly *74*

Bulkeley *22,74*

Bulkley *227*

Bulkley, T. *227*

Bullard *68*

Buller *74*

Buller, Edw. *15*

Bullock (pl) *13*

Burbridge *74*

Burgess *75*

Burgh *75*

de Burgh *75*

Burgoyne *20,22, 75,227*

Burk *75*

Burke *75*

Burke Birth. *153*

Burn 77
Burne 38-40,68,75
Burnell 10,22,27,75
Burnell Of   31
Burnett 75,228
Burniston 30,75
Burns 75
Burns Beirne 75
Burns, John 41
Burr 20,75
Burrilow 75
Burrowes 76,225
Burrows 76
Burt 76,223
Burton 24,27,76,
    223-27-28
Burton, T. 228
Busby 76
Bush 76,225
Bushell 76,224
Buston 76,223
Butler 38-40
Butler 9,10,22,
    76,224-5-6
Butler Or   19
Butler, Robt. 27
Butler, Wm. 225
Butterfield 76
Butterly 38-40,76
Butterton 76
Buttler 76
Bygins 76,226
Bygins, John 226
Byland 76
Byrne 75
O Byrne 10...,22
O'Byrne, Byrnes 77
Byrne, Ed. 24
Byrne, John 14
Byrne, T. 13
Byrnes 75
Byron 77
Bysse 77
Bysse, Robt. 31
MacCaba 77
MacCabe 77
Caddell 77
Caddle 77,228
Caddle, J. 228

Cadell 9,10,77
Cadmore 77,225
Cadwell 77,225
Cady 77
MacCafferky 78
MacCaffrey 78
Caffreys 78
Cahan 140-1
O Cahan 78
Cahane 78, 140
O Cahassy 81
Cahere Of 19
Cahil 78
McCahil 78
O Cahill 78
Cain 140-1
Calaghan 78
Calahan 78
Calan 79
Calbs 78, 218
Caldbeck 28, 78
Caldwell 78
McCall 78, 82
O Callaghan 20,34,78
Callahan 78
Callan 79
Callen 38-40,79
MacCallery 79
Callihan 78
Callin 38-40,79
Callisher 79, 218
MacCalshender 54
Calwell 78
Candit 79, 223
Cane 141
MacCann 79
McCann 37
Cannan 79, 118
Cannon 118
O Cannon 79
Canny 79
Cantrel 79
Cantwell 79
Capper 79
Capper, Edw. 32
Carberry 27, 79
Carbery 227-8
Carbery, J. 228

Carbry 79
Carden 79
Carden House 27
Cardiff 79
Cardiffsbridge 31
Cardyff 79, 225
Carew 18, 79
Carew, Ray. 16
McCarey 80
O Carey 80
Carey, G. 32
Carey, Geo. 15
O Carey   10
Caricke 225
Carie 80
Carleton 80
Carley 80
Carlis 80
Carlton 80
Carmichael 19,80
Carnett 80
Carney 141
McCarney 141
Carol 81
O Carolan 80
Caroll 81
Carpenter 80
Carr 80,226
Carr, G. 226
Carre 80,226
Carrick 24,80
McCarrig   80
Carrigan 91
Carrol 81
Carrolan 80
Carroll 38-40
MacCarroll 81
O Carroll 81
O Carroll Arms 52
Carrothers 81
Carruthers 81
Carson 81
Cart 81,229
Cart, Nich. 229
Carte 81
Carte, Nich. 31
Carter 81
MacCartney 81,154

Carton 81
Caruthers 81
Cary 80
Casaday 82
Casement 81
Casey 38-40,82
MacCasey 81
O Casey Cassy 81
Cashell 81
Cashell Of 19
Caskin 81
O Cassidy 82
Cassilly 82
Cassy 38-40
Castleknock 31
Castleton 82
Casy 38-40,81-2
Catelyn 82
Catholic 34
Catholic 44
Caufield 82
Caulfield 82,118,
    224
Cavan 82
Cavanagh 38-40,
    82,141
Cavenah 38-40
MacCawell 82
Cawldwell 78
Cecil 82
Census 1659 37,223
Chabner 82,227
Chaffee 82
Chalkwright 82
Chamberlain 19,29,
    32,83
Chamberlayne 83
Chamberlyn 229
Chambers 24,83,
    225-6
Chambres 83
Champines 83,225
Chandlee 83
Chandler 83,225
Chandley 83
Chapman 83
Chapman, R. 23
Charlton 83,224
McChayer 83

Chaytor 83
Cheevers 14,16,83
Cheevers, H. 11
Chesterman 83
Cheswright 226
Chetten 84
Chichester 84,226
Chidley 229
Chiefs 10
Chillam 29,84
Christian 84,225
Church 35
Church Records 43
de Clahull 27,84
Claiborne 85
Clairborne 85
Clairke 84
Clanmaliere 10
Clapham 84,226
Clare 84,97
de Clare 84
Claridge 84
Clarke 38-40,84,
223..28,
Clarke, T. 228
Clarkins 84
Classon 20,84
Clausson 84
Clay 84,227
Clayhull 84
Claypoole 84,223
Clayton 84
Cleabear 84,226
Cleare 225
Cleary 84
Clemens 84,225
Clements 23,84
Clench 85
Clere 84,225
Clibborn 85
Cliborne 85
Cliff 85,223
Cliff, John 223
Clinch 85
Clinch, Wm. 24,227
Clinchey 85
Clinton 85
Clontarf Battle 34

McClory 121
McCloskey 85
Clotworthy 85,225
McCloud 85
Clovan 86
Cloven 86
McCluskey 85
Coal 86
Coalman 86
Coan 85-6,218
Coat Of Arms 43
Coates 85
Coats 85
Cobb 11
Cobbe 85
Coch 123
Cochrane 85
Cocks 92
Coddington 86,228
Coen 85-6
Coffee 86
O Coffey 86
Cogan 9,10
Coghill 11,20,86
Coghill, M. 34
MacCoghlan 86
Coghlane 86
Cogley 176
Cohalan 86
Cohen 85,86,218
Colavin 78.88
Colby 86
Colcott 86
Coldwell 78
Cole 22,86,226
Coleman 38-40, 223
O Coleman 86
Coleman, R. 223
Coley 87
MacColgan 87
O Colgan 10
Colgen 87
Colgun 87
Coligan 87
Collen 87
Collett 87
Colley, Cooley 87
Colley, Richd. 18

Collie 87
Collier 87,223
Colligan 87
Collins 87
Collis 87
MacColly 87
Colman 86
Colvan 88
Colven 88
Colvil 88
Colville 88
Colvin 88
Colyer 87
Combes 88,223
MacCombs 134
Comerford 88
Commerford 88
Commins 88
Commons 94
Compton 88
Comyn 94
Comyns 88
Comyns Of 28
Conaway 89
Condran 88
Condron 88
Conel 88
Conley 88
Conly 88,225
MacConmara 165
Connaghan 94
Conneely 88
Connell 88
O Connell 29,33,88
Connell, J. 229
Connell, John 31
O Conner 89
O Connoll 88
Connolly 88
O Connolly 88
Connoly 88
O'Connoly viii
Connor 38-40
O'Connor 89
O Connor Arms 52
O Connor Offaley 10
Conol 88
Conolly 89

Conolly Of 22
Conolly, Wm. 29
Conoly 88
Conor 89
O'Conor 31
O Conor, Rod. 36
Conran 88,89
Conrane 89
Conroy 89,144
Conry 144
Constantine 89
Contents Page v
Conway 89
McConway 89
O Conway 89
Coogan Cogan 89
Cooke 26,46,89,
224..27
Cooke, V. 224
Cool 92
McCool 92
Cooley 18
Cooly 87
Coonahan 89,92
Coonan 89
O Cooney 89
Coony 89
Cooper 89
Coot 90
Coote 16,90,
224...29
Cope 90
Cope Of 29
Copeland 90
Cor, Nich. 14
Corballis 45,90
Corbally 38-40,
45,90
Corban 90
Corbane 90
Corbett 90, 229
Corbett, Miles 229
Corckron 90
Corcoran 85, 90
MacCorcoran 90
O Corcoran 90
Corey 90, 223
Corigan 91
MacCormack 90

McCormack 90
McCormick 90
Cornwalsh 20,30,90
Corr Castle 30
Corr Corry 90
Corra 90
Corregan 91
Corrican 91
Corrie 90
O Corrigan 91
Corry 90-1
Corscadden 91
Cory 24,91
O'Cosgrave 91
Cosgrove 91
Cossart 91
MacCostello 91
Costellow 91
MacCostigan 91
Costigin 91
Costillo 91
Costleloe 225
Costolloe 91
Cosyn 22,91
Cotes 85
MacCotter 91
O Cotter 91
Cottingham 91
Cottle 22,91.227
Cotton 91, 223-25-29
Cotton, R. 229
Cottor 91
MacCottyr 91
Coughlan 86
Coulter 92
Coultry 92
Counihan 94
de Courcey 97
Courtney 92
Cowell 92
Cowhey 86
Cowhig 86
Cowley 87
Cowman 92
Cowse 92,227
Cox 29,92, 223-27
Cox, Capt. W. 227

Coy 92
MacCoy 136
McCoy 92
Coyle 92
Crabb 92,218
Crafton 92
Cramby 92,225
Cramer 20,92-3
Crampton 15,92
Cranwell 92,223
Crary 92
MacCrea 177
Creamer 93,226
Creamor 93
Creary 92
Creemer 93
Creighton 93
Critchet 93
Crofton 93,225
Crole 93
Crolly 93
Croly 93
Cromwellia 36
Crosbie 93
Crosby 93,226
Crosby, Lady 224
Cross 93
Crostenton 93,225
Crowe 19,29,93
O Crowley 93
Crowly 93
Cruise 31,38-40
Cruise 9,10,15,93
Cruise Family 16
Cruiserath 31
Crum (pl) 28
Crump 93
Crump, Geof. 23
Cruse 93
Cruys 93
Crych 223
Crych, John 223
Cudahey 94
Cudahy 94
Cuddahy 94
Cuddihy 94
Cudihy 94
Cuff 94,223-26

Cuff, James 223
Cuggeran 85
O Cuinn 176
Culhane 87
Cullane 87
Cullen 87
O Cullen 10,94
Cullenswood 20
Cullin 94
McCullin 94
Culloon 94
Cumming 94
Cummings 94
Cummins 88,94
Cunningham 94
MacCurley 94
Curling 94
Curr 90
Curragh 94
Curran 94
Curran, J. P. 22
Curraugh 94
Curren 226
Currid 94
Curry 90
Curson 94
Cursun 10
Curtis 29,94
Cusack 9,10,95, 227
Cusack Of 14
Cusacke 95
Cusake 95
Cussack 95
Cussacks 20
Cuthbert 95
Cutter 95
Cyrch 95
D'aungiers 58
D'erley 105
Dag 95
Dagg 95
MacDaid 99
Daily 95
Dalkey (pl) 14
Daltin 95
Dalton 95
Daly 38-40

O'Daly 95
Damer 95
Damer, Joseph 33
Danagher 95
Danaher 95-6,
Dancer 95,228
Dancer, T. 228
Dandridge 95
Danes 34
Daniel 95,101
McDaniel 24,37, 101
Daniell 95,228
McDaniell 38-40
Daniell And 38-40
Daniell 38-40
Dannaher 95-6
MacDarcey 96
O Darcey 96
Darcy 9,10,96
Dardes 96
Dardis 96
Dargan 45,96
Dargen 96
Darin 96
Darlas 96
Darlases 24
Darley 96
Darley, Rev. 32
Darling 96,226
Darly 96
Dason 96,223
Daton 96
Dauson 96,223
Davidson 218
Davidson Of 96
Davies 24,96-7
Davies, John 29
Davieson 96,218
Davine 99
Davis 38-40,97, 218,226
Davis Eng. & 38-40
Davis, Paul 226
Davis, Rouse 229
Davison 96-9
MacDavitt 99
Davys 26, 96-7
Davys, C. 33

Dawe 97	Degane 98	Desutun 193	Doil 103
Dawe Of 23	Degrenan 124	Deuswell 31,99	Dolan 100-04
Dawkins 97,227	Dejean 19,98	Devane 99	Dolane 100-04
Dawley 95	Delacy 98	Develin 99	Dologhan 100
Dawly 95	Delafeld 111	Deveneis 23,99	Dolphin 28,101
Dawson 96-7	Delafield 111	Devery 99	Dolphyn 101
Dawson, John 29	Delahide 32,98	Devin 99	Doly 101
Dayley 95	Delahoid 98	O'Devine 99	Doly, Etc.. 38-40
De Arci 96	Delahoyd 228	Devitt 99	Dolyphy 28
De Bathe 9,10	Delahoyde 9,11,90	McDevitt 99	Domvile 27,101
De Bray 97	Delahyde 98	O'Devlin 99	Domvile Arms 52
De Bray, Robt. 23	Delamain 45	Devry 99	Domviles 15
De Clahull 97	Delane 98	Dewylde 210	Domville 11,22,101
De Clare 97	O'Delaney 98	Dexter 99	Donahoe 102
De Courcey 97	Delap 98	Diamond 100,218	Donal 101
De Courcy 30	Delarupe 180	Diamonte 100	McDonald 101
De Coursey 11,97	Delasale 99,225	Dick 100	Donaldson 102
De Flamstead 97	Delasalle 99,182	Dickinson 20,100	Donel 101
De Groot 97	Delees 146	Dickson 100	Donelan 101
De Hose 136	Dellany 98	Diggs 100,225	Donell 101
De Hyndeberge 97	Delong 152	Dillane 98,100	McDonell 37
De La Feldes 31	Dempsey 99	Dillion 100	Donell And 38-40
De Lacy 10,19,34	ODempsey 10	Dillon 9,10,22	Donely 102
De London 97	ODempsie Of 10	Dillon 225,229	Dongan 30,101
De Long 97	Den 24,99	Dillon, Dillion 100	Donlan 101
De Marisco 97	Denn 99,227	Dillon, James 229	Donlon 101
De Moenes 22,97	Denn, J. 227	Dillon, Luke 229	Donn 38-40,101
De Mora 19,97	Dens Family 23	Dillon, Martin 31	Donnell 101
De Tasagart 98	Dent 99,225	Dimond 100	MacDonnell 10,101
De Verdon 98	Denughent 168	Dioderici 34,100	O'Donnell 101
De Verneuil 98	Depoher 174	Directories 44	McDonnell 23
De Walhope 98	Depreston 174	Divelin 99	Donnellan 228
Deagan 98	Derbon 99,223	Divine 99	O'Donnellan 101
Dealy 95	Derevell 178	Dix 46,100	ODonnelly 102
Dean 98-9,227	Derideleford 179	Dixon 20,100	Donneybrook 19
Dean, J. 227	Dermitt 99	Dixson 223,225	Donnogh 102
Deane 98,225	McDermitt 99	Doane 100	O'Donoghoe viii
Deane Family 20-8	Dermody 99	Dobson 100,226,-8	Donohoe 10,102
Dearing 98	MacDermot 99	Dobson, I. 228	Donohue 102
Deave Deaves 98	Dermott 38-40,99	Dobson, Isaac 19	McDonold 101
Debart 98,223	Deroley 181	Dobson, J. 226	Dooal 103
Debart, J. 223	Derpatrick 16,99	Dockerell 100	Doody 102
Deburgh 75	Derpatrick Of 23	Dockrell 100	Doogan 102-04
Dee 98,225	Derry 99,224	Dodd 102	Doohey 104
Deegan 98	Derry, A. 224	Dodson 100,223	Doolan 100-02
Deering 22,98	Desmineer 99	Doe 100	Doolen 103
Defreyne 116	Desmineers 225	Dogherty 20,100	O'Dooley 102
Defullam 117	Desminiers 99	Doherty 18,100	Doolin 102-03

Dooling 103
Dooly 103
O'Doran 102
Dorane 102
Dore 102
Doren 102
Dores 102,223
Dorgan 96
Dorian 102
Dorland 102
Douces 26,102
Doud 102
Doude 226
McDougall 30,102
Dougherty 100
Doughty 224-26
Doulough's 112
Dousse 103
Dover 102
O'Dowd 102
Dowdall 9,10,31, 102
Dowdall 38-40, 225-28
Dowdall, Geo. 225
Dowding 226
Dowds 102
Doweing 38-40
Dowey 104
Dowlin 103
O'Dowling 103
Dowly 102
Downes 19
Downs 103
Dowse 103
Doyle 38-40, 103,226
McDoyle 103
ODoyle 103
Doyne 18,103
ODoyne 104
Drake 9,10,103
Drake, John 36
Drape 27,103
Draycott 33,103
Drean 53
Drew 103
Drewery 103
Drewry 103
Dromgold 103,226

Dromgoole 103
Druery 103
Drumgoold 103
Drumgoole 103
Drury 223
Drury, Drew 103
Dryland 103
Dublin Arms 230
Dublin City 42
Dublin Map vi
Dublin, N. H. 41
Dublin, Ohio 41
Duchamine 103
Ducker 104
Duddy 102
Dudley 104
Dudly 104,224
Duff 11,38-40, 104,224
Duffe 104
Duffey 104
Duffie 104
ODuffy 10,104
Dugan 98,104
O'Duggan 104
Duggen 104
Duhig 104
Dulane 104
Dulany 98
Dun 104
Dundon 104
Dundrum 14,104
Dungan 104,226
Dunleary (pl) 13
Dunlop 45
Dunn 38-40,104
ODunn 10
Dunne 38-40
O'Dunne 104
Dunphy 104
Durdin 104
Durham 104
Dustin 104
Dutch 104,218
Dutton 105,225
Dwier 105
Dwire 105
O'Dwyer 105

Dwyre 105
Dyas 105
Dyle 103
Eagan 105,141
MacEagan 156
Eagen 141
Eager 105
Earhart 105
Earl 106
Earle 226
Earley 105
Early 105,223
Eastwood 105,226
Eaton 24, 107
Eaves 108
Eblani 34
Eccles 33,105
Eccles Mount 33
Ecklin 105
Edkins 105, 223
McEdmond 37
Edmonds 105
Edmounds 105
Edwards 105, 223-29
Edwards, R. 13
Egan 105,141
MacEgan 141
Egar 105
Egerton 105
Egerton, T. 33
Egyr 105
Eirill 106
Ekin 53,105,224
MacElhar 80
Elias 24,105
Eliott 105
Elison 106
Elkin 105,218
Ellard 105
Elliot 105
Elliott 105-6
Ellis 30,106,227
Ellis, Owen 227
Ellison 55,106
Elliston 106
Ellot 105
Ellott 106,227

Ellrington 106
Elrington 106
Elrington, R. 13
Elshinder 54
Elward 106,223
MacElwoo 108
Emery 106
Emmet Burial 183
Emmett 106
Emmett, Dr. 20
Empson 106
Empson, Wm. 32
England 106
England, John 32
English 38-40,106
Englonde 106
L'Englys 106
MacEninry 132
Ennes 106
Ennis 28,106
Ennis Ennos 38-40
Enniss 106
Ennoss 106
Enos 31,106
Epstein 106,218
Erley 105
Erlich 106,218
Errill 106
Erskine 107
Espinasse 107
Espinasse, W. 14
Eton 107,223
Euleston 107
Eustace 9,10,27, 107,200
Eustace   27
Eustace, J. 11
Eustace Of   23
Eustice 107
Evans 10,107
Evers 108,223
Eves 108
MacEvoy 108
Ewing 108
Exham 108
Exham House 27
Exshaw 108
Exshaw, John 20

Fade *108*
de Fae *110*
Fagan *viii,33,110*
MacFagan *10*
OFagan *10*
Fagan Arms *52*
Fagan Fagon *108*
Fagans *13*
Fagon, C. *229*
Faile *109*
Fairbrother *33,109*
Fairview *109*
Falconer *109,110*
Falk *109,210, 218*
Falkiner *110*
Falkiner *28,31, 109,110*
Falkner *109*
Fallard *109,225*
Fallek *109,218*
Famine, The *41*
Fannin *45*
Fant *116*
Farel *109*
Farelly *109*
Farely *109*
McFarland *109*
Farley *109,224*
Farmer *109*
Farral *109*
Farrall *38-40*
Farrel *109*
Farrell *38-40*
OFarrell *14.109*
O'Farrelly *109*
Farris *110*
Faucett *110*
Faulkiner *109*
Faulkner *109,110*
Fawcett *110*
Fawcetts *15*
Fay *110,116,226*
Faye *110*
Fearnely *110,227*
Featherston *110*
Fee *110,116*
Feehan *118*
Feeheny *136*

Fegan *110*
Feghan *110*
Feighan *111*
Feild *111*
Felan *205*
de la Feldes *31*
Fenell *110*
Fenelon *110*
Fenlon *110*
Fennell *110,225*
Fennelly *110*
Ferguson *110*
Feritter *110*
Ferly *109*
Ferneley *28,110*
Ferneley, Ph. *32*
Fernelly *110*
Ferrall *109*
Ferrely *109*
Ferreter *110*
Ferris *110*
Ferris, Gilb. *31*
Ferriter *110*
Ferry *110*
Fetherston *15,110*
Fey *110,116, 136*
Ffolliott *23,110*
OFiachra *10*
Fian *118*
Fians *111*
Field *111*
Fieragh *22,111*
Figgis *111*
OFihelly *111*
Fingal (pl) *34*
Finglas *9,10,22,111*
Finlay *111*
Finlay Family *28*
MacFinn *111*
O'Finn *111*
Finnellan *110*
Finnucane *111*
Finucane *111*
Fisher *111,225*
Fisher, Geo. *225*
Fitch *112*
Fits *162*
Fitz *112,162*

Fitz Rery *111*
Fitzgerald *38-40*
Fitzgerald *18,19,22, 112,224*
Fitzgerrald *112*
Fitzgerrold *112*
Fitzgibbon *30,112*
Fitzharris *112*
Fitzharry *112*
Fitzhenry *112*
Fitzmaurice *18*
Fitzpatrick *112*
Fitzrichard *14,112*
Fitzrory *111*
Fitzrury *111*
Fitzsimmons *112*
Fitzsimon *33,112*
Fitzsimons *10,23, 28,145*
Fitzsimon *14*
Fitzstephen *191*
Fitzsymon *112*
Fitzwilliam *9...11, 18..20*
Fitzwilliam *30,113*
Fitzwilliams *113,224, 229*
Fitzwm Arms *52*
Flamstead *19,113*
Flanagan *113*
O'Flanagan *113*
Flang *113*
Flanigan *113*
Fleming *10,31,114*
Flemming *38-40*
Flemming *9,114,224*
Flemmyng *114*
Flemon *114*
Fletcher *114,224*
Flinn *114*
Flood *13,114,195*
Flower *114,226,228*
Flower, J. *228*
Floyd *114,223*
Flynn *114*
Foard *115*
Foester *114,227*
O'Fogarty *114*
Fogerty *114*

Foley *110*
O'Foley *114*
Foli *114*
Font *116*
Fookes *114,225*
Fooley *114*
Fooluiah *114*
Foorde *115*
Foot *115*
Foot, J. *22*
Foot, Lundy *22*
Foran *115*
OForan *115*
Forane *115*
Forbes, *115*
Ford *29,225*
Ford, Sir R. *225*
Forde *115*
Forester *115*
OForhane *115*
Format *48*
Forrest *115,225*
Forster *115*
Forster, G. *228*
Forster, J. *33*
Forsters *27*
Forth *115,224-28*
Forth, Sir A. *32*
Fortick *33,115*
Fortick, Sir W. *19*
Fossett *115*
Foster *10,19, 114-15*
Foules *115,223*
Founbaine *115,223*
Fount *116*
Fountain *20*
Fountaine *116,225*
Founts Family *23*
Fowloo *114*
Fowly *114*
Fownes *29,116*
Fox *116*
Fox, Sir P. *28*
Fox, Thomas *18*
Foxall *116,225*
Foxwich *116,223*
Foy *110,116,227*
Foy, Dr. *227*

Foye 116,227
Foyle 116
Foyll 116
Foynes 111
Frail 116
Frain 116
Frame 116
Frampton 116
France, In 36
Frances 116
Francis 116,226
Frane 116
Frank 116
Frankel 117,218
Franklin 117,223
Franks 116-17
Fraser 117
Frazer 117
Frazier 117
Freeman 117,225
Freeme 31,117
Frein 116
French 117,225
French Family 14
French, M. 225
French, Robt. 32
Frend 24,117
Freyn 116
de Freyne 33
Frieudman 117,218
Fry 117
Fryer 117,226
Fulham 38-40,117, 225
Fullam 38-40,117
Fullard 117
Fuller 117
Fullerton 118
Fulton 118,224
Fyan 10,118
Fyans 111-18
Fye 116
Fyenell 110
Fyne 118
Fynes 10,118
Gaban 13,118
Gaban, John 13
Gadell 77

Gaffey 118
O'Gaffney 118
Gage 118
Gahagan 119
Gainor 119
Gaisford 30,118
Gaisford Arms 52
Galagher 118
Galbelly 118,226
Gall 118
Gallagher 118
O'Gallagher 118
Gallaher 118
Galligan 121
Gallougher 118
Galvey 20,118
Gann 118
McGann 118
Gannon 79
MacGannon 118
Gardiner 118
Garlan 118
Garland 118
McGarland 118
Garner 118,226
Garner, Dr. 226
Garnet 11,119
Garnett 32,80
Garrett 38-40,119
Garrey 119
Garrie 119
Garrihy 119
Garrity 120
Garry 119
MacGarry 119
Gartland 118
Garvey 119
Garvey, James 14
Gaskin 81,119
Gaughney 118
Gaul 190
Gavan 119
Gavan, Henry 33
Gay 119,224
Gayner 119
Gaynor 119
MacGee, Magee 119
Geering 20,119

Gegan 119
Gehegan 119
O'Gelbroin 119
Genealogy 43
Genese 119,218
MacGenis 125
Gennitt 119
MacGeogh 123
Geoghan 119
MacGeoghegan 119
Geography 34
George 119
George, Denis 19
MacGeraghty 120
Gerity 120
Gernan 120
Gernon 26,110,120
Gernon Slain 30
Gerrard 120
Gerrity 120
Gerry 120,224
Gerry, Dr. 224
Gerty 120
Ghee 119
McGhee 119
Gibbons 120
Gibbons, John 27
Gibbs 120
Giblin 120
Gibner 120
Gibney 120
Gibsen 120
Gibson 120,228-9
Gibson, R. 229
Giffard 120
Giffard, John 19
Gifford 120
MacGilamchlmg 23
MacGilamochl' viii
MacGilamochl' 121
Gilbert 120,218,225
Gilbert, Wm. 13
Gilbroin 119
OGilbroin 10,120
Gilcolm 10,120
Giles 126
Gilfoil 120
Gilfoyle 125

MacGilfoyle 120
Gill 120
MacGill 120,155
McGill 120
Gillen 121
MacGilligan 121
MacGilloway 108
MacGilpatrick 112
Gilpin 121
Gilroy 144
Gilstrap 121
Gilthorpe 121
Giltrap 121
Ginnaw 142
Gipsey 120
Gitt Elson 121,218
Givney 120
Glascord 121,223
Glasnevin (pl) 33
Gleason 121
O'Gleeson 121
Glenn 121
Glenny 121
Glissane 121
Glorney 121
McGlory 121
McGlorye 37,38-40
MacGloughlin 147
Glover 121,223
Glover, G. 13
Glynn 121
Goch 123
Godd 121,218
Godiman 24,121
Goff 121-3
MacGoffrey 78
Gogarty 114
Going 188
Gold 122
Golding 122
Goodiman 121
Goodman 14,15, 121-2
Goodman, J. 14
Goodmans 16
Goodrich 122
Goodwin 122
Goragh 122,226

Goragh, Wm. 226
Gorden 122
Gordon 122
Gore 122
Gorer 122,218
MacGorhain 188
Gormaly 122
Gorman 122,225
MacGorman 122
O'Gorman 122
O'Gormley 122
Gormly 38-40
Gormon 122
Gormooly 122
Gothimer 122,218
Gotler 122,218
Gouge 122-3,223
Gough 10,18,122-3
Gough, Wm. 30
Goulbee 123
Goulborne 123.225
Gould 123,224
Goulding 23,123
Gowen 123
Grace 9,10,123
Graddy 123
Gradon 227
O'Grady 123
Grafton 123
Graham 20,24,123
Grahams 123
MacGrane 155
McGrane 123
Grange 123
Grannell 179
Gratan 124
Grattan 9,11,30,124
Gratten 124
Graves 124,223
Graveston 44
Gray 124
Graydon 124,227
Gready 123
Greeley 124
Green 124
Green 29,226
Greenan 124
Greene 124,227

Greene, Rchd. 22
Greene, Wm. 227
Greenhow 124
Gregorie 124
Gregory 124
Gregry 124
Grennan 124
Gressingham 124
MacGretten 124
Grible 24,125
Grierson 125
Griffen 125
Griffin 125
Griffon 125
Grimes 122
Grogan 125
Groggan 125
Grolliax 125,225
Groot 218
de Groot 125
Grugan 125
Grugane 125
Grumby 125
Gryffith 125,227
McGue 123
Guilfoyle 120,125
Guiness Arms 52
Guinness 22,125
McGuinness 125
MacGuire 125,155
McGuirk 125
Guiy 125-6,223
Gurk 125
McGurke 125
Gurling 125
Gutch 125,223
Guthrie 126
Guy 125-6
MacGwyer 155
McGwyer 125
Gyles 126,228
Gyles, John 228
Habbagan 134
Hacket 14
Hacket, Simon 16
Hacketsisland 15
Hackett 30,126
MacHackett 126

Hadsor 126
Hagan 126
OHagan 11
Hagans 133
Hagen 126
Haghan 130
Haines 126
Hairt 129
O'Hairt viii
Haket 126
Hakett 126
McHale 126
Halfpenny 126
Haliday 126,134
Hall 20,126, 224,228
Hall, Sam. 228
Hallaghan 126
Halley 126
Halligan 126
Hallighan 126
Halloway 55
Hallowel 126
Hally 131
Halpen 126
Halpenny 126
Halpin 126
OHaly 131
Hamilton 11,31,127
Hamilton, J. 32
Hancock 127
Hand 127
Handcock 22,127
Handcocks 23
Handy 127
Hanebry 132
Hanes 127
Hankes 127
Hankshaw 127,226
Hanlan 127
O'Hanlon 127
Hannagan 127
Hannigan 127
O'Hanraghty 127
Hanratty 127
Hanstede 26.127
Hanway 127,224
O'Hara 127

Harah 127
Harborne 127,224
Harbourne 27,127
Harburne 127
Hard 127-8
Hardiman 128
Harding 127,226
Harding, Dr. 23,228
Hardy 128,225
Harford 38-40
Harford 30,128
Harington 128-9,223
Harisson 129
Harkin 128
Harkins 128
Harknett 128
Harman 11,128,224
Harmel 128,218
Harmon 128
Harnet 128,224
Harnett 224
Haroid 128
Harold 14,20,22,128
Harold, Walter 13
Harolds 19
Harolds Cross 28
Harp 128
Harper 128
Harpor 128
Harpur 31,128
Harrihy 129
Harrington 33,128-9, 227
Harris 129,218,223
Harrisen 129
Harrison 129,224
Harrold 128
Harroughten 129
Harson 129,224
Hart 129,224
O'Hart viii,129
Harte 129
Harte Of   27
O'Hartley 129
Hartly 129
Hartney 129,226
Hartpole 26,129
Harty 128

Harvey *130,227*
Harvy *130,224-5,*
Haskins *57*
Haslam *130*
Hasler *130*
Hasler, Sir J. *14*
Hasselham *130,225*
Hassler *130*
Hast *130,223*
Hatchell *20,130*
Hatchell, J. *20*
Hate *130*
Hatfield *130,223*
Hatter *130,226*
Hatton *130*
Haubois *130*
Haubois, A. *29*
Haughton *130,224*
Haven *130*
Haward *130,228*
Hawkins *22,27,30,*
131,227
Hawkins Arms *230*
Hawkshaw *131*
OHawrde *135*
Hayden *131*
Haydon *131,223-25*
Hayes *131*
Haynes *126*
Hays *131*
Hayward *130*
OHea *10,131*
OHealihy *131*
O'Healy *131*
Heas *131*
Heath *131*
Heavisid *20,131*
Hellen *131*
Hellen, Robt. *19*
OHely *131*
Hemphill *131*
Hemsworth *131*
Henchy *132*
Henderson *131*
Hendrick *131*
McHendrick *131*
Henebry *132*
Henesy *132*

Henneberry *132*
O'Hennessy *132*
Hennesy *132*
Hennigan *127*
Henrick *131*
MacHenry *132*
McHenry *132*
OHenry *132*
Henry I I *34*
Hensey *132*
OHeoghy *133*
Heraghty *129*
Herbert *132,224*
Herbert, V. *41*
Hereford *128*
Herlihy *136*
Herman *132,218*
Hert *129*
Hertford *128*
Hervey *130*
Hervie *130*
Hesse *132,218*
Hetherington *132*
Hetheringtons *24*
Hewet *132*
Hewetson *132*
Hewett *132*
Hewison *132*
Hewitt Hewett *132*
Hewson *132,136*
Hewson, Col. *26*
Heynham *132,226*
Heys *131*
Hiatt *132*
Hiatt, Love *14*
O'Hickey *132*
Hickie *132*
Hicks *132*
Hickson *132,226*
Hicky *132*
Hide *137*
Hide, Nich. *26*
Higby *133*
Higgens *133*
O'Higgin *133*
Higgins *133*
Higins *133*
Hilan *137*

Hiland *137*
Hill *133,224-25*
Hill, George *18*
Hill, Wm. *224-25*
Hillard *133*
Hilliard *133*
Hillyard *133*
Hilton *133*
Hilyard *133*
Hines *137*
Hoadly *133*
Hoagman *133,218*
Hoar *135*
Hoare *133-5*
Hoban *133*
Hobb *134*
Hobkins *134*
Hobson *133*
Hodges *133,225*
Hodgkins *133,226*
Hodser *133,226*
Hoey *133*
Hogain *133*
O'Hogan *133*
Hogane *133*
Hogart *135*
Hogen *133*
Hogin *133*
Holden *133*
Holder *133*
Holder, Pat. *27*
Holford *133,223*
Holian *135*
Holiday *126,134*
Holland *134*
Hollande *134*
Hollaway *134,227*
Holliday *126,134*
Holloway *55*
Hollywood *9,10,134,*
229
Holme *134*
Holmes *134*
Holmes, S. *29*
Holmpatrick *31,134*
Holohan *134-5*
Holt *134-5*
Homes *134*

Hone *134*
Hone, Nath. *19*
OHoneen *124*
Hood *134*
Hood, Robin *28*
Hook *134*
Hooke *134,225*
Hooker *134,224*
Hookes *134,223-4*
Hoop *134*
Hopkins *134,225-27*
Hore *14,133-5*
Hore, John *13*
Horish *135,228*
Horish, Wm. *228*
Horten *135*
Horton *135*
De Hose *136*
OHosey *136*
Hotten *130*
Houghton *130*
Houlihan *135*
O'Houlihan *135*
Hoult *135,226*
Houneen *124*
Houssaye *136*
How *20,135*
Howard *130,135,*
224-26
Howell *19*
McHowell *135*
Howell Family *23*
Howell, Peter *15*
Howlett *135*
Howse *135*
Howth *9,10,135*
Howth, Earl Of *30*
Hoy *131*
Huband *135*
Hudson *22,32,136,*
227
Huggard *136*
OHugh *131*
Hughe *136*
Hughes *136,227*
Hughes, John *227*
Hughs *38-40*
Hughs *223-4,226*
Huguenot *13*

Huguenots 43
Hulihan 135
Hull 133
Humfrey 136
Humphries 136,218
Humphry 136
Humphrys 136
Huneen 124
Hunt 19,31,116, 136,226
Hunte 136
Hunter 136
Huntington 136
O Hure 135
O'Hurley 136
Hurly 136
Hussey 9,10,136
Hussy 136
Hutchinson 27,137, 224-6
Hutchison 137
Hyatt 132
Hyde 137
Hylan 137
Hyland 137
Hyndeberge 19,137
Hynebry 132
Hynes 137
Ievers 137
Immaulouz 137
Immaulouz 22
Immigration 41
Ince 137
Inglefield 137
Invasions 9
Irish Army List 36
Irishtown 27
Irwin 33,137
Isaacs 137,218
Israel 137,218
Iver 137
McIver 137
Ivers 137
Ivors 137
Ivory 137
Jackson 24,137
Jackson, E. 20
Jackson, H. 20
Jackson, J. 30

Jacob 138,218
Jaffery 138
Jaffray 138
Jaffray, Alex. 20
Jaffrey 138
McJames 225
Jameson 30,138
Jamieson 138
Jamison 138
Jamisone 138
Jans 138
Jans, Robert 19
Jarvis 138
Jeffery 138,223
Jefford 138,223
Jeffry 138
Jenings 138
Jenkins 138
Jenkinson 138
Jennings 138
Jephson 138
Jephson, J. 32
Jerety 120
Jervice 138,224
Jewish Cem't'ry 34
Jewish 218
Jewish Records 44
Joakes 138,223
Joanes 138
Joanes, H. 228
Jocelyn 19,138
Joel 139,218
John 139,225
Johns 139
Johnson 139,225
Johnson, R. 225
Johnsons 23
Johnston 20,139
Johnstone 139
Joley 139
Jolley Jolly 139
Jolliff 139
Joly 139
Jones 225-28-29
Jones 29,33,140, 223
Jones, Allen 225
Jones, Henry 23
Jones, James 226

Jones, John 22
Jones, M. 227
Jones, Michell 229
Jones, Morgan 24
Jones, Morgan 227
Jones, Owen 226
Jones, T. 28,228
Jones, Theo. 26,227
Jones, Wm. 13,223
Jordan 229
MacJordan 140
Jordan, John 31
Joy 140
Joy, Henry 22
Juckes 138
Judah 140,218
Judd 140
Judge 140
July 139
Kain 140-1
Kaine 140
Kane 140-1
O Kane 78
Kaplan 140,218
Kary 80
Kasey 81
Kavanagh 141
Kavanaugh 141
Kay 141,224
MacKay 136
Kay, Thomas 224
Kealey 141-4
Kealy 141-4,227
Kean 78,141
Keane 78
Keane Kane 141
Keaney 143
Keany 143
O'Kearney 141
Kearns 141-4
Kearogan 141
Kearon 144
Kearovan 38-40, 141
Keary 80
Keating 141,225
Keatinge Burial 27
Keavanagh 141

Keavenagh - 38-40
O'Keefe 141
O Keeffe 141
Keegan 141
MacKeegan 156
Keeley 141
Keely 142-4
MacKeenan 142
O'Keenan 142
Keerin 144
Keeting 141
Keevan 141
Kegley 176
Keherney 141
Kehily 142
Kehoe 143
Keife 141
Keightley 29
Keightly 142
Keily 141-2-4
Kellett 142
Kellie 141-2
Kellie, John 19
Kelly 38-40,141, 223-6
O'Kelly viii,142
Kelly, John 226
Kellye 142
MacKen 142
Kenah 142
Kendal 142
Kendal, John 14
Kenedie 142
Kenedy 38-40
Kenedy 142,223-4-5
Kenedy, T. 225
MacKenna 142
Kennagh 142
Kennan 31,142-3
Kenneday 142
O'Kennedy 142
Kennedy, Dr. 22
Kennedy, J. 24
Kennedy, R. 27
Kennon 79,118
Kenny 24,223
O'Kenny 143
Kent 143

McKenzie 143
McKenzy 143
M'Keo 143
Keogh 143
MacKeogh 143
Keogh, John 28
Keoghe 143
Keon 142
Keough 143
Kerdiff 31,143
Kerdiff, W. 32
Kerin 144
Kerke 143,225
Kerley 94
Kerlin 80
McKern 143
Kernahan 143
Kernan 38-40
McKernan 143
Kernes, Irish 36
Kerovan 145
Kerr 80
Kerrane 80,144
Kerris 143,229
Kerris, Gilb. 229
Kerwan 145
Kett 143,224
Kettle 143
Keveny 118
MacKey 143,155
McKibben 143
McKibbin 143
OKibbon 143
McKibbons 143
Kickham 143,223
Kid 143
Kidd 143
MacKie 143
Kieley 144
Kiely 144
O'Kieran 144
Kiernan 143
MacKiernan 144
McKiernan 144
Kilgobbin (pl) 23
Kilmainham 29
Kilmartin 157
Kilmore 144

Kilmore, Roger 18
Kilmurray 164
MacKin 142
Kinaghan 144
Kinahan 19,144
Kinahane 144
Kinane 142
Kinchella 145
King 20-2, 144,223-27
King, John 227
Kingsbury 144
Kingsmill 144
Kingston 144
Kingstone 144
Kingstown 13
MacKinnawe 115
Kinnealy 88
Kinney 143
Kinnie 143
Kinsela 145
Kinsella 145
Kinsellagh 145
Kirk 143
Kirke 143
Kirkpatrick 34,145
O'Kirwan 145
Kirwin 145
Kithinyman 145,223
Knally 165
McKneight 145
Knight 223-4
McKnight 145
Knight, N. 223
Knot 145,225
Knott 145
Knowels 145
Knowlan 167
Knowland 167-8
Knowle 145
Knowles 145
Knowls 145
Knox 145
Koch 92
Kotter 91
Kramer 93
Krowley 93
MacKy 155

MacKynega 36
Kyrvan 145
L'englys 106
La Touche 11,18, 22,145
Labhles 148
Lacey, De Lacy 146
Lacie 146
Lacy 146,148
Lacye 146
Laghanstown 15
Lagthenan 14,146
Lahiff 146
Laird 146
Lally 150,163
Lalor 146
O'Lalor 146
Lamb 146
Lambart 146,224
Lambart, J. 228
Lambert 15,146,229
Lamberton 146
Land Records 45
Landa 146
Landers 146
Landmarks 35
Landy 146
Lane 147,225
Langdale 147.225
Langham 147
Langtry 147
Lapham 147
Larcher 56
Larkan 224
Larkan, Ez. 224
Larkin 147
Lasch 147,218
Latimer 147
Lattimer 147
MacLaughlin 147, 158
OLaughlin 153
Laundy 38-40,146-7
Laurance 148,190
Laurence 147,190
Lavelle 147
Law 147
Lawces 38-40,147
Laweless 148

Lawler 38-40,146
Lawles 148,226
Lawless 45
Lawless 9,10,23-4-7, 33,148,226
Lawless, T. 14
Lawlis 38-40
Lawlor 13,24,146
Lawndy 146
Lawrance 148,190
Lawrence 147-8,229
Lawrenson 30,148
Lawson 148
Layfield 148
Layfield, Lewis 32
Lazarus 148,218
Le Brun 20,148
Le Fevre 148
Le Hunt 136
Lea 148-9
Lea, T. 30,229
Leach 149
Leacy 148
Leake 31,148,229
Leake, N. 229
Leash 146
Leason 149
Lecch 148,226
Lecchfield 148,226
Lecora 149
Lecora, Lt. 223
Ledwich 149
Ledwidge 149
Ledwitch 149
Ledwith 149
Lee 148,218
MacLee 149
O'Lee 149
Lee, Jonas 225
Leech 148-9,226
Leech, R. 19
Leechfield 148,226
Leedom 24,149
Leeson 11,33,149
Leeson Family 20
Lefroy 149
STLeger 150
Lehman 150,218

Leinster *34*
Leischman *150,218*
Lely *33,150*
Lemon *150*
Lemond *150,223*
Lenard *150*
Lenglas *106*
Lennan *38-40*
OLennan *150*
O'Lennon *150*
Lentaigne *150*
Lentaigne Arm *230*
Leonard *150*
Leopardstown *16*
Leperstown *16*
Leporter *174*
Lesaw *150,225*
Leuett *224*
Leuett Levitt *150*
Levenston *150,218*
Levett *150*
Levi *150,218*
Levingston *150-1,218*
Lewis *150-3,218, 224*
Leynagh *154*
Liffey River *34*
Lightburne *150*
Lightburne, Dr *15*
Lightfoot *30,151*
Lincoln *151*
Lindley *151*
Linegar *151*
Linegar *32*
Linkfield *151*
Linnane *150*
Linton *151*
Lisle *154*
Littell *151*
Litten *151*
Little *151,154,223*
Little, F. *223*
Litton *151*
Litton, Wm. *19*
Livinglyhurst *13,151*
Livingston *151*
Livingstone *151*
Lloyd *151,223*
Locations *34*

Loch *151*
OLochalinn *153*
Lockard *151,226*
Locke *151,225,228*
Locke, Capt. *225*
Locke Family *24*
Locke, John *228*
Lockhart *151*
Lockwood *33,151*
Locumbe *16,151*
Locumbe, J. *19*
Lodlowe, E. *228*
Loftis *152*
Loftus *224-5-7*
Loftus *11,20,22*
Loftus, D. *225*
Loghenan *16,152*
OLoghlen *153*
Loghlin *38-40,152*
Lombard *152*
de London *19*
Long *97,152,224*
Long, Gerald *14*
McLongahan *152*
Longan *152*
Longervile *152*
Longley *152*
OLorcain *147*
OLorcan *147*
Lord *152,224*
Lorde *152*
Lorkan *147*
Losse *152*
Loughery *153*
MacLoughlin *147*
McLoughlin *152*
OLoughlin *152-3*
Loughlinstown *15*
Loughnan *152*
Loughnane *152*
Louis *150-3,218*
Lovelace *24,153*
Lovell *153*
Low *153*
Lowe *153*
Lowery *153*
Lowry *153*
Lowther *153,226*

Lucan Parish *26*
Lucas *226*
Lucy *148*
Ludlow *153,226*
Ludlowe *153*
Lupton *153*
Lushe *24,153*
Luthera *44*
Lutrell *154*
Lutrellstown *26*
Lutterell *154,229*
Luttrell *9,11,26-7, 154,228*
Luttrells *22*
Lynacar *154,226*
Lynagh *154*
Lynam *154*
Lynan *154*
Lynch *38-40,154*
Lynchy *38-40,154*
Lynsey *154,227*
Lyons *154,218*
Lysle *154*
Lyttle *151,154*
Mac *101*
Macabe *77*
Macanna *79*
Macartney *14,154*
Macavaddy *155*
Maccan *38-40*
Mack *101*
Mackay *136,155*
Mackie *143*
Macklean *155*
Macklean, J. *18*
Macky *155*
Maconchie *155*
Maconchy *155*
Madagane *155*
O'Madden *155*
Maddicks *155*
Maddin *224*
Maddox *155*
Madigan *155*
Magee *46,119*
Magennis *125*
Magg *155,225*
Maghan *155*

Magher *155*
Magill *155*
Magilligan *121*
Maginn *111*
Magphinn *111*
Magrane *155*
Maguire *125,155*
Maguirke *125*
Maheir *155*
Maher *155-8*
Mahon *155*
MacMahon *155*
McMahon, W. *20*
Mahoney *155*
McMahoney *155*
Mahowne *38-40*
O'Mahowne *155*
Mahowney *155*
Maine *155,158*
Mainey *161*
Makagan *156*
Makagan, P. *23*
Makay *92*
Maklelan *156*
Malahide (pl) *59*
Malley *158*
Mallone *38-40,156*
Malloone *156*
Malone *38-40*
O'Malone *156*
Malone, Rchd. *31*
Malpas *156*
Man *156*
O'Mangan *156*
Manghan *156*
Mangin *156*
Maning *156*
Manion *156*
Manley *156*
Manly *156,228*
Mann *155-6*
Manney *156,223*
Manney, R. *223*
Mannin *156*
Manning *13,156*
Mannion *156*
OMannion *156*
Map, Ordnance *12*

Mapas *156*	Maule, T. *223*	Merry, C. *14*	Moffat *160*
Mape *156*	Maura *156*	Merrygan *159*	Moffitt *160*
Mapes *156,225*	Mautner *158,218*	Mervin *159,225*	Moir *161*
Mara *155-6*	Maxwell *158,223*	Merwin *159*	Molesworth *11,161*
O Mara *158*	May *158-9*	Messit *19,159*	Molleneaux *161*
Marah *158*	Mayhugh *158*	Methodist *43*	Mollenex *161,226*
Marcus *156,218*	Mayler *158*	Metzenberg *159,218*	Molley *161*
Mardell *157*	Mayne *158*	Mey *24,27,159*	Molloy *161*
Marienhoff *156,218*	Mayne, Edw. *19*	Meyrick *159*	O'Molloy *161*
de Marisco *22*	Maynes *155-8*	Michael *190*	Molyneaux *161*
Mark *157*	Mayo *158*	Michell *159,160,226*	Molyneux *28,161*
Markam *156,224*	Mayrick *159*	Mickle *159*	O'Monagha *161*
Markey *157*	Mayson *158*	Middleton *159*	Monck *33*
Markham *156,223-4*	O Meachair *155*	Mildmay *159*	Money *161*
Marks *157,218*	Meagher *158*	Miler *160*	Mongan *156*
O'Marky *157*	Meaney *161*	Milis *160*	Monk, Gen. *23*
Marlow *157*	Meany *161*	Milis, John *14*	Monks *161*
Marra *158*	Meara *156*	Mill *160*	Monnaughan *161*
Marsden *157*	O'Meara *158*	Millar *160*	Monohan *161*
Marshal *157*	Meath *158*	Millea *161*	Montpelier *13*
Marshall *24,157,224*	Medlicott *14,158*	Miller *160,226-27*	Mooney *161*
le Marshall *24-6*	Mee *158*	Miller, H. *227*	O'Mooney *161*
Marshall, R. *13*	Mee, Giles *226*	Miller, T. *226*	Moor *161*
Marshell *157*	Meegan *158*	Milligen *163*	Moore *38-40,22,223*
Martell *157*	O'Meehan *158*	Milliken *163*	Moore, C. *34*
Marten *157*	McMeekin *158*	Millington *160*	O'Moore Moor *161*
Martin *38-40,224*	Meeny *161*	Millinton *160,225*	O Moore Of Leix *10*
Martin, *157*	O Meera *158*	Mills *160*	Moorhouse *161*
Martin, H. *226*	Mehegan *158*	Milmay *159*	Moory *161,224*
Martin, Henry *226*	Meighan *158*	Milmo *159*	Mora *97*
Martine *38-40*	Meilor *158*	Milmoy *159*	de Mora *19*
Martyn *38-40,157*	Melaghlin *147,158*	Minchin *14,160*	Moran *161-62*
Marvin *159*	Melden *159*	Miner *160*	Moran, John *13*
Marward *9,10,157*	Meldiric *24,159*	Missett *160*	More *161*
Marwards *157*	Meldon *159*	Missett, Walt. *19*	O More *161*
Mason *157,*	Melville *159*	Missit *159*	More, Boyles *32*
226,229	Menarry *165*	Mitchel *160*	Mores *162*
Mason, John *229*	Mercer *159,226*	Mitchell *33,159,160*	Morey *161*
Mason, Thom. *20*	Mercer Family *15*	Mockler *160*	Morgan *15,225-26-28*
Massey *157*	Mercier *159*	Moclare *160*	O'Morgan *162*
McMaster *157*	Merdith, Maj. *226*	Mocter *160*	Morgan, Wm. *228*
Masterson *157*	Meredeth *159,226*	Mocton *160*	O Moriarty *10*
Mathew *28*	Meredith *159,226*	Mocton, Ellena *16*	Mornington *188*
Mathewes *158*	Merrick *159*	O'Modarn *viii,10,160*	Moroly *162,223*
Mathews *158*	Merricke *159,223*	Modern *160*	Morphy *38-40,162*
Matthews *158*	Merrigan *159*	Moelet *160*	Morran *38-40,161-2*
Maughan *155*	Merrion (pl) *18*	Moenes *22,160,163*	Morres *162*
Maule *158,223*	Merry *159*	Moenes, Wm. *28*	Morris *162*

Morris, M. *162*
Morris, Thom. *29*
Morrison *162*
Morrisson *162*
Morse *162*
Mortimer *162*
Mortomer *162,226*
Morton *162*
Morvill *18,162*
Moseley *162,218*
Moses *162,218*
Mossom *162*
Mossoms *15*
O Mothan *22,162*
Mould *226*
Mould *162,223*
Moulds *19*
Moxon *162*
Moyle *163*
Moynes *163,223*
Muckleborne *163, 223*
Muir *161-3*
Mulally *163*
Mulchinock *163*
Mulderick *159*
Mulderrick *24*
Mulgan *163*
Mulhal *163*
Mulhall *163*
Mulholland *134*
Mulhuddart Pl *31*
Mullagen *163*
O'Mullally *163*
Mullaly *163*
Mullan *163*
Mullane *163*
Mullee *161*
Mullen *163*
O Mullen *10*
O'Mullens *viii*
O'Mulligan *163*
Mullin *163*
Mullins *163*
Mullooly *163*
Mulloy *161*
Mulready *178*
Mulrooney *181*

O Mulryan *182*
Muncke *225*
Muncks *161*
Munks *161*
Munn *33,163*
Munson *163*
Muonks *161*
O Murcain *163*
Murcan *163*
O Murcan *10*
Murdoch *164*
Murdock *164*
Mac Muregain *viii*
Mac Muregain *163*
Murhila *136*
Murily *136*
Murphy *38-40,24, 162-4,*
Murphy, Capt. *41*
Murphy, E. *13*
O Murphy Of *10*
Murphy, Sam. *15*
Murphystown *15*
Murray *164*
Murrey *38-40*
Murrihy *164*
Murry *164*
Mc Murry *164*
Murta *164*
Murtagh *23,164*
O Murtagh *10*
Murtaugh *164*
O Murtha *10*
O'Murtogh *viii*
Muschamp *31,164*
Music, Sheet *50*
Mustan *164*
Mustian *164,229*
Myers *13,164,218*
Mynagh *164*
Mynagh,j. *18*
Nagle *164*
Nailor *165*
Naish *165*
Mac Nally *165*
Mc Nally *55*
Nally Of *23*
Nally, Wm. *20*

McNamara *165*
Names Listed *37*
Nangle *9,11,164-65*
Naper *165*
Naper, Robt. *27*
Napier *165*
Nary *165*
Mac Nary *165*
Nash *165*
Nash Arms *230*
Nashe *165*
Nasse *165*
Nathan *165,218*
Mc Naul *165*
Navill *165,226*
Navill, Tho. *226*
Naylor *165*
Neagle *164*
Neale *38-40,166*
Mac Neale *166*
O Neale *38-40,166*
Mac Neale Arms *52*
Neary *166*
Mac Neary *165*
Mac Nebury *15,166*
Neel *166*
Neele *166*
Neil *166*
O'Neill *166*
O'Neill, Sir B. *26*
Neills *28*
Neilson *166*
Neish *165*
Mc Nelly *165*
Nelson *166*
Nerwich *166,218*
Nesbitt *166*
Nettervill *166*
Netterville *9,10,166*
Nettervilles *32*
Nevill *166*
Neville *166*
New York *41*
Newcastle *24*
Newcom *166*
Newcomb *166*
Newcome *166*

Newcomen *22,27,30, 166,227*
Newcoment *167,226*
Newell *145*
Newenham *34,167*
Newenham, E. *13*
Newman *167,218,223*
Newmen *167*
Newspapers *45*
Newtownpark *14*
Nichlas *167*
Nicholas *167,225*
Nicholls *167,223*
Nicholson *167*
Nielson *166*
Nihill *166-7*
Nixon *167*
Nixon, Capt. *31*
Nobel *167*
Nogent *168*
O'Nolan *167*
Nolte *168*
Nolty *168*
Norecone *167*
Norse Names *30*
North *167,224*
Norton *167,225*
Norwegian *35*
Nott *145*
Nottingham *27,168*
de Nottingham *26*
Nottinghams *45*
Nowlan *24,168*
O Nowlan *167*
Nowland *38-40,168*
Nowlane *38-40*
Nowlin *168*
Noy *29,168*
Noyce *168*
Nuel *168,218*
Nugent *22,168*
Nugent, I. *32*
Nughent *168*
Nulty *224*
Mc Nulty *165,168*
Nutley *23,168*
Nuttall *168*
Nutterville *166*

Oakley *168*
Ob *168,223*
Odlum *168*
Odlum, Wm. *33*
Ogan *133*
Ogham Stone *202*
Opolinser *168,218*
Orde *169*
Orde, A. *28*
Ordnanc *17,21,25*
Orr *169,226*
Orson *169,226*
Othyr *19,169*
Ouldley *57*
Outlaw *148*
McOwen *169*
Owen, John *31*
Owen(s) *169*
Owens *169,225-6*
Owenson *169*
Ownyan *169,229*
Padmore *169,223*
Page *169*
Paget *169*
Paine *169,223*
Paisley *169,171*
Palfery *169,224*
Paling *169*
Pallace *169*
Pallas *169*
Pallatio (del) *169*
Palles *169*
Palliser *20,169*
Pallys *169*
Palmer *9,10,169, 223-25*
Palmerston Pl *27*
Parish (pl) *35*
Parker *170*
Parkinson *170*
Parnall *170,225*
Parnell *20*
Parry *170*
Parsons *11,22-4, 170,227*
Parsons, W. *24*
Parvin *170*
Pasco *170*
Patrick *112*

Patrickson *14,170*
Patton *170*
Payne *169-70*
Payne, John *15*
Peachen *170,226*
Peake *171,223*
MacPeake *171*
Pearce *172*
Pearse *172*
Pearson *171*
Peasley *171,227*
Peasley, Capt. *27*
Peche *26,171*
Pedelow *26,171*
Peepes *171,224*
Peirce *172*
Pemberton *171*
Pender *174*
Pendergas *174*
Pendergast *171-74*
Pendy *174*
Pennefather *29,171*
Pennington *171,226*
Pennsylvania *41*
Penny *171*
Penoyx *171,227*
Pentenny *223*
Penteny *171,223-29*
Penteny, J. *229*
Peppard *11,33,171*
Peppard, W. *23*
Pepper *171*
Periodicals *45*
Perkens *171*
Perkins *171*
Perrier *172*
Perrin-hatchell *20*
Perry *172*
Perry, Anth. *19*
Pers *172*
Petticrew *172*
Pettit *172*
·Phalen *205*
Phellane *205*
Pheopoes *9,172*
Phepoe *10*
Phepoes *10,172*
Philadelphia *41*

Philip *26*
Philips *172*
Phillip *218*
McPhillip *172*
Phillipps *223-24-26*
Phillipps, Lady *223*
Phillips *172,218*
Phillpot *172,223*
Phipps *172*
Phipps, C. *41*
Picket *172*
Picknall *172,224*
MacPierce *172*
Piers *172*
Pierson *171*
Piggott *172*
Pigott *172*
Pilson *172*
Pim *172*
Pin *172,223*
Pine *175*
Pinson *172,223*
Pippard *26,172*
Pitts *172,223*
Place Names *219*
Playford *173,223*
Plunket *10,173,225*
Plunkets *11*
Plunkett *38-40,229*
Plunkett *9,31,173,225*
Plunkitt *173*
Pocklington *173*
Pocklingtons *15*
Pockrich *173*
Pockrich, R. *29*
De Poher *174*
Polak *218*
Polak Of *173*
Polexfield *173,224*
Pollack *173,218*
Pollard *173*
Pollock *173*
Ponsonby *22,173*
Pontoney *173,224*
Pony *173,224*
Poole *173,224*
Pooley *24,173*
Pooly *173,223*

Poope *173,223*
Poope, Capt. T. *223*
Poor *174*
Poors *174*
Pope *173*
Porcel *175*
Porter *31,174*
Porter, H. *229*
Porterstown *31*
Portreue *227*
Poter *174*
Pott *174,227*
Potter *174,223*
Potts *174*
Potts, James *20*
Poudyhard *174,225*
Povey *32,174*
Powell *120,174,226*
Powell Family *15*
Power *174*
Powers *174*
Powre *174*
Prendergast *174*
Presbyteria *43*
Preston *9..11,174, 223*
De Preston *174*
Prestons *23*
Price *22,175, 224..226*
Prigget *175,226*
Principal *37*
Prinn *175,227*
Pritchet *175,223*
Probey *32*
Proby *175*
Prosser, The *27*
Prossor *175*
Purcell *28,175,227*
Purcill *175*
Purdon *175*
Purdon, Wm. *33*
Purdy *175*
Purefoy *175*
Purfield *175*
Pursell *175*
Purshell *175*
Purtill *175*
Putland *11,175*

Putland, John *33*
Pyn *175*
Pyn, Nicholas *14*
Pyne *175*
Quade *201*
McQuade *201*
Quail *176*
Quaker   *44*
Qualter *203*
Quane *175*
Quartermas *33,175*
Quayle *176*
Queale *176*
MacQueale *176*
Queally *142*
Queen *176*
Quen *176*
Quenedy *142*
O'Quigley *176*
Quill *92,209*
Quilly *209*
MacQuilly *92*
Quin *176*
Quinn *38-40,225*
O'Quinn *176*
Quinne *38-40,176*
M'Quirk *125*
Quirke *226*
Radcliffe *20,176*
Radman *177*
Rafter *176*
Raftery *176*
ORaftery *176*
Ragan *178*
ORagher *176*
Rainllow *176,223*
Ram *176*
Ramsey *176,223*
Randall *20,176*
Randell *176*
MacRannall *179*
McRannall *179*
Ransford *176*
Raphson *13,176*
Rath *24,176*
Rathborne *31,33, 176*
Rathbourne *176*

Rathburne *176,218*
Raw *177*
Rawlings *176*
Rawlingson *177,224*
Rawlinson *177,225-27*
Rawlinson, J. *225*
Rawson *11,177*
Raygan *178*
Raynor *177,227*
Rea *177*
Read *177*
Reade *178*
Readeinge *177,227*
Reader *177*
Ready *177*
Reagan *178*
Reagh *177*
Real *177-9*
Really *177-8*
OReally *177*
Realy *38-40,177*
ORealy *177*
Reaves *182*
Reavy *177*
O'Reddan *177*
Reddin *177*
Reddington *177*
Reddy *177*
Reddy, Dr. R. *29*
Redesdale *16,177*
Redmon *177*
Redmond *177*
Redmont *177*
Redmun *177*
Reed *178*
Reede *178*
Reegan *178*
Reel *177*
Reese *178*
Reeues *225-6*
Reeues Reeves *177*
Reeves *182*
ORegan *viii,178*
Reid *177-8*
Reilly *28,178*
O'Reilly *18,178-9*
Reily *178*
Reis *178,218*

Relick *178,226*
Relly *178*
ORelly *178*
Relly, Barnaby *22*
Renourd *178*
Renourd, Col. *33*
Renvelstown *31*
Renville *31,178*
Research Aids *49*
Revell *178*
de Revell *24*
Reyley *178*
Reyly *38-40,178, 227*
Reyly, Moses *24*
Reynolds *24,179,225*
Reynor *179*
Rhode Island *41*
Rhys *175-9*
ORiagain *viii*
Riall *177-9*
Riall, Capt. *23*
Rice *175-9*
Rich *179,223*
Richard *179,223*
McRichard *223*
Richards *179*
Richards, J. *20*
Richardsen *179, 206, 228*
Richt *179,223*
Richt, Mr. *223*
Rickard *30,179*
Riddell *179*
Riddle *179*
Rideleford *16,18, 22,179*
Rider *179,225*
Rider, John *28*
Ridgate *179*
Rielly *179*
Rigg *180*
Rigg, A. *226*
Right *209*
Riley *177-8-9*
Rind *182*
Ringsend (pl) *18*
Rinkel *180*
Rinkle *19,180*

Roach *180*
Roachforde *180*
Roark *181*
Roarke *181*
Roarty *176*
Robenson *180*
Robert *180,224*
Robert, Wm. *224*
Roberts *180,223-26*
Roberts, Dr. *13*
Roberts   *23*
Roberts, Hugh *226*
Robinsen *180*
Robinson *15,24,180, 218-27*
Robotham *180,224*
Roch *180*
Roche Roach *180*
Rocheford *180*
Rochestown *14*
Rochford *180*
Rochfort *15,180*
Rock *180*
Rodan *177*
Rodgers *180*
Roe *38-40,223*
Roe, Anthony *223*
Roebuck (pl) *20*
Rogers *19,180*
Rogerson *33,180*
Rohan *181*
Roice *179*
Rokeby *26,181*
Rolandson *181*
De Roley *181*
Rolles *181*
O'Ronan *181*
Ronane *181*
Roney *181,223*
Rooke *181*
O'Rooney *181*
Roony *181*
Rooth *181*
Rorke *181*
Rorque *181*
ORory *180*
Roseingrave *13,181*
Rosengrane *181,226*

Rosengrave *181*
Rosenstein *218*
Rosenstein *181*
Rosenthal *218*
Rosenthal *181*
Ross *181*
Rossiter *181*
Rosswell *181*
Roth *181*
Rothes *181*
Rothwell *181*
Rouane *182*
Roughan *181*
Round Towers *35*
McRourke *181*
O'Rourke *181*
Rowlandson *181*
Rowles *181,229*
Rowles, Wm. *31*
Rowley *33,181*
O Rowley *181*
Rowley Arms *52*
Rowly *181-2*
Royan *182*
Roynane *181*
Ruan *182*
Rubinstein *182,218*
Ruddan *177*
Ruddanes *177*
Ruddy *177,182*
Rudman *182,218*
Rueff *182,218*
Runey *181*
Rupe *180*
Rusell *182*
Russel *182*
Russell *38-40*
Russell *24,182, 228-29*
Russell, Capt. *41*
Russell Family *26*
Russell, J. *228-9*
Russell, P. *228*
Ruth *181*
Ruthe *181*
Rutledge *24,182*
Rutter *182*
Rutty *182*

Rutty, J. *29*
Ryan *38-40*
Ryan, John *29*
O'Ryan, *182*
Ryder *179*
Ryley *179*
Rynd *182*
Rysback *182*
Rysbrack, M. *32*
Ryves *182*
Ryves House *27*
Sagart *98*
Saggart *23*
Salaman *183-8*
Sale *182*
Sall *182*
Salmon *183,188, 218-25*
Saltinsball *183,225*
Sampson *183,218*
Sampson, Lt. *31*
Samson *183*
Samuelson *183,218*
Sanchy *183*
Sancky *183,223*
Sand *183*
Sanders, *183*
Sanderson *183*
Sandes *183*
Sandford *183,226*
Sandheim *183,218*
Sands *183,224, 226*
Sandwith *183*
Sandymount *18*
Sandys *183*
Sanford *183*
Sankey *183,224*
Sanky *183*
Sarsefeld *184*
Sarsfield *9..11,26, 184*
Saul *182*
Savadge *184,225*
Savage *184*
Savage, T. *33*
Savauge *184*
Sawey *184*
Say *184*

Sayers *184*
Scally *184*
Scarborough *24-6,184, 228*
Scarborrough *227*
Schmidt *188*
Scott *184*
Scriven *184*
Scullin *184*
Scullion *184*
Scully *184*
O'Scully *184*
Sculy *184*
Scurlagh *31,185*
Scurlock *24,185*
Scurlogh *185*
Seagrave *9,45, 185,226*
Seaman *185,223*
Seapoint *13*
Seargent *185*
Sears *184*
Seden *185,223*
Sedgraue *185,228*
Sedgrave *185*
Sedgrave *27*
Sedgrave, T. *26*
Seery *185*
Segerson *185*
Segrave *10,32,185*
Segrave, Nich. *20*
Semple *185*
Sergeant *185,225*
Sergent *185,226*
Serjeant *185*
Serjeant, Robt. *18*
O Serky *186*
Seward *185,229*
Shackleford *185*
Shakleton *185*
Shalloo *186*
Shallowe *186*
Shamrock *41*
Shanahy *116*
Shane *185,223*
Sharket *186*
O'Sharkey *186*
Sharp *186*
Sharry *186*

Sharvin *186*
Shaw *11,186,226*
Shaw, Capt. *223*
Shaw, Robt. *20*
Shawe *186*
Shea *19,186*
Sheaperd *186,224*
Sheapheard *224*
Sheapherd *186*
Sheilds *186*
Sheils *186*
Shelley *186*
Shelloe *186*
Shelly *186*
Shelton *186,224*
Shepherd *186*
Sheppard *45*
Sherdan *186*
Sherden *186*
Sherding *186,225*
Sherdon *186*
Shergoll *30,186*
O'Sheridan *186*
Sherlock *26,186*
Sherlog *186*
Sherodan *186*
Sherry *186*
O Sherry *186*
Sherwin *186*
McShery *186*
O Shiel *186*
Shields *186*
Shillingford *28,186*
Shinnock *116*
Shipcott *187,224*
Shiply *187*
Shippy *187*
Ships *41*
Shipsen *187*
Shipton *187*
Shipward *187*
Shore *187,227*
Shore, Wm. *20*
Short *187,226*
Shortall *187*
Shuldham *187*
Shurlock *187*
Shurlog *187,223*

MacShurton 140
Siev 187,218
Sigerson 185
Simmons 187
Simmonscourt 18
Simons 187,193,218
Simple 185
Singleton 34,187
Sinnot 187
Sinnott 187,193
Sinton 187
Sirr 187
Sisk 187
Siske 187
MacSiurtan 140
MacSkally 184
Skelly 184-7-8
OSkelly 184
Skelten 187
Skelton 187,226
Skiddy 188
Skully 184-88
Slater 188
Slator 188
Slingsby 26,188
Smallman 188
Smidt 188,218
Smith 11,32,188
Smith Of   27
Smith, Sir M. 16
Smith, Thom. 15
Smithe 188
Smothe 188
Smothe Family 18
Smullen 188
Smyth 228-29
Smyth 38-40,
     224-5-6
Smyth, Col. 229
Smyth, Dr. 226
Smyth, G. 229
Smyth, J. 227
Smyth, J. 225-7-8
Smyth, Robt. 228
Smythe 38-40,188
Smythe, Rev. 27
Solomon 183,188,
     218
Somers 189,192

Somerville 189
Sommerford 189
Sommers 189
Soolivan 192
Soople 192
Sources 46
Southwell 22,189
Southy 189,226
Sowthick 189
Sparrow 189
Speers 189
Speght 189
Spelling   43
Spellings 48
Spence 189,226
Spencer 189
Spiers 189
Spiro 189,218
Spranger 189,226
Spring 189,227
Springe 189
Springer 189
Springham 189,225,
     228
Sproule 189
Sprule 189
St. George 224-5
St. John 24,189
St. Lawrence 9..11,30,
     190
St. Lawrence 228,229
St Lawrence   52
St. Michael 22,190
St Michan's 183
Stafford 190
Staford 190
Stanford 190,225
Stanihurst 10,190
Stanihurt 9,190
Stanley 190,224-5
Stannard 20,190
Stanton 190,224
Stanyhurst 190
Stanyhurst, J. 13
Stapleton 190
Starky 190
Staughton 191,223
Staunton 190-1
Stavenhagen 191,218

Steel 191
Steele 191,226
Steill 191
OSteille 191
Stellman 191,218
Stephen 191
Stephens 191
Stephens,   29
Stephens, T. 33
Stephenson 191,225
Sterling 191,227
Sterne 19,191
Stevenson 191
Steward 191,223
Stewart 191
Stewart Arms 230
Stibbe 191,218
Stiles 191,225-6
Stillorgan 16
Stoakes 224
Stock 191
Stock, Stephen 19
Stoke 191
Stokes 191
Stokes, Dr. W. 30
Stopford 191,226
Storey 192
Storton 192,223
Stoughton 192,224-27
Stowell 192
Stoyte 19,192
Strabane 192
Strange 192
Strangman 192
Straughton 192,228
Strettle 192
Strickland 192
Strieley 192
Strong 192
Strongbow 54
Stryny 192,223
Stuart 191
Styles 192
Styles House 27
Sueterby 28,192
Sulivan 192
Sulliban 192
O'Sullivan 192

Sulyvant 192
Summars 192,224
Summer 192,225
Summerly 189
Summers 189
Suppel 192
Suppels 192
Supple Suppels 192
Surdeville 193
Surnames 36-7
Sutton 30,193
Sutton House 30
de Sutun 193
Swan 193,224
Swan, Wm. 33
Swanton 193
Sweetman 9,10,193,
     229
Sweteman 193
Swift 30,46,193
Swift's Birth. 194
Swifte 193
Swinfeild 193,228
Swinfield, N. 13
Swinfield Of   14
Swinfield, R. 228
Swords 193
Symons 187,193,
     218,224
Synge 193
Synnott 187,193
Synot 187
Synott 187,193
Synyres 193,223
Taa 194
Taafe 194
Taaffe 194
Tacker 194,223
Taff 194
Taffe 194
McTague 197
Tailer 195
Tailor 195
Taite 195
Talant 194,223
Talant, Pat. 223
Talbot 225-27-28
Talbot 9,10,22,
     194-5

Talbot Of   27
Talbot, Wm. 228
Talbots 11
Talbott 227
Tallaght (pl) 22
Tallent 194
Tallon 195
Tally 195
Taney Parish 19
Tansey 195
Tansy 195
OTapa 193
Tappy 193
Tara Tribes viii
de Tasagart 23
Tasker 195
Tate 195
Tatton 195
Tatton Family 33
Taunton 19,195
McTavish 196
Tayler 195
Taylor 228-9
Taylor 10,22,33,
    195,223-4
Taylor Arms 230
Taylor, C. 27
Taylor, Ed. 229
Taylor, H. 229
Taylor, J. 13
Taylor, T. 226
Tayte 195
McTeague 197
Tedcastle 195
Tedcastle, R. 22
Teebay 32,195
Teeling 195
Teesdale 197
Teige 197
McTeigue 37
Teirney 197
Telyng 195
Temple 11,27,196,
    223,226
Temple Family 20
MacTernan 144
Terrell 196
Terry 94,196
Tew 11,196

Thackerly 196
Theswell 196,225
Thomas 196
Thomas, Wm. 22
Thompson 196
Thomson 196
Thornhill 13,196
Thornton 196,
    223-5-6
Thornton, M. 41
Thorton 196
Thunder 30,196
Thunder Of 27
Thurgood 196
Thwaites 19,28,
    196,226
Tichborne 32,197,
    224-6
Tickell 197
Tickell's House 33
Tiege 197
Tiernan 144,197
O'Tierney 197
Tierny 197
Tighe 197
MacTighe   197
Tighe, S. 31
Timmin 197
Timmins 197
Timmons 197
Timon 197
Tingham 197
Tingham, Ed. 29
Tipperstown 14
Tirell 200
Tisdall 197
Toal 198
Tobbine 197
Tobias 197,218
Tobin 197
Tobine 197
Tobyn 197
Tobynn 197
Tomey 197
Tomin 197
Tomlins 197,224
Tomlinson 20
Tomson 196
Tone 197

Tong 197
Tonge 197
Tongue 197
Tonstall 197,224
Toogood 198,225
OTool 198
Toole 38-40
OToole 10...,198
OToole Family 16
OTooles 34
Tooley 198
Toomey 197-8-9
Toomy 199
Topham 198
Totten 198
Tottenham 198
Tottericke 198,226
Touche 22,198
La Touche 198
Toulson 198,224
Toumey 198
Towers 33,198,229
Towers, T. 229
Townsend 198
Townshend 13,198
Towson 15,198
Toye 198,227
Tracey 198
Tracing Roots 43
O'Tracy 198
Trail 29,198
Trainer 199
Trainor 199
Trant 9,11,22,
    198
Trasey 198
Travers 11,14,16,
    199,225-28
Traverse 199
MacTraynor 199
Treacy 11,198
Treanor 199
Trench 199
Trench, A. 28
McTrenor 199
Tressy 198
Triar 199,228
Triar, R. 228
Tribal Names vii

Tristam 30
Tristam, Ship 41
Truelock 199
Truelocke 199
Trulock 18,199
Trum (pl) 28
Tuhill 198
Tuinon 199,224
Tuite 9,11,199
Tullamore 199
Tullamore, Ld. 34
Tully 199
MacTully 195
OTully 195
Turley 94
Turner 199
Turner, Robt. 19
Tweddell 199
Tweddell, G. 27
Tweedy 46,199
Twigg 19,199
Twigley 176
Twomey 197-8
O'Twomey 199
Twomy 199
Tynte 200
Tynte Family 22
Tyrel, George 15
Tyrell 46,196,200
Tyrell, Hugh 10
Tyrell Of   31
Tyrrell 9,10,200
Tyth 200,226
Uniack 200
Usher 9,11,27,200
Usher 224-25-27-29
Usher, A. 227
Usher, Geo. 229
Ussher 14,18,19,
    28,33,200
Ussher, Geo. 13
Ussher Of   14
Ustace 107,200-25
Uustice 223
Valentia, Lord 29
Valentine 200
Vance 200
Vancoulster 201

Vanderpuer *201,227*
Vaughan *201-24-27, 228-29*
Vaughan, E. *228*
Vavasor *201*
Vavasour *201*
MacVeagh *108*
de Verdon *19*
Verneuil *19,201*
Vernon *11,201*
Vernon Arms *52*
Vernor *201*
Verschoyle *201*
Verscoyle *226*
Verveer *201*
Verveer House *27*
Vesey *201*
Vesey Burial *26*
Viking *9,34,35*
Vincent *201,227*
Vincent, T. *27*
Vipoint *201*
Vipont, C. *33*
Vizard *201,226*
Voyzin *201*
Wade *38-40,201-23 -24-25-26*
Wade, H. *223*
Wadsworth *201*
Wafer *204*
Waight *201,223*
Wainman *201,224*
Waite *201*
Wakefield *202,228*
Walcot *20,202*
Walcott *202*
Waldren *202*
Waldron *30,202*
Wale *202*
Walhope *19*
Walis *202*
Walker *202*
Wall *9,10,202*
Wallace *202*
Wallis *22,202,224*
Wallis, Ralph *226*
Walls *202*
Walse *27,202*

Walsh *38-40,10,15, 202,223-28*
Walsh Alias *14*
Walsh, Henry *20*
Walsh, Robt. *16*
Walsh   Welsh *203*
Walshe *9,203*
Walshes *16,19*
Walshman *203,228*
Walter *203*
MacWalter *203*
Walters *203*
Walton *203,223*
Wamought *203,224*
Wandesford *203*
Wandesforde *23*
Ward *20,203,223, 225,227*
MacWard *203*
Ward, Peter *227*
Ward, Thomas *20*
Ware *32,204,224*
Warren *9,10,23,32, 204,223-27*
Warren, A. *223*
Warren, Maj. *227*
Warren   *14*
Warren, Wm. *229*
Warrens *31*
Warrren, W. *34*
Wasberry *226*
Wasbery *204,226*
Waterhouse *204, 224-26*
Watson *204,227*
Watson, John *227*
Watts *204*
Watts, J. *223*
Waybrent *204,225*
Wayman *204,225*
Wayte *201*
Weafer *204*
Weatherhead *204*
Weaver *204*
Webb *204,223-25*
Webber *204,227*
Webber, John *227*
Webster *204*
Weever *204*

Welch *203*
Weld *28,204*
Weldon *204,225*
Wellesley *204*
Wellmore *208*
Wells *204*
Welsh *viii,38-40*
Welsh Birth *22*
Wenman *11,205*
Wenwell *205,223*
Werthheim *205,218*
Wesby *223*
Wesley *18,205*
Wespey *27,205*
Westbury *205*
Westby *205*
Westby Arms *52*
Westen *205*
Westenra *205*
Westinra *205*
Weston *205,224*
Wetherall *205,224*
Whalan *205*
Whaley *225*
Whaly *205,225*
Wharton *24,205*
Whately *16,205*
Whatton *205*
Wheeler *205*
Whelen, *205*
Whetlock *205,225*
Whight *206*
Whitchurch *206,224*
White *223,225,228*
White *9,10,24,32, 38-40,206-7*
White, Luke *22-6*
White, Nich. *26*
White, Rich. *29*
White, T. *228*
Whitechurch *206*
Whitefield *206,228*
Whitegrove *206*
Whitehead *206*
Whites *26*
Whiteside *206*
Whitfield *206*
Whitgrove *206,223*

Whithead *206*
Whitihell *206,225*
Whitmore *206,225*
Whitshed *22,206*
Whitside *206*
Whittingham *18,206*
Whitwell *206*
Whitwell, N. *32*
Whyte *14,206,207*
Whyte, John *22*
Whytes *26*
Wickombe *207,228*
Wicombe *207*
Wiggstead *207*
Wight *18,207*
Wighte *207*
Wilcocks *27,207*
Wilcox *207,223*
Wild *207*
Wild Geese *36*
Wilde *210*
Wilders *210*
Wiles *207*
Wiley *207,210*
Wilkinson *207*
Wilkinson   *28*
Wilks *20,207*
Willan *207*
Willes *207*
Willes, E. *13*
McWilliam *207*
Williams *38-40,45, 207,227*
Williams, Mr. *14*
Williamson *207*
Willion *24,207*
Willis *207*
Willison *208*
Willmer *208*
Willmore *208*
Willouby *208*
Willouby, Col. *32*
Willoughby *208,229*
Wills *208,218*
Wills, Dublin *44*
Willson *208*
Wilson *15,208, 224,227*
Wimsey *208*

Wingfield 208
Winslow 208
Winstanley 19,208
Withams 208,224
Withington 208
Wizard 208,225
Woder 11,208
Wogan 9,10,208
Wogane 208
Wolf 208,210
Wolfe 22,208
Wolfe Of   28
Wolferston 16,109
Wolverston 13,15,
45,209
Wolverston, W 14
Wood 209
Wood, Val. 228
Woodcock 209
Woodfin 209
Woodfin, J. 20
Woodlock 9,10,209
Woodlocks 31
Woodruff 209
Woods 209,224-28
Woods, James 228
Woodside 209
Woodward 209
Woodward, R. 19
Woolverston 209,228
Workman 209,226
Wormington 209
Worship 209,226
Worth 209
Worth, Judge 22
Worthington 209
Woulfe 208
Wray 177
Wright 209,223
Wright, Rev. 15
Wybrant 226
Wybrants 210
Wyburne 210,227
Wye 45,210
Wye Of Belfast 15
Wyld 210
Wylder 210
Wyles 207

Wylie 210
Wyly 207,210
Wyndham 32,210
Wynn 210
Wynne 30,210,229
Wynne, Peter 229
Wythir 14,210
Yates 210,224
Yates, James 224
Yearwood 210
Yeates 210
Yeates, Isaiah 18
Yeats 210
Yelverton 28,210
Yerward 24
Yerwood 210
Young 210-25-26
Young, Gerald 15

Dublin Research Tip

Records of the Rotunda

Many of us doing research on Irish families in the Dublin area have run into a brick wall while looking for births/ deaths/ marriages in the mid 1700's to the 1850's...

I suggest you look into sources like the registers of the Rotunda Maternity Hospital, a charity operation that was begun around 1756. The rumors suggesting that all Irish children were born at home was simply not true. The LDS (Latter Day Saints) Family Research Centers have films available which recorded most of the Registers of Labour Patients from 1797 to 1882. Each woman who checked into the hospital gave her name, age, husbands name and occupation, parish they were in , entry date, delivery date, sex of child, and in a few cases the christening name of the child.

This collection is rich with information of all kinds - and if you are fortunate, I would estimate that if any of your Irish were average folks - not of any wealth, and lived in the Irish section (the 'Liberties'), that possibly as many as 80-85% of the births will be found there. The only real downside is the effort - but most serious genealogists have a lot of time!

One can watch the emergence of families, their locations, occupations, when their children were born and other probable family members. Also you can watch the spelling of names change, and witness at first hand why so many names - spelled at different times by different nuns/nurses were simply adopted by many of the semiliterate Irish of those times. In my case, as the handwriting (yes- all entries were handwritten - and in some cases almost scribbled) changes from duty shift to duty shift, I found that some nurses spelled ALL Dunn/Dunnes with an 'e' and several others would spell all of them without the 'e'.

So - if you hear anyone arguing or discussing the exact or correct spelling of a surname, you will see that it really depended on who could write- and how they decided to write it. I know, for instance that my grandfather, who was born in Dublin made an 'X' or cross for his signature in the death entries of his parents. On the page I have which has 6-7 death entries, every one of them were signed with an 'X'!

In the mid 19th century you will even find the address of many families included - thus forming a valuable database of Dublin families. *(based upon information researched by Harry Dunne, found in the Journal of Irish Families, March 1999.)*

Notice

Published by the Irish Genealogical Foundation Press.
Updates and comments on all IGF publications appear in,
and should be directed to OLochlainns Journal of Irish
Families, our monthly membership publication. Write us at
Box 7575, Kansas City, Missouri, 64116 U.S.A..
Email: Mike@Irishroots.com
Visit our home page at: www.Irishroots.com
Full Catalog on Request.